Handbook of Culture and Creativity

FRONTIERS IN CULTURE AND PSYCHOLOGY

Series Editors
Michele J. Gelfand
Chi-yue Chiu
Ying-yi Hong

Books in the Series

Culture and Group Processes
Edited by Masaki Yuki and Marilynn Brewer

Handbook of Culture and Consumer Behavior
Edited by Sharon Ng and Angela Y. Lee

Handbook of Imagination and Culture
Edited by Tania Zittoun and Vlad Glăveanu

Handbook of Culture and Memory
Edited by Brady Wagoner

Handbook of Culture and Creativity
Edited by Angela K.-Y. Leung, Letty Y.-Y. Kwan, and Shyhnan Liou

Handbook of Culture and Creativity

Basic Processes and Applied Innovations

EDITED BY

ANGELA K.-Y. LEUNG

LETTY Y.-Y. KWAN

AND

SHYHNAN LIOU

OXFORD
UNIVERSITY PRESS

Oxford University Press is a department of the University of Oxford. It furthers
the University's objective of excellence in research, scholarship, and education
by publishing worldwide. Oxford is a registered trade mark of Oxford University
Press in the UK and certain other countries.

Published in the United States of America by Oxford University Press
198 Madison Avenue, New York, NY 10016, United States of America.

Library of Congress Cataloging-in-Publication Data
Names: Leung, Angela K.-Y., 1979– editor. | Kwan, Letty Y.-Y., editor. | Liou, Shyhnan, editor.
Title: Handbook of culture and creativity: basic processes and applied innovations /
edited by Angela K.-Y. Leung, Letty Y.-Y. Kwan, Shyhnan Liou.
Description: New York, NY : Oxford University Press, [2018] |
Series: Frontiers in culture and psychology | Includes bibliographical references and index.
Identifiers: LCCN 2017048279 | ISBN 9780190455675 (hardcover : alk. paper) |
ISBN 9780190455682 (pbk. : alk. paper)
Subjects: LCSH: Culture. | Creative ability—Social aspects.
Classification: LCC HM621 .H3445 2018 | DDC 306—dc23
LC record available at https://lccn.loc.gov/2017048279

9 8 7 6 5 4 3 2 1

Paperback printed by Webcom, Inc., Canada
Hardback printed by Bridgeport National Bindery, Inc., United States of America

CONTENTS

CONTRIBUTORS

Kevin Au
Center for Entrepreneurship
The Chinese University of Hong Kong
Hong Kong

Chi-Ying Cheng
School of Social Sciences
Singapore Management University
Singapore

Chi-yue Chiu
Department of Psychology
The Chinese University of Hong Kong
Hong Kong

Roy Y. J. Chua
Department of Organisational
    Behaviour & Human Resources
Singapore Management University
Singapore

Marta K. Dowejko
School of Business
Hong Kong Baptist University
Hong Kong

Liane Gabora
Department of Psychology
University of British Columbia
Kelowna, British Columbia, Canada

Vlad Petre Glăveanu
Department of Communication and
    Psychology
Aalborg University
Aalborg, Denmark

Brandon Koh
School of Social Sciences
Singapore Management University
Singapore

Letty Y.-Y. Kwan
Department of Psychology
The Chinese University of Hong Kong
Hong Kong

Angela K.-Y. Leung
School of Social Sciences
Singapore Management University
Singapore

Chun-Chi Lin
Department of Psychology
National Taiwan University
Taipei, Taiwan

Shyhnan Liou
Institute of Cultural Creative
    Industries Design
National Cheng Kung University
Tainan, Taiwan

Todd Lubart
Department of Psychology
Paris Descartes University
Paris, France

Jing Luo
School of Psychology
Capital Normal University
Beijing, China

Ella Miron-Spektor
William Davidson Faculty of
  Industrial Engineering and
  Management
Technion-Israel Institute of
  Technology
Haifa, Israel

Lay See Ong
School of Social Sciences
Singapore Management University
Singapore

Susannah B. F. Paletz
Center for Advanced Study of
  Language
University of Maryland
College Park, Maryland, USA

Ivica Pavisic
Department of Psychology
Bowling Green State University
Bowling Green, Ohio, USA

Baoguo Shi
School of Psychology
Capital Normal University
Beijing, China

Dean Keith Simonton
Department of Psychology
University of California, Davis
Davis, California, USA

Yi Wen Tan
School of Social Sciences
Singapore Management University
Singapore

Fon Wiruchnipawan
Leadership Development
Charoen Pokphand Group Co., Ltd.
Thailand

Yingzhao Xiao
Center for Entrepreneurship
The Chinese University of Hong Kong
Hong Kong

Chia Han Yang
Institute of Cultural Creative
  Industries Design
National Cheng Kung University
Tainan, Taiwan

Frontier Research on Culture and Creativity: An Overview

To elucidate the meaning of the cultural perspective of creativity, Glăveanu (2010) has defined creativity as:

> a complex socio-cultural-psychological process that, through working with "culturally-impregnated" materials within an intersubjective space, leads to the generation of artifacts that are evaluated as new and significant by one or more persons or communities at a given time. (p. 11)

This perspective highlights that culture and creativity mutually inform each other. Creative acts emerge from dialogical interaction with cultural norms, expectations, and artifacts; culture is evolved and transformed in the generative process of creativity. To enrich the cultural perspective of creativity, the 12 chapters of the present volume share a common objective to provide a thorough and in-depth analysis of the relationship between culture and creativity. Contributed by expert culture and creativity scholars, many of whom are either authors of the citation classics or the most recent empirical research in the field, the edited volume presents an systematic inquiry into the cultural processes of creativity and innovation. Epitomizing the value of diversity in promoting creativity, this volume benefits from the authors' cultural diversity (they come from North America, Asia, and Europe) and their disciplinary diversity (they are experts from psychology, business management, organizational behavior, communication, design, or computational modeling).

The volume starts with two chapters that shed new light on extensive research to showcase the reciprocal nature of culture processes and creativity, Leung and Koh (Chapter 1) propose the Complementary Model of Culture and Creativity (CMCC) to put into perspective how a broader, connected cultural experience aids people to destabilize cultural stereotypes, to oscillate between cultural perspectives, and to integrate discrepant ideas from different cultural sources. Empirical evidence is discussed to support that these cognitive processes bring about discernible creative advantages. Gabora (Chapter 2) reviews evidence from agent-based modeling to support a communal exchange perspective to cultural evolution, which places creativity and innovation at the heart of cultural change. As such, creativity fuels cultural evolution and vice versa.

In the second section, four chapters dovetail very nicely with the perspective of contextualizing creativity. Based on a systematic review of existing historiometric inquiries, Simonton (Chapter 3) has identified some key factors that contribute to the emergence of creative geniuses and the production of creative masterpieces across (creative) times and places. In Chapter 4, based on cross-national data Chiu and Kwan argued for the importance of institutional support and institutional trust as enabling contextual factors to promote a country's innovative performance. Understanding the socio-cultural embeddedness of creativity also highlights the importance of not reducing the processes of creative production at the national level to those at the individual and team levels. Although evidence on the creative advantages of multicultural experience and cultural diversity abounds for individuals and groups, Kwan and Chiu (Chapter 5) presented their cross-national data that reveal that cultural diversity in a nation is negatively related to its innovative performance and human development. Of import, they found that a nation could benefit from an open economy to mitigate these adverse effects of cultural diversity. Glăveanu and Lubert (Chapter 6) take a cultural psychology perspective and characterize creativity as a process whereby the material and symbolic environment of individuals, groups, and societies are continuously revitalized. Based on this perspective, they present qualitative research findings to illustrate the creative processes underlying the creative expressions of the professional groups of artists, scientists, and designers.

The third section offers unique perspectives on the creative benefits of multicultural or diversifying experiences. In line with Glăveanu and Lubert (Chapter 6)'s idea, Paletz and colleagues (Chapter 8) also recognize that every established profession or discipline is associated with distinct meaning systems and social identities. They go on to identify factors that affect the creative performance of multidisciplinary and multicultural teams. Ong, Tan, and Cheng (Chapter 10) add to the analysis by focusing on the moderating role of multicultural identity integration in the link between multicultural experience and creative performance. Shi and Luo (Chapter 7) and Wiruchnipawan & Chua (Chapter 9) examine the cognitive, metacognitive, and interpersonal factors that mediate or moderate the creative benefits of multiculturalism. After providing a critical review on the cultural differences in creativity and the lay conceptions of creativity, Shi and Luo (Chapter 7) present cognitive neuroscience evidence related to bilingualism and creativity, and identify perceptual chunking as a major obstacle to insight problem solving. Putting a focus on the cooperative nature of creative pursuits, Wiruchnipawan and Chua (Chapter 9) discuss a balanced view of how intercultural interactions expand creative potential and how intercultural tensions undermine such potential. They then suggest ways of how individuals can reap the creative benefits of engaging in intercultural dyadic collaboration and working in multicultural teams.

In the final section, two chapters apply the theme of the earlier sections to understanding the creative industries in Taiwan and Hong Kong. In Liou and Chia's chapter (Chapter 11), they discuss the challenges of transdisciplinary collaboration and relate these challenges to the development of creative cultural industries in Taiwan. They also recommend some strategies to meet these challenges. The role of institutional support in innovation and entrepreneurship (a topic in Chapter 4) is richly illustrated in Dowejko, Au, and Xiao's chapter (Chapter 12). In their detailed analysis, they apply a novel lens of time orientation to understand Hong Kong's challenges in nurturing innovative entrepreneurship despite the affluence of the city.

Together, the 12 chapters offer a multi-level, multi-disciplinary, and multi-method probe on the bidirectional relationship between culture and creativity. Balancing between basic research and applications in business and design, this volume provides important insights to lay the foundation for an integrated psychological science of culture and creativity.

Angela K.-Y. Leung
Letty Y.-Y. Kwan
Shyhnan Liou

REFERENCE

Glăveanu, V. (2010). Paradigms in the study of creativity: Introducing the perspective of cultural psychology. *New Ideas in Psychology, 28*, 79–93.

PART ONE

Culture and Creativity

Reciprocal Relationships

The Role of Culture
in Creative Cognition

ANGELA K.-Y. LEUNG AND BRANDON KOH ■

Being asked during an interview why some products are great, the late CEO of Apple Inc., Steve Jobs, put it this way:

> Creativity is just connecting things. When you ask creative people how they did something, they feel a little guilty because they didn't really do it, they just saw something. It seemed obvious to them after a while. That's because they were able to connect experiences they've had and synthesize new things. And the reason they were able to do that was that they've had more experiences or they have thought more about their experiences than other people. Unfortunately, that's too rare a commodity. A lot of people in our industry haven't had very diverse experiences. So they don't have enough dots to connect, and they end up with very linear solutions without a broad perspective on the problem. The broader one's understanding of the human experience, the better design we will have. (The Wired Interview, 1993)

Jobs talked about creativity as all about experience. A broader, connected human experience provides an impetus to break down existing conceptual boundaries, to oscillate between a variety of perspectives, or to synthesize a multitude of ideas, which are largely creativity-supporting processes. The Apple iPod provides an illustrative example of how a broader understanding of experience creates the revolutionary "Walkman of the twenty-first century" (Simon & Young, 2005). Officially released in October 2001, Jobs described iPod as a device that puts "1,000 songs in your pocket" with its 5 GB hard drive (Hormby, 2013). iPod is a creation that breaks away from the set concept of the then big and clunky Walkman. It was designed with the vision of providing huge storage capacity as an external disk drive to play music, which showed a flexible switching of perspectives by engineering the device as both a music player and a digital storage disk. Ranging from its engineering to aesthetic design to user interface, iPod exemplifies creative idea synthesis that recombines seemingly incompatible ideas in ways most people would not even imagine.

In this chapter, we propose a theoretical framework to put into perspective how creativity can be instigated by cultural experience, a form of experience that is of paramount importance to human existence. We posit that a broader, connected *cultural* experience provides an impetus to break down cultural confines, to oscillate between a variety of cultural perspectives, or to synthesize a multitude of ideas from different cultures, and these processes in turn bring about discernible enduring benefits to creativity.

THE COMPLEMENTARY MODEL OF CULTURE AND CREATIVITY

We propose a theoretical model to explain the role of culture in creativity (see Figure 1.1). The complementary model of culture and creativity (CMCC) examines three pairs of contrasting forces that describe the ways how individuals manage their cultural experiences can have an impact on their creative pursuits. Based on the model, we argue that the effects of culture on creativity are influenced by three bidimensional psychological processes: (1) stereotyping versus destabilizing cultural norms, (2) fixating on one cultural mindset versus alternating between cultural frames, and (3) distancing from versus integrating cultures. We further posit that destabilizing cultural knowledge, alternating between cultural frames, and integrating multiple cultures are more creativity enhancing, in that they serve to confer greater advantage to stimulate generation of more unconventional and novel ideas. Conversely, the opposing tendencies of stereotyping

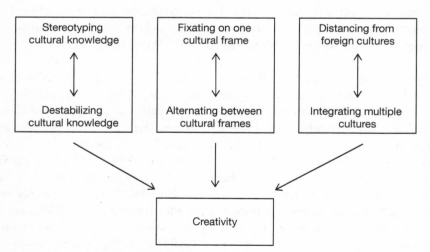

Figure 1.1. Complementary model of culture and creativity (CMCC).

cultural knowledge, fixating on a single cultural frame, and distancing from foreign cultures are commonly understood as more creativity hampering.

Nevertheless, we want to highlight that those relatively creativity-hampering orientations remain useful in the creative process. Creativity is often culturally embedded to operate with a consensual basis (Chiu & Kwan, 2010). Therefore, when individuals access the stereotypical creativity-related norms in the culture or dwell on the local cultural mind frame, the salient cultural knowledge they attend to could still provide an important reference point for idea generation and selection.

STEREOTYPING VERSUS DESTABILIZING CULTURAL KNOWLEDGE

As a form of well-learned stereotypes or generalized expectations, knowledge about a culture can become deeply ingrained and automatized. Socializing into the stereotypic conventions and mandates of a culture facilitates cultural members' sense making and interpersonal coordination, because they highlight the culturally normative ways of thinking and behaving (Chiu & Hong, 2006). However, as much as culture-specific knowledge aids psychological and social coordination, it instills a sense of structure that can constrain or impair generative and creative thoughts. We, therefore, argue that destabilizing the established and habitually accessible ways of thinking and acting that are predominant in a given culture confers the capacity to break set and to exercise flexible thinking among individuals (Nijstad, De Dreu, Rietzschel, & Baas, 2010).

The Creativity-Enhancing (Creativity-Hampering) Effect of Destabilizing (Stereotyping) Cultures

It is widely understood that stereotypical schemas commonly found in a given culture are effective and efficient heuristics meant to help people make sense of frequently occurring events in that culture (Rosch, 1978). Efficiency aside, thoughts invoked by stereotypes usually lack originality. Not surprisingly, individuals who rely on stereotypical heuristics under time pressure or cognitive load are more likely to have their creativity constrained (Antes & Mumford, 2009; De Dreu, Nijstad, Baas, Wolsink, & Roskes, 2012). Even experts were found to be less creative in their subject domain, presumably because they have developed heuristic solutions or stereotypical views through their extensive experience, and they kept fixating on them even in novel situations (Wiley, 1998).

Even with a clear goal of generating truly original ideas, creative work is often anchored on existing schemata normally experienced in everyday life. When passenger rail trains were first implemented in the United States in the 1830s, they were modeled directly after horse-drawn stagecoaches with conductors sitting outside the train cabin. Although directly transferring the design of the horse-pulled stagecoach to the rail train had facilitated implementation of railway travel, many conductors sitting outside the train cabin fell off and were killed at the time (Ward, 2007; White, 1978). This example is in line with what Ward and colleagues (2002) proposed as the *path of least resistance*. In a given culture, many paths of least resistance dominate different domains of thoughts. During idea generation many people are susceptible to these paths of least resistance by first retrieving typical instances of a known concept and subsequently attempting to modify them (Ward, Patterson, Sifonis, Dodds, & Saunders, 2002). For instance, participants who were asked to imagine animals from other planets with "wings" tended to also include "feathers" rather than "fur"; similarly, the feature "scales" also coincided highly with "fins" and "gills." These findings suggest how people would conform to the stereotypical schemas of bird and fish (Ward, 1994).

Our culture has made accessible many stereotypes, schemas, and exemplars to provide structure and predictability, but stereotype-driven thoughts can often constrain generative and creative thinking. It follows that countering these predominant stereotypes in the culture can potentially boost creative functioning. One way to destabilize or loosen the constraints of norms, stereotypes, worldviews, and practices that are seldom challenged in a given culture is through adequate immersion in multiple cultures. It was theorized that multicultural diversity could foster the creative process that brings into being something both novel and useful by challenging and resolving stereotypical expectations (Crisp & Turner, 2011; Leung & Chiu, 2008, 2010; Leung, Maddux, Galinsky, & Chiu, 2008; Maddux & Galinsky, 2009).

In line with the basic tenet in the creative cognition approach (Finke, Ward, & Smith, 1992; Ward, Smith, & Vaid, 1997), the acquisition of different cultural knowledge systems through extensive multicultural exposure is key to destabilizing bounds of culture. We argue that destabilizing cultural bounds is initiated by bringing together disparate ideas from different cultural sources, giving multicultural individuals a broader knowledge base at their disposal to experiment with creative pursuits (Cheng, Sanchez-Burks, & Lee, 2008; Chiu, Leung, & Hong, 2010; Leung et al., 2008). It follows that when structured and routinized mindsets are destabilized and disrupted, multicultural navigators might start to appreciate seemingly incompatible perspectives and become more prepared to explore and exploit the interrelations of incongruent concepts from different cultures (Maddux & Galinsky, 2009). This can further promote their integrative complexity—the capacities to differentiate and integrate competing cultural elements (Suedfeld, Tetlock, & Streufert, 1992; Tadmor & Tetlock, 2006), as well as their conceptual expansion ability—the capacity to broaden conceptual boundaries of an existing concept by combining it with other seemingly irrelevant concepts (Ward et al., 1997). Mastering these creativity-supporting processes can strengthen the generalized ability to think creatively across domains (Leung & Chiu, 2010).

Related arguments were put forward by Crisp and Turner (2011) in their categorization-processing-adaptation-generalization (CPAG) model. The central proposition of the model predicts that if social or cultural diversity is experienced under the right conditions, which go in the order of (a) the diversity experience challenges existing stereotypical expectations (i.e., categorization), (b) the perceivers are motivated and competent to resolve the stereotypical inconsistencies through suppressing stereotypes and producing generative thoughts (i.e., processing), and (c) the perceivers repeatedly engage in such inconsistency resolution processes (i.e., adaptation), then (d) they will be capable of developing generalized cognitive flexibility to spontaneously inhibit stereotype-based knowledge and exhibit generative thinking in future diversity encounters (i.e., generalization).

To elaborate on the CPAG model, the *categorization* component concerns how the diversity experience categorizes individuals (e.g., majority vs. minority group members). Such categorization makes apparent the categorized group (e.g., the minorities) as being inconsistent with the dominant norm and provokes deeper cognitive processing to resolve the inconsistency. For example, the research on minority opinions offers support that categorization increases inconsistency salience, which then triggers more divergent thinking and detection of novel solutions (e.g., Nemeth, 1986; Nemeth & Kwan, 1985; Nemeth & Wachtler, 1983). In the face of categorization, individuals must have the cognitive resources and motivation to engage in the *processing* of inconsistency resolution and to proceed to the subsequent stages. Otherwise, they will focus on one categorical frame without seeing the need to resolve inconsistencies. Notably, although both categorization and processing are effortful processes, they can become cognitively easier with *adaptation* or repeated engagement. Individuals can adapt to repeated resolution of stereotypical inconsistencies by automatically inhibiting stereotype activation and inducing divergent thought process to, say, form less biased individuated impressions (Hall & Crisp, 2005; Hutter & Crisp, 2005). Finally, *generalization* occurs when the process of inconsistency resolution is repeatedly engaged over time and to be applied to other domains. It is through the generalization process that multicultural individuals achieve higher levels of cognitive flexibility and become more adept at generative thinking across multiple domains of behavior and judgment (Crisp & Turner, 2011).

Empirical Evidence

The creative benefits of breaking away from the stereotypic and structured ways of thinking and behaving in a culture are evidenced from both historiometric and psychometric research. According to Simonton (2008), historiometric investigations are conducted at the aggregate or individual level. At the aggregate level, creative activities in a given nation or civilization are analyzed over historical time. For example, analyses revealed that countries tended to experience creativity influx after the periods they underwent nationalistic revolts and rebellions (e.g., the Golden Age of Greece appeared after the revolt against the Persian Empire and the Greek civilization was fragmented into different city-states; Simonton, 1975), they opened their civilization to foreign immigrants (e.g., Chinese Buddhist monks, Korean artists, and Christian missionaries entered the Japanese territory; Simonton, 1997, 2000), or they had their citizens travel or study in foreign soils. In many of these circumstances, the inflows of foreign influences led to the emergence of a polyglot civilization within the nation-state and that often accompanied prominent creative activities among its citizens.

At the individual level, historiometric researchers seek to examine characteristics of specific creative personalities. For example, historiometric investigations of over 300 eminent twentieth-century personalities (Goertzel, Goertzel, & Goertzel, 1978), Nobel laureates (Moulin, 1955), and US scientists (Levin & Stephan, 1999) showed that most creative geniuses appeared to have been either foreign born, lived overseas, or studied abroad. Based on large databases, historiometric inquiries provide support that shaking up the structured ways of life might fuel creativity (see Chapter 3: Cultural-Historiometric Studies of Creativity, this volume).

Psychometric investigations that compare individuals' performance in creativity tests are more common in the field of psychology (Simonton, 2008). For example, both correlational and experimental studies demonstrated that individuals spending longer (vs. shorter) time living in a foreign country or experiencing joint (vs. single) culture activation (or minimal intercultural contacts) scored higher on various creativity tests that measure performance in generating original ideas or coming up with creative insights (Leung & Chiu, 2008, 2010; Maddux & Galinsky, 2009). People are often bound to familiar or frequently activated knowledge in their culture. Exposure toward or activation of foreign cultures could free them from these cultural restraints and allow them to "think outside the box."

Studies on the cognitive and emotional mechanisms underlying the multicultural experience–creativity link also support the theorization that destabilizing cultures could be creativity enhancing. In terms of cognitive process, research has shown that Caucasian American participants with richer multicultural experiences were more inclined to appropriate ideas from foreign (vs. local) cultures in a creative idea expansion task (Leung & Chiu, 2010; Study 3). The task required them to freely sample some sayings authored by American, Chinese, or Turkish scholars in order to receive inspirations for expanding a preliminary research proposition about promoting happiness. Multicultural American students were more likely to recruit Chinese and Turkish sayings, which were supposedly to be more foreign to them, than local American sayings. Another study found that those participants who obtained a higher multicultural experience score tended to spontaneously retrieve culturally unconventional gift ideas that other people in their community did not readily generate (e.g., poetry, donation in their friend's name; Leung & Chiu, 2010, Study 2). These findings attest to the creative value of destabilizing cultural conventions when people are willing to break free from their culture's normative mental sets.

In terms of emotional process, it is reasonable to imagine that destabilizing cultures could put much strain on individuals, at least during the early stage of breaking away from familiar cultural mindsets. When examining the role of emotions on creativity, Cheng, Leung, and Wu (2011) posited that (a) cognizing the juxtaposition and the accompanied dissonance of seemingly conflicting ideas from dissimilar cultures could induce negative emotions, (b) negative emotions have been shown to enhance cognitive complexity (e.g., Forgas, 2007; Isen, Daubman, & Nowicki, 1987; Sinclair, 1988), and (c) enhanced cognitive complexity is conducive for creative capability (Tadmor, Tetlock, & Peng, 2009). To test the emotional underpinning of the relationship between joint culture activation and creativity, they found that Singaporean Chinese students under the dual (vs. single) cultural exposure condition showed a reduced amount of positive emotions, which in turn promoted greater creative flexibility, thus offering partial support for the proposed meditation. In another study, they recruited Taiwanese participants who had relatively fewer multicultural experiences and a stronger degree of cultural ambivalence than Singaporeans. As hypothesized, Taiwanese participants' negative emotions significantly mediated the relationship between local–foreign cultural exposure and creative performance. Of import, participants in this study were either exposed to a self-relevant local (Taiwanese) culture and a foreign (American) culture (i.e., the local-foreign cultural exposure condition) or to two foreign cultures (Indian and American cultures; i.e., the dual–foreign cultural exposure condition). Given that exposure to two foreign cultures did not produce the same creative benefit, it would be intriguing to consider the possibility that while foreign cultural immersion can destabilize conventions of a self-relevant local culture for harnessing its creative advantage, exposure to two foreign cultures does not pose the same destabilizing and creativity-enhancing effects if people are not actually bounded by the imperatives of these foreign cultures.

Although cultural pluralism provides a conducive environment to catalyze people's creativity by destabilizing routinized cultural conventions, the realization of this potential is largely predicated on people's receptivity to cultural heterogeneity and their ability to learn from and engage in the new culture. Openness to experience, as a relatively chronic personality disposition, supports intercultural learning and promotes integrative responses in intercultural settings (Leung & Chiu, 2010; Leung, Qiu, & Chiu, 2014). Being one of the Big Five personality traits, individual variability in openness to experience is reflected in one's tendencies to seek out and appreciate new experiences and ideas, to take risks, and to entertain alternatives (Costa & McCrae, 1992; McCrae & Costa, 1987). Intuitively, open-minded individuals should be more receptive to novel cultural experiences and more easily "let go" of well-learned stereotypic cultural knowledge. Their close-minded counterparts, in contrast, are more likely to resist inflows of foreign cultures. They fear that new ideas and practices from unfamiliar cultures will contradict and challenge established social norms and cognitive structures in the local communities, thus bringing about uncertainty and ambiguity to their everyday sense making.

Consistent with this contention, Leung and Chiu (2010) showed that openness to experience modulated the multicultural experience–creativity link, such that participants with richer intercultural contacts performed better in creativity tasks only if they were open to experience. When their European American participants were asked to generate novel uses of a garbage bag or to retrieve exemplars in the conceptual domain of "occupation," only those who reported more extensive intercultural experiences *and* higher openness to new experience came up with more unusual uses of a garbage bag (both in terms of number and strategy) or more normatively inaccessible occupations (e.g., dialect coach).

To demonstrate the important role of multicultural learning, in one study, Maddux, Adam, and Galinsky (2010, Study 1) randomly primed individuals with either within-culture learning experiences or multicultural learning experiences. Whereas making within-culture learning experiences salient was expected to activate routinized, preexisting, and chronically accessible responses, priming multicultural learning experiences was expected to challenge culturally constrained assumptions and destabilize habitual cognitive structures and behaviors. In another study, Maddux and colleagues (2010, Study 2) further tested the nuances of multicultural learning by priming *functional* multicultural learning or within-culture learning experiences, highlighting the learning of the underlying reasons or functions why people from a different culture or their own culture behave the way they do. Across both studies, results indicated that multicultural learning, in particular those experiences that involved functional learning, stimulated creative problem solving. In yet another study with a longitudinal design, Maddux, Bivolaru, Hafenbrack, Tadmor, and Galinsky (2014) recruited a sample of highly international MBA masters students and showed the practical value of multicultural engagement, which captures individuals' ability to actively engage in understanding and learning a new culture in a multicultural environment. Participants' degree of multicultural engagement raised their integrative complexity, which in turn predicted job market success in terms of increasing their professional opportunities.

Besides individuals' predispositions to endorse an open attitude toward and to learn from and engage in the new culture, it is also effective to consider how situationally induced interventions can help individuals break their mental set from accustomed ways of thinking and acting. One way to facilitate breaking of mental sets and approaching problems from multiple perspectives is to induce a dissimilarity (vs. similarity) comparison mindset. As prior research suggested, some creativity-supporting capacities attest to whether individuals can recognize and subsequently reconcile and combine cultural discrepancies to make novel connections between ideas (Tadmor et al., 2009). A dissimilarity processing mindset can highlight cultural differences in norms and values, and it can motivate the creative processes of acknowledging and recombining discrepant cultural perspectives to bring about new insights (Cheng & Leung, 2012; see also Mussweiler, 2003; Mussweiler & Damisch, 2008). As further argued, the cultures should be distinctive enough, or of sufficiently large perceived cultural distance, in order to energize the dissimilarity comparison mindset to induce heightened creative processing (Cheng & Leung, 2012). Across two studies, Cheng and Leung (2012) showed support for the predictions that participants undergoing dual cultural primes featuring two cultures with high levels of perceived cultural distance solved more creative insight problems when they personally predisposed to or were experimentally induced to adopt a dissimilarity (vs. similarity) comparison mindset.

Another relevant line of research examined whether inducing counterstereotypical thinking, arguably an intervention to highlight differences not normally encountered in a given culture, can enhance divergent creativity (Gocłowska & Crisp, 2013). The research is based on the premise that exposure to counterstereotypes (e.g., a female mechanic) would discourage individuals to use any easily accessible knowledge, but this effect is qualified by individuals' personal need for structure (PNS; Neuberg & Newsom, 1993). If individuals feel uncomfortable abandoning stereotypic thoughts or seeing their cherished generalized expectations being challenged (i.e., those high in PNS; Hutter, Crisp, Humphreys, Waters, & Moffitt, 2009), they would react against stereotype-inconsistent information and would not harness the creative benefit. As hypothesized, the study showed that only low-PNS participants became more flexible and original in a divergent thinking task after thinking of a counterstereotypic (vs. stereotypic) target (see also Goclowska, Baas, Crisp, & De Dreu, 2014; Goclowska, Crisp, & Labuschagne, 2012, for similar results).

FIXATING ON A SINGLE CULTURAL FRAME VERSUS ALTERNATING BETWEEN CULTURAL FRAMES

It is reasonable to argue that individuals who adhere to mainly one cultural identity or have not acquired much cultural knowledge at their disposal will readily act upon or fixate on their habitual ways of thinking or behaving. However, some individuals are identified as alternating biculturals who tend to oscillate between dual cultural identities based on situational demands (LaFromboise, Coleman, & Gerton, 1993). As alternating biculturals have two or more possible ways to categorize themselves, the identity that the situation activates and deems applicable will serve to call out the identity-defining cognitive and behavioral reactions (Gocłowska & Crisp, 2014). Similarly, for those individuals who have gained extensive knowledge of two or more cultures, it is widely understood that they would exhibit cultural frame-switching—a process that depicts how bicultural or multicultural individuals flexibly alternate between cultural frames to act congruently with the meaning systems and behavioral rules salient in the situation press (Hong, Morris, Chiu, & Benet-Martinez, 2000).

Empirical evidence abounds to illustrate the effects of cultural frame-switching. For example, as demonstrated by Fu and colleagues (2007), Hong Kong Chinese biculturals could switch correspondent moral inferences to cues from American or Chinese culture spontaneously even within the same experimental session. In the last decade, the cultural frame-switching phenomenon was replicated with a multitude of dependent measures, including self-concept and values (Ross, Xun, & Wilson, 2002), behavioral decisions in economics games (Wong & Hong, 2005), attributional judgments (Benet-Martinez, Leu, Lee, & Morris, 2002; Hong et al., 2000), personality profiles (Ramírez-Esparza, Gosling, Benet-Martínez, Potter, & Pennebaker, 2006), conformity of judgments (Mok & Morris, 2010b), and evaluative forecasts of others' behavior (Mok & Morris, 2011), to name just a few. We posit that alternating between cultural mind frames, as opposed to fixating on the conventionalized mental sets of a single culture, has an important role to play in promoting creative performance.

The Creativity-Enhancing (Creativity-Hampering) Effect of Cultural Alternation (Fixation)

Normative understanding of creativity resides in our culture. As Morris and Leung (2010, p. 322) put it, "culture does not shape an individual's creative behavior, as is popularly imagined, by imprinting fixed mentalities, worldviews, or talents. Culture shapes behavior largely through social norms, contexts that cue them, and motives that drive individuals to follow, ignore, or invert them." Instead of adhering to a trait account that portrays East Asians as predispositioned to conformity and Westerners to uniqueness, Morris and Leung (2010) put forward a normative account that East Asians prioritize the usefulness norm and Westerners the novelty norm (see also Lubart, 1999; Noriko, Fan, & Van Dusen, 2001).

Erez and Nouri (2010) further theorized that the cultural normative orientations toward different facets of creativity are linked to specific cultural values, with the East Asian culture's dominant values of collectivism, high uncertainty avoidance, and high power distance supporting the expression of usefulness and the Western culture's dominant values of individualism, low uncertainty avoidance, and low power distance supporting novelty (see also Brewer & Chen, 2007; Jones & Davis, 2000; Miron, Erez, & Naveh, 2004; Morrison & Milliken, 2003). Of import, as individuals are motivated by accountability concerns, it was found that cultural variations in generating novel versus useful ideas were accentuated in social contexts, such as working in the presence of peers or supervisors (vs. working alone; e.g., Nouri, Erez, Rockstuhl, & Ang, 2008).

Consonant with a normative approach to creativity, Miron-Spektor, Paletz, and Lin (2015) discussed how the cultural logic of face—the public-self as construed by others' views—undermines creativity. A cultural logic is a normative syndrome that organizes a culture with a constellation of shared beliefs, values, and practices around a particular theme (e.g., face, honor, individualism), giving people a sense of coherence and logical consistency to derive meanings from being a member of the culture (see Leung & Cohen, 2011; also Triandis, 1994). Although a given culture is likely to have multiple cultural logics in operation, some logics are the more dominant organizing syndrome of the culture, and the face logic is identified as more prevailing within the East Asian culture. Specifically, Miron-Spektor and colleagues' (2015) results showed that the face cultural logic weakens the novelty dimension of creativity, but not necessarily the appropriateness or the usefulness dimension. It is because people who are concerned with face are more likely to take the perspective of others (Liu, Friedman, Barry, Gelfand, & Zhang, 2012) and to feel more at ease with generating appropriate ideas as opposed to highly novel ideas that may threaten consensus and convention, or heighten risk and uncertainty.

Culturally normative expectations of orienting creativity toward novelty versus usefulness align with the theorizing that Western culture fosters breakthrough innovation and East Asian culture fosters incremental innovation (Herbig & Palumbo, 1996; Morris & Leung, 2010). Whereas breakthrough innovation boldly introduces more radical disruptions to existing ideas for bringing about novel inventions, incremental innovation improves current ideas or products with gradual extensions for upgrading their usefulness (Morris & Leung, 2010). Based on this perspective that emphasizes the culturally consensual norms of creativity, Chiu and Kwan (2010) commented that a fruitful way to understand the role of culture on creativity is to examine cultural differences in lay constructions of what creativity and innovation entail. Taken together, based on the normative account of creativity, we theorize that switching between normative frames of creativity is more likely to enrich idea generation than fixating on one normative orientation that narrows the scope of what constitutes creativity.

Another important research area corroborating the creativity-enhancing effect of cultural alternation or switching is bilingualism. Presumably, multicultural experiences are reciprocally linked to bilingualism or even multilingualism. An extensive exposure to multiple cultures is advantageous to the acquisition of second-language competency, and a bilingual/multilingual experience involves socializing people with speaking different languages, which is often an integral part of multicultural experiences. It was argued that bilingual individuals (who are often biculturals) are more adept at cultural frame-switching (Gocłowska & Crisp, 2014), as they were often found to possess more superior executive control to manage conflicting information and to switch between changing task demands (Bialystok & Viswanathan, 2009).

Extant research suggests that the many cognitive benefits of bilingual experience, including creativity, stem from bilinguals keeping both of their native and second languages activated and regularly switching between the two languages (Abutalebi & Green, 2007; Bialystok, 2009; Green, 1998). Whenever bilinguals process words or semantics, they experience neurocognitive activations in both languages, a phenomenon known as parallel language activation, resulting in crosslinguistic competition where concepts of the nontarget language must be suppressed for fluent speech production (Blumenfeld & Marian, 2013; Giezen, Blumenfeld, Shook, Marian, & Emmorey, 2015). This puts a greater demand on bilinguals' attentional and inhibitory control and hence sharpens these control processes, so that they can suppress coactivation of both the target and nontarget languages (Starreveld, De Groot, Rossmark, & Van Hell, 2013).

In addition, research identified that switching between languages contributes to both syntactic and lexical flexibility. Syntactically, bilinguals are more aware of the languages' structural flexibility (e.g., the form change of verb in Spanish depends on emotional state, personal volition, or uncontrollable chance). Semantically, bilinguals recognize the lack of conceptual equivalence between languages. This enriches their semantic networks because shared, but not identical conceptual representations spread broader activation to additional unrelated concepts from different categories (Paradis, 1997). This automatic process of spreading activation across richer associations is coined as *language-mediated concept activation* (see Altarriba & Basnight-Brown, 2007; Kroll & De Groot, 1997; Kroll & Tokowicz, 2005), which presumably supports bilinguals' more superior creative development (Mohanty & Babu, 1982; Simonton, 2008). Together, higher creative functioning among bilinguals (vs. monolinguals) might ensue from better cognitive control and higher language-afforded flexibility to aid switching between different languages.

Empirical Evidence

In view of the normative emphasis of different creativity dimensions in different cultures, it is reasonable to argue that fixating on one normative view debilitates creativity because the norm prioritizes one facet of creativity but ignores another. Dunlap-Hinkler, Kotabe, and Mudambi (2010) carried out a field study to examine the temporal trend of the new applications to the Food and Drug Administration submitted by 98 companies between 1992 and 2002. Of the 1,699 total applications, they found that companies with an established track record of focusing on incremental innovations had lower levels of breakthrough innovations from 1992 to 2002, suggesting that companies that used to incrementally innovate by specializing in extending or complementing an existing product line were less successful to radically innovate by starting a new cycle of technological change. Thus, the existing cultural expectation or practice of the company may have limited the kind of innovation it can pursue.

It is interesting to consider adherence to creativity norms in relation to the socio-ecological notions of cultural tightness versus looseness that exert different degrees of demand on norm adherence (Gelfand, Nishii, & Raver, 2006; Triandis, 1989). Tight cultures are characterized by very clear and strong norms and a strict enforcement of sanctioning norm deviance. In contrast, loose cultures are characterized by greater acceptance of diversity of norms and tolerance for deviant behaviors. Through socializing individuals to fixate on cultural norms and to develop psychological characteristics emphasizing discipline and caution, cultural tightness is believed to stabilize norms and to inhibit divergent thinking (Chua, Roth, & Lemoine, 2015). As Chua and colleagues (2015) argued, cultural tightness aligns with an adaptor cognitive style to reference on established and existing ideas in order to achieve incremental innovation; conversely, cultural looseness aligns with an innovator cognitive style to introduce radical changes in order to achieve breakthrough innovation (see also Kirton, 1994). Further, in the context of pursuing foreign creativity projects that require divergent thinking to go beyond local norms, the constraining effect of cultural tightness on foreign creativity tasks would be magnified. With field data collected from participants working on an online crowdsourcing platform, their findings supported that cultural tightness undermined foreign creative task performance, with cultural distance between the local and foreign cultural environments exacerbating the negative relationship. Nevertheless, participants coming from tight cultures were more likely to succeed at local creative tasks because being knowledgeable of local cultural norms that are strong and unambiguous presented them a distinct advantage of benefiting local tasks. Together, the demand on strict norm adherence in tight cultures could be detrimental to creativity when the creativity tasks are tailored to foreign cultural needs; however, cultural tightness increases individuals' likelihood of creative engagement in and creative success at local creativity tasks.

As fixation on one normative expectation of creativity is likely to be creativity hampering, it follows that when individuals can alternate between normative views, they are more likely to express creativity more optimally by considering both novelty and appropriateness. One study supported the context-specific alternating strategy among individuals with higher bicultural identity integration (BII) who perceived their two affiliated cultures to be compatible and in harmony (Mok & Morris, 2010a). Asian Americans with integrated bicultural identity (i.e., higher BII) responded assimilatively by generating more novel ideas after being primed with American (vs. Asian) cultural cues, although their lower BII counterparts responded contrastively by generating fewer novel ideas. Biculturals' tendency to flexibly switch between different cultural orientations of creativity suggests that they could be versatile to spontaneously express novelty or usefulness in their idea as signaled by situational demands, or even incorporate both creativity facets into the idea depending on which identity is made salient during different times within the idea generation stage. To summarize, the lay conception of creativity pertinent in the culture provides a reference point that can constrain the source of idea generation (either fixating on novelty or usefulness). With an extensive amount of foreign cultural experiences, coupled with a perceived sense of compatibility with biculturality, people may more readily go beyond local cultural norms and switch their creative cognitive styles based on environmental signals, thus expanding their creative bandwidth.

Apart from the degree of dual identity integration, it is important to consider individuals' motivated cognitive needs that affect their tendency to fixate on or oscillate between the perceptual and habitual sets of a culture. One motivated need concerns the epistemic need for cognitive closure (NFCC), which reflects individuals' urge for seeking firm answers and adhering to cultural conventions in order to attain order and predictability when rendering judgments or making decisions (Chao, Zhang, & Chiu, 2009; Fu et al., 2007; Leung, Kim, Zhang, Tam, & Chiu, 2012). An acute need for cognitive closure can be situationally induced when individuals are pressurized to make quick judgments under time pressure (Chiu, Morris, Hong, & Menon, 2000). One study showed that when time pressure heightened participants' need for epistemic closure, more exposure to foreign culture tended to decrease an individual's willingness to appropriate intellectual resources from other cultures to expand an improvised idea about happiness into a creative one (Leung & Chiu, 2010). However, when the participants did not feel pressurized to hurry through the task, replicating previous findings, more multicultural experience was accompanied by a greater readiness to sample ideas from unfamiliar cultures and incorporate them in the creatively expanded idea. In another study, when European American participants were asked to list exemplars of fruit, those with higher (vs. lower) levels of NFCC tended to access normatively accessible fruits in their own culture, but not those that are also common in other cultural settings (e.g., durian, rhubarb; Ip, Chen, & Chiu, 2006).

Another motivated need pertains to the need for existential security, as seen when individuals are motivationally driven to assuage existential anxiety by upholding cultural imperatives and protecting the integrity of their culture (Pyszczynski, Greenberg, & Koole, 2004; Pyszczynski, Greenberg, Solomon, Arndt, & Schimel, 2004). By defending and adhering to the normative mandates of their own culture, people would experience symbolic immortality through the continuity of their cultural tradition. With the same creative expansion task mentioned earlier, Leung and Chiu (2010) found in another study that, among participants in the mortality salience condition, exposure to foreign cultures was unrelated to how favorably they evaluated the ideas from foreign cultures, which were potential sources of creative inspirations to expand the impoverished idea. When mortality threat was not activated, the more exposure to foreign cultures, the more favorably participants rated the foreign ideas. In summary, both the needs for epistemic and existential security can drive individuals to freeze on or affirm the value of local cultural mandates.

Regarding the empirical support for the creative benefit of linguistic switching, one research study examined different, but interconnected aspects of bilingual experience concerning (a) second language aptitude, (b) the age of second language acquisition, and (c) the length of immersion in the new culture where second language acquisition takes place (Kharkhurin, 2008). Findings suggested that these aspects uniquely promoted bilinguals' creative performance. Specifically, by comparing Russian-English bilingual immigrants and English monolingual native speakers, partial correlational analyses revealed that second language exposure at a younger age and longer cultural immersion significantly increased fluency (i.e., a greater number of new ideas generated) and flexibility (i.e., a higher ability to simultaneously activate multiple seemingly unrelated concepts from distant categories). Further, both linguistic fluency and length of cultural immersion were positively associated with elaboration (i.e., a higher ability to keep concepts active during creative thought processes). Notably, bilinguals did not show superiority in idea originality by producing more unique and original ideas. Kharkhurin (2008) reasoned that bilingual experience might not directly promote creativity, but rather those creativity-supporting processes that underlie success generation of creative ideas.

In another study, Lee and Kim (2011) compared balanced against less balanced Korean American bilinguals who differ in the degree to which they are equally proficient in both languages. They showed that balanced (vs. less balanced) bilinguals performed more creatively in the Torrance Test of Creative Thinking, regardless of their age and gender. Even stronger support for the creativity-enhancing effect of linguistic alternation comes from the study of bilingual code switching, defined as "the alternation and mixing of different languages in the same episode of speech production" (Kharkhurin & Wei, 2015, p. 153). As expected, bilinguals who were habitual code switchers surpassed their nonhabitual counterparts in creative thinking (Kharkhurin & Wei, 2015).

DISTANCING FROM FOREIGN CULTURES VERSUS INTEGRATING MULTIPLE CULTURES

In the face of multiple cultures, some individuals might choose to keep a distance from foreign cultures and maintain a strong attachment with their ethnic culture, whereas others may choose to forge integrations between cultures or even go beyond mere integration to create a third, hybrid culture. Findings are generally in favor of the discernible creative benefits of cultural integration, but some recent research has started to bring some novel insights to demonstrate the creative potential of cultural distancing.

The Creativity-Enhancing (Creativity-Hampering) Effect of Cultural Integration (Distancing)

Past research suggests that individuals' cultural identity or their use of cultural knowledge might progress from distancing to alternation to integration. In a four-stage model of cultural identification (Amiot, de la Sablonniere, Terry, & Smith, 2007), the first two stages—anticipatory categorization and categorization—are analogous to cultural distancing, with individuals identifying with only one of the two affiliated cultures. Individuals in the third stage, compartmentalization, are alternating biculturals who hold two separate cultural identities and act in a way that is context dependent. Finally, integration is a stage where individuals attain an integrated identity as they identify with multiple cultures simultaneously and reconcile cultural conflicts more completely. In a similar model, Gocłowska and Crisp (2014) further extend the integration stage into a broadening stage that produces a more inclusive self-concept. A broadened self-definition facilitates accessibility and integration of concepts, thus benefiting creative performance.

According to the notion of BII, levels of identity integration are perceived to differ on a continuum (Benet-Martinez, Leu, Lee, & Morris, 2002). Specifically, the construct of BII captures two independent and exogenous dimensions: the dimension of *cultural distance* pertains to the degree to which individuals perceive the two cultural identities as blended and compatible (vs. dissociated and incompatible), and the dimension of *cultural conflict* pertains to the degree to which individuals feel that the two cultures are in harmony (vs. conflicting). The two dimensions are mainly derived from people's subjective perception and experience of cultural compatibility and harmony, but not objective differences between the original and receiving cultures (Benet-Martinez, 2010).

Why and how does an integrated identity confer creative advantage? According to Gocłowska and Crisp (2014), alternation works best only when individuals can keep the two cultural worlds separate, but not when they face upfront situations of culture mixing where two or more cultures collide at the same time and in the same space. Culture mixing situations might challenge alternating biculturals to resolve intra-individual conflicts and to maintain belongingness with multiple cultures, thereby threatening their cohesive self-identity (Amiot et al., 2007; Walsh, Shulman, Feldman, & Maurer, 2005). However, integration is conducive for fostering creativity under conditions of culture mixing as integrating biculturals are more adept at blending both of their identities; for example, Indian transnational youths in Canada experiment with a creative fusion of ethnic Indian and Western attire for displaying their blended cultural identity (Somerville, 2008). To integrate conflicting gender-role identities, a woman might manage two seemingly nonoverlapping identities of being a mother and an engineer by broadening her self-definition to be a "professional woman" (Amiot et al., 2007; Gocłowska & Crisp, 2014). Furthermore, if the to-be-combined identities are seemingly incongruent (e.g., combining the identities of "a Harvard graduate" and "a carpenter"), individuals might become aspired to assume an *emergent* identity (e.g., a Harvard-educated carpenter who is a highly skilled and creative entrepreneur; Amiot et al., 2007). Prior research has also demonstrated that integrating disparate ideas that belong to two or more cultures is a powerful way to stimulate idea generation (Wan & Chiu, 2002).

As seen from the earlier examples, adhering to an integrated bicultural experience attests to several creativity-enhancing implications (to put it differently, assuming a cultural distancing position may hamper the opportunity to capitalize on these implications). First, as people are socialized to take up their culture's perceptual and mental sets, they often fall into a habitual way to work with the same assumptions and look at problems from a similar perspective (Chiu & Kwan, 2010). Cultural integration entails developing a deeper relationship with the dual cultures and an engagement with incongruent cultural perspectives (e.g., Huang & Galinsky, 2011; Saad, Damian, Benet-Martínez, Moons, & Robins, 2013; Tadmor, Galinsky, & Maddux, 2012). Second, when combined, these incongruent cultural perspectives will trigger higher levels of cognitive flexibility, mental-set breaking, and expansion of conceptual boundaries of existing knowledge (Godart, Maddux, Shipilov, & Galinsky, 2015; Leung et al., 2008; Maddux et al., 2014; Morris, Mok, & Mor, 2011; Tadmor et al., 2009). Third, integration paves the way to eventually develop a broadened, inclusive, and superordinate sense of self-definition for increasing receptivity to an expanded scope of cognitions, norms, and values (e.g., Amiot et al., 2007; Gaertner et al., 2000; McFarland, Brown, & Webb, 2013). Through integration, individuals can recategorize their multiple cultural or social identities into one unified identity characterized by a higher order conceptual category (e.g., a new generation Indo-Canadian, a professional woman, a creative carpentry entrepreneur; Amiot et al., 2007; Gocłowska & Crisp, 2014). As a consequence, coherently forging an integration of the discrepant identities boosts individuals' creative potentiality through the production of some fused novel concepts, widening the base of cognitions to accommodate counternormative possibilities, and loosening identity boundaries to generate emergent properties that are not inherently linked with the original identities.

Empirical Evidence

Benet-Martínez, Lee, and Leu (2006) examined bicultural Chinese American and monocultural Anglo-American students' free associations about Chinese and American cultural representations. Results showed that bicultural participants were more cognitively complex than their monocultural counterparts, with their descriptions of each culture incorporating different perspectives and their evaluations featuring both differentiated and integrated properties. In another study that used the same methodology, the researchers compared students with lower versus higher levels of BII, and interestingly results revealed that the free descriptions of lower (vs. higher) BII participants were higher in cognitive complexity. The researchers reasoned that bicultural individuals, particularly those with incompatible cultural identities, are under a constant need to monitor conflicting demands between the two cultures, and over time they have developed higher cognitive complexity to systematically process and elaborate on cultural cues (see also Botvinick, Braver, Barch, Carter, & Cohen, 2001).

Notably, lower BII individuals' higher cognitive complexity in cultural representations does not necessarily carry over to benefit their creativity. As shown in another study (Cheng et al., 2008), Asian Americans and female engineers with higher (vs. lower) levels of BII performed more creatively in tasks that were identity relevant (e.g., developing fusion dishes using both Asian and American ingredients, designing a communication device targeted for female users). As performing well in these tasks requires drawing upon identity-related knowledge domains, higher BII individuals are at an advantage to simultaneously recruit knowledge from two compatible social identities to creatively enrich their solutions.

In line with this finding, another study showed that bicultural individuals who adopted an integrationist strategy of acculturation (i.e., they identified highly with both the mainstream and ethnic cultures) displayed higher integrative complexity, which was further shown to mediate the relationship between their dual cultural identification and creative advantages, including more adept performance in laboratory creativity tasks, greater workplace innovation, higher promotion rates, and more positive reputations at work (Tadmor et al., 2012). These findings did not emerge for those who identified with only one culture through adopting the assimilation or separation strategy. Interestingly, improvements to integrative flexibility and creativity were also observed among individuals who adhered to a marginalization strategy that is associated with low identification with both cultures.

It is worth a closer look at the unexpected finding that biculturals who adopted the marginalization strategy could be more creative. Indeed, recently researchers have paid more attention to this neglected group who marginalizes from both their heritage culture and the receiving culture. The notion of marginalization has long been associated with a pejorative connotation, which prompted some researchers to reconsider marginalization as actually depicting cultural independence or cosmopolitanism (Cannon & Yaprak, 2002; Gillespie, McBride, & Riddle, 2010; Glaser, 1958; Kim, 1988; Razzouk & Masters, 1986; Rudmin & Ahmadzadeh, 2001). Other researchers have incorporated a new acculturation orientation—individualism—to Berry's original framework of integrationism, assimilationism, separationism, and marginalization (see the Interactive Acculturation Model [IAM] proposed by Bourhis, Moise, Perreault, & Senecal, 1997). Accordingly, they identified individualists as those "who define themselves and others based on their personal characteristics rather than on their group membership" (Bourhis, Barrette, El-Geledi, & Schmidt, 2009, p. 444). Although individualists, like marginalists, are not concerned with identifying with both their native and the receiving cultures, they are distinct from the marginalists in showing higher tendencies to emphasize personal qualities and aspirations, to downplay group ascriptions, and to interact with other immigrants and members of the dominant group alike in a nondifferentiating manner (Bourhis et al., 2009).

Denoting a lack of strong identification with either culture, it was theorized that cultural individualists or cosmopolitans could transcend any cultures, acquire a stronger sense of self-efficacy, and develop a more secure self-identity (Bennett, Passin, & McKnight, 1958; Gillespie et al., 2010; Nash & Schaw, 1962). In line with this reasoning, accumulating evidence supports that cultural independence or cosmopolitanism is associated with positive socio-psychological outcomes, such as better sociocultural adaptation to a second culture (Kosic, 2002), attaining above-average school performance (Saruk & Gulutsan, 1970), being successful professionals at work (Kim, 1988), developing autonomous worldviews and higher creative potential that transcend particular cultures (Cannon & Yaprak, 2002), exhibiting more complex thinking and better discriminatory capability to select the best aspects of different cultures for improving performance (Tadmor et al., 2009), and displaying highly sought-after qualities such as rationality, objectivity, logical thinking, and effective management skills (Mol, 1963). Further, Gillespie and colleagues (2010) showed that their Mexican participants who pursued integration or cultural independence were more likely to be upper-level managers than their counterparts who identified strongly with either the Mexican culture or the new American culture brought by American employees working in their companies. In the school setting, Bourhis and colleagues (2009) found that both local European American and African American students and immigrant Asian and Hispanic students attending a multicultural university in Los Angeles had more harmonious intercultural relations if they endorsed integrationism and individualism, but more problematic and conflicting relations if they endorsed the other three acculturation orientations.

One may find that the general support for the creative benefits of cultural integration is paradoxical to the finding that some form of cultural distancing (e.g., individualism, independence, or cosmopolitanism) is also creativity inducing. To reconcile these seemingly contradictory results, we argue that people's orientation or motivation toward cultural learning might matter more than whether they choose to identify with certain cultures (as cultural identifications form the basis for their acculturation attitude such as integrationism and marginalization). Our argument is based on two propositions. First, in the literature an important distinction is made between multicultural *knowledge* and multicultural *identity*, in that individuals with extensive exposure to a multicultural environment could acquire sufficient knowledge about diverse cultures, but they do not necessarily uphold a sense of identification, attachment, or loyalty with the cultures to which they are exposed (Benet-Martinez, 2010; Benet-Martinez & Haritatos, 2005; Hariatos & Benet-Martinez, 2002; Hong, Wan, No, & Chiu, 2007). The relationship between multicultural knowledge and multicultural identity is also likely to be asymmetrical, as people tend to be knowledgeable about the cultures they identify with, but they might not identify with the cultures that they are knowledgeable of.

Second, in their comprehensive review of the literature on cosmopolitanism and development efforts of a Cosmopolitan Orientation Scale (COS), Leung, Koh, and Tam (2015) derived some essential qualities or orientations of being a cosmopolitan individual (cultural openness, global prosociality, respect for cultural diversity). Among the three dimensions, *cultural openness* is often identified as the most defining feature that exemplifies the cosmopolitan core in existing measurements (Hannerz, 1990; Roudometof, 2005; Szerszynski & Urry, 2002). Cosmopolitans are open, both intellectually and aesthetically, and they have an outward stance toward divergent cultural experiences (Beck, 2002; Hannerz, 1990). With their regular travel experiences and intercultural interactions, they easily feel at home when abroad (Konrád, 1984) and are usually culturally competent to participate skillfully in different cultures (Pichler, 2011). They are often open-minded intellectuals, or so-called cultural omnivores, who are highly receptive to engage with and learn through people, places, and experiences that belong to other cultures and to seek mental stimulations through foreign cultural encounters (Brett & Moran, 2011; Lizardo, 2005).

Based on these propositions, we posit that cultural distancing is not necessarily antithetical to cultural learning. One might choose not to strongly attach to or identify with any cultures, but maintain a strong cultural learning orientation to acquire knowledge from diverse cultural sources and uphold a cosmopolitan orientation driven by a sense of world openness. Above all, what matters to enhancing individuals' creative bandwidth is their motivation to remain open to the rich intellectual resources made available by different cultures, rather than their degree of identification with these cultures.

IMPLICATIONS AND CONCLUSION

Throughout the manuscript, we have argued and presented empirical evidence that destabilizing cultural norms, alternating between cultural frames, or integrating disparate cultural identities/ideas offers individuals an advantage to promote their creative cognition. However, we want to highlight that it is not our intention to interpret the proposed CMCC that relying on cultural stereotypes, fixating on one cultural frame of mind, or distancing from foreign cultures is not useful for the creative process. According to the process model of creativity proposed by Chiu and Kwan (2010), the production of creative ideas pertains to three successive stages of knowledge creation: (a) authoring new ideas; (b) selecting, editing, and marketing ideas; and (c) idea acceptance in the market. We posit that focusing attention toward the (accurate) creativity-related stereotypes pertinent in a given culture can provide the idea producers much needed cultural knowledge to anchor the authoring of original ideas. Stereotypical expectations of the lay creativity construction in the culture can also provide them the normative basis for idea selection, editing, and marketing. In other words, attending to the cultures' stereotypical creativity conception can aid idea producers to engage in audience design (Clark, Schreuder, & Buttrick, 1983; Clark & Wilkes-Gibbs, 1986; Isaacs & Clark, 1987), which is the process of adjusting idea generation and its accompanying selection, editing, and marketing processes toward the normative knowledge of the idea recipients in that culture. By harnessing a common ground, audience design can heighten the chance of eventual acceptance of the ideas in the cultural marketplace.

These arguments are consonant with Chua and colleagues' (2015) finding, which showed that familiarity with and adherence to local cultural norms conferred creative advantages for idea producers, particularly when strong and clear norms were enforced in the local culture (i.e., a tight culture). In addition, the evaluations of usefulness and novelty are relative to a culture. The assessment of usefulness is relative to the demands and needs of the prospective audience or users embedded in a given culture, whereas the assessment of novelty is relative to what is known currently in the culture (Chiu & Kwan, 2010). As a consequence, orienting toward the culturally consensual knowledge about creativity can impact on the evaluative judgments of an idea's usefulness and novelty.

Based on the intersubjective representation approach, we also noted that people who are more strongly identified with a culture tend to align their personal values with the collective representation of those cultural norms that are intersubjectively perceived to be distinctively important for that culture (Chiu, Gelfand, Yamagishi, Shteynberg, & Wan, 2010). Therefore, individuals who are strong identifiers of their own culture, regardless of whether they keep a distance from or identify with other foreign cultures, can discern the intersubjective representations of the creative norms endorsed in their culture. They can apply this culturally consensual knowledge to benefit different stages of the creative process. Furthermore, as we have discussed even for those who hold a distancing orientation from both the native culture and other foreign cultures (i.e., those identified as marginalists, individualists, independents, or cosmopolitans), research has shown preliminary evidence that they could transcend cultural bounds to be creatively inspired—a discovery that adds to the negative socio-psychological adaptation outcomes commonly found among those who adopt a marginalization strategy to disidentify with both the ethnic and host cultures.

To sum up, the complementary model of culture and creativity proposed here seeks to identify the important role of culture in creative cognition and to recognize the different socio-psychological variables that are part of this complex culture–creativity nexus. As the next chapter will present, creativity also assumes an important role to participate in various cultural processes. Creativity resides in a culture, and the way culture emerges, stabilizes, and evolves is embedded in processes of knowledge creation. We hope that our model will inspire future research to provide more nuanced insights on the mutual and dynamic relationship between culture and creativity.

REFERENCES

Abutalebi, J., & Green, D. (2007). Bilingual language production: The neurocognition of language representation and control. *Journal of Neurolinguistics*, *20*, 242–275.

Altarriba, J., & Basnight-Brown, D. M. (2007). Methodological considerations in performing semantic-and translation-priming experiments across languages. *Behavior Research Methods*, *39*(1), 1–18.

Amiot, C. E., de la Sablonniere, R., Terry, D. J., & Smith, J. R. (2007). Integration of social identities in the self: Toward a cognitive-developmental model. *Personality and Social Psychological Review*, *11*(4), 364–388.

Antes, A. L., & Mumford, M. D. (2009). Effects of time frame on creative thought: Process versus problem-solving effects. *Creativity Research Journal*, *21*(2-3), 166–182.

Beck, U. (2002). The cosmopolitan society and its enemies. *Theory, Culture, & Society*, *19*(1-2), 17–44.

Benet-Martinez, V. (2010). Multiculturalism: Cultural, social, and personality processes. In K. Deaux & M. Snyder (Eds.), *Handbook of personality and social psychology* (pp. 623–648). New York, NY: Oxford University Press.

Benet-Martinez, V., & Haritatos, J. (2005). Bicultural identity integration (BII): Components and psychosocial antecedents. *Journal of Personality*, *73*(4), 1015–1049.

Benet-Martínez, V., Lee, F., & Leu, J. (2006). Biculturalism and cognitive complexity expertise in cultural representations. *Journal of Cross-Cultural Psychology*, *37*(4), 386–407.

Benet-Martinez, V., Leu, J., Lee, F., & Morris, M. W. (2002). Negotiating biculturalism: Cultural frame switching in biculturals with oppositional versus compatible cultural identities. *Journal of Cross-Cultural Psychology*, *33*(5), 492–516.

Bennett, J., Passin, H., & McKnight, R. (1958). *In the search of identity: Overseas scholars in the United States*. Minneapolis: University of Minnesota.

Bialystok, E. (2009). Bilingualism: The good, the bad, and the indifferent. *Bilingualism: Language and Cognition*, *12*(1), 3.

Bialystok, E., & Viswanathan, M. (2009). Components of executive control with advantages for bilingual children in two cultures. *Cognition*, *112*(3), 494–500.

Blumenfeld, H. K., & Marian, V. (2013). Parallel language activation and cognitive control during spoken word recognition in bilinguals. *Journal of Cognitive Psychology*, *25*(5), 547–567.

Botvinick, M. M., Braver, T. S., Barch, D. M., Carter, C. S., & Cohen, J. D. (2001). Conflict monitoring and cognitive control. *Psychological Review*, *108*(3), 624–652.

Bourhis, R. Y., Barrette, G., El-Geledi, S., & Schmidt, R. (2009). Acculturation orientations and social relations between immigrant and host community members in California. *Journal of Cross-Cultural Psychology*, *40*(3), 443–467.

Bourhis, R. Y., Moise, L. C., Perreault, S., & Senecal, S. (1997). Towards an interactive acculturation model: A social psychological approach. *International Journal of Psychology, 32*(6), 369–386.

Brett, J., & Moran, A. (2011). Cosmopolitan nationalism: Ordinary people making sense of diversity. *Nations and Nationalism, 17*(1), 188–206.

Brewer, M. B., & Chen, Y. (2007). Where (Who) are collectives in collectivism? Toward conceptual clarification of individualism and collectivism. *Psychological Review, 114*(1), 133–151.

Cannon, H. M., & Yaprak, A. (2002). Will the real-world citizen please stand up! The many faces of cosmopolitan consumer behavior. *Journal of International Marketing, 10*(4), 30–52.

Chao, M. M., Zhang, Z.-X., & Chiu, C.-y. (2009). Adherence to perceived norms across cultural boundaries: The role of need for cognitive closure and ingroup identification. *Group Processes & Intergroup Relations, 13*(1), 69–89.

Cheng, C.-y., & Leung, A. K.-y. (2012). Revisiting the multicultural experience-creativity link: The effects of perceived cultural distance and comparison mind-set. *Social Psychological and Personality Science, 4*(4), 475–482.

Cheng, C.-y., Leung, A. K.-y., & Wu, T. Y. (2011). Going beyond the multicultural experience-creativity link: The mediating role of emotions. *Journal of Social Issues, 67*(4), 806–824.

Cheng, C.-y., Sanchez-Burks, J., & Lee, F. (2008). Connecting the dots within creative performance and identity integration. *Psychological Science, 19*(11), 1178–1184.

Chiu, C.-y., Gelfand, M. J., Yamagishi, T., Shteynberg, G., & Wan, C. (2010). Intersubjective culture the role of intersubjective perceptions in cross-cultural research. *Perspectives on Psychological Science, 5*(4), 482–493.

Chiu, C.-y., & Hong, Y. y. (2006). *The social psychology of culture.* New York, NY: Psychology Press.

Chiu, C.-y., & Kwan, L. Y. Y. (2010). Culture and creativity: A process model. *Management and Organization Review, 6*(3), 447–461.

Chiu, C-y., Leung, A. K.-y., & Hong, Y-y. (2010). Cultural processes: An overview. In A. K.-y. Leung, C-y. Chiu, & Y-y. Hong (Eds.), *Cultural processes: A social psychological perspective* (pp. 3–39). New York, NY: Cambridge University Press.

Chiu, C., Morris, M. W., Hong, Y., & Menon, T. (2000). Motivated cultural cognition: The impact of implicit cultural theories on dispositional attribution varies as a function of need for closure. *Journal of Personality and Social Psychology, 78*, 247–259.

Chua, R. Y., Roth, Y., & Lemoine, J.-F. (2015). How culture impacts creativity: Cultural tightness, cultural distance, and global creative work. *Administrative Science Quarterly, 60*(2), 189–227.

Clark, H. H., Schreuder, R., & Buttrick, S. (1983). Common ground at the understanding of demonstrative reference. *Journal of Verbal Learning and Verbal Behavior, 22*(2), 245–258.

Clark, H. H., & Wilkes-Gibbs, D. (1986). Referring as a collaborative process. *Cognition, 22*(1), 1–39.

Costa, R. T., & McCrae, R. R. (1992). *Revised NEO Personality Inventory (NEO PI-R) and NEO Five-Factor Inventory (NEO-FFI) professional manual.* Odessa, FL: Psychological Assessment Resources.

Crisp, R. J., & Turner, R. N. (2011). Cognitive adaptation to the experience of social and cultural diversity. *Psychological Bulletin, 137*(2), 242–266.

De Dreu, C. K., Nijstad, B. A., Baas, M., Wolsink, I., & Roskes, M. (2012). Working memory benefits creative insight, musical improvisation, and original ideation through maintained task-focused attention. *Personality and Social Psychology Bulletin, 38,* 656–669.

Dunlap-Hinkler, D., Kotabe, M., & Mudambi, R. (2010). A story of breakthrough versus incremental innovation: Corporate entrepreneurship in the global pharmaceutical industry. *Strategic Entrepreneurship Journal, 4,* 106–127.

Erez, M., & Nouri, R. (2010). Creativity: The influence of cultural, social, and work contexts. *Management and Organization Review, 6*(3), 351–370.

Finke, R. A., Ward, T. B., & Smith, S. M. (1992). *Creative cognition: Theory, research, and applications.* Cambridge, MA: MIT Press.

Forgas, J. P. (2007). When sad is better than happy: Negative affect can improve the quality and effectiveness of persuasive messages and social influence strategies. *Journal of Experimental Social Psychology, 43*(4), 513–528.

Fu, J. H.-y., Morris, M. W., Lee, S.-l., Chao, M., Chiu, C.-y., & Hong, Y.-y. (2007). Epistemic motives and cultural conformity: Need for closure, culture, and context as determinants of conflict judgments. *Journal of Personality and Social Psychology, 92*(2), 191.

Gaertner, S. L., Dovidio, J. F., Banker, B. S., Houlette, M., Johnson, K. M., & McGlynn, E. A. (2000). Reducing intergroup conflict: From superordinate goals to decategorization, recategorization, and mutual differentiation. *Group Dynamics: Theory, Research, and Practice, 4*(1), 98.

Gelfand, M. J., Nishii, L. H., & Raver, J. L. (2006). On the nature and importance of cultural tightness-looseness. *Journal of Applied Psychology, 91*(6), 1225.

Giezen, M. R., Blumenfeld, H. K., Shook, A., Marian, V., & Emmorey, K. (2015). Parallel language activation and inhibitory control in bimodal bilinguals. *Cognition, 141,* 9–25.

Gillespie, K., McBride, J. B., & Riddle, L. (2010). Globalization, biculturalism and cosmopolitanism: The acculturation status of Mexicans in upper management. *International Journal of Cross Cultural Management, 10*(1), 37–53.

Glaser, D. (1958). Dynamics of ethnic identification. *American Sociological Review, 23*(1), 31–40.

Goclowska, M. A., Baas, M., Crisp, R. J., & De Dreu, C. K. (2014). Whether social schema violations help or hurt creativity depends on need for structure. *Personality and Social Psychology Bulletin, 40*(8), 959–971.

Goclowska, M. A., & Crisp, R. J. (2013). On counter-stereotypes and creative cognition: When interventions for reducing prejudice can boost divergent thinking. *Thinking Skills and Creativity, 8,* 72–79.

Goclowska, M. A., & Crisp, R. J. (2014). How dual-identity processes foster creativity. *Review of General Psychology, 18*(3), 216–236.

Goclowska, M. A., Crisp, R. J., & Labuschagne, K. (2012). Can counter-stereotypes boost flexible thinking? *Group Processes & Intergroup Relations, 16*(2), 217–231.

Godart, F. C., Maddux, W. W., Shipilov, A. V., & Galinsky, A. D. (2015). Fashion with a foreign flair: Professional experiences abroad facilitate the creative innovations of organizations. *Academy of Management Journal, 58*(1), 195–220.

Goertzel, M. G., Goertzel, V., & Goertzel, T. G. (1978). *300 eminent personalities: A psychosocial analysis of the famous.* San Francisco, CA: Jossey-Bass.

Green, D. W. (1998). Mental control of the bilingual lexico-semantic system. *Bilingualism: Language and Cognition, 1*(2), 67–81.

Hall, N. R., & Crisp, R. J. (2005). Considering multiple criteria for social categorization can reduce intergroup bias. *Personality and Social Psychology Bulletin, 31*(10), 1435–1444.

Hannerz, U. (1990). Cosmopolitans and locals in world culture. *Theory, Culture, & Society, 7*(2), 237–251.

Hariatos, J., & Benet-Martinez, V. (2002). Bicultural identities: The interface of cultural, personality, and socio-cognitive processes. *Journal of Research in Personality, 36,* 598–606.

Herbig, P. A., & Palumbo, F. A. (1996). Innovation—Japanese style. *Industrial Management & Data Systems, 96*(5), 11–20.

Hong, Y. y., Morris, M. W., Chiu, C. y., & Benet-Martinez, V. (2000). Multicultural minds: A dynamic constructivist approach to culture and cognition. *American Psychologist, 55*(7), 709–720.

Hong, Y. y., Wan, C., No, S., & Chiu, C. y. (2007). Multicultural identities. In S. Kitayama & D. Cohen (Eds.), *Handbook of cultural psychology.* New York, NY: Guilford.

Hormby, T. (2013). A history of the iPod: 2000 to 2004. Retrieved September 16, 2015, from lowendmac.com/2013/ipod-history-origin-2000-2004/

Huang, L., & Galinsky, A. D. (2011). Mind–body dissonance conflict between the senses expands the mind's horizons. *Social Psychological and Personality Science, 2*(4), 351–359.

Hutter, R. R., & Crisp, R. J. (2005). The composition of category conjunctions. *Personality and Social Psychology Bulletin, 31*(5), 647–657.

Hutter, R. R. C., Crisp, R. J., Humphreys, G. W., Waters, G. M., & Moffitt, G. (2009). The dynamics of category conjunctions. *Group Processes & Intergroup Relations, 12*(5), 673–686.

Ip, G. W.-m., Chen, J., & Chiu, C.-y. (2006). The relationship of promotion focus, need for cognitive closure, and categorical accessibility in American and Hong Kong Chinese university students. *The Journal of Creative Behavior, 40*(3), 201–215.

Isaacs, E. A., & Clark, H. H. (1987). References in conversation between experts and novices. *Journal of Experimental Psychology: General, 116*(1), 26.

Isen, A. M., Daubman, K. A., & Nowicki, G. P. (1987). Positive affect facilitates creative problem solving. *Journal of Personality and Social Psychology, 52,* 1122–1131.

Jones, G. K., & Davis, J. (2000). National culture and innovation: Implications for locating global R&D operations. *Management International Review, 40,* 1–39.

Kharkhurin, A. V. (2008). The effect of linguistic proficiency, age of second language acquisition, and length of exposure to a new cultural environment on bilinguals' divergent thinking. *Bilingualism: Language and Cognition, 11*(2), 225–243.

Kharkhurin, A. V., & Wei, L. (2015). The role of code-switching in bilingual creativity. *International Journal of Bilingual Education and Bilingualism, 18*(2), 153–169.

Kim, U. (1988). *Acculturation of Korean immigrants to Canada.* Queen's University. Kingston, Ontario.

Kirton, M. (1994). *Adaptors and innovators: Styles of creativity and problem solving.* New York, NY: Routledge.

Konrád, G. (1984). *Antipolitics*. San Diego, CA: Harcourt.

Kosic, A. (2002). Acculturation attitudes, need for cognitive closure, and adaptation of immigrants'. *Journal of Social Psychology, 142*(2), 179–201.

Kroll, J. F., & De Groot, A. M. B. (1997). Lexical and conceptual memory in the bilingual: Mapping form to meaning in two languages. In A. M. B. De Groot & J. F. Kroll (Eds.), *Tutorials in bilingualism: Psycholinguistic perspectives* (pp. 169–199). Mahwah, NJ: Lawrence Erlbaum.

Kroll, J. F., & Tokowicz, N. (2005). Models of bilingual representation and processing. In J. F. Kroll & A. M. B. De Groot (Eds.), *Handbook of bilingualism: Psycholinguistic approaches* (pp. 531–553). New York, NY: Oxford University Press.

LaFromboise, T., Coleman, H. L., & Gerton, J. (1993). Psychological impact of biculturalism: Evidence and theory. *Psychological Bulletin, 114*, 395–412.

Lee, H., & Kim, K. H. (2011). Can speaking more languages enhance your creativity? Relationship between bilingualism and creative potential among Korean American students with multicultural link. *Personality and Individual Differences, 50*(8), 1186–1190.

Leung, A. K.-y., & Chiu, C.-y. (2008). Interactive effects of multicultural experiences and openness to experience on creative potential. *Creativity Research Journal, 20*(4), 376–382.

Leung, A. K.-y., & Chiu, C.-y. (2010). Multicultural experience, idea receptiveness, and creativity. *Journal of Cross-Cultural Psychology, 41*(5-6), 723–741.

Leung, A. K.-y., & Cohen, D. (2011). Within- and between-culture variation: Individual differences and the cultural logics of honor, face, and dignity cultures. *Journal of Personality and Social Psychology, 100*(3), 507–526.

Leung, A. K.-y., Kim, Y. H., Zhang, Z. X., Tam, K. P., & Chiu, C.-y. (2012). Cultural construction of success and epistemic motives moderate American-Chinese differences in reward allocation biases. *Journal of Cross-Cultural Psychology, 43*(1), 46–52.

Leung, A. K.-y., Koh, K., & Tam, K.-P. (2015). Being environmentally responsible: Cosmopolitan orientation predicts pro-environmental behaviors. *Journal of Environmental Psychology, 43*, 79–94.

Leung, A. K.-y., Maddux, W. W., Galinsky, A. D., & Chiu, C.-y. (2008). Multicultural experience enhances creativity: The when and how. *American Psychologist, 63*(3), 169–181.

Leung, A. K.-y., Qiu, L., & Chiu, C.-y. (2014). The psychological science of globalization. In V. Benet-Martinez & Y. y. Hong (Eds.), *Handbook of multicultural identity: Basic and applied perspectives* (pp. 181–201). Oxford, UK: Oxford University Press.

Levin, S. G., & Stephan, P. E. (1999). Are the foreign born a source of strength for U.S. science? *Science, 285*, 1213–1214.

Liu, L. A., Friedman, R., Barry, B., Gelfand, M. J., & Zhang, Z.-X. (2012). The dynamics of consensus building in intercultural and intercultural negations. *Administrative Science Quarterly, 57*(2), 269–304.

Lizardo, O. (2005). Can cultural capital theory be reconsidered in the light of world polity institutionalism? Evidence from Spain. *Poetics, 33*(2), 81–110.

Lubart, T. I. (1999). Creativity across cultures. In R. J. Sternberg (Ed.), *Handbook of creativity* (pp. 339–350). New York, NY: Cambridge University Press.

Maddux, W. W., Adam, H., & Galinsky, A. D. (2010). When in Rome . . . Learn why the Romans do what they do: How multicultural learning experiences facilitate creativity. *Personality and Social Psychology Bulletin, 36*(6), 731–741.

Maddux, W. W., Bivolaru, E., Hafenbrack, A. C., Tadmor, C. T., & Galinsky, A. D. (2014). Expanding opportunities by opening your mind multicultural engagement predicts job market success through longitudinal increases in integrative complexity. *Social Psychological and Personality Science, 5*(5), 608–615.

Maddux, W. W., & Galinsky, A. D. (2009). Cultural borders and mental barriers: The relationship between living abroad and creativity. *Journal of Personality and Social Psychology, 96*(5), 1047–1061.

McCrae, R. R., & Costa, P. T., Jr. (1987). Validation of the five-factor model of personality across instruments and observers. *Journal of Personality and Social Psychology, 52*(1), 81.

McFarland, S., Brown, D., & Webb, M. (2013). Identification with all humanity as a moral concept and psychological construct. *Current Directions in Psychological Science, 22*(3), 194–198.

Miron, E., Erez, M., & Naveh, E. (2004). Do personal characteristics and cultural values that promote innovation, quality, and efficiency compete or complement each other? *Journal of Organizational Behavior, 25*(2), 175–199.

Miron-Spektor, E., Paletz, S. B. F., & Lin, C.-C. (2015). To create without losing face: The effects of face cultural logic and social-image affirmation on creativity. *Journal of Organizational Behavior, 36*(7), 919–943.

Mohanty, A. K., & Babu, N. (1982). Bilingualism and metalinguistic ability among kond tribals in Orissa, India. *Journal of Social Psychology, 121*, 15–22.

Mok, A., & Morris, M. W. (2010a). Asian-Americans' creative styles in Asian and American situations: Assimilative and contrastive responses as a function of bicultural identity integration. *Management and Organization Review, 6*(3), 371–390.

Mok, A., & Morris, M. W. (2010b). An upside to bicultural identity conflict: Resisting groupthink in cultural ingroups. *Journal of Experimental Social Psychology, 46*(6), 1114–1117.

Mok, A., & Morris, M. W. (2011). Forecasting good or bad behaviour: A non-transparent test of contrastive responses to cultural cues. *Asian Journal of Social Psychology, 14*(4), 294–301.

Mol, J. J. (1963). The function of marginality. *International Migration, 1*(2), 175–177.

Morris, M. W., & Leung, K. (2010). Creativity east and west: Perspectives and parallels. *Management and Organization Review, 6*(3), 313–327.

Morris, M. W., Mok, A., & Mor, S. (2011). Cultural identity threat: The role of cultural identification in moderating closure responses to foreign cultural inflow. *Journal of Social Issues, 67*(4), 760–773.

Morrison, E. W., & Milliken, F. J. (2003). Guest editor's introduction: Speaking up, remaining silent: The dynamics of voice and silence in organizations. *Journal of Management Studies, 40*(6), 1353–1357.

Moulin, L. (1955). The Nobel prizes for the sciences from 1901–1950: An essay in sociological analysis. *British Journal Of Sociology, 6*, 246–263.

Mussweiler, T. (2003). Comparison processes in social judgment: Mechanisms and consequences. *Psychological Review, 110*, 472–489.

Mussweiler, T., & Damisch, L. (2008). Going back to Donald: How comparisons shape judgmental priming effects. *Journal of Personality and Social Psychology, 95,* 1295–1315.

Nash, D., & Schaw, L. (1962). Personality and adaptation in an overseas enclave. *Human Organization, 21*(4), 252–263.

Nemeth, C. J. (1986). Differential contributions of majority and minority influence. *Psychological Review, 93*(1), 23.

Nemeth, C. J., & Kwan, J. L. (1985). Originality of word associations as a function of majority vs. minority influence. *Social Psychology Quarterly, 48*(3), 277–282.

Nemeth, C. J., & Wachtler, J. (1983). Creative problem solving as a result of majority vs minority influence. *European Journal of Social Psychology, 13*(1), 45–55.

Neuberg, S. L., & Newsom, J. T. (1993). Personal need for structure: Individual differences in the desire for simpler structure. *Journal of Personality and Social Psychology, 65*(1), 113–131.

Nijstad, B. A., De Dreu, C. K., Rietzschel, E. F., & Baas, M. (2010). The dual pathway to creativity model: Creative ideation as a function of flexibility and persistence. *European Review of Social Psychology, 21*(1), 34–77.

Noriko, S., Fan, X., & Van Dusen, L. (2001). A comparative study of creative thinking of American and Japanese college students. *The Journal of Creative Behavior, 35*(1), 24–36.

Nouri, R., Erez, M., Rockstuhl, T., & Ang, S. (2008). *Creativity in multicultural teams: The effects of cultural diversity and situational strength on creative performance.* Paper presented at the The Academy of Management Annual Meeting, Anaheim, CA.

Paradis, M. (1997). The cognitive neuropsychology of bilingualism. In J. F. Kroll (Ed.), *Tutorials in bilingualism: Psycholinguistic perspectives* (pp. 331–354). Hillsdale, NJ: Erlbaum.

Pichler, F. (2011). Cosmopolitanism in a global perspective: An international comparison of open-minded orientations and identity in relation to globalization. *International Sociology, 27*(1), 21–50.

Pyszczynski, T., Greenberg, J., & Koole, S. L. (2004). Experimental existential psychology: Exploring the human confrontation with reality. In J. Greenberg, S. L. Koole, & T. Pyszczynski (Eds.), *Handbook of experimental existential psychology* (pp. 3–9). New York, NY: Guilford.

Pyszczynski, T., Greenberg, J., Solomon, S., Arndt, J., & Schimel, J. (2004). Why do people need self-esteem? A theoretical and empirical review. *Psychological Bulletin, 130*(3), 435–468.

Ramírez-Esparza, N., Gosling, S. D., Benet-Martínez, V., Potter, J. P., & Pennebaker, J. W. (2006). Do bilinguals have two personalities? A special case of cultural frame switching. *Journal of Research in Personality, 40,* 99–120.

Razzouk, N. Y., & Masters, L. (1986). *Cultural marginality in the Arab world: Implications for Western marketers.* New York, NY: de Gryyteiz.

Rosch, E. (1978). Principles of categorization. In E. Rosch & B. B. Lloyd (Eds.), *Cognition and categorization* (pp. 27–48). Hillsdale, NJ: Erlbaum.

Ross, M., Xun, W. Q. E., & Wilson, A. E. (2002). Language and the bicultural self. *Personality and Social Psychology Bulletin, 28*(8), 1040–1050.

Roudometof, V. (2005). Transnationalism, cosmopolitanism and glocalization. *Current Sociology, 53*(1), 113–135.

Rudmin, F. W., & Ahmadzadeh, V. (2001). Psychometric critique of acculturation psychology: The case of Iranian migrants in Norway. *Scandinavian Journal of Psychology*, *42*(1), 41–56.

Saad, C. S., Damian, R. I., Benet-Martínez, V., Moons, W. G., & Robins, R. W. (2013). Multiculturalism and creativity effects of cultural context, bicultural identity, and ideational fluency. *Social Psychological and Personality Science*, *4*(3), 369–375.

Saruk, A., & Gulutsan, M. (1970). Academic performance of students and the cultural orientation of their parents. *Alberta Journal of Educational Research*, *16*(3), 189–195.

Simon, W. L., & Young, J. S. (2005). *iCon: Steve Jobs, the greatest act in the history of business*. Somerset, NJ: John Wiley & Sons.

Simonton, D. K. (1975). Sociocultural context of individual creativity: A transhistorical time-series analysis. *Journal of Personality and Social Psychology*, *32*, 1119–1133.

Simonton, D. K. (1997). Foreign influence and national achievement: The impact of open milieus on Japanese civilization. *Journal of Personality and Social Psychology*, *72*, 86–94.

Simonton, D. K. (2000). Creativity: Cognitive, developmental, personal, and social aspects. *American Psychologist*, *55*, 151–158.

Simonton, D. K. (2008). Bilingualism and creativity. In J. Altarriba & R. R. Heredia (Eds.), *An introduction to bilingualism: Principles and processes* (pp. 147–166). New York, NY: Lawrence Erlbaum.

Sinclair, R. C. (1988). Mood, categorization breadth, and performance appraisal: The effects of order of information acquisition and affective state on halo, accuracy, information retrieval, and evaluations. *Organizational Behavior and Human Decision Processes*, *42*(1), 22–46.

Somerville, K. (2008). Transnational belonging among second generation youth: Identity in a globalized world. *Journal of Social Sciences*, *10*, 23–33.

Starreveld, P. A., De Groot, A. M. B., Rossmark, B. M. M., & Van Hell, J. G. (2013). Parallel language activation during word processing in bilinguals: Evidence from word production in sentence context. *Bilingualism: Language and Cognition*, *17*(2), 258–276.

Suedfeld, P., Tetlock, P. E., & Streufert, S. (1992). Conceptual/integrative complexity. In C. P. Smith (Ed.), *Motivation and personality: Handbook of thematic content analysis* (pp. 393–400). New York, NY: Cambridge University Press.

Szerszynski, B., & Urry, J. (2002). Cultures of cosmopolitanism. *The Sociological Review*, *50*(4), 461–481.

Tadmor, C. T., Galinsky, A. D., & Maddux, W. W. (2012). Getting the most out of living abroad: Biculturalism and integrative complexity as key drivers of creative and professional success. *Journal of Personality and Social Psychology*, *103*(3), 520–542.

Tadmor, C. T., & Tetlock, P. E. (2006). Biculturalism a model of the effects of second-culture exposure on acculturation and integrative complexity. *Journal of Cross-Cultural Psychology*, *37*(2), 173–190.

Tadmor, C. T., Tetlock, P. E., & Peng, K. (2009). Acculturation strategies and integrative complexity the cognitive implications of biculturalism. *Journal of Cross-Cultural Psychology*, *40*(1), 105–139.

Triandis, H. C. (1989). The self and social behavior in differing cultural contexts. *Psychological Review*, *96*(3), 506–520.

Triandis, H. C. (1994). *Culture and social behavior*. New York, NY: McGraw-Hill.

Walsh, S., Shulman, S., Feldman, B., & Maurer, O. (2005). The impact of immigration on the internal processes and developmental tasks of emerging adulthood. *Journal of Youth and Adolescence, 34*(5), 413–426.

Wan, W., & Chiu, C. y. (2002). Effects of novel conceptual combination on creativity. *The Journal of Creative Behavior, 36*, 227–241.

Ward, T. B. (1994). Structured imagination: The role of conceptual structure in exemplar generation. *Cognitive Psychology, 27*, 1–40.

Ward, T. B. (2007). Creative cognition as a window on creativity. *Methods, 42*(1), 28–37.

Ward, T. B., Patterson, M. J., Sifonis, C. M., Dodds, R. A., & Saunders, K. N. (2002). The role of graded category structure in imaginative thought. *Memory & Cognition, 30*, 199–216.

Ward, T. B., Smith, S. M., & Vaid, J. (1997). Conceptual structures and processes in creative thought. In T. B. Ward, S. M. Smith, & J. Vaid (Eds.), *Creative thought: An investigation of conceptual structures and processes* (pp. 1–27). Washington, DC: American Psychological Association.

White, J. H. (1978). *The American railroad passenger car*. Baltimore, MD: Johns Hopkins University Press.

Wiley, J. (1998). Expertise as a mental set: The effect of domain knowledge in creative problem solving. *Memory & Cognition, 26*, 716–730.

The Wired Interview. (1993). Steve Jobs: The next insanely great thing. Retrieved September 19, 2015, from archive.wired.com/wired/archive/4.02/jobs_pr.html

Wong, R. Y., & Hong, Y. Y. (2005). Dynamic influences of culture on cooperation in the prisoner's dilemma. *Psychological Science, 16*(6), 429–434.

2

The Creative Process
of Cultural Evolution

LIANE GABORA ■

If I have seen further, it is by standing on the shoulders of giants.
—Isaac Newton, 16th century

Even this saying itself is a variant of a similar statement attributed to Bernard of Chartres in the 12th century, and it inspired the title for a book by Steven Hawking and an album by Oasis. Creative ideas beget other creative ideas and, as a result, modifications accumulate. We see an overall increase in the complexity of cultural novelty over time, a phenomenon sometimes referred to as the *ratchet effect* (Tomasello, Kruger, & Ratner, 1993). Although we may never meet the people or objects that creatively influence us, by assimilating what we encounter around us and bringing to bear our own insights and perspectives, we all contribute in our own way, however small, to a second evolutionary process: the evolution of culture.

This chapter explores how we can better understand culture by understanding the creative processes that fuel it, and better understand creativity by examining it from its cultural context. First, we look at some theoretical frameworks for how culture evolves and what these frameworks imply for the role of creativity. Then we will see how questions about the relationship between creativity and cultural evolution have been addressed using an agent-based model. We will also discuss studies of how creative outputs are influenced, in perhaps unexpected ways, by other ideas and individuals, and how individual creative styles "peek through" cultural outputs in different domains.

A SCIENTIFIC FRAMEWORK FOR CULTURAL EVOLUTION

Darwin vastly enhanced our understanding of the organismal world by integrating scattered biological knowledge into an evolutionary framework, enabling us to see how species fit together in a unified "tree of life." His feat even improved our ability to make predictions about what kinds of underlying mechanisms were at work and what traits or species we might expect in particular environments. Because art, technology, languages, and customs change over time in a manner seemingly reminiscent of biological evolution, it seems reasonable to view culture as a second evolutionary process. This section gives a brief overview of two theories of cultural evolution, and discusses what these theories imply for our understanding of creativity.

Cultural Evolution as a Selectionist Process

Biological evolutionary processes can be seen as consisting of two components: the *generation* of new variants, and the differential survival or *selection* of some of those variants, such that they live long enough to produce offspring. Darwin's explanation focused not on the generation of variants but on the selection of some fraction of them, which is why it is sometimes referred to as a *selectionist* theory. He posited that biological change is due to the effect of differential selection on the distribution of heritable variation in a population; those with adaptive traits live longer, have more offspring, and are "selected" for, and therefore, their traits proliferate in future generations. Thus, a selectionist process works through competitive exclusion among *existing* variants; it is not a mechanism that affects how variants are generated in the first place. In fact, it assumes that variants are generated randomly, for to the extent that variation is not randomly generated, the distribution of variants reflects whatever was biasing the generation away from random in the first place, not survival of the fittest. Notice also that the theory operates on the timescale of generations, as it requires at a minimum an entire generation for change to occur.

The reason a selectionist explanation is applicable in biology is that in biological evolution there are two kinds of traits: (1) *inherited traits* (e.g., blood type or eye color), which are transmitted vertically from parent to offspring by way of the genes; and (2) *acquired traits* (e.g., a tattoo, or knowledge of someone's name), which are obtained during an individual's lifetime, and which are sometimes called *epigenetic* because they are not transmitted vertically through the genes. Because acquired traits are not passed down (e.g., you do not inherit your mother's tattoo), in biological evolution, the fast intragenerational transmission of acquired traits does not drown out the slow, intergenerational transmission of inherited traits. In other words, a Darwinian explanation works when the longterm (i.e., intergenerational) impact of *acquired* change is negligible relative to that of *inherited* change; otherwise the first, which can operate over minutes, overwhelms the second, which requires generations.

Attempts to develop a scientific framework for cultural evolution initially attempted to frame it as a selectionist process (Aunger, 2000; Boyd & Richerson, 1985; Gabora, 1996). However, this was difficult to reconcile with the high frequency of altruism in human societies (wouldn't genes that support altruism be selected against?) and, when examined closely, the selectionist theory is incompatible with basic facts about how culture evolves (Fracchia & Lewontin, 1999; Gabora, 2004, 2011, 2013; Gabora & Kauffman, in press; Temkin & Eldredge, 2007). In cultural evolution there is no mechanism for discarding acquired change (e.g., once one cup had a handle, all cups could have handles). Therefore, acquired change accumulates orders of magnitude faster than, and overwhelms, change due to the mechanism Darwin proposed: differential replication of variants in response to selection. Moreover, to the extent that the *generation* of novelty deviates from random chance, change is due to whatever is causing that deviation in the first place rather than to *selection* of fitter variants. In short, cultural change is acquired, not inherited, and it is generated not randomly, but through strategy and intuition. Therefore, a Darwinian theory of creative cultural evolution has been found to be inappropriate (Gabora, 2004, 2008a, 2011, 2013; Gabora & Kauffman, 2016).

Cultural Evolution as a Communal Exchange Process

This analysis prohibits a selectionist, but not an evolutionary, framework for culture. Even in the biological realm we are only just starting to appreciate the key role played by non-Darwinian epigenetic processes (Kauffman, 1993; Koonin, 2009; Koonin & Wolf, 2012; Lynch, 2007; Woese, 2002; Woese & Goldenfeld, 2009). Research on the origin of life suggests that early life consisted of autocatalytic protocells that evolved through a non-Darwinian process of *communal exchange*, and that natural selection emerged later from this more haphazard, ancestral evolutionary process (e.g., Gabora, 2006; Hordijk, Steel, & Kauffman, 2012; Segre, 2000; Vetsigian, Woese, & Goldenfeld, 2006; Wächtershäuser, 1997). Communal exchange is more haphazard than selection, and does not require a self-assembly code (such as the genetic code). What it requires is structure that is (1) *self-organizing*: its components generate new components through their interactions, (2) *self-replicating*: through duplication of components it can reconstitute an entity like itself, and (3) *interactive*: entities exchange components. Table 2.1 provides a summary of the similarities and differences between natural selection and communal exchange. Both have mechanisms for preserving continuity and for introducing novelty. However, whereas natural selection is a high-fidelity Darwinian process and the structure that self-replicates is DNA-based self-assembly instructions, communal exchange is a low-fidelity Lamarckian process, and the structure that replicates is an autopoietic network. Only communal exchange allows transmission of acquired traits. Communal exchange is the proposed mechanism by which early life evolved, as well as the mechanism by which culture evolves, and some aspects of present-day life, such as horizontal

Table 2.1. SIMILARITIES AND DIFFERENCES BETWEEN TWO EVOLUTIONARY
FRAMEWORKS: NATURAL SELECTION AND COMMUNAL EXCHANGE

	Natural Selection	Communal Exchange
Unit of self-replication	DNA	Autopoietic network
Mechanism for preserving continuity	DNA replication; proofreading enzymes, etc.	Retention of horizontally transmitted information
Mechanism for generating novelty	Mutation; recombination; replication errors; pseudo-genes	Faulty duplication of autopoietic structure; transmission errors; innovation
Self-assembly code	Yes	No
High fidelity	Yes	No
Transmission of acquired traits	No	Yes
Type of process	Darwinian	Lamarckian (by some standards)
Evolutionary processes it seeks to explain	Biological	Early life; horizontal gene transfer (HGT); cultural

SOURCE: From Gabora (2013).

gene transfer. A schematic illustration of both evolution through a selectionist process and evolution through communal exchange is provided in Figure 2.1.

If even biological life initially evolved not through a selectionist process but through communal exchange, it seems reasonable that cultural evolution would get established through this simpler, more haphazard process (Gabora, 2000a, 2013). Adults share ideas with children such that eventually they develop their own self-organized network of understandings, at which point they can adapt ideas to their own needs and perspectives, and thereby contribute creatively to culture. We can refer to such a web of understandings as a *worldview*. A worldview is self-regenerating: An adult shares concepts, ideas, attitudes, stories, and experiences with children (and other adults), influencing little by little the formation of other worldviews. Thus, through interactions among its parts, a worldview not only responds to perturbations but also reconstitutes itself. Each worldview takes form through the influence of many others, though some, such as those of relatives and teachers, may predominate. Children expose fragments of what was originally the adult's worldview to different experiences and different bodily constraints, thereby forging unique internal models of the relation of self to world.

Thus, the human mind dynamically reconfigures itself to achieve a more stable configuration, and it acts in ways that cause such reconfigurations to proliferate; it possesses the necessary structure for evolution through communal exchange, as illustrated schematically in Figure 2.2. The more information a mind encodes, the

Evolution through natural selection

Lineage A

Individual in generation 1	
Individual in generation 2	
More individuals in generation 3	

Lineage B

Individual in generation 1	
Individual in generation 2	
No individuals in generation 3	

Evolution through communal exchange

Lineage A

Individual 1	
Individual 2	

Lineage B

Individual 1	

Figure 2.1. Top: Schematic depiction of evolution through natural selection. Each individual has a genotype, represented by a small circle, and a phenotype, represented by a larger circle encompassing the small circle. Phenotypic change acquired over a lifetime, indicated by increasingly lighter gray, is not passed on, as indicated by the fact that in lineage A the individual born in generation 2 did not inherit the lighter gray the parent acquired by the time it had offspring. Lineage A outcompetes lineage B as indicated by the fact that by generation 3 there are no individuals left in lineage B. Evolution relies on *competition among* individuals rather than *transformation of* individuals. Bottom: Evolution through *communal exchange* involves the duplication and transformation of variants. There is no distinction between phenotype and genotype, and acquired characteristics are transmitted, as shown by how in lineage A, Individual 2 has the light gray its "parent" acquired over its lifetime. Death does not have the same finality since, given the right conditions, an inert individual could potentially reconstitute itself, as in Lineage B. Therefore, the term "generations" is not meaningful. Acquired change is transmitted. Communal exchange relies more on *transformation of* individuals than *competition among* individuals. Biological evolution involves both communal exchange and natural selection. With respect to cultural evolution, the matter is still a subject of discussion but many, including the author, believe it evolves solely through communal exchange. (From Gabora, 2013)

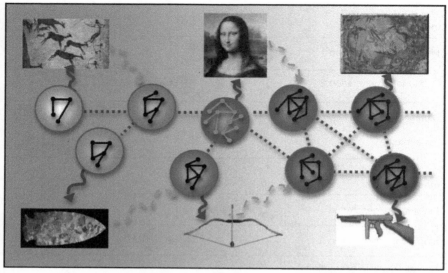

Figure 2.2. Schematic depiction of how worldviews evolve, not through *survival of the fittest* but *transformation of all*. *Worldviews* transform as a consequence of psychological entropy-reducing restructuring and communal exchange. Individuals are represented by spheres and their internal models of the world, or *worldviews*, are represented by networks within the spheres. Patterns of social transmission are indicated by dashed lines. Creative contributions to culture are indicated by wavy arrows from creator to artifact. Learning through exposure to artifacts is indicated by wavy dashed arrows. Worldviews and patterns of social transmission tend to become more complex over time. Individuals such as the one with the network on the far right are more compelled than others to reframe what they learn in their own terms, potentially resulting in a more unique or nuanced worldview. Such "self-made" individuals are more likely to have an effect on culture (e.g., through the creation of artifacts), which may influence the formation of new worldviews long after they have died. This is indicated by the diffusion of segments from self-made individuals to other individuals, either indirectly by way of exposure to the Mona Lisa, or directly by way of exposure to its creator. (From Gabora, 2013)

greater the variety of ways this knowledge base can be reconfigured. Its configuration is revealed through behavioral regularities in how it expresses itself and responds to situations, and in the creative outputs it generates. Note that although this process does not involve selection in its technical sense (i.e., change due to the effect of differential selection on the distribution of heritable variation across a population), selection as the term is used in everyday parlance may play a role (i.e., individuals may be selective about which aspects of their worldviews they share or assimilate).

For minds to evolve through communal exchange, they must be organized such that, for any given concept or idea, there exists *some* pathway (e.g., a chain of associations, or deductive reasoning) by which it could potentially interact with and modify any other given concept or idea. The concepts and ideas must form an integrated whole; that is, they must be able to interact with and modify others not just in the same local cluster (as in comparing one dress to another) but across clusters (as in cross-domain analogy). Thus, a big question is: How did the human mind acquire this kind of structure?

EVOLUTION OF THE CAPACITY FOR CHAINING AND REDESCRIPTION

Let us first consider how the mind acquired the capacity to modify thoughts and ideas by thinking about them in the context of other thoughts and ideas that are similar, that is, in the same local knowledge domain. Merlin Donald (1991) suggested that the enlarged cranial capacity of our *Homo erectus* ancestors 1.7 million years ago enabled them to voluntarily retrieve and modify memories independent of environmental cues (sometimes referred to as "autocuing"), a capacity he referred to as *self-triggered recall and rehearsal*, and which ushered forth a transition to a new mode of cognitive functioning. Thus, while *Homo habilis* was limited to the "here and now," *Homo erectus* could *chain* memories, thoughts, and actions into more complex ones and progressively modify them, thereby gaining new perspectives on past or possible events, and even mime or reenact them for others. The notion of self-triggered recall bears some resemblance to Hauser et al.'s (2002) idea that what distinguishes human cognition from that of other species is the capacity for recursion, and to Penn, Penn, Holyoak, and Povinelli's (2008) concept of *relational reinterpretation*, the ability to reinterpret higher order relations between perceptual relations.

Donald's proposal has been shown to be consistent with the structure and dynamics of associative memory (Gabora, 2000b, 2010a). Neurons are sensitive to primitive stimulus attributes or "microfeatures," such as sounds of a particular pitch or lines of a particular orientation. Experiences encoded in memory are *distributed* across cell assemblies of neurons, and each neuron participates in the encoding of many experiences. Memory is also *content addressable:* Similar stimuli activate overlapping distributions of neurons. With larger brains, experiences could be encoded in more detail, enabling a transition from coarse-grained to fine-grained memory. Fine-grained memory enabled concepts and ideas to be encoded in more detail; that is, there were more ways in which distributed sets of microfeatures could overlap. Greater overlap enabled more routes for self-triggered recall, and it paved the way for streams of abstract thought. Ideas could now be reprocessed until they fit together with cognitive structures already in place, allowing for the emergence of local clusters of mutually consistent ideas, and thus for a more coherent internal model of the world, or worldview (Gabora, 1999; Gabora & Steel, 2017).

EVOLUTION OF CAPACITY FOR CROSS-DOMAIN THINKING

At this point it was possible to think about an idea in relation to other closely related ideas and thereby forge clusters of mutually consistent ideas, which allowed for a narrow kind of creativity, limited to minor adaptations of existing ideas. But the mind was not integrated, nor truly creative, until it could forge connections between seemingly disparate ideas, such as in the formation of analogies. How did this come about?

One proposal is that it was due to the onset in the Middle/Upper Paleolithic of *contextual focus* (CF): the ability to shift between different modes of thought—an explicit *analytic mode* conducive to logical problem solving, and an implicit *associative mode* conducive to insight and breaking out of a rut (Gabora, 2003). Whereas dual processing theories generally attribute abstract, hypothetical thinking solely to a more recently evolved "deliberate" mode (e.g., Evans, 2003), according to the CF hypothesis, abstract thought is possible in either mode, but it will have a different character in the two modes (flights of fancy versus logically constructed arguments) (Sowden, Pringle, & Gabora, 2014). CF thus paved the way for integration of different domains of knowledge (Mithen, 1998). It has been proposed that CF was made possible by mutation of the FOXP2 gene, which is known to have undergone human-specific mutations in the Paleolithic era (Chrusch & Gabora, 2014). FOXP2, once thought to be the "language gene," is not uniquely associated with language. The idea is that, in its modern form, FOXP2 enabled fine-tuning of the neurological mechanisms underlying the capacity to shift between processing modes by varying the size of the activated region of memory.

IMPLICATIONS OF CULTURAL EVOLUTION FRAMEWORK FOR CREATIVITY

The communal exchange theory of cultural evolution suggests a theory of creativity, sometimes referred to as honing theory, according to which peoples' uniquely structured webs of understanding, or *worldviews*, are the basic units of cultural evolution. It is through the "honing" of creative ideas that worldviews transform and evolve. In other words, the creative process reflects the natural tendency of a worldview to seek a state of dynamic equilibrium by exploring perspectives and associations until the worldview achieves a more stable state than it started with. A creative outcome (e.g., a painting) can be an *external* manifestation of *internal* cognitive restructuring brought about through immersion in a creative task. The creator may see and feel the world differently afterward, which is why creativity can be transformative, and why expressive art therapies are gaining prominence. Not all creative outputs involve extensive cognitive restructuring; some are minor variations on a theme, and others outright imitations, which is why a creative work cannot be fully understood outside of its cultural context.

COMPUTATIONALLY MODELING THE EVOLUTION OF CULTURAL NOVELTY

It is difficult to test experimentally hypotheses about how the creative abilities underlying cultural transitions evolved. Agent-based modeling is a computational methodology in which artificial agents can be used to represent interacting individuals. It enables us to address questions about the workings of collectives such as societies. It is particularly valuable for answering questions of this sort which lie at the interface between anthropology and psychology, owing both to (1) the difficulty of experimentally manipulating a variable, such as the average amount by which one invention differs from its predecessor and observing its impact on cumulative culture over time, and (2) the sparseness of the premodern archaeological record. Although methods for analyzing archaeological remains are becoming increasingly sophisticated, they cannot always distinguish among different theories.

EVOC (for EVOlution of Culture) is a computational model of cultural evolution that consists of neural network-based agents that invent new actions and imitate actions performed by neighbors (Gabora, 1995, 2008b). The assemblage of ideas changes over time not because some replicate at the expense of others, as in natural selection, but through inventive and social processes. Agents can learn generalizations concerning what kinds of actions are useful, or have a high "fitness," with respect to a particular goal, and use this acquired knowledge to modify ideas for actions before transmitting them to other agents. A model such as EVOC is a vast simplification, and results obtained with it may or may not have direct bearing on complex human societies, but it allows us to vary one parameter while holding others constant and thereby test hypotheses that could otherwise not be tested. It provides new ways of thinking about and understanding what is going on.

EVOC exhibits typical evolutionary patterns, such as (1) a cumulative increase in the fitness and complexity of cultural outputs over time, and (2) an increase in diversity as the space of possibilities is explored followed by a decrease as agents converge on the fittest possibilities, as illustrated in Figure 2.3. EVOC has been used to model how the mean fitness and diversity of cultural elements is affected by factors such as population size and density, and borders that affect transmission between populations, as well as the questions reported here pertaining to creativity.

Modeling Hypothesized Cognitive Breakthroughs Underlying Cultural Transitions

Recall Donald's hypothesis that cultural evolution was made possible by the onset of the capacity for one thought to trigger another, leading to the chaining and progressive modification of thoughts and actions (Donald, 1991). This was tested in EVOC by comparing runs in which agents were limited to single-step actions to runs in which they could chain ideas together to generate multistep actions (Gabora, Chia, & Firouzi, 2013). As illustrated in Figure 2.4, chaining increased the mean fitness and diversity of cultural outputs across the artificial society. Whereas chaining and no-chaining runs both converged on optimal actions, without chaining this set was static, but with chaining it was in constant flux as ever-fitter actions were found. Whereas without chaining there was a ceiling on mean fitness of actions, with chaining there was no such ceiling, and chaining also enhanced the effectiveness of the ability to learn trends. These findings support the hypothesis that the ability to chain ideas together can transform a culturally static society into one characterized by open-ended novelty.

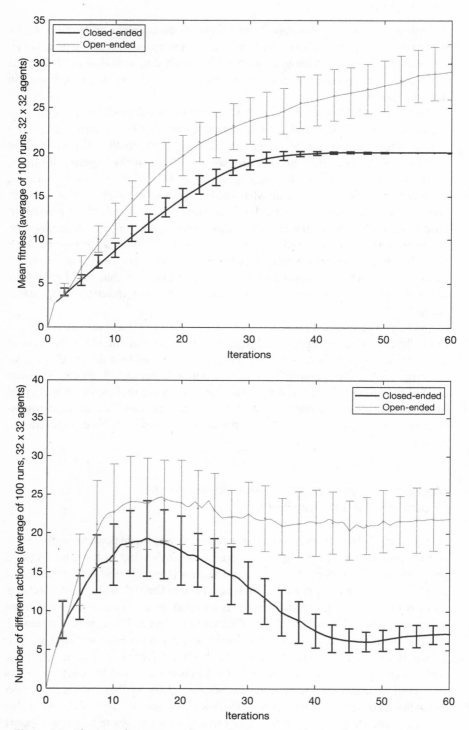

Figure 2.3. The typical increase in fitness of cultural outputs over time (top) and increase in diversity as the space of possibilities is being explored followed by a decline as the society converges on the fittest (bottom). These graphs also demonstrate the effect on fitness and diversity is an open-ended space of possibilities.

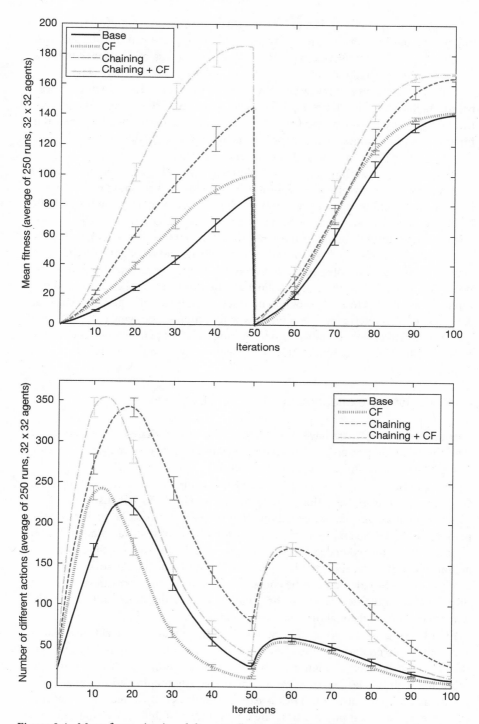

Figure 2.4. Mean fitness (top) and diversity (bottom) of cultural outputs across the artificial EVOC society with both chaining and CF, chaining only, CF only, and neither chaining nor CF. Data are means of 500 runs. (From Gabora & Smith, submitted)

The hypothesis that the onset of CF brought about a second cognitive transition underlying the human capacity to evolve complex culture was also tested with EVOC (Gabora, Chia, & Firouzi, 2013). When the fitness of an agent's outputs was low, it temporarily shifted to a more divergent mode by increasing α: the degree to which a newly invented idea deviates from the idea on which it was based. As illustrated in Figure 2.4, both mean fitness of actions across the society increased with CF, as hypothesized, and CF was particularly effective when the fitness function changed, which supports its hypothesized utility in breaking out of a rut and adapting to new or changing environments.

These findings show how a cultural evolutionary framework can provide a valuable perspective on creativity. Note, however, that although chaining made the variety of novel outputs open ended, and this became even more pronounced with CF, these novel outputs were nonetheless predictable. Chaining and CF did not open up new cultural niches in the sense that, for example, the invention of cars created niches for the invention of things like seatbelts and stoplights. EVOC in its current form could not solve *insight problems*, which require restructuring the solution space. Nonetheless, these results illustrate the effectiveness of chaining and CF. Building on a related research program in concept combination (e.g., Aerts, Gabora, & Sozzo, 2013), models of concepts provide further support, showing that CF is conducive to making creative connections by placing concepts in new contexts (Gabora & Aerts, 2009; Gabora & Kitto, 2013; Veloz, Gabora, Eyjolfson, & Aerts, 2011).

Impact of Creative Leadership on Cultural Evolution

Throughout history there have been leaders who were imitated more frequently than the common person. An interesting question is: What is the impact of leadership on creativity and the evolution of culture?

This question was also investigated in EVOC using the *broadcasting* function. Broadcasting allows the action of a leader to be visible to not just immediate neighbors but all agents, thereby simulating the effects of media, such as public performances, television, or the Internet, on patterns of cultural change. When broadcasting is turned on, each agent adds the broadcaster as a possible source of actions it can imitate. A particular agent can be chosen as the broadcaster before the run, or the broadcaster can be chosen at random, or the user can specify that the agent with the fittest action is the broadcaster. Broadcasting can be intermittent or continuous throughout the duration of a run.

Broadcasting produced a modest increase in the fitness of actions, but it accelerates convergence on optimal actions, thereby consistently reducing diversity. This can be seen in Figure 2.5 by comparing column 1 with no leader to column 2 with one leader. Here we see the previously mentioned increase in diversity as the space of possibilities is explored followed by a decrease as agents converge on the fittest possibilities. The total number of different actions after 20 iterations decreases from eight to five when a leader is introduced, and the percentage of agents executing the most popular action increases from 41% to 84%. Thus, leadership accentuates the normal plummet in diversity.

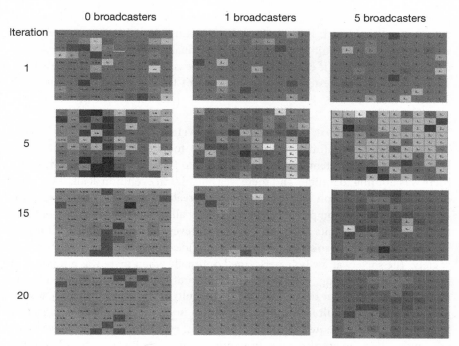

Figure 2.5. Diversity of actions over a run with 0, 1, and 5 broadcasters. Different actions are represented by differently colored cells. In all cases there is an increase followed by a decrease in diversity over time (moving down any column from the first iteration at the top to the 20th at the bottom), but this becomes less pronounced with additional leaders. In these experiments, broadcasters were chosen at random in every iteration, and when there were multiple broadcasters available to imitate, agents selected the broadcaster whose action was most similar to their own. (Adapted from Gabora, 2008b)

Figure 2.5 also shows the impact of a dictatorial style of leadership (one broadcaster) versus a more distributed style of leadership (multiple leaders). As we go from one leader to five leaders, the total number of different actions after 20 iterations increases from five to nine, and the percentage of agents executing the most popular action decreases from 84% to 31%. Thus, the leadership-induced decrease in diversity is mitigated by a more distributed leadership.

The effectiveness of creative versus uncreative styles of leadership was also investigated. Creative leadership increased the mean fitness of cultural outputs only when nonleaders were relatively uncreative, and it increased the diversity of outputs only early in a run during initial exploration of the space of possibilities (Leijnen & Gabora, 2010).

Balancing Creativity With Continuity

Cultural evolution, like any evolutionary process, requires a balance of change and continuity. While creative individuals generate the novelty that fuels cultural evolution, absorption in their creative process impedes the diffusion of proven solutions, effectively rupturing the fabric of society. Thus, it was hypothesized that a society in which creative (novelty-injecting) individuals are interposed with imitating (continuity-maintaining) individuals ensures both that new ideas come about and that, if effective, they are not easily lost by society as a whole. This hypothesis was tested in EVOC in a set of three experiments (Gabora & Tseng, 2017).

VARYING THE RATIO OF INVENTING TO IMITATING

To investigate the optimal ratio of inventing to imitating, the invention-to-imitation ratio was systematically varied from 0 to 1. When agents never invented, there was nothing to imitate, and there was no cultural evolution at all. If the ratio of invention to imitation was even marginally greater than 0, not only was cumulative cultural evolution possible, but eventually all agents converged on optimal outputs. When all agents always invented and never imitated, the mean fitness of cultural outputs was also suboptimal because fit ideas were not dispersing through society. The society as a whole performed optimally when there was a mixture of inventing and imitating, with the optimal ratio of the two being approximately 1:1, with the exact value depending on the difficulty of the fitness function; for example, with the difficult fitness function shown in Figure 2.6, it was significantly lower than 1:1. This showed that, as in biological evolution, culture evolves most efficiently when the novelty-generating process of creativity is tempered with the continuity-fostering process of imitation.

VARYING THE RATIO OF CREATORS TO CONFORMERS

The finding that very high levels of creativity can be detrimental for society led to the hypothesis that there is an adaptive value to society's ambivalent attitude toward creativity; society as a whole may benefit from a distinction between the conventional workforce and what has been called a "creative class" (Florida, 2002). This was investigated by introducing two types of agents: *conformers*, who only obtained new actions by imitating, and *creators*, who obtained new actions either by inventing or imitating (Gabora & Firouzi, 2012). A given agent was either a creator or an imitator throughout the entire run, and whether a given creator invented or imitated in a given iteration fluctuated stochastically. We could systematically vary C, the proportion of creators to imitators in the society, and p, how creative the creators were. As illustrated in Figure 2.7, we observed a tradeoff between C and p, thus providing further evidence that society as a whole functions optimally when creativity is tempered with continuity.

SOCIAL REGULATION OF HOW CREATIVE PEOPLE ARE

We then hypothesized that society as a whole might perform even better with the ability to adjust creativity in accordance with their perceived creative success, through mechanisms such as selective ostracization of deviant behavior unless accompanied by the generation of valuable cultural novelty, and encouraging of successful creators. A first step in investigating this was to determine whether it is algorithmically possible to increase the mean fitness of ideas in a society by

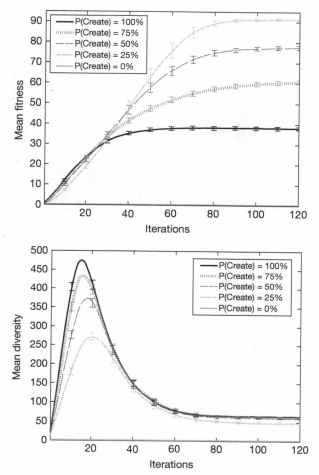

Figure 2.6. Fitness (top) and diversity (bottom) of cultural outputs with different ratios of inventing to imitating.

enabling them to self-regulate how creative they are. To test the hypothesis that the mean fitness of cultural outputs across society increases faster with social regulation (SR) than without it, we increased the relative frequency of invention for agents that generated superior ideas and decreased it for agents that generated inferior ideas (Gabora & Tseng, 2014). Thus, when SR was on, if relative fitness was high, the agent invented more; if it was low, the agent imitated more. $p(C)$ was initialized at 0.5 for both SR and non-SR societies.

When social regulation was introduced into the artificial society, the mean fitness of cultural outputs was higher, as shown in Figure 2.8. The typical pattern was observed with respect to diversity, or number of different ideas: an increase in diversity as the space of possibilities is explored followed by a decrease as agents converge on fit actions. However, this pattern occurred earlier, and was more pronounced, in societies with SR than societies without it.

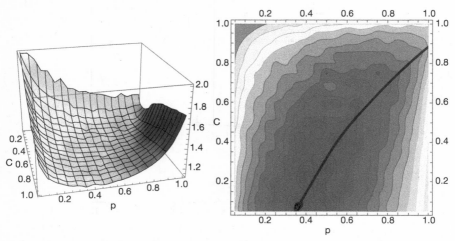

Figure 2.7. The effect of varying the percentage of creators, C, and how creative they are, *p*, on the mean fitness of ideas in EVOC. Three-dimensional graph (left) and contour plot (right) for the average mean fitness for different values of C and *p* using discounting to ensure that the present value of any given benefit with respect to idea fitness diminishes as a function of elapsed time before that benefit is realized. The z-axis is reversed to obtain an unobstructed view of surface; therefore, lower values indicate higher mean fitness. The line in the contour plot shows the position of a clear ridge in fitness landscape indicating optimal values of C and *p* that are submaximal for most {C, *p*} settings; that is, a tradeoff between how many creators there are and how creative they should be. The results suggest that excess creativity at the individual level can be detrimental at the level of the society because creators invest in unproven ideas at the expense of propagating proven ideas. The same pattern of results was obtained analyzing just one point in time and using a different discounting method (not shown). (Adapted from Gabora & Firouzi, 2012)

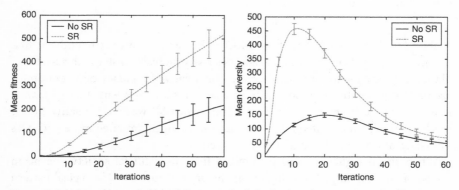

Figure 2.8. Mean fitness (left) and diversity (right) of cultural outputs across all agents over the duration of the run with and without social regulation. Data are averages across 250 runs. (From Gabora & Tseng, 2014)

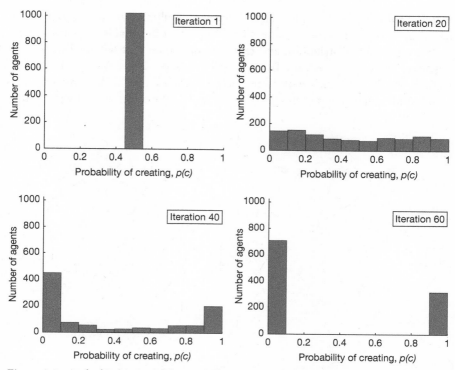

Figure 2.9. At the beginning of the run, all agents created and imitated with equal probability. Midway through, their *p(C)* values were distributed along the range from 0 to 1. By iteration 60 they had segregated into two distinct groups: conformers (with *p(C)* from 0 to 0.1) and creators (with *p(C)* from 0.9 to 1). (From Gabora & Tseng, 2014)

As illustrated in Figure 2.9, societies with SR ended up separating into two distinct groups: one that primarily invented, and one that primarily imitated. Thus, the observed increase in fitness can indeed be attributed to increasingly pronounced individual differences in their degree of creative expression over the course of a run. Agents who generated superior cultural outputs had more opportunity to do so, whereas agents who generated inferior cultural outputs became more likely to propagate proven effective ideas rather than reinvent the wheel.

DOCUMENTING OUR CULTURAL ANCESTRY

The application of phylogenetic techniques derived from Darwinian approaches to culture present a distorted picture of cultural history as branching rather than network-like, because they do not incorporate horizontal transmission and blending. Also, because they incorporate only measurable attributes, they do not capture relatedness that resides at the conceptual level (e.g., mortars and pestles are highly related despite little similarity at the attribute level). To deal with this, the communal exchange theory of culture inspired a new technique for chronicling material cultural history, which has been used on multiple data sets. This method has been shown to generate a pattern of cultural ancestry that is more congruent with geographical distribution and temporal data than that obtained with phylogenetic approaches (Gabora, Leijnen, Veloz, & Lipo, 2011; Veloz, Tempkin, & Gabora, 2012). An example of a small set of data in Figure 2.10 shows how the communal exchange representation is weblike—it allows for not just vertical but

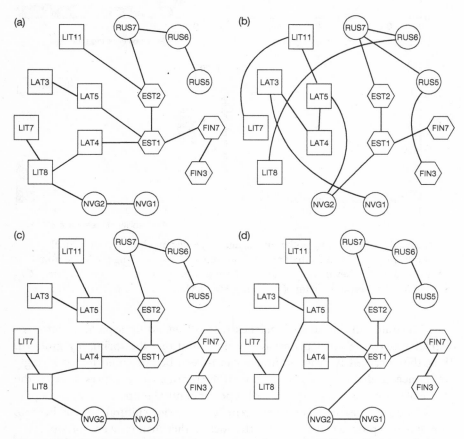

Figure 2.10. Similarity graphs based on conceptual network analysis of Baltic psalteries (a kind of stringed musical instrument) under different perspective-weighting schemes. By incorporating not just physical characteristics but also conceptual attributes (such as those pertaining to sacred symbolic imagery), and weighting them differently, it was possible to resolve ambiguities obtained with the phylogenetic approach and generate a lineage more consistent with other historical data. (a) Physical attributes only; (b) symbolism; (c) physical attributes and symbolism (equal weights); (d) physical attributes (25% weight) and symbolism (75% weight). Each node corresponds to a single artifact. Node shapes indicate ethnolinguistic groups: Slavic (circle), Finnic (hexagon), and Baltic (square). Shaded nodes designate archaeological instruments (10–13 cc); remaining nodes correspond to ethnographical instruments (17–20 cc). (From Veloz, Tempkin, & Gabora, 2012)

also horizontal lines of descent—not branching, as would be imposed on it by a phylogenetic representation, which allows for only vertical lines of descent.

UNDERSTANDING CREATIVE WORKS IN THEIR CULTURAL CONTEXT

We now examine studies with real humans that explore in various ways the interplay between creativity and the cultural milieu.

Cross-Domain Recognizability of Creative "Essence"

To what extent is a creative idea an abstract Platonic essence, and to what extent is it something that could only emerge from within the constraints of a specific domain? This question has implications for the evolution of culture, because the greater the extent to which ideas are not tied to their manifestation in any particular domain, the greater the extent to which creative novelty can reflect influences from diverse sources.

In a study that set out to investigate this empirically, it was demonstrated that when pieces of music were reinterpreted as paintings, naïve participants were able to correctly identify at significantly above chance which piece of music inspired which painting (Ranjan, 2014; Ranjan, Gabora, & O'Connor, 2014). Although the medium of expression is different, something of its essence remains sufficiently intact for an observer to detect a resemblance between the new work and the source that inspired it. This result lent empirical support to the largely anecdotal body of evidence that cross-domain influence is a genuine phenomenon, and it suggested that, at their core, creative ideas are less domain dependent than is generally assumed. It did not, however, provide evidence that the phenomenon extends beyond the artificial conditions of such a study, nor did it give an indication of how prevalent it is.

Cross-Domain Influences on Innovation

Who or what influenced your creative output? Anecdotal reports and case studies (e.g., Feinstein, 2006) are one method of getting answers to this question. However, we are exposed to so many different people and objects in our lives that we may not be completely conscious of whom or what influences our creative outputs. We are beginning to be able to corroborate anecdotal reports with machine-learning techniques designed to resolve lines of influence (Saleh, Abe, & Elgammal, 2014), but these techniques are not yet able to discern cross-domain influences, wherein a creator in one domain (e.g., artist) is influenced by another domain (e.g., music).

Because Darwinian theories assume strictly vertical transmission and do not allow different "species" of cultural artifacts to "mate," they are incompatible with

Table 2.2. PERCENTAGE OF CROSS-DOMAIN (CD), WITHIN-
DOMAIN NARROW (WD-n), WITHIN-DOMAIN BROAD (WD-b), AND
UNCERTAIN (U) INFLUENCES

	CD	WD-n	WD-b	U
% of Total	47%	27%	8%	18%

SOURCE: From Gabora and Carbert (2015).

cross-domain influence. In contrast, communal exchange theory predicts that cross-domain influence not only *exists*; it fuels cultural innovation. In a project designed to test between these competing predictions, 66 creative individuals in a variety of disciplines were asked to list as many influences on their creative work as they could (Gabora & Carbert, 2015). Results strongly suggest that cross-domain influences are in fact more widespread than within-domain influences, even when broad within-domain influences (e.g., technology influenced by music) as well as narrow within-domain influences (e.g., music influenced by other music) are taken into account (Table 2.2).

Cross-Domain Recognizability of Creative Style

If creative output reflects not just chance or expertise but the idiosyncratic process of wrestling with personally meaningful issues to forge an integrated worldview, one might expect creative individuals to have a characteristic style or "voice," a distinctive facet of their personality that is recognizable not just within domains but across domains. Empirical support has been obtained for this prediction (Gabora, 2010b; Gabora, O'Connor, & Ranjan, 2012; Ranjan, 2014). Art students were able to identify at significantly above-chance levels which famous artists created pieces of art they had not seen before. They also identified at significantly above-chance levels which of their classmates created pieces of art they had not seen before. More surprisingly, art students also identified the creators of nonpainting artworks that they had not seen before. Similarly, creative writing students were able to identify at significantly above-chance levels passages of text written by famous writers that they had not encountered before and passages of text written by their classmates that they had not encountered before. Perhaps most surprising of all, creative writing students also identified at significantly above-chance levels which of their classmates created particular works of visual art, that is, they recognized the personal style of a creative writer in a domain *other than* writing.

Creativity is sometimes thought to be "domain specific" because expertise or eminence in one creative endeavor is rarely associated with expertise or eminence in another (Baer, 1996; Tardif & Sternberg, 1988). Although polymaths exist, famously creative scientists are rarely famously creative artists. However, the results summarized in the previous paragraph support the view that creative achievement can be characterized in terms of, not just expertise or eminence, but the ability to express what we genuinely are through whatever media we have at our disposal. When looked at this way, creativity does appear to be more domain-general than it was believed to be.

APPLICATIONS OF RESEARCH ON THE CULTURAL EVOLUTION OF CREATIVITY

Finally, let us briefly mention how research on creativity in a cultural context is being used to model one kind of cognitive process by which people find creative solutions to practical problems: *exaptation*. The concept of exaptation comes from biology, where it refers to the situation wherein a trait that originally came about to solve one problem is co-opted for another use. Exaptation has been shown to play a pivotal role in economics (Dew, Sarasvathy, & Ventakaraman, 2004), and a preliminary attempt has been made to develop a mathematical model of exaptation that can be applied across disciplines (Gabora, Scott, & Kauffman, 2013). Applied to culture, it refers to the situation wherein a different context suggests a new use for an existing item. The approach provides a formal model of what Rothberg (2015) calls Janusian thinking, which involves achieving a creative outcome by looking at something from a different perspective. Waste recycling is an interesting form of cross-domain creative influence because of its applications to sustainability efforts. An item that is a wasteful byproduct in one context is found to be useful in a different context. The approach has been used to model the creative restructuring of a concept in a new context when it is considered from another perspective (Gabora & Carbert, 2015). A similar approach can be taken to data transformation, in which data in one format are changed to a different format while preserving the content so that the data can be put to a different purpose or made easier to interpret or understand (as in the visualization of astronomical data).

CONCLUSIONS

To understand how culture evolves, one must understand the creative processes that fuel cultural innovation. This chapter provided an overview of ways in which creativity and cultural evolution interact, and ways in which theoretical investigations and empirical studies of both can mutually inform one another. The chapter merely touches the tip of the iceberg of this fascinating topic. It will be exciting to see what the coming decade brings as we move ahead on the exciting journey toward understanding the lineages of creative influence that result in not just the artistic masterpieces that inspire us and the technological achievements that connect us but the ideas, gadgets, and jokes we encounter each day that make life simpler or just make us smile.

ACKNOWLEDGMENTS

This research was supported in part by a grant from the Natural Sciences and Engineering Research Council of Canada. Thanks to Simon Tseng, Stefan Leijnen, and Hadi Firouzi for the contributions to EVOC.

REFERENCES

Aerts, D., Gabora, L., & Sozzo, S. (2013). How concepts combine: A quantum theoretical model. *Topics in Cognitive Science, 5*, 737–772.

Aunger, R. (2000). *Darwinizing culture*. Oxford, UK: Oxford University Press.

Boyd, R., & Richerson, P. (1985). *Culture and the evolutionary process*. Chicago, IL: University of Chicago Press.

Baer, J. (1996). The effects of task-specific divergent-thinking training. *Journal of Creative Behavior, 30*, 183–187.

Chrusch, C., & Gabora, L. (2014). A tentative role for FOXP2 in the evolution of dual processing modes and generative abilities. In *Proceedings of the 36th meeting of the Cognitive Science Society* (pp. 499–504). Austin, TX: Cognitive Science Society.

Dew, N., Sarasvathy, S., & Ventakaraman, S. (2004). The economic implications of exaptation. *Journal of Evolutionary Economics, 14*, 69–84.

Donald, M. (1991). *Origins of the modern mind: Three stages in the evolution of culture and cognition*. Cambridge, MA: Harvard University Press.

Evans, J. S. B. (2003). In two minds: dual process accounts of reasoning. *Trends in Cognitive Science, 7*, 454–459.

Feinstein, J. S. (2006). *The nature of creative development*. Stanford, CA: Stanford University Press.

Fracchia, J., & Lewontin, R. C. (1999). Does culture evolve? *History and Theory, 38*, 52–78.

Gabora, L. (1996). A day in the life of a meme. *Philosophica, 57*, 901–938.

Gabora, L. (1999). Weaving, bending, patching, mending the fabric of reality: A cognitive science perspective on worldview inconsistency. *Foundations of Science, 3*, 395–428.

Gabora, L. (2000a). Conceptual closure: Weaving memories into an interconnected worldview. *Annals of the New York Academy of Sciences, 901*, 42–53.

Gabora, L. (2000b). Toward a theory of creative inklings. In R. Ascott (Ed.), *Art, technology, and consciousness* (pp. 159–164). Bristol, UK: Intellect Press.

Gabora, L. (2003). Contextual focus: A cognitive explanation for the cultural transition of the Middle/Upper Paleolithic. In *Proceedings of the 25th annual meeting of the Cognitive Science Society* (pp. 432–437). Hillsdale, NJ: Lawrence Erlbaum.

Gabora, L. (2004). Ideas are not replicators but minds are. *Biology & Philosophy, 19*, 127–143.

Gabora, L. (2006). Self-other organization: Why early life did not evolve through natural selection. *Journal of Theoretical Biology, 241*, 443–450.

Gabora, L. (2008a). The cultural evolution of socially situated cognition. *Cognitive Systems Research, 9*, 104–113.

Gabora, L. (2008b). Modeling cultural dynamics. In *Proceedings of the Association for the Advancement of Artificial Intelligence (AAAI) Fall Symposium 1: Adaptive Agents in a Cultural Context* (pp. 18–25). Menlo Park, CA: AAAI Press.

Gabora, L. (2010a). Revenge of the "neurds": Characterizing creative thought in terms of the structure and dynamics of human memory. *Creativity Research Journal, 22,* 1–13.

Gabora, L. (2010b). Recognizability of creative style within and across domains: Preliminary studies. In R. Camtrabone & S. Ohlsson (Eds.), *Proceedings of the Annual Meeting of the Cognitive Science Society* (pp. 2350–2355). Austin, TX: Cognitive Science Society.

Gabora, L. (2011). Five clarifications about cultural evolution. *Journal of Cognition and Culture, 11,* 61–83.

Gabora, L. (2013). An evolutionary framework for culture: Selectionism versus communal exchange. *Physics of Life Reviews, 10,* 117–145.

Gabora, L., & Aerts, D. (2009). A model of the emergence and evolution of integrated worldviews. *Journal of Mathematical Psychology, 53,* 434–451.

Gabora, L. & Carbert, N. (2015). Cross-domain influences on creative innovation: Preliminary Investigations. In R. Dale, C. Jennings, P. Maglio, T. Matlock, D. Noelle, A. Warlaumont & J. Yashimi (Eds.), *Proceedings of the 37th Annual Meeting of the Cognitive Science Society* (pp. 758–763). Austin, TX: Cognitive Science Society.

Gabora, L., Chia, W., & Firouzi, H. (2013). A computational model of two cognitive transitions underlying cultural evolution. In *Proceedings of the 35th annual meeting of the Cognitive Science Society* (pp. 2344–2349). Austin, TX: Cognitive Science Society.

Gabora, L., & Kauffman, S. (in press). Toward an evolutionary-predictive foundation for creativity. *Psychonomic Bulletin & Review.*

Gabora, L., & Kitto, K. (2013). Concept combination and the origins of complex cognition. In E. Swan (Ed.), *Origins of mind: Biosemiotics series, Vol. 8* (pp. 361–382). Berlin, Germany: Springer.

Gabora, L., Leijnen, S., Veloz, T., & Lipo, C. (2011). A non-phylogenetic conceptual network architecture for organizing classes of material artifacts into cultural lineages. In *Proceedings of the 33rd annual meeting Cognitive Science Society* (pp. 2923–2928). Austin, TX: Cognitive Science Society.

Gabora, L., O'Connor, B., & Ranjan, A. (2012). The recognizability of individual creative styles within and across domains. *Psychology of Aesthetics, Creativity, and the Arts, 6,* 351–360.

Gabora, L., Scott, E., & Kauffman, S. (2013). A quantum model of exaptation: Incorporating potentiality into biological theory. *Progress in Biophysics & Molecular Biology, 113,* 108–116.

Gabora, L., & Steel, M. (2017). Autocatalytic networks in cognition and the origin of culture. *Journal of Theoretical Biology, 431,* 87–95.

Gabora, L., & Tseng, S. (2014). Computational evidence that self-regulation of creativity is good for society. In P. Bello, M. Guarini, M. McShane, & B. Scassellati (Eds.), *Proceedings of the 36th Annual Meeting of the Cognitive Science Society* (pp. 2240–2245). Austin TX: Cognitive Science Society.

Gabora, L., & Tseng, S. (2017). The social benefits of balancing creativity and imitation: Evidence from an agent-based model. *Psychology of Aesthetics, Creativity, and the Arts, 11*(4), 457–473.

Hauser, M. D., Chomsky, N., & Fitch, W. T. (2002). The faculty of language: What is it, who has it and how did it evolve? *Science, 298,* 1569–1579.

Hordijk, W., Steel, M., & Kauffman, S. (2012). The structure of autocatalytic sets: Evolvability, enablement, and emergence. *Acta biotheoretica, 60*(4), 379–392.

Kauffman, S. (1993). *Origins of order.* New York, NY: Oxford University Press.

Koonin, E. V. (2009). Darwinian evolution in the light of genomics. *Nucleic Acids Research, 37*, 1011–1034.

Koonin, E. V., & Wolf, Y. I. (2012). Evolution of microbes and viruses: a paradigm shift in evolutionary biology? *Frontiers in cellular and infection microbiology, 2.*

Leijnen, S., & Gabora, L. (2010). An agent-based simulation of the effectiveness of creative leadership. In R. Camtrabone & S. Ohlsson (Eds.), *Proceedings of the Annual Meeting of the Cognitive Science Society* (pp. 955–960). Austin TX: Cognitive Science Society.

Lynch, M. (2007). The frailty of adaptive hypotheses for the origins of organismal complexity. *Proceedings of the National Academy of Science USA, 104*, 8597–8604.

Mithen, S. (1998). *Creativity in human evolution and prehistory.* London, UK: Routledge.

Ranjan, A. (2014). *Understanding the creative process: Personal signatures and cross-domain interpretations of ideas.* Doctoral dissertation: University of British Columbia.

Ranjan, A., Gabora, L., & O'Connor, B. (2013). The Cross-domain re-interpretation of artistic ideas. In M. Knauff, M. Pauen, N. Sebanz, & I. Wachsmuth (Eds.), *Proceedings of the 35th Annual Meeting of the Cognitive Science Society* (pp. 3251–3256). Austin TX: Cognitive Science Society.

Rothenberg, A. (2015). *Flight from wonder: An investigation of scientific creativity.* Oxford, UK: Oxford University Press.

Saleh, B., Abe, K & Elgammal, A. (2014). Knowledge discovery of artistic influences: A metric learning approach. In *Proceedings of the Fifth International Conference on Computational Creativity.* Palo Alto, CA: Association for the Advancement of Artificial Intelligence.

Segre, D. (2000). Compositional genomes: Prebiotic information transfer in mutually catalytic noncovalent assemblies. *Proceedings National Academy Science USA, 97*, 4112–4117.

Sowden, P., Pringle, A., & Gabora, L. (2014). The shifting sands of creative thinking: Connections to dual process theory. *Thinking & Reasoning, 21*, 40–60.

Tardif, T. Z., & Sternberg, R. J. (1988). What do we know about creativity? In R. J. Sternberg (Ed.), *The nature of creativity: contemporary psychological perspectives* (pp. 429–440). Cambridge, UK: Cambridge University Press.

Temkin, I., & Eldredge, N. (2007). Phylogenetics and material cultural evolution. *Current Anthropology, 48*, 146–153.

Tomasello, M., Kruger, A. C., & Ratner, H. H. (1993). Cultural learning. *Behavioral and Brain Science, 16*, 495–511.

Veloz, T., Gabora, L., Eyjolfson, M., & Aerts, D. (2011). A model of the shifting relationship between concepts and contexts in different modes of thought. *Lecture Notes in Computer Science 7052: Proceedings of the Fifth International Symposium on Quantum Interaction.* Berlin, Germany: Springer.

Veloz, T., Tempkin, I., & Gabora, L. (2012). A conceptual network-based approach to inferring cultural phylogenies. In *Proceedings of 34th meeting of Cognitive Science Society* (pp. 2487–2492). Austin, TX: Cognitive Science Society.

Vetsigian, K., Woese, C., & Goldenfeld, N. (2006). Collective evolution and the genetic code. *Proceedings National Academy Science, 103*, 10696–10701.

Wächtershäuser, G. (1997). The origin of life and its methodological challenge. *Journal of Theoretical Biology, 187*, 483–494.

Woese, C. R. (2002). On the evolution of cells. *Proceedings National Academy Science,* *99,* 8742–8747.

Woese, C. R., & Goldenfeld N. (2009). How the microbial world saved evolution from the scylla of molecular biology and the charybdis of the modern synthesis. *Microbiology and Molecular Biology Reviews, 73,* 14–21.

Creativity in Sociocultural Contexts

3

Cultural-Historiometric Studies of Creativity

DEAN KEITH SIMONTON ■

Creativity researchers have long made the distinction between "little-c" and "Big-C" creativity (Simonton, 2013). The former is most often associated with everyday creativity at home and work, whereas the latter is most frequently identified with making a creative contribution to a culturally valued domain, such as science, philosophy, literature, art, or music. Those Big-C creators who have made enduring contributions to the histories of civilizations may then be called *creative geniuses*. Indeed, the greatest Big-C creators largely *define* a given civilization's intellectual and artistic history (Murray, 2003). What would the Italian Renaissance be without Leonardo da Vinci, Michelangelo, and Raphael? These three artistic geniuses were highly praised in their own time, and they continue to be acclaimed today (Ginsburgh & Weyers, 2006). This close correspondence was acknowledged by the anthropologist Alfred Kroeber in his 1944 *Configurations of Culture Growth*, in which he assessed the rise, growth, and decline of cultures according to the magnitude of creative genius appearing at a particular time and place (see also Gray, 1958, 1961, 1966; Murray, 2003). Similarly, when the sociologist Pitirim Sorokin (1937–1941) sought to measure the "culture mentality" of a civilization in a given period, he could find no better recourse than to examine the comings and goings of Big-C creators, especially in philosophy (see also Klingemann, Mohler, & Weber, 1982; Simonton, 1976b).

Now, two implicit features of creative genius must be made more explicit. First, Big-C creators are distributed across nations, cultures, and civilizations, permitting cross-national, cross-cultural, and cross-civilization studies (Simonton, 2003a). For instance, Kroeber (1944) studied creative achievements in ancient Egypt, Mesopotamia, Persia, Greece, and Rome, as well as India, China, Japan, medieval Islam, and modern Europe. More recently, Murray (2003) examined creative genius in European, Islamic, Indian, Chinese, and Japanese civilizations.

Sometimes these comparative studies explicitly entail direct "East-versus-West" comparisons (Murray, 2014; Simonton & Ting, 2010). For instance, Simonton and Ting (2010) compared the characteristics of creators in both European and Chinese civilizations, finding convergence (with respect to precocity, productivity, age, versatility, and life span) but also divergence (regarding formal education and mental illness). Creativity in civilizations will sometimes have differences reflecting cultural contrasts, such as Europe having more linguistic diversity but less cultural stability than China.

Second, within any given nation, culture, or civilization, Big-C creators are distributed across a historical timeline—most often spanning a century or more. The best illustration is probably Chinese civilization, which exhibits a cultural continuity that dates back millennia (Simonton, 1988). To be sure, Chinese culture has gone through numerous transformations, especially the arrival of Buddhism, various "barbarian" invasions, and the advent of communism. Even so, it is telling that despite all of those historical changes, when the People's Republic of China finished constructing the world's fifth tallest sculpture in 2007, the sculpture depicted not Mao Zedong or Karl Marx, but rather Yan Di and Huang Di, two of the earliest emperors of ancient China. That would be comparable to the current Egyptian government building a massive monument to the Pharoah Khufu, who had built the Great Pyramid of Giza, when only the Coptic minority has even the remotest connection with the nation's pharaonic past. In any case, this second feature of creative genius permits the transhistorical study of how Big-C creativity fluctuates over the course of a culture's history (Simonton, 2003b).

These cultural and historical distributions have a critical connection. On the one hand, when we speak of different nations or civilizations, it is obvious that they are not culturally distinct. Japanese civilization cannot be discussed without any reference to Chinese civilization because much of the former culture was heavily influenced by the latter culture, via the process of cultural diffusion (Simonton, 1975c), a diffusion process that often transpired through Korea as the intermediary (Simonton, 1997c). Likewise, Roman civilization was heavily dependent on Greek civilization: The grandeur that was Rome was partly built on the glory that was Greece. Because the diffusion of cultural traits—such as artistic images and philosophical issues—takes time, that process has a definite temporal component. Indeed, rather than refer to Greek and then Roman civilization, often the two cultures will be arranged in an overlapping sequence, and then be termed Graeco-Roman civilization (e.g., Gray, 1958). Moreover, because the Roman Empire gave way to the Byzantine Empire, the Holy Roman Empire, and eventually modern Europe, the whole sequence may be styled European or even Western civilization. In a sense, it is again possible to speak of long-term cultural diffusion, a diffusion from the Eastern Mediterranean to the Western Mediterranean, and hence, eventually to Western Europe through Latin-Christian (Catholic) culture and to Eastern Europe through Greek-Christian (Orthodox) culture. As a result, both French and Russian cultures can be traced ultimately back to Homeric Greece, albeit by sometimes rather circuitous routes and tenuous threads (cf. Quigley, 1979; Toynbee, 1946). Therefore, transhistorical research of any substantial duration—usually extending a century or more—must necessarily be considered cross-cultural research as well. Victorian Great Britain does not represent the same sociocultural system as post–World War II Great Britain.

The issue now becomes, how can one study Big-C creativity across both time and space, or cultural innovation across history and geography? I know only one method, a method known as either historiometry or historiometrics (Simonton, 1990b). Any alternative method will leave out some crucial element. For example, psychometric assessments and interview techniques can be applied to contemporary creative geniuses but not to historical ones, and even cross-cultural studies of highly creative contemporaries are largely limited to Westernized nations where such scientific research is culturally accepted. Even then, pure logistic problems will restrict the investigation to a single nation. To illustrate, in Roe's (1953) major study of 64 eminent scientists, only one was born outside the United States and all were between 31 and 60 years old at the time of assessment, indicating that the sample largely represents the same time and place—namely, the mid-20th century United States. In comparison, one historiometric study of 2,016 eminent scientists obtained a sample that encompassed antiquity to the present day and all major continents except Antarctica (Simonton, 1991a). Plus, the sample was several times larger!

What is a historiometric study?

DEFINITION OF HISTORIOMETRY

Although the term "historiometry" was first coined more than a century ago (Woods, 1909, 1911), it did not receive a formal definition until many decades later (Simonton, 1990b, 2014a). For the purposes of this chapter, this definition holds that historiometric studies are engaged in testing nomothetic hypotheses about human thought, emotion, and behavior by applying quantitative analyses to biographical and historical data regarding multiple historic cases. This mouthful of words can be untangled by discussing the following concepts separately: nomothetic hypotheses, quantitative analyses, and multiple historic cases.

Nomothetic Hypotheses

A hypothesis is *nomothetic* when it refers to general laws, patterns, or regularities. For example, the commonplace conjecture that "cultural creativity is promoted by economic prosperity" counts as a nomothetic hypothesis (Durant & Durant, 1968; Kavolis, 1964; Norling, 1970). The statement is devoid of "names, dates, and places" that require the insertion of proper nouns and calendrical numbers. For instance, it is possible to convert the foregoing hypothesis into the more *idiographic* claim that "the rise of Florentine Renaissance art and architecture in the 15th and 16th centuries was promoted by the enormous wealth accumulated by the Medici Bank." Notice that this last proposition can be subsumed under the first as a special case of a general law. Indeed, if the nomothetic statement is empirically valid, then it can be said to provide an explanation for the idiographic observation, should it also prove empirically valid. This kind of explanation is sometimes referred to as a "Hempelian covering law" (Simonton, 1990b; see Hempel, 1965).

Nomothetic hypotheses in historiometric research are certainly more limited than what are found in the physical sciences. When Isaac Newton proposed the universal law of gravitation, he argued that it applied not just to objects falling on the earth but also to the planets rotating around the sun. Furthermore, his gravitational law claimed considerable predictive precision, so much so that it was eventually used to predict the existence of a new planet, Neptune. In contrast, the "laws of history" depart in two significant ways.

First, historiometric laws are invariably *statistical* rather than deterministic. That is, the supposed laws cannot explain all or even most of the variance in the criterion of interest. That limitation ensues from the fact that most cultural and historical phenomena have multiple causes, each adding its own little contribution to the overall explanation. In the case of the creativity–prosperity relation, for example, cultural activity is influenced by many factors besides pure economic growth. The Byzantine Empire was far richer than the Athenian Empire, yet it is the latter rather than the former that contained the Golden Age of Greek civilization. The simple statistical nature of historiometric hypotheses holds at the level of the individual Big-C creator. Even Thomas Carlyle, the conspicuous 19th-century proponent of the "Great Person Theory" of history (Carlyle, 1841), admitted, "Fame, we may understand, is no sure test of merit, but only a probability of such" (Carlyle, 1893/1928, p. 179). Indeed, some historiometric inquiries scrutinize the extent to which the eminence of creative genius is independent of actual creative contributions. An example is the eminence boost apparently obtained from dying tragically young, such as what happened to Wolfgang Amadeus Mozart and Franz Schubert (Simonton, 1976a).

Second, historiometric laws must always be constrained by certain *boundary conditions*. That is, the statistical association can only be expected to hold for cultures or historical periods that satisfy prerequisite circumstances. Perhaps the most obvious illustration is that a culture has to attain a given level of cumulative complexity before Big-C creativity can even be said to exist (Carneiro, 1970; Peregrine, Ember, & Ember, 2004). Below that level, full-time creators in any domain do not even appear. In the main, the culture usually has to evolve to the point of becoming a full-fledged civilization, with a writing system to record historical events and with sufficient urbanization in which those events take place. Other boundary conditions recognize that even civilizations can differ in specific cultural orientations, such as the apparent tendency for Western civilizations to be more individualistic and Eastern civilizations more collectivistic (Sorokin, 1937–1941; Triandis, 1995). This contrast has repercussions regarding the relation between political context and sociocultural creativity: An individualistic culture responds differently to an imperial regime than does a collectivistic culture. Where the former culture favors political fragmentation, the latter prefers political integration, with corresponding repercussions for Big-C creative activity (Simonton & Ting, 2010).

Quantitative Analyses

If nomothetic hypotheses are to be properly tested, then quantification is mandatory (Simonton, 2003c). This quantification consists of two parts: the *measurement* of the implied variables along a quantitative scale and the *analysis* of those measurements using statistics—given that the law or regularity is presumed to be statistical rather than deterministic. For example, suppose a researcher conjectures that international war is antithetical to cultural creativity (Norling, 1970). Both of these variables are intrinsically quantitative. On the one hand, war can vary from total peace (the zero point), to local and minor military conflicts, to worldwide conflagrations, such as occurred during World War II. This variation can be assessed a number of ways, such as the number of casualties incurred or battles fought (e.g., Wright, 1965). On the other hand, cultural creativity can also fluctuate across time and vary across space, as indicated by the number of Big-C creators or creative products generated by those creators (e.g., Price, 1978). Given these two quantified variables, the next step is to gauge the magnitude of association—by hypothesis negative—between the two. The most straightforward analysis would be to calculate the Pearson product–moment correlation between the two variables (e.g., Naroll et al., 1971; Simonton, 1976c).

In truth, the statistical analyses used in historiometric studies are most often far more complicated than merely calculating the simple "zero-order" bivariate correlation (Simonton, 1990b). These methods include multiple regression analysis, latent-variable modeling, time-series analysis, and multilevel modeling. Besides controlling for various potential artifacts and spurious relations, these methods enable the researcher to test directly if the findings are cross-culturally and transhistorically invariant. To illustrate, the tendency in literary creativity for poets to produce their best work at younger ages than prose authors was shown to be universal across time (from antiquity to the present) and across civilization areas (Western, Near Eastern, and Far Eastern; Simonton, 1975a), meaning that the contrast is intrinsic to the artistic medium (see also Simonton, 1997b, 2007b).

Multiple Historic Cases

Quantitative analyses of even the simplest kind are impossible without having a sufficient number of cases on which the key variables are accessed. Indeed, the methodological norm is to have far more cases than variables so that there are sufficient degrees of freedom to conduct the necessary statistics. For example, a multiple regression analysis is impossible unless the number of variables is less than the number of cases. In any event, very often historiometric studies begin with a large sample of individual creators, the size ranging between dozens to thousands (Simonton, 1990b). In this respect, historiometric studies of creativity do not differ from other studies of creativity using psychometric or experimental methods. The individual is still the unit of analysis, but the creators are exclusively Big-C rather than little-c. Every single creator in a historiometric sample has made history. Nonetheless, historiometric research often uses cases defined by units that are either much smaller or much bigger.

On the small side are those historiometric inquiries that use creative products as the unit of analysis. These products can include plays, poems, songs, symphonies, films, journal articles, books, discoveries, inventions, and so forth (e.g., Derks, 1989; Jackson & Padgett, 1982; Martindale, 1990; Simonton, 1989; Thagard, 2012; Zickar & Slaughter, 1999). Sometimes the studies will concentrate on the creative productions of a single creator (e.g., Derks, 1994; Kozbelt, 2005; Kozbelt & Burger-Pianko, 2007; Simonton, 1987). Furthermore, at times the products will be broken down into parts, rendering the units even smaller, such as stanzas in poems or melodies in compositions (e.g., Cerulo, 1988; Simonton, 1980b, 1990a).

On the large side are those historiometric studies that aggregate creators (or their products) either into years, decades, generations, or centuries (e.g., Murray, 2003; Price, 1978; Sorokin & Merton, 1935), into nations or civilizations (e.g., Candolle, 1873; Cattell, 1903), or some combination of the two (e.g., Lehman, 1947; Naroll et al., 1971; Yuasa, 1974).

This flexibility in defining the historic cases is a central asset of historiometric research on creativity. This method alone can span from the creativity of an individual melody to that of an entire civilization. Thus, the unit of analysis can be tailored to the specific nomothetic hypotheses. To illustrate, if the hypothesis concerns the characteristics of creative masterworks, then the product will be chosen as the unit of analysis, but if the hypotheses involve the circumstances that produce Golden Ages, then the generation will be selected.

HISTORY OF HISTORIOMETRY

Given the intrinsic fascination of Big-C creativity, it should come as no surprise that historiometry can be considered the oldest approach to the scientific study of creative genius. The first published investigation appeared in 1835, when Quetelet examined the relation between creative productivity and age in a sample of eminent French and British dramatists. Thirty years later, Galton (1865) conducted the first historiometric inquiry concerning whether genius is "born or made," a study that culminated in his 1869 *Hereditary Genius*, the first classic monograph using the method (Woods, 1909; see also Bramwell, 1948). Galton's work inspired additional research in the beginning of the 20th century, most notably by Cattell (1903) and Ellis (1904). Like Galton, these historiometric researchers included eminent leaders as well as creators. One advantage of the inclusiveness of this sample is that the leaders provide a comparison group of historic cases, providing a baseline for understanding the creative geniuses (e.g., Ludwig, 1992; Post, 1994; Simonton, 1976a; Simonton & Song, 2009). Such inclusively defined samples are also found in Cox's (1926) *Early Mental Traits of Three Hundred Geniuses*, perhaps the most ambitious historiometric study ever conducted (Richardson & Simonton, 2014).

Given that the preceding investigations were mostly conducted by psychologists, the unit of analysis was the individual. Other social scientists have preferred larger, aggregate units, such as whole nations or civilizations sliced into decades or centuries. In fact, the very first such investigation was published only a few years after Galton's 1869 contribution, namely, Candolle's (1873) cross-national inquiry regarding the political, economic, sociological, cultural, religious, and educational factors underlying the emergence of scientific genius. However, unlike Galton, Candolle had no immediate successors, so it was not until the 1930s and 1940s that researchers returned to quantitative studies of the sociocultural context of Big-C creativity (e.g., Lehman, 1947; McGuire, 1976; Schneider, 1937; Sorokin, 1937–1941). This alternative tradition was then extensively developed in the 1970s (e.g., Naroll et al., 1971), especially with the advent of generational time-series analyses (Simonton, 1984b; e.g., Simonton, 1975b).

A more recent development in historiometric research was the emergence of various content analytical methods for scrutinizing historiometric samples of creative products (Cerulo, 1984, 1988, 1989; Martindale, 1975). Especially critical is the appearance of computerized content-analytical programs (e.g., Derks, 1994; Paisley, 1964; Stirman & Pennebaker, 2001). These programs include both general purpose software, such as LIWC (Linguistic Inquiry and Word Count; e.g., Stirman & Pennebaker, 2001) and more specialized programs such as RID (Regressive Imagery Dictionary; e.g., Derks, 1994). Although computerized content analysis was first applied to literary text, eventually the technique was used to scrutinize other kinds of creative products, such as music compositions (e.g., Kozbelt & Burger-Pianko, 2007; Petrie, Pennebaker, & Sivertsen, 2008; Simonton, 1980b).

In the past decade or so, historiometry has been radically changed by the expansion of the Internet, and especially the appearance of online databases. Where once the historiometrician had to spend days in libraries and archives checking out books, photocopying pages, and taking notes on index cards, now Big-C creativity can often be studied by directly downloading the necessary information onto a computer. For instance, a considerable amount of recent research on cinematic creativity has been conducted using databases on critical evaluations, movie awards, box office performance, and film characteristics (see Simonton, 2011b, for a review). As increasingly more historical and biographical data become readily available on the Internet, the potential for historiometric research should expand substantially.

OVERVIEW OF EMPIRICAL RESEARCH

Given that historiometric research on creativity is well over a century old, it is not surprising that the resulting literature has become far too vast to summarize in a brief chapter. Indeed, three decades ago it took a whole book to review the cumulative findings (Simonton, 1984c), and considerably more research has been published since then (cf. Simonton, 1999a). Hence, I can do no more here than to provide an overview that treats what we have learned about creative geniuses, creative masterworks, and creative times and places.

Creative Geniuses

Because creative genius is usually defined in terms of achieved eminence in a culturally valued domain, one of the first issues often concerns how to assess achieved eminence (Cattell, 1903; Murray, 2003). Although such assessments can be based on measures as diverse as archival space measures, expert ratings, and disciplinary awards, research indicates that alternative assessments tap into the same latent variable, what has been called Galton's G (Simonton, 1991c). This single Big-C factor exhibits high internal consistency, reliability, is highly stable over time, and appears to be cross-culturally robust (Farnsworth, 1969; Ginsburgh & Weyers, 2014; Over, 1982; Rosengren, 1985; Simonton, 1991a; Vermeylen, van Dijck, & de Laet, 2013). This is not to say that historical trends and ethnocentric biases never intrude, but only that they tend to account for a small proportion of the variance and that it is easy to introduce the appropriate controls (Simonton, 1990b; cf. Runco, Kaufman, Halladay, & Cole, 2010; Whipple, 2004). For example, Candolle (1873) controlled for ethnocentric bias in the assessment of scientific genius by restricting the measure to eminence achieved outside the scientist's own country (viz. membership in foreign academies).

If individual variation in eminence becomes the gauge of the magnitude of Big-C creativity, the obvious next question is what factors predict eminence? The potential answers can be grouped into two main categories: differential and developmental.

Differential factors concern individual differences in behavior, cognition, or personality. A prominent example is creative productivity, a variable that is often considered the defining characteristic of creative genius (Albert, 1975). This variable actually contains several subsidiary variables, such as output rate and lifetime output, that provide critical predictors of creative eminence (R. A. Davis, 1987; Dennis, 1954; Simonton, 1977b, 1991a, 1991b, 1997c). Among cognitive factors, the most obvious is general intelligence or "IQ" (Cox, 1926; Simonton & Song, 2009; Walberg, Rasher, & Hase, 1978). Personality also plays an important role (Cox, 1926; Thorndike, 1950), such as openness to experience, as manifested in broad interests, voracious reading, versatility, and receptiveness to new ideas (Cassandro & Simonton, 2010; McCrae & Greenberg, 2014; Root-Bernstein et al., 2008; Sulloway, 2014; White, 1931). Of special interest and importance is the extensive research on the "mad-genius" hypothesis, research that finds some positive relation between psychopathological symptoms and creative eminence, especially in the arts (Juda, 1949; Karlsson, 1970; Kaufman, 2000–2001, 2001, 2005; Ko & Kim, 2008; Ludwig, 1992, 1998; Post, 1994; Ramey & Weisberg, 2004; Simonton,

2014c; Stirman & Pennebaker 2001; Weisberg, 1994). Also of particular interest is the relation between alcoholism and literary genius (W. M. Davis, 1986; Ludwig, 1990; Post, 1996; Schaller, 1997).

Developmental factors are even more diverse and long ranging. Such factors can extend from birth, with the work on genetics (Bramwell, 1948; Galton, 1869), to death, with the work on life expectancies (Cassandro, 1998; Kaufman, 2003; Kaun, 1991; McCann, 2001; Simonton 1997a)—literally from cradle to grave. Between these two endpoints are numerous other developmental variables involving family environment (Berry, 1981; Clark & Rice, 1982; Eisenstadt, 1978; Rothenberg & Wyshak, 2004; Schubert, Wagner, & Schubert, 1977; Sulloway, 1996; Terry, 1989; Walberg, Rasher, & Parkerson, 1980), gender (Kaufman, 2001; Simonton, 1992a, 2008b; Stariha & Walberg 1995), and formal education or professional training (Gieryn & Hirsh, 1983; Hayes, 1989; Simonton, 1991b, 2000). Finally, but most crucially, is the historiometric research on career trajectories, particularly the ages at which creative geniuses tend to produce their masterpieces (Galenson, 2005; Ginsburgh & Weyers, 2005; Jones, Reedy, & Weinberg, 2014; Kozbelt, 2014; Lehman, 1953; McKay & Kaufman, 2014; Raskin, 1936; Simonton, 1977a, 1991a, 1991b, 1992b, 2007a; Wray, 2003, 2004; Zusne, 1976). As observed earlier, the very first historiometric study ever published was devoted to this very question (Quetelet, 1835/1842). Career age leaves an imprint on other features of Big-C creativity as well, such as shifts in artistic style and openness to new ideas (Hull, Tessner, & Diamond, 1978; Lindauer, 2003; Simonton, 1986, 1987).

Creative Masterworks

Because Big-C creators are largely identified by the creative masterworks that define their careers, it is essential to take the creative product as the unit of analysis as well. Unfortunately, historiometric studies of this kind are less frequent than those that focus on creative geniuses. Nonetheless, these relatively few studies have led to some important findings. For example, just as evaluations of Big-C creators tend to be highly stable and consistent across history and cultures, the same applies to the creative products on which their reputations rest. Thus, an opera's reception in its opening season (including how many different language translations the libretto received) predicts its popularity before modern audiences even more than a century later (Simonton, 1998b; see also Simonton, 1989). Of course, if this stability and consensus did not appear for individual products, it would be difficult to imagine how there could be a stable consensus on the Big-C creators. In addition, analyses of creative products have helped detect some of the attributes that lead to their impact. These analyses have been most successful in literature (Harvey, 1953; Martindale et al., 1988; Simonton, 1986, 1989, 1990a) and music (Kozbelt & Burger-Pianko, 2007; Simonton, 1980b, 1995), but also some recent predictive successes have been seen in cinema (for review, see Simonton, 2011b). Somewhat ironically, it is far more difficult to decipher the basis for high-impact publications in the sciences. Even so, single creative contributions to science have provided the foundation for extensive inquiries into multiple discoveries and inventions (Brannigan & Wanner, 1983a, 1983b; Simonton, 1979). This distinctive event occurs when two or more creators independently, and often simultaneously, make the same contribution.

Finally, creative products have been analyzed to determine the cognitive processes involved in Big-C creativity. In the sciences, this research will often rely on notebooks, whereas in the arts the investigation will often focus on sketches (e.g., Simonton, 2012; Tweney, 1989). A particularly conspicuous example is the empirical work on Picasso's sketches for *Guernica* (Damian & Simonton, 2011; Simonton, 2007b; Weisberg, 2004). This historiometric research lends support to the conjecture that Campbell's (1960) blind-variation and selective-retention (BVSR) theory of creativity may provide the universal process underlying all Big-C creativity (Simonton, 2011a, in press). BVSR encompasses all of those processes and procedures in which low-probability ideational combinations are generated without prior knowledge of their utility values and then tested to determine those combinations with the highest utilities (Simonton, 2010). The universality of BVSR transcends not just creative domains but also historical periods and socio-cultural systems. The reason for this universality is that it constitutes the only way to make discoveries and conceive inventions that go beyond established domain-specific expertise.

Creative Times and Places

The emergence of creative genius and their products is necessarily contingent on the historical period and geographical location. This fact was first empirically demonstrated in Candolle's classic 1873 historiometric investigation, an inquiry that was conducted in direct response to Galton's (1869) extreme genetic determinism. Candolle specifically studied the distribution of great scientists in the years 1750, 1789, 1829, and 1869 for the United States and the main European nations (Britain, France, Germany, Italy, Switzerland, Holland, Spain, Portugal, Russia, Poland, and the Scandinavian countries). It was clear that each nation showed its distinctive rise and fall, so that the center of scientific genius would change across time (see also Kroeber, 1944; Lehman, 1947; Simonton, 2016; Yuasa, 1974).

As mentioned earlier, Candolle also tried to identify the factors in each time and place responsible for these shifts (albeit without using quantitative methods). Other historiometric research has also attempted to discern the historical and sociocultural factors that generate these Big-C creativity clusters across time and place. Some of these inquiries concentrate on external factors, that is, influences that impinge on the creative individual from outside the domain itself, such as international and domestic peace, economic prosperity, political freedom, cultural values, and prevailing ideology (Bernholz & Vaubel, 2004; Berry, 1999; Kuo, 1986, 1988; Martindale, 1975, 1990; Murray, 2003; Simonton, 1976b, 1976e, 1980a, 1992a; Sorokin, 1937–1941). Other studies focus on internal factors, that is, influences that operate from within a given creative domain. Examples include the availability of role models and mentors, domain-specific social networks, and changes in scientific paradigms or artistic conventions (Hellmanzik, 2014; Ko & Kim, 2008; Martindale, 1990; Simonton, 1975b, 1984a, 1988, 1992c). Naturally, some investigators deliberately combine both internal and external variables to determine their relative importance in the emergence of creative genius (Murray, 2003; Simonton, 1975b; Simonton & Tang, 2010).

Lastly, I should note that sometimes these various units of analysis can be combined to produce hybrid historiometric designs. Not only can individual creators be investigated in historical and sociocultural contexts (Simonton, 1976d, 1996), but even creative products can be examined in the doubled context of the individual creator and the sociocultural context, yielding a three-level analysis (Kozbelt, 2014; Simonton, 1980b). As Big-C creativity is inherently a multilevel phenomenon, these more complex designs hold great promise in the future.

EVALUATION

Although the preceding overview provides only the barest sketch of the vast research literature using historiometric methods, it should prove sufficient to permit a brief evaluation of its advantages and disadvantages in the study of creativity. The main advantages have been put forth at the very beginning of this chapter. Unless someone invents a bona fide time machine, historiometry provides the *only* method available for studying Big-C creativity without imposing any arbitrary restrictions regarding civilization area or historical period—especially the latter. For instance, when Simonton (1975a) wanted to study the age at which literary geniuses produced their greatest works, he picked historiometry because it permitted him to include almost all of the masterpieces of world literature, from ancient Greek and Latin to modern European literatures and from Arabic and Persian to Chinese and Japanese literatures. That breadth across time and space then ensured that any results would be transhistorically and cross-culturally invariant.

The foregoing example illustrates another advantage of historiometric research: the capacity to study questions that could not be easily answered otherwise. In the case of Simonton's (1975a) inquiry, the investigator wanted to look at how life span influenced the age at which literary geniuses produce their best work. Logically, that question requires that all members of the sample be deceased. Although this might be achieved in a longitudinal study that waits until the entire sample passes away, that approach is not very efficient (cf. Duggan & Friedman, 2014). The research subjects can even outlive the researcher! Moreover, many other crucial questions about Big-C creativity similarly seem to require historiometric responses. Indeed, almost any nomothetic hypothesis that contains the word "genius" must be considered prime material for a historiometric inquiry. After all, historiometry was originally invented to develop the "psychology of genius" (Woods, 1911, p. 568). Hence, a question such as "Is genius mad?" would seem to necessitate historiometric study (Simonton, 2014c). Although genius might be alternatively defined in terms of an exceptional IQ score (Terman, 1925–1959), a psychometric study of the relation between IQ and psychopathology would not address this question directly, and the answers might not even be the same. High-IQ people might easily be more mentally healthy while creative geniuses might be much less so. Given that IQ provides a very tenuous measure of general intelligence, and that general intelligence represents only a tiny part of Big-C creativity, the two alternative definitions cannot possibly be the same. So they need not correlate with the same variables at all.

A unique advantage of historiometry is worth noting as well: It provides the only practical method for studying creativity that can obtain what have been called *significant samples* (Simonton, 1999b). Such samples occur whenever the historic cases represent the entire available population of Big-C creators that satisfy the given sampling criteria regarding domain, time, and place (Murray, 2003). For example, historiometicians have studied *all* recipients of a Nobel Prize, *all* movies nominated for major cinematic award, or *all* sonnets by William Shakespeare. Because these historic cases can be exactly identified, the investigations do not suffer from the problems of sampling error that so often undermine studies that depend on a small sample drawn from a much larger population. Indeed, significance tests become largely irrelevant when exact replication becomes possible (Simonton, 2014d).

Even some of the supposed disadvantages of historiometric research cannot be accepted without qualification. For instance, it is certainly true that historiometry, as a correlational method, cannot support secure inferences of causal effects. Yet this deficiency in internal validity is counterbalanced by its superior external validity: Historiometric findings generalize to the real world because the data come directly from the real world. No extrapolations are necessary. Another objection is that because the historical record superficially seems to be dominated by European "dead white males," historiometric conclusions must also be restricted to that tiny subset of humanity (cf. Murray, 2014). Yet that objection overlooks the fact that history is richly populated by non-Europeans and by both females and persons of color (and some even still living). Consequently, it is possible to focus an entire historiometric sample on an otherwise underrepresented group. Such studies have included eminent woman psychologists (Simonton, 2008b) and female Japanese creative writers (Simonton, 1992a), as well as gender-neutral samples of highly creative African Americans (Damian & Simonton, 2015; Simonton, 1998a, 2008a), Arabs (Sorokin & Merton, 1935), Hindus (Schaefer, Babu, & Rao, 1977), Chinese (Kuo, 1986, 1988; Niu & Kaufman, 2005; Simonton, 1988; Simonton & Ting, 2010), and Japanese (Simonton, 1996, 1997c). For instance, Simonton (1992a) showed how the prominence of Japanese women literary creators in a given generation was contingent on the extent to which the culture was dominated by Confucian philosophy and militaristic ideology—two milieus antithetical to female achievement. In general, any culture or subculture that produced a historical record of their creative contributions can provide data for a historiometric study of Big-C creativity. That stipulation provides the only essential boundary condition.

To be sure, the historical record tends to become increasingly unreliable as we push back into the remote past. The Chinese emperors Yan Di and Huang Di, who were commemorated in the 2007 PRC monument, and as noted at the beginning of the chapter, are both embedded in the mists of legend. And the ancient civilizations of the Maya, Inca, and even much of pre-Muslim India have yet to be fully fathomed by modern archeology and historiography, if they ever will be. Nevertheless, it must be recognized that the historical record is continuing to grow at an accelerating pace. Better yet, that rapidly expanding record is becoming ever more accessible via Internet databases and archives. When these trends are coupled with the enhanced sophistication of the available statistical methods, an optimistic perspective on the continued progress of historiometric research becomes inevitable. Regardless of cultural origins, all of the Big-C creators who are active today, no matter where in the world they reside, can readily provide the historic cases of the future.

CONCLUSION

It is always dangerous to become a prophet—to predict the future. Yet I will still prophesize that historiometric research will continue to have a long history. Already the oldest scientific method for studying creativity (exceptional or otherwise), the technique will always attract those researchers who wish to take advantage of its unique advantages. Anyone who wants to study the Big-C creators of every civilization and in every historical period has no other choice. Particularly today, as cultures almost everywhere often seem to be moving toward a more homogeneous civilization—courtesy largely of modern technology—historiometric research provides the only means for studying Big-C creators who owned no computers or smartphones.

REFERENCES

Albert, R. S. (1975). Toward a behavioral definition of genius. *American Psychologist*, *30*, 140–151.

Bernholz, P., & Vaubel, R. (Eds.). (2004). *Political competition, innovation and growth in the history of Asian civilizations*. Northampton, MA: Elgar.

Berry, C. (1981). The Nobel scientists and the origins of scientific achievement. *British Journal of Sociology*, *32*, 381–391.

Berry, C. (1999). Religious traditions as contexts of historical creativity: Patterns of scientific and artistic achievement and their stability. *Personality & Individual Differences*, *26*, 1125–1135.

Bramwell, B. S. (1948). Galton's "Hereditary Genius" and the three following generations since 1869. *Eugenics Review*, *39*, 146–153.

Brannigan, A., & Wanner, R. A. (1983a). Historical distributions of multiple discoveries and theories of scientific change. *Social Studies of Science, 13*, 417–435.

Brannigan, A., & Wanner, R. A. (1983b). Multiple discoveries in science: A test of the communication theory. *Canadian Journal of Sociology, 8*, 135–151.

Campbell, D. T. (1960). Blind variation and selective retention in creative thought as in other knowledge processes. *Psychological Review, 67*, 380–400.

Candolle, A. de (1873). *Histoire des sciences et des savants depuis deux siècles*. Geneve, Switzerland: Georg.

Carlyle, T. (1841). *On heroes, hero-worship, and the heroic*. London, UK: Fraser.

Carlyle, T. (1893). Goethe. In *Critical and miscellaneous essays* (Vol. 1, pp. 172–222). London, UK: Chapman & Hall. (Work originally published 1828)

Carneiro, R. L. (1970). Scale analysis, evolutionary sequences, and the rating of cultures. In R. Naroll & R. Cohn (Eds.), *A handbook of method in cultural anthropology* (pp. 834–871). New York, NY: Natural History Press.

Cassandro, V. J. (1998). Explaining premature mortality across fields of creative endeavor. *Journal of Personality, 66*, 805–833.

Cassandro, V. J., & Simonton, D. K. (2010). Versatility, openness to experience, and topical diversity in creative products: An exploratory historiometric analysis of scientists, philosophers, and writers. *Journal of Creative Behavior, 44*, 1–18.

Cattell, J. M. (1903). A statistical study of eminent men. *Popular Science Monthly, 62*, 359–377.

Cerulo, K. A. (1984). Social disruption and its effects on music: An empirical analysis. *Social Forces, 62*, 885–904.

Cerulo, K. A. (1988). Analyzing cultural products: A new method of measurement. *Social Science Research, 17*, 317–352.

Cerulo, K. A. (1989). Variations in musical syntax: Patterns of measurement. *Communication Research, 16*, 204–235.

Clark, R. D., & Rice, G. A. (1982). Family constellations and eminence: The birth orders of Nobel Prize winners. *Journal of Psychology, 110*, 281–287.

Cox, C. (1926). *The early mental traits of three hundred geniuses*. Stanford, CA: Stanford University Press.

Damian, R. I., & Simonton, D. K. (2011). From past to future art: The creative impact of Picasso's 1935 *Minotauromachy* on his 1937 *Guernica*. *Psychology of Aesthetics, Creativity, and the Arts, 5*, 360–369.

Damian, R. I., & Simonton, D. K. (2015). Psychopathology, adversity, and creativity: Diversifying experiences in the development of eminent African Americans. *Journal of Personality and Social Psychology, 108*, 623–636.

Davis, R. A. (1987). Creativity in neurological publications. *Neurosurgery, 20*, 652–663.

Davis, W. M. (1986). Premature mortality among prominent American authors noted for alcohol abuse. *Drug and Alcohol Dependence, 18*, 133–138.

Dennis, W. (1954, September). Bibliographies of eminent scientists. *Scientific Monthly, 79*, 180–183.

Derks, P. L. (1989). Pun frequency and popularity of Shakespeare's plays. *Empirical Studies of the Arts, 7*, 23–31.

Derks, P. L. (1994). Clockwork Shakespeare: The Bard meets the Regressive Imagery Dictionary. *Empirical Studies of the Arts, 12*, 131–139.

Duggan, K. A., & Friedman, H. S. (2014). Lifetime biopsychosocial trajectories of the terman gifted children: health, well-being and longevity. In D. K. Simonton (Ed.), *The Wiley handbook of genius*. Oxford, UK: Wiley.

Durant, W., & Durant, A. (1968). *The lessons of history*. New York, NY: Simon & Schuster.

Eisenstadt, J. M. (1978). Parental loss and genius. *American Psychologist, 33*, 211–223.

Ellis, H. (1904). *A study of British genius*. London, UK: Hurst & Blackett.

Farnsworth, P. R. (1969). *The social psychology of music* (2nd ed.). Ames, IW: Iowa State University Press.

Galenson, D. W. (2005). *Old masters and young geniuses: The two life cycles of artistic creativity*. Princeton, NJ: Princeton University Press.

Galton, F. (1865). Hereditary talent and character. *Macmillan's Magazine, 12*, 157–166, 318–327.

Galton, F. (1869). *Hereditary genius: An inquiry into its laws and consequences*. London, UK: Macmillan.

Gieryn, T. F., & Hirsh, R. F. (1983). Marginality and innovation in science. *Social Studies of Science, 13*, 87–106.

Ginsburgh, V., & Weyers, S. A. (2005). Creativity and life cycles of artists. *Journal of Cultural Economics, 30*, 91–107.

Ginsburgh, V., & Weyers, S. A. (2006). Persistence and fashion in art: Italian Renaissance from Vasari to Berenson and beyond. *Poetics, 34*, 24–44.

Ginsburgh, V., & Weyers, S. A. (2014). Evaluating excellence in the arts. In D. K. Simonton (Ed.), *The Wiley handbook of genius*. Oxford, UK: Wiley.

Gray, C. E. (1958). An analysis of Graeco-Roman development: The epicyclical evolution of Graeco-Roman civilization. *American Anthropologist, 60*, 13–31.

Gray, C. E. (1961). An epicyclical model for Western civilization. *American Anthropologist, 63*, 1014–1037.

Gray, C. E. (1966). A measurement of creativity in Western civilization. *American Anthropologist, 68*, 1384–1417.

Harvey, J. (1953). The content characteristics of best-selling novels. *Public Opinion Quarterly, 17*, 91–114.

Hayes, J. R. (1989). *The complete problem solver* (2nd ed.). Hillsdale, NJ: Erlbaum.

Hempel, C. G. (1965). *Aspects of scientific explanation, and other essays in the philosophy of science*. New York, NY: Free Press.

Hellmanzik, C. (2014). Prominent modern artists: Determinants of creativity. In D. K. Simonton (Ed.), *The Wiley handbook of genius*. Oxford, UK: Wiley.

Hull, D. L., Tessner, P. D., & Diamond, A. M. (1978, November 17). Planck's principle: Do younger scientists accept new scientific ideas with greater alacrity than older scientists? *Science, 202*, 717–723.

Jackson, J. M., & Padgett, V. R. (1982). With a little help from my friend: Social loafing and the Lennon-McCartney songs. *Personality and Social Psychology Bulletin, 8*, 672–677.

Jones, B. F., Reedy, E. J., & Weinberg, B. A. (2014). Age and scientific genius. In D. K. Simonton (Ed.), *The Wiley handbook of genius* (pp. 422–450). Oxford, UK: Wiley.

Juda, A. (1949). The relationship between highest mental capacity and psychic abnormalities. *American Journal of Psychiatry, 106*, 296–307.

Karlsson, J. I. (1970). Genetic association of giftedness and creativity with schizophrenia. *Hereditas, 66*, 177–182.

Kaufman, J. C. (2000-2001). Genius, lunatics and poets: Mental illness in prize-winning authors. *Imagination, Cognition & Personality, 20*, 305–314.

Kaufman, J. C. (2001). The Sylvia Plath effect: Mental illness in eminent creative writers. *Journal of Creative Behavior, 35*, 37–50.

Kaufman, J. C. (2003). The cost of the muse; poets die young. *Death Studies, 27*, 813–821.

Kaufman, J. C. (2005). The door that leads into madness: Eastern European poets and mental illness. *Creativity Research Journal, 17*, 99–103.

Kaun, D. E. (1991). Writers die young: The impact of work and leisure on longevity. *Journal of Economic Psychology, 12*, 381–399.

Kavolis, V. (1964). Economic correlates of artistic creativity. *American Journal of Sociology, 70*, 332–341.

McKay, A. S., & Kaufman, J. C. (2014). Literary geniuses: Their life, work, and death. In D. K. Simonton (Ed.), *The Wiley handbook of genius*. Oxford, UK: Wiley.

Klingemann, H.-D., Mohler, P. P., & Weber, R. P. (1982). Cultural indicators based on content analysis: A secondary analysis of Sorokin's data on fluctuations of systems of truth. *Quality and Quantity, 16*, 1–18.

Ko, Y., & Kim, J. (2008). Scientific geniuses' psychopathology as a moderator in the relation between creative contribution types and eminence. *Creativity Research Journal, 20*, 251–261.

Kozbelt, A. (2005). Factors affecting aesthetic success and improvement in creativity: A case study of musical genres in Mozart. *Psychology of Music, 33*, 235–255.

Kozbelt, A. (2014). Music creativity over the life span. In D. K. Simonton (Ed.), *The Wiley handbook of genius*. Oxford, UK: Wiley.

Kozbelt, A., & Burger-Pianko, Z. (2007).Words, music, and other measures: Predicting the repertoire popularity of 597 Schubert lieder. *Psychology of Aesthetics, Creativity, and the Arts, 1*, 191–203.

Kroeber, A. L. (1944). *Configurations of culture growth*. Berkeley: University of California Press.

Kuo, Y. (1986). The growth and decline of Chinese philosophical genius. *Chinese Journal of Psychology, 28*, 81–91.

Kuo, Y. (1988). The social psychology of Chinese philosophical creativity: A critical synthesis. *Social Epistemology, 2*, 283–295.

Lehman, H. C. (1947). National differences in creativity. *American Journal of Sociology, 52*, 475–488.

Lehman, H. C. (1953). *Age and achievement*. Princeton, NJ: Princeton University Press.

Lindauer, M. S. (2003). *Aging, creativity, and art: A positive perspective on late-life development*. New York, NY: Kluwer Academic/Plenum.

Ludwig, A. M. (1990). Alcohol input and creative output. *British Journal of Addiction, 85*, 953–963.

Ludwig, A. M. (1992). Creative achievement and psychopathology: Comparison among professions. *American Journal of Psychotherapy, 46*, 330–356.

Ludwig, A. M. (1998). Method and madness in the arts and sciences. *Creativity Research m Journal, 11*, 93–101.

Martindale, C. (1975). *Romantic progression: The psychology of literary history*. Washington, DC: Hemisphere.

Martindale, C. (1990). *The clockwork muse: The predictability of artistic styles*. New York, NY: Basic Books.

Martindale, C., Brewer, W. F., Helson, R., Rosenberg, S., Simonton, D. K., Keeley, A., Leigh, J., & Ohtsuka, K. (1988). Structure, theme, style, and reader response in Hungarian and American short stories. In C. Martindale (Ed.), *Psychological approaches to the study of literary narratives* (pp. 267–289). Hamburg, Germany: Buske.

McCann, S. J. H. (2001). The precocity-longevity hypothesis: Earlier peaks in career achievement predict shorter lives. *Personality and Social Psychology Bulletin, 27*, 1429–1439.

McCrae, R. R., & Greenberg, D. M. (2014). Openness to experience. In D. K. Simonton (Ed.), *The Wiley handbook of genius* (pp. 222–243). Oxford, UK: Wiley.

McGuire, W. J. (1976). Historical comparisons: Testing psychological hypotheses with cross-era data. *International Journal of Psychology, 11*, 161–183.

Murray, C. (2003). *Human accomplishment: The pursuit of excellence in the arts and sciences, 800 B.C. to 1950.* New York, NY: HarperCollins.

Murray, C. (2014). Genius in world civilization. In D. K. Simonton (Ed.), *The Wiley handbook of genius* (pp. 586–608). Oxford, UK: Wiley.

Naroll, R., Benjamin, E. C., Fohl, F. K., Fried, M. J., Hildreth, R. E., & Schaefer, J. M. (1971). Creativity: A cross-historical pilot survey. *Journal of Cross-Cultural Psychology, 2*, 181–188.

Niu, W., & Kaufman, J. C. (2005). Creativity in troubled times: Factors associated with recognitions of Chinese literary creativity in the 20th century. *Journal of Creative Behavior, 39*, 57–67.

Norling, B. (1970). *Timeless problems in history.* Notre Dame, IN: Notre Dame Press.

Over, R. (1982). The durability of scientific reputation. *Journal of the History of the Behavioral Sciences, 18*, 53–61.

Paisley, W. J. (1964). Identifying the unknown communicator in painting, literature and music: The significance of minor encoding habits. *Journal of Communication, 14*, 219–237.

Peregrine, P. N., C. R. Ember, & M. Ember (2004). Universal patterns in cultural evolution: An empirical analysis using Guttman scaling. *American Anthropologist, 106*, 145–149.

Petrie, K. J., Pennebaker, J. W., & Sivertsen, B. (2008). Things we said today: A linguistic analysis of the Beatles. *Psychology of Aesthetics, Creativity, and the Arts, 2*, 197–202.

Post, F. (1994). Creativity and psychopathology: A study of 291 world-famous men. *British Journal of Psychiatry, 165*, 22–34.

Post, F. (1996). Verbal creativity, depression and alcoholism: An investigation of one hundred American and British writers. *British Journal of Psychiatry, 168*, 545–555.

Price, D. (1978). Ups and downs in the pulse of science and technology. In J. Gaston (Ed.), *The sociology of science* (pp. 162–171). San Francisco, CA: Jossey-Bass.

Quételet, A. (1842). *A treatise on man and the development of his faculties.* New York, NY: Franklin. (Edinburgh translation of 1835 French original)

Quigley, C. (1979). *The evolution of civilizations: An introduction to historical analysis* (2nd ed.). Indianapolis, IN: Liberty Press.

Ramey, C. H., & Weisberg, R. W. (2004). The "poetical activity" of Emily Dickinson: A further test of the hypothesis that affective disorders foster creativity. *Creativity Research Journal, 16*, 173–185.

Raskin, E. A. (1936). Comparison of scientific and literary ability: A biographical study of eminent scientists and men of letters of the nineteenth century. *Journal of Abnormal and Social Psychology*, *31*, 20–35.

Richardson, A., & Simonton, D. K. (2014). Catharine Morris Cox Miles and the lives of others (1890-1984). In A. Richardson & J. L. Jolly (Eds.), *A century of contributions to gifted education: Illuminating lives* (pp. 101–114). London, UK: Routledge.

Roe, A. (1953). *The making of a scientist*. New York, NY: Dodd, Mead.

Root-Bernstein, R., Allen, L., Beach, L. Bhadula, R., Fast, J., Hosey, C., . . . Weinlander, S. (2008). Arts foster scientific success: Avocations of Nobel, National Academy, Royal Society, and Sigma Xi members. *Journal of the Psychology of Science and Technology*, *1*, 51–63.

Rosengren, K. E. (1985). Time and literary fame. *Poetics*, *14*, 157–172.

Rothenberg, A., & Wyshak, G. (2004). Family background and genius. *Canadian Journal of Psychiatry*, *49*, 185–191.

Runco, M. A., Kaufman, J. C., Halladay, L. R., & Cole, J. C. (2010). Changes in reputation and an index of genius, eminence, and creative talent. *Historical Methods*, *43*, 91–96.

Schaefer, J. M., Babu, M. C., & Rao, N. S. (1977). Sociopolitical causes of creativity in India 500 B.C.–1800 A.D.: A regional time-lagged study. Paper presented at the meeting of the International Studies Association, St. Louis.

Schaller, M. (1997). The psychological consequences of fame: Three tests of the self-consciousness hypothesis. *Journal of Personality*, *65*, 291–309.

Schneider, J. (1937). The cultural situation as a condition for the achievement of fame. *American Sociological Review*, *2*, 480–491.

Schubert, D. S. P., Wagner, M. E., & Schubert, H. J. P. (1977). Family constellation and creativity: Firstborn predominance among classical music composers. *Journal of Psychology*, *95*, 147–149.

Simonton, D. K. (1975a). Age and literary creativity: A cross-cultural and transhistorical survey. *Journal of Cross-Cultural Psychology*, *6*, 259–277.

Simonton, D. K. (1975b). Sociocultural context of individual creativity: A transhistorical time-series analysis. *Journal of Personality and Social Psychology*, *32*, 1119–1133.

Simonton, D. K. (1975c). Galton's problem, autocorrelation, and diffusion coefficients. *Behavior Science Research*, *10*, 239–248.

Simonton, D. K. (1976a). Biographical determinants of achieved eminence: A multivariate approach to the Cox data. *Journal of Personality and Social Psychology*, *33*, 218–226.

Simonton, D. K. (1976b). Do Sorokin's data support his theory?: A study of generational fluctuations in philosophical beliefs. *Journal for the Scientific Study of Religion*, *15*, 187–198.

Simonton, D. K. (1976c). Interdisciplinary and military determinants of scientific productivity: A cross-lagged correlation analysis. *Journal of Vocational Behavior*, *9*, 53–62.

Simonton, D. K. (1976d). Philosophical eminence, beliefs, and zeitgeist: An individual-generational analysis. *Journal of Personality and Social Psychology*, *34*, 630–640.

Simonton, D. K. (1976e). The sociopolitical context of philosophical beliefs: A transhistorical causal analysis. *Social Forces*, *54*, 513–523.

Simonton, D. K. (1977a). Creative productivity, age, and stress: A biographical time-series analysis of 10 classical composers. *Journal of Personality and Social Psychology*, *35*, 791–804.

Simonton, D. K. (1977b). Eminence, creativity, and geographic marginality: A recursive structural equation model. *Journal of Personality and Social Psychology, 35,* 805–816.

Simonton, D. K. (1979). Multiple discovery and invention: Zeitgeist, genius, or chance? *Journal of Personality and Social Psychology, 37,* 1603–1616.

Simonton, D. K. (1980a). Techno-scientific activity and war: A yearly time-series analysis, 1500-1903 A.D. *Scientometrics, 2,* 251–255.

Simonton, D. K. (1980b). Thematic fame, melodic originality, and musical zeitgeist: A biographical and transhistorical content analysis. *Journal of Personality and Social Psychology, 38,* 972–983.

Simonton, D. K. (1984a). Artistic creativity and interpersonal relationships across and within generations. *Journal of Personality and Social Psychology, 46,* 1273–1286.

Simonton, D. K. (1984b). Generational time-series analysis: A paradigm for studying sociocultural influences. In K. Gergen & M. Gergen (Eds.), *Historical social psychology* (pp. 141–155). Hillsdale, NJ: Lawrence Erlbaum.

Simonton, D. K. (1984c). *Genius, creativity, and leadership: Historiometric inquiries.* Cambridge, MA: Harvard University Press.

Simonton, D. K. (1986). Popularity, content, and context in 37 Shakespeare plays. *Poetics, 15,* 493–510.

Simonton, D. K. (1987). Musical aesthetics and creativity in Beethoven: A computer analysis of 105 compositions. *Empirical Studies of the Arts, 5,* 87–104.

Simonton, D. K. (1988). Galtonian genius, Kroeberian configurations, and emulation: A generational time-series analysis of Chinese civilization. *Journal of Personality and Social Psychology, 55,* 230–238.

Simonton, D. K. (1989). Shakespeare's sonnets: A case of and for single-case historiometry. *Journal of Personality, 57,* 695–721.

Simonton, D. K. (1990a). Lexical choices and aesthetic success: A computer content analysis of 154 Shakespeare sonnets. *Computers and the Humanities, 24,* 251–264.

Simonton, D. K. (1990b). *Psychology, science, and history: An introduction to historiometry.* New Haven, CT: Yale University Press.

Simonton, D. K. (1991a). Career landmarks in science: Individual differences and interdisciplinary contrasts. *Developmental Psychology, 27,* 119–130.

Simonton, D. K. (1991b). Emergence and realization of genius: The lives and works of 120 classical composers. *Journal of Personality and Social Psychology, 61,* 829–840.

Simonton, D. K. (1991c). Latent-variable models of posthumous reputation: A quest for Galton's G. *Journal of Personality and Social Psychology, 60,* 607–619.

Simonton, D. K. (1992a). Gender and genius in Japan: Feminine eminence in masculine culture. *Sex Roles, 27,* 101–119.

Simonton, D. K. (1992b). Leaders of American psychology, 1879–1967: Career development, creative output, and professional achievement. *Journal of Personality and Social Psychology, 62,* 5–17.

Simonton, D. K. (1992c). The social context of career success and course for 2,026 scientists and inventors. *Personality and Social Psychology Bulletin, 18,* 452–463.

Simonton, D. K. (1995). Drawing inferences from symphonic programs: Musical attributes versus listener attributions. *Music Perception, 12,* 307–322.

Simonton, D. K. (1996). Individual genius and cultural configurations: The case of Japanese civilization. *Journal of Cross-Cultural Psychology, 27,* 354–375.

Simonton, D. K. (1997a). Achievement domain and life expectancies in Japanese civilization. *International Journal of Aging and Human Development*, *44*, 103–114.

Simonton, D. K. (1997b). Creative productivity: A predictive and explanatory model of career trajectories and landmarks. *Psychological Review*, *104*, 66–89.

Simonton, D. K. (1997c). Foreign influence and national achievement: The impact of open milieus on Japanese civilization. *Journal of Personality and Social Psychology*, *72*, 86–94.

Simonton, D. K. (1998a). Achieved eminence in minority and majority cultures: Convergence versus divergence in the assessments of 294 African Americans. *Journal of Personality and Social Psychology*, *74*, 804–817.

Simonton, D. K. (1998b). Fickle fashion versus immortal fame: Transhistorical assessments of creative products in the opera house. *Journal of Personality and Social Psychology*, *75*, 198–210.

Simonton, D. K. (1999a). Creativity from a historiometric perspective. In R. J. Sternberg (Ed.), *Handbook of creativity* (pp. 116–133). Cambridge, UK: Cambridge University Press.

Simonton, D. K. (1999b). Significant samples: The psychological study of eminent individuals. *Psychological Methods*, *4*, 425–451.

Simonton, D. K. (2000). Creative development as acquired expertise: Theoretical issues and an empirical test. *Developmental Review*, *20*, 283–318.

Simonton, D. K. (2003a). Creative cultures, nations, and civilizations: Strategies and results. In P. B. Paulus & B. A. Nijstad (Eds.), *Group creativity: Innovation through collaboration* (pp. 304–328). New York, NY: Oxford University Press.

Simonton, D. K. (2003b). Kroeber's cultural configurations, Sorokin's culture mentalities, and generational time-series analysis: A quantitative paradigm for the comparative study of civilizations. *Comparative Civilizations Review*, *49*, 96–108.

Simonton, D. K. (2003c). Qualitative and quantitative analyses of historical data. *Annual Review of Psychology*, *54*, 617–640.

Simonton, D. K. (2007a). Creative life cycles in literature: Poets versus novelists or conceptualists versus experimentalists? *Psychology of Aesthetics, Creativity, and the Arts*, *1*, 133–139.

Simonton, D. K. (2007b). The creative process in Picasso's *Guernica* sketches: Monotonic improvements or nonmonotonic variants? *Creativity Research Journal*, *19*, 329–344.

Simonton, D. K. (2008a). Childhood giftedness and adulthood genius: A historiometric analysis of 291 eminent African Americans. *Gifted Child Quarterly*, *52*, 243–255.

Simonton, D. K. (2008b). Gender differences in birth order and family size among 186 eminent psychologists. *Journal of Psychology of Science and Technology*, *1*, 15–22.

Simonton, D. K. (2010). Creativity in highly eminent individuals. In J. C. Kaufman & R. J. Sternberg (Eds.), *Cambridge handbook of creativity* (pp. 174–188). New York, NY: Cambridge University Press.

Simonton, D. K. (2011a). Creativity and discovery as blind variation: Campbell's (1960) BVSR model after the half-century mark. *Review of General Psychology*, *15*, 158–174.

Simonton, D. K. (2011b). *Great flicks: Scientific studies of cinematic creativity and aesthetics*. New York, NY: Oxford University Press.

Simonton, D. K. (2012). Foresight, insight, oversight, and hindsight in scientific discovery: How sighted were Galileo's telescopic sightings? *Psychology of Aesthetics, Creativity, and the Arts*, *6*, 243–254.

Simonton, D. K (2013). What is a creative idea? Little-c versus Big-C creativity. In J. Chan & K. Thomas (Eds.), *Handbook of research on creativity*. Cheltenham Glos, UK: Edward Elgar.

Simonton, D. K. (2014a). Historiometric studies of genius. In D. K. Simonton (Ed.), *The Wiley handbook of genius* (pp. 87–106). Oxford, UK: Wiley.

Simonton, D. K. (2014b). The mad (creative) genius: What do we know after a century of historiometric research? In J. C. Kaufman (Ed.), *Creativity and mental illness* (pp. 25–41). New York, NY: Cambridge University Press.

Simonton, D. K. (2014c). More method in the mad-genius controversy: A historiometric study of 204 historic creators. *Psychology of Aesthetics, Creativity, and the Arts, 8*, 53–61.

Simonton, D. K. (2014d). Significant samples—not significance tests! The often overlooked solution to the replication problem. *Psychology of Aesthetics, Creativity, and the Arts, 8*, 11–12.

Simonton, D. K. (2016). Scientific genius in Islamic civilization: Quantified time series from qualitative historical narratives. *Journal of Genius and Eminence, 1*, 4–13.

Simonton, D. K. (2017). Domain-general creativity: On producing original, useful, and surprising combinations. In J. C. Kaufman, J. Baer, & V. P. Glăveanu (Eds.), *Cambridge handbook of creativity across different domains* (pp. 41–60). New York, NY: Cambridge University Press.

Simonton, D. K., & Song, A. V. (2009). Eminence, IQ, physical and mental health, and achievement domain: Cox's 282 geniuses revisited. *Psychological Science, 20*, 429–434.

Simonton, D. K., & Ting, S.-S. (2010). Creativity in Eastern and Western civilizations: The lessons of historiometry. *Management and Organization Review, 6*, 329–350.

Sorokin, P. A. (1937-1941). *Social and cultural dynamics* (Vols. 1–4). New York, NY: American Book.

Sorokin, P. A., & Merton, R. K. (1935). The course of Arabian intellectual development, 700-1300 A.D. A study in method. *Isis, 22*, 516–524.

Stariha, W. E., & Walberg, H. J. (1995). Childhood precursors of women's artistic eminence. *Journal of Creative Behavior, 29*, 269–282.

Stirman, S. W., & Pennebaker, J. W. (2001). Word use in the poetry of suicidal and nonsuicidal poets. *Psychosomatic Medicine, 63*, 517–522.

Sulloway, F. J. (1996). *Born to rebel: Birth order, family dynamics, and creative lives.* New York, NY: Pantheon.

Sulloway, F. J. (2014). Openness to scientific innovation. In D. K. Simonton (Ed.), *The Wiley handbook of genius* (pp. 546–563). Oxford, UK: Wiley.

Terman, L. M. (1925-1959). *Genetic studies of genius* (5 vols.). Stanford, CA: Stanford University Press.

Terry, W. S. (1989). Birth order and prominence in the history of psychology. *Psychological Record, 39*, 333–337.

Thagard, P. (2012). Creative combination of representations: Scientific discovery and technological invention. In R. Proctor & E. J. Capaldi (Eds.), *Psychology of science: Implicit and explicit processes* (pp. 389–405). New York, NY: Oxford University Press.

Thorndike, E. L. (1950). Traits of personality and their intercorrelations as shown in biographies. *Journal of Educational Psychology, 41*, 193–216.

Toynbee, A. J. (1946). *A study of history* (abridged by D. C. Somervell, Vols. 1–2). New York, NY: Oxford University Press.

Triandis, H. C. (1995). *Individualism & collectivism*. Boulder, CO: Westview.

Tweney, R. D. (1989). A framework for the cognitive psychology of science. In B. Gholson, W. R. Shadish, Jr., R. A. Neimeyer, & A. C. Houts (Eds.), *The psychology of science: Contributions to metascience* (pp. 342–366). Cambridge, UK: Cambridge University Press.

Vermeylen, F., van Dijck, M., & de Laet, V. (2013). The test of time: Art encyclopedias and the formation of the canon of the 17th-century painters in the Low Countries. *Empirical Studies of the Arts, 31*, 81–105.

Walberg, H. J., Rasher, S. P., & Hase, K. (1978). IQ correlates with high eminence. *Gifted Child Quarterly, 22*, 196–200.

Walberg, H. J., Rasher, S. P., & Parkerson, J. (1980). Childhood and eminence. *Journal of Creative Behavior, 13*, 225–231.

Weisberg, R. W. (1994). Genius and madness? A quasi-experimental test of the hypothesis that manic-depression increases creativity. *Psychological Science, 5*, 361–367.

Weisberg, R. W. (2004). On structure in the creative process: A quantitative case-study of the creation of Picasso's *Guernica*. *Empirical Studies of the Arts, 22*, 23–54.

Whipple, E. M. (2004). Eminence revisited. *History of Psychology, 7*, 265–296.

White, R. K. (1931). The versatility of genius. *Journal of Social Psychology, 2*, 460–489.

Woods, F. A. (1909, November 19). A new name for a new science. *Science, 30*, 703–704.

Woods, F. A. (1911, April 14). Historiometry as an exact science. *Science, 33*, 568–574.

Wray, K. B. (2003). Is science really a young man's game? *Social Studies of Science, 33*, 137–149.

Wray, K. B. (2004). An examination of the contributions of young scientists in new fields. *Scientometrics, 61*, 117–128.

Wright, Q. (1965). *A study of war* (2nd ed.). Chicago, IL: University of Chicago Press.

Yuasa, M. (1974). The shifting center of scientific activity in the West: From the sixteenth to the twentieth century. In N. Shigeru, D. L. Swain, & Y. Eri (Eds.), *Science and society in modern Japan* (pp. 81–103). Tokyo, Japan: University of Tokyo Press.

Zickar, M. J., & Slaughter, J. E. (1999). Examining creative performance over time using hierarchical linear modeling: An illustration using film directors. *Human Performance, 12*, 211–230.

Zusne, L. (1976). Age and achievement in psychology: The harmonic mean as a model. *American Psychologist, 31*, 805–807.

4

National and Historical Variations in Innovation Performance

A Country-Level Analysis

CHI-YUE CHIU AND LETTY Y.-Y. KWAN ■

In his 2010 National Security Strategy Report, US President Barack Obama emphasized the strategic value of advances in science and technology for national development: "Reaffirming America's role as the global engine of scientific discovery and technological innovation has never been more critical . . . Our renewed commitment to science and technology . . . will help us protect our citizens and advance US national security priorities" (Office of Science and Technology Policy, the White House, 2010).

The need to boost innovation is present not only in developed economies but also in newly advanced economies such as Brazil, Russia, India, and China (BRIC countries). In these countries, innovation may be the key to maintaining rapid economic growth and escaping the middle-income trap—the threat that a rapidly developing economy will get stuck when its per capita gross national product reaches the middle-income range (US$10,000–12,000 at 2010 prices) after the economy's initial comparative advantages (e.g., cheap labor) have been fully exploited (Chiu, Liou, & Kwan, 2016).

Innovation performance differs across nations. Within the same nation, innovation performance also varies across time. The Global Innovation Index (GII; Dutta, 2011, 2012; Dutta & Lanvin, 2013) tracked the annual innovation performance of more than 100 countries since 2007. Figure 4.1 shows the percentile ranks of three Scandinavian countries (Denmark, Finland, and Sweden), the G7 countries (developed economies), and the BRIC countries (rapidly developing economies) between 2007 and 2013. Relatively speaking, the Scandinavian and G7 countries had higher innovation performance than did the BRIC countries. In

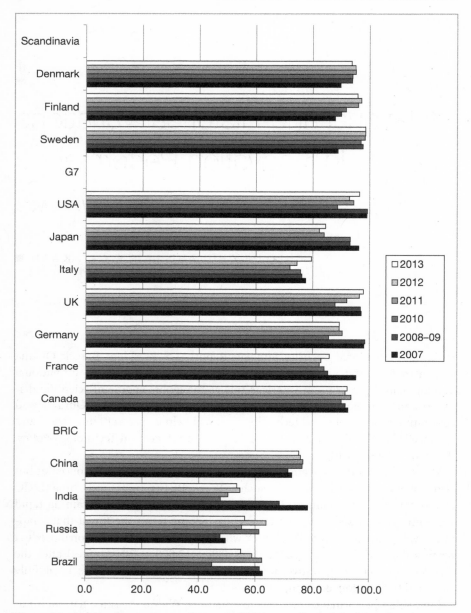

Figure 4.1. Relative innovation performance (GII percentile ranks) of Scandinavian countries (Denmark, Finland, Sweden), G7 countries (developed economies), and the BRIC countries (rapidly developing economies) between 2007 and 2013.

the second section of the present chapter, we will review some recent findings on the factors that explain these cross-national variations in innovation performance.

As also shown in Figure 4.1, while the relative innovation performance of the Scandinavian countries has improved steadily since 2007, the relative innovation performance in several G7 countries (Japan, Germany, and France) had declined. Among the BRIC countries, the relative innovation performance of India and Brazil has declined, whereas that of China has been fairly stable. Long-term historical fluctuations in a nation's innovation performance have received a lot of research attention in the social sciences (see Simonton & Ting, 2010). These fluctuations were not random; they were systematically linked to a set of cultural, political, and institutional factors. In the second section of this chapter, we also discuss some cultural, political, and institutional factors that explain historical variations in a country's innovation performance.

Although recent studies have uncovered some distal cultural and institutional factors that may explain cross-national and historical variations in innovation performance, relatively little is known about the proximal psychological factors that explain these variations. To address this knowledge gap, in the third section of this chapter, using the multinational data from the GII, we focus on the extent to which people in a country rely on financial institutions to mitigate risks in daily life as a proximal predictor of innovation performance at the national level. We argue that the tendency to rely on formal institutions to mitigate risks in everyday life reflects the level of institutional trust, which is a factor that contributes to both cross-national and historical variations in innovation performance. We further argue that institutional trust plays a particularly important role in promoting innovation in countries that lack strong institutional support for innovation.

CROSS-NATIONAL AND HISTORICAL VARIATIONS IN INNOVATION PERFORMANCE

Cross-National Variations

Two major factors that explain cross-national variations in innovation performance are the supply and quality of global talents and the presence of institutional support for innovation (e.g., law and order; protection of intellectual property rights) in the country (Kwan & Chiu, 2015). However, how these two factors impact innovation performance in a country is not straightforward.

For example, availability of global talents can increase a country's innovation performance through increasing the amount of cultural diversity in the country (see Erez et al., 2013; Han, Peng, Chiu, & Leung, 2010). An extensive amount of research has been carried out to understand how cultural diversity affects the creative performance of individuals and groups (see Leung, Maddux, Galinsky, & Chiu, 2008). This research shows that exposure to ideas from dissimilar cultures evokes negative affect or cognitive dissonance, which in turn motivates creative problem solving (Cheng & Leung, 2013; Cheng, Leung, & Wu, 2011). Multicultural experiences are particularly beneficial to creative performance among people who are open to experience (Chen et al., in press; Leung & Chiu, 2010).

However, the beneficial effects of multicultural experiences on individual and team creativity are attenuated when individuals or team members have strong identification with their own culture and a strong desire for conventionalized solutions to problems (Leung & Chiu, 2008). These results are applicable across levels of analysis. At the country level, recent findings show that higher levels of cultural diversity predict higher innovation performance. However, when fault lines have been formed between competing cultural groups within a country, intergroup competition can eradicate the creative benefits of cultural diversity (Zhan, Bendapudi, & Hong, 2015; see also Chiu, Kwan, & Liou, 2013; Li, Kwan, Liou, & Chiu, 2013).

How the supply and quality of talents contribute to innovation performance depends also on the type of innovation. In a multinational study, Bendapudi, Zhan, and Hong (2015) predicted a country's innovation performance from its quality of primary and secondary education, measured through the Program for International Student Assessment (PISA). In this study, the investigators distinguished between two types of innovation outputs: knowledge and technology outputs and creative outputs. Knowledge and technology outputs refer to knowledge and applications generated from scientific and technological research, whereas creative outputs refer to products, goods, and services from the creative industries (Stupples, 2014). The investigators argue that availability of high-quality talents may be enough to drive creation of knowledge and technology outputs. However, a culture that privileges self-expansive values (self-direction, stimulation, hedonism, universalism, and benevolence) is also needed to motivate generation of creative outputs. Consistent with their hypothesis, irrespective of whether self-expansive values are prioritized in a country, as long as it has high-quality education that grows talents, the country tends to have high performance in knowledge and technology outputs. However, quality of education predicts performance in creative outputs only in countries that emphasize self-expansive values.

Chiu et al. (2016) further break down knowledge and technology outputs into incremental innovations and frame-breaking or radical innovations. They argued and found that supply and quality of global talents are enough for the generation of incremental innovation; a country's incremental innovation performance is predictable from the quality of its human capital alone. However, good performance in radical innovations requires both high-quality human capital as well as the presence of institutional support for innovation, which consists of democratic, legal, and political institutions that protect freedom of expression and the innovators' proprietary rights to their intellectual and financial properties (Kwan & Chiu, 2015). As Kwan and Chiu (2015) put it, "Innovation outputs with global influence are often transformational innovation that disrupts existing technology, transforms existing markets, and creates new ones . . . Producing transformational innovation requires both strong institutional support and rich human capital resources. In contrast, not all newly created knowledge has significant global impact. Mere presence of human capital may be sufficient for producing a high volume of innovation outputs, although institutional support can enhance the efficiency of human capital in knowledge creation" (p. 1065).

HISTORICAL VARIATIONS

Innovation performance varies across countries. Within a country, innovation performance is not static. For example, China was a world champion in invention before the middle of the Ming Dynasty (1368–1644). However, it has failed to maintain its global leadership since then. This phenomenon has been referred to as the Needham Puzzle. Augier, Guo, and Rowen (in press) attributed the phenomenon to three cultural factors in China: (a) the underdevelopment of the scientific method, (b) lack of educational diversity and ideational fluidity, and (c) lack of openness to the outside world in China after the mid-1600s. Liou, Kwan, and Chiu (in press) attributed the decline of technological innovation in China to the country's defensive responses to external threats and fatal infectious diseases, the shift of emphasis from rationalism to subjectivism in Confucianism, and propagation of moral particularism after the middle of the Ming Dynasty.

More systematic analysis of the factors that influence historical variations in a country's creative performance (Simonton & Ting, 2010; see also Chapter 5 of this volume) reveals that in both Eastern and Western histories, a country's creative performance increased when there were political instability and conflicts and when role models were available, probably because political conflicts destabilized established structures, institutions, and norms, whereas availability of champions inspired new ideas. Nonetheless, political fragmentation, civil disturbances, and prevalence of ideology had more beneficial effects on creative performance in the West than in the East. In the West, political fragmentation and civil disturbances often resulted in greater cultural heterogeneity and tolerance of diversity; whereas in the East, the desire for political unification and ideological uniformity often followed relatively brief periods of political fragmentation and civil disturbances. In addition, the ideologies in the West (e.g., individualism, empiricism) encourage both self-expression and scientific creativity, whereas those in the East (e.g., Confucianism) do not.

THE ROLE OF INSTITUTIONAL TRUST

Thus far, we have focused on the distal historical, cultural, and institutional factors that affect innovation performance of a certain country at a certain period. We now move on to discuss some more proximal psychological factors that may influence innovation performance of a country.

An extensive amount of research has been carried out to identify the proximal psychological factors that mediate cultural differences in the creative performance of individuals and teams (Chiu & Kwan, 2010). However, it is still unclear how distal institutional factors and proximal psychological factors jointly influence innovation performance at the country level. In this section, we will use institutional support for innovation and trust in institutions as an example to illustrate the theoretical utility of examining their joint effect on innovation performance.

Institutional Support and Institutional Trust

We argued in the first section of this chapter that institutional support is of critical importance to the generation of innovation, particularly radical innovation. However, some writers believe that institutional support for innovation can stimulate innovation only when people trust the institutions (Dixit, 2004; Granovetter, 1985). To these writers, institutional trust mediates the effect of institutional support on innovation performance.

Other writers contend that institutional trust is important only when institutional support for innovation is absent (Peng, 2003; Tan, Tang, & Veliyath, 2009). Institutional support for innovation is present in most developed economies. However, in most transforming economies, institutional support for innovation is not established yet. In these economies, trust in the country's emerging institutions plays a critical supporting role in the country's innovation performance. In short, there should be a negative interaction effect of institutional support and institutional trust on innovation performance.

A third view is that institutional support and institutional trust have mutually supportive effects on a country's innovation. According to this view, the presence of strong institutional support mitigates the risks of trusting the institutions (Cook, Hardin, & Levi, 2005; North, 1990). At the same time, institutional trust increases the efficiency of institutional regulation by improving coordination and reducing transaction costs in social exchanges (Chiu & Kwan, 2015; Luhmann, 1979). Thus, institutional support and institutional trust should have a positive interaction effect on innovation performance. That is, the beneficial effect of institutional support on innovation performance should be more pronounced when institutional trust is high (vs. low). Likewise, the beneficial effect of institutional trust on innovation performance should be more salient at the presence of strong institutional support (positive interaction effect). To reconcile these alternative views, we carried out and report next a study that examined the interaction effect of institutional support and institutional trust on country level innovation performance.

Proxy for Institutional Support and Institutional Trust

As mentioned earlier, institutional support for innovation refers to the presence of democratic, legal, and political institutions that protect freedom of expression and the innovators' proprietary rights to their intellectual and financial properties. When left alone to pursue selfish maximizing goals, individuals often exploit the common good for selfish gains, resulting in corruption in the society (Chiu & Kim, 2011; Murmann, Aldrich, Levinthal, & Winter, 2003; Singh & Lumsden, 1990). To coordinate individual behaviors in complex societies, democratic, legal, and political institutions emerged to encourage cooperation and punish defections, resulting in more transparent governance in the society. A proxy for the presence of institutional support is the corruption perception index published by Transparency International (http://www.transparency.org/research/cpi/over-view). First launched in 1995 and published annually, the transparency index (also known as the corruption perception index) captures the perceptions of analysts, businesspeople, and experts in countries around the world on how corrupt their public sectors are. Countries with higher scores on the transparency index are perceived to be less corrupt. The level of perceived corruption in a country may fluctuate across years. To capture the presence or absence of stable, formal institutions that assure transparency in governance, in our analysis, for each country, we took the average of the transparency index between 2001 and 2010 as a proxy measuring the level of institutional support in a country. The stability of the transparency index across 10 years as measured by the Cronbach's coefficient of international consistency (α) was .997. To establish the validity of the transparency index as a measure of institutional support for innovation, we correlated the transparency index with three measures of institutional support for innovation in the 2014 Global Innovation Index (GII; Dutta, Lanvin, & Wunsch-Vincent, 2014): institutional support in the political environment ($r = .85$, $N = 141$), institutional support in the regulatory environment ($r = .80$, $N = 141$), and institutional support in the business environment ($r = .78$, $N = 141$). The high correlations between the transparency index and the GII indices of institutional support for innovation attest to the validity of the transparency index as a measure of institutional support.

We used the average annual percentage of GDP people in a country spent on non–life insurance premium between 2002 and 2011 as a proxy measure of institutional trust. In social sciences, trust involves the following characteristics: The trustor is willing to rely on and give up control over the actions of the trustee in the management of a situation that may affect the trustor's future outcomes. Consequently, the trustor accepts the risk of failure or harm to him or her if the trustee will not behave as expected (Mayer, Davis, & Schoorman, 1995). Institutional trust refers to the willingness of the trustor to rely on and give up control over the actions of formal institutions (as opposed to other noninstitutional trustees) in the management of a situation that may affect the trustor's future outcomes. Insurance is a mechanism through which an insured party transfers to a formal financial institution the risk of loss or damage caused by events beyond the control of insured party. That is, the insured party trusts that a financial institution will fulfill its obligation to compensate for the loss of damage caused by events beyond the insured party's control. Thus, the amount of non–life insurance consumption of a country seems to be a reasonable proxy for institutional trust in that country.

In our analysis, we did not use life insurance consumption as a measure of institutional trust because life insurance is also an investment instrument used to mitigate the effect of inflation, and the best predictors of the amount of life insurance consumption in a country are its GDP and inflation rate (Beck & Webb, 2003). Country-level data on annual percentage of GDP spent on non–life insurance and life insurance premiums are available from World Bank (http://data.worldbank.org/indicator). The 10-year (2001–2010) stability coefficient (Cronbach's α) was

.99 for both non–life insurance spending and life insurance spending. The zero-order correlation between non–life insurance consumption and life insurance consumption was .67 ($N = 167$), and their partial correlation after controlling for per capita GDP and inflation was .34. When we analyzed the relationship of non–life insurance consumption and innovation performance, we controlled the effects of life insurance consumption, per capita GDP, and inflation.

Does Institutional Trust Mediate the Effect of Institutional Support on Innovation?

In our analysis, we used the percentile ranks of the GII from 2011 to 2013 (Dutta, 2011, 2012; Dutta & Lanvin, 2013) as the outcome variables, which capture the overall levels of development and performance in innovation in over 100 countries or regions. To test the hypothesis that institutional trust mediates the effect of institutional support on innovation performance, we regressed innovation performance in 2011, 2012, and 2013 on institutional support (mean of the transparency index from 2001 to 2010), controlling for per capita GDP (mean of 2001–2010) and inflation (mean of 2001–2010). As in Kwan and Chiu (2015), although GII data are available since 2007, we used data from 2011 to 2013 only for four reasons. First, only a much smaller number of countries were included in the 2007–2011 GII study. Second, different scaling methods were used to construct the GII before 2011. Third, independent audits had not been performed on the GII data published before 2011. Finally, 17 out of the 81 indicators used in the GII had been adjusted or revised since 2014. Note that the predictors and control variables were measured (2001–2010) before the dependent variables were measured (2011–2013).

As shown in Model 1 of Table 4.1, Table 4.2, and Table 4.3, there was a highly significant positive effect of institutional support on innovation performance. Next, we added institutional trust (non–life insurance consumption) as another independent variable and life insurance consumption as a control variable to the regression equations (Model 2 of Table 4.1, Table 4.2, and Table 4.3). The predicted positive effect of institutional trust on innovation performance was significant. The positive effect of institutional support on innovation performance remained highly significant, although its effect sizes (as reflected in the sizes of the regression coefficients) were slightly reduced. That is, the presence of institutional support was still a good predictor of innovation performance after controlling for institutional trust. Nonetheless, as shown in Figure 4.2, there was a significant indirect effect of institutional support on innovation performance through institutional trust.

In short, on the one hand, to some extent, the presence of institutional support predicts higher levels of institutional trust, which in turn are accompanied by higher levels of innovation performance. On the other hand, institutional support can also directly impact innovation performance without going through institutional trust.

Table 4.1. PREDICTING COUNTRIES' GLOBAL INNOVATION INDEX PERCENTILE RANKS IN 2011 BY INSTITUTIONAL SUPPORT AND INSTITUTIONAL TRUST: UNSTANDARDIZED REGRESSION COEFFICIENTS AND STANDARD ERRORS

	Model 1	Model 2	Model 3
Predictors			
Institutional support (IS)	9.87 (1.32)***	7.95 (1.34)***	7.18 (1.28)***
Institutional trust (IT)		11.18 (2.60)***	11.61 (2.45)***
IT x IS			−3.81 (0.98)**
Control variables			
GPA/capita	0.09 (0.14)	−0.07 (1.42)	0.21 (0.15)
Inflation	−0.41 (0.44)	−0.55 (0.44)	−0.48 (0.41)
Life insurance consumption		0.45 (0.79)	0.41 (0.24)
Intercept	7.22	4.02	6.52
R^2 adjusted	.69	.73	.76
N	125	115	115

NOTE: The proxy for institutional support is the transparency index and that for institutional trust is non–life insurance consumption.

* $p < .05$, ** $p < .01$, *** $p \le .0001$.

Table 4.2. PREDICTING COUNTRIES' GLOBAL INNOVATION INDEX PERCENTILE RANKS IN 2012 BY INSTITUTIONAL SUPPORT AND INSTITUTIONAL TRUST: UNSTANDARDIZED REGRESSION COEFFICIENTS AND STANDARD ERRORS

	Model 1	Model 2	Model 3
Predictors			
Institutional support (IS)	10.21 (1.24)***	8.46 (1.28)***	7.65 (1.20)***
Institutional trust (IT)		9.42 (2.38)***	9.95 (2.20)***
IT x IS			−4.31 (0.91)***
Control variables			
GPA/capita	0.05 (0.14)	−0.06 (0.14)	0.27 (0.14)
Inflation	−0.71 (0.35)	−0.72 (0.35)*	−0.62 (0.32)
Life insurance consumption		0.45 (0.76)	0.46 (0.70)
Intercept	9.40	6.25	8.52
R^2 adjusted	.72	.75	.79
N	139	125	125

NOTE: The proxy for institutional support is the transparency index and that for institutional trust is non–life insurance consumption.

* $p < .05$, ** $p < .01$, *** $p \le .0001$.

Table 4.3. Predicting Countries' Global Innovation Index Percentile Ranks in 2013 by Institutional Support and Institutional Trust: Unstandardized Regression Coefficients and Standard Errors

	Model 1	Model 2	Model 3
Predictors			
Institutional support (IS)	9.10 (1.31)***	6.97 (1.41)***	6.51 (1.32)***
Institutional trust (IT)		7.43 (2.38)***	9.66 (2.28)***
IT x IS			−3.97 (0.91)***
Control variables			
GPA/capita	0.16 (0.14)	0.11 (0.14)	0.36 (0.15)
Inflation	−0.61 (0.37)	−0.60 (0.37)	−0.44 (0.35)
Life insurance consumption		0.82 (0.83)	0.61 (0.77)
Intercept	12.06	11.44	10.92
R^2 adjusted	.66	.69	.73
N	139	126	126

NOTE: The proxy for institutional support is the transparency index and that for institutional trust is non–life insurance consumption.

* $p < .05$, ** $p < .01$, *** $p \le .0001$.

Joint Effect of Institutional Support and Institutional Trust

Next, because institutional trust does not fully mediate the effect of institutional support on innovation performance, it is legitimate to examine the joint effect of institutional support and institutional trust on innovation performance. We did so by adding the interaction of institutional support and institutional trust in the regression equations (Model 3 of Table 4.1, Table 4.2, and Table 4.3). We centered institutional support and institutional trust at their respective mean and used the product of the two centered variables to form the interaction term. The interaction was negative and significant. Figure 4.3 depicts the expected value of innovation performance when the two independent variables were high (one standard deviation above their respective mean) or low (one standard deviation below their respective mean). When a country had both low institutional support and low institutional trust, its expected level of innovation performance was significantly below those countries that had either high institutional support or high institutional trust. In addition, the effect of institutional trust was significant only when institutional support was weak. With the presence of strong institutional support, the effect of institutional trust was not statistically discernible. These results support the idea that institutional trust is important only when institutional support for innovation is absent.

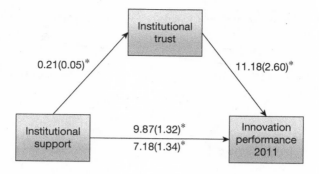

Sobel'z for indirect effect = 3.00*

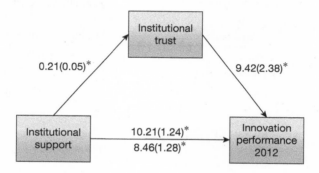

Sobel'z for indirect effect = 2.88*

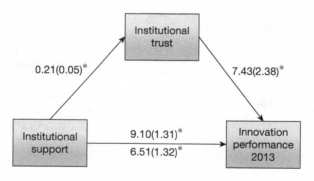

Sobel'z for indirect effect = 2.51*

Figure 4.2. Institutional trust (non–life insurance consumption) partially mediated the effect of institutional support (transparency) on innovation performance. * $p < .01$.

Predicting Short-Term Change in Innovation Performance

Because we had innovation performance data from 2011 to 2013, we also tested whether institutional support and institutional trust predicted short-term change in a country's innovation performance. First, we tested whether institutional

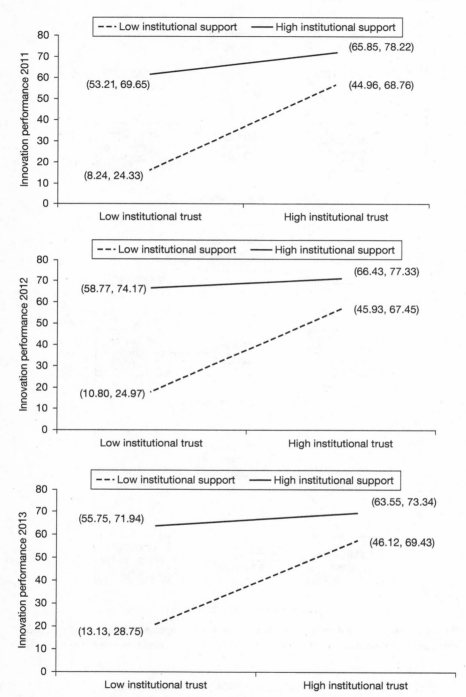

Figure 4.3. Joint effect of institutional support (transparency) and institutional trust (non–life insurance consumption) on innovation performance, 2011–2013. Shown in parentheses are the 95% confidence intervals of the estimated values.

support predicted change in innovation performance. As shown in Table 4.4, when innovation performance in 2012 was regressed on institutional support, controlling for per capita GDP and inflation and innovation performance in 2011, the effect of institutional support was not significant. The same nonsignificant effect of institutional support was obtained when innovation performance in 2013 was regressed on institutional support, controlling for per capita GDP and inflation and innovation performance in 2011 or 2012. In short, although institutional support predicted cross-national differences in innovation performance (see section on "Does Institutional Trust Mediate the Effect of Institutional Support on Innovation?"), it did not predict cross-national change in innovation performance from one year to next one or two years. This is not surprising because formal institutions in a country tend to be stable and do not change much within a short period of time. Because the effect of institutional support was not significant in these analyses, we did not test the mediation hypothesis.

Finally, we tested the joint effect of institutional support and institutional trust on short-term change in innovation performance by including in the regression described in the previous paragraph the main effect of institutional trust and the interaction of institutional support and institutional trust as predictors and life insurance consumption as a control variable. As shown in Table 4.5, the interaction significantly predicted the expected level of innovation performance in 2012 and

Table 4.4. INSTITUTIONAL SUPPORT DID NOT PREDICT CHANGE IN INNOVATION PERFORMANCE OVER YEARS: UNSTANDARDIZED REGRESSION COEFFICIENTS AND STANDARD ERRORS

Dependent Variable	Innovation Performance 2012	Innovation Performance 2013	Innovation Performance 2013
Predictors			
Institutional support (IS)	0.87 (0.58)	0.51 (0.78)	−0.20 (0.68)
Control variables			
GPA/capita	−0.01 (0.05)	0.02 (0.07)	0.04 (0.06)
Inflation	−0.51 (0.16)*	−0.48 (0.22)*	0.03 (0.16)
Innovation performance 2011	0.86 (0.03)***	0.89 (0.04)***	
Innovation performance 2012			0.98 (0.04)***
Intercept	8.92	10.11	0.58
R^2 adjusted	.96	.92	.94
N	123	123	136

NOTE: The proxy for institutional support is the transparency index.

* $p < .05$, ** $p < .01$, *** $p \leq .0001$.

Table 4.5. JOINT EFFECTS OF INSTITUTIONAL SUPPORT AND INSTITUTIONAL TRUST
ON CHANGE IN INNOVATION PERFORMANCE OVER YEARS: UNSTANDARDIZED
REGRESSION COEFFICIENTS AND STANDARD ERRORS

	Innovation Performance 2012	Innovation Performance 2013	Innovation Performance 2013
Predictors			
Institutional support (IS)	0.79 (0.53)	0.10 (0.77)	−0.31 (0.72)
Institutional trust (IT)	2.42 (0.99)*	3.84 (1.44)**	0.78 (1.24)
IT x IS	−1.43 (0.38)***	−1.15 (0.55)*	0.30 (0.51)
Control variables			
GPA/capita	0.08 (0.06)	0.09 (0.08)	0.02 (0.08)
Inflation	−0.57 (0.15)**	−0.63 (0.22)	0.007 (0.17)
Life insurance consumption	−0.17 (0.27)	−0.38 (0.40)	−0.09 (0.36)
Innovation performance 2011	0.81 (0.04)***	0.83 (0.05)***	
Innovation performance 2012			0.99 (0.05)***
Intercept	9.27	10.24	0.34
R^2 adjusted	.97	.99	.94
N	113	113	122

NOTE: The proxy for institutional support is the transparency index and that for institutional trust is non-life insurance consumption.

$^*p < .05,$ $^{**}p < .01,$ $^{***}p \le .0001.$

2013 beyond and above the expected level of innovation performance in 2011. The interaction did not predict the expected level of innovation performance in 2013 beyond and above the expected level of innovation performance in 2012, probably because there was very little change in the countries' relative innovation performance in these 2 years; the correlation between innovation performance in 2012 and 2013 was close to perfect ($r = .97$).

Figure 4.4 illustrates the nature of the significant interactions. The vertical axis depicts positive or negative deviation of innovation performance in 2012 or 2013 from the expected level of innovation performance based on 2011 performance. Only countries that were low in both institutional support and institutional trust showed significantly negative change in relative innovation performance. In addition, institutional trust had significant positive effect on innovation performance change only when institutional support was absent.

In summary, as mentioned in "Institutional Support and Institutional Trust," theoretically, institutional support and institutional trust affect a country's innovation performance in several ways. Our analysis clarified the relationship of

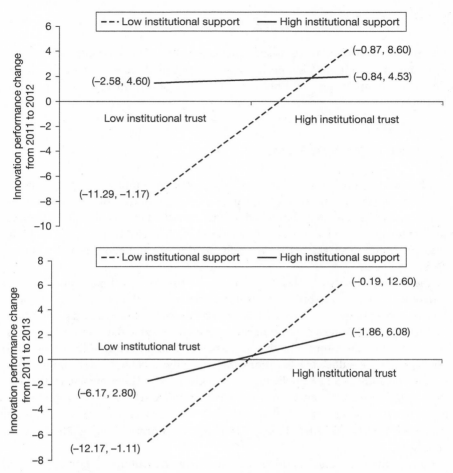

Figure 4.4. Joint effect of institutional support (transparency) and institutional trust (non–life insurance consumption) on change in innovation performance from 2011 to 2012 and 2013. Shown in parentheses are the 95% confidence intervals of the estimated values.

institutional support, institutional trust, and innovation performance. The significant but small indirect effect of institutional trust indicates that institutional trust is not necessary for institutional support to impact innovation performance. However, in a country that has low levels of institutional support and institutional trust, its level of innovation performance tends to be low and declining. Institutional support is present in most developed economies. In these economies, innovation performance tends to be high and will remain at high levels even when institutional trust is low. However, institutional support for innovation is not well established in many transforming economies. For transforming economies that do not have formal institutional support for innovation, its innovation performance depends critically on whether people in these countries trust the evolving institutions in the countries.

CONCLUSIONS

In the present chapter, we discussed some factors that explain country and historical differences in innovation performance. In this final section, we discuss some theoretical contributions and policy implications of our selective review of the literature.

The Culture–Creativity Puzzle

As shown in Figure 4.1, there are marked differences in innovation performance across countries. However, past research on cross-cultural differences in individual and group creativity has failed to find consistent cross-cultural differences in people's performance in standardized tests of creativity (Chiu & Kwan, 2010; Erez, in press; Li et al., 2013). We refer to this phenomenon as the culture–creativity puzzle.

There are at least two ways we solve this puzzle. First, although people from different cultures have similar levels of performance, cultures differ in the normative conceptions of creativity. For example, novelty is a necessary condition for creativity in Western cultural norms; it is inconceivable that something that is not an original creation is creative. In Eastern cultural norms, both novelty and applicability are sufficient conditions for creativity; a creative idea could be an original creation or a new application of an existing idea (Loewenstein & Mueller, in press). Cultural differences in creative performance arise when cultural norms are salient in the context, such as when people work on a creativity task in a group versus alone (Li et al., 2013; Liou & Lan, in press; Morris & Leung, 2010; Nouri et al., 2015).

Our analysis suggests another way to solve the culture–creativity puzzle. Specifically, our results show that country differences in innovation performance are more strongly related to cultural and institutional factors (Liou et al., in press), which cannot be reduced to individual or group processes. For example, countries that are able to attract, nurture, and retain global talents will have a greater supply of global talents to support innovation (Kwan & Chiu, 2015). Countries that value openness more will benefit more from the cultural diversity of their global talents. In contrast, prevalence of localism and concern over security in culturally diverse countries will lead to cultural clashes and exacerbate intercultural tension, which in turn will eradicate the potential creative benefits of cultural diversity (Zhan et al., 2015). In addition, emphasizing self-expansive values supports the pursuit of creative outputs (Bendapudi et al., in press). The presence of institutional support for innovation empowers the talents in the country to attempt radical innovations (Chiu et al., in press; Kwan & Chiu, 2015). In short, analyzing country and historical variations in innovation performance at the country level draws psychologists' attention to the previously overlooked macro-level determinants of innovation performance.

Interactive Effects of Institutional Support and Institutional Trust

In the section "Institutional Support and Institutional Trust," we introduced three possible ways institutional support and institutional trust can jointly influence a country's innovation performance. First, institutional trust mediates the effect of institutional support on innovation performance (the mediation hypothesis). Second, institutional trust is important only when institutional support for innovation is absent (the compensation hypothesis). Third, institutional support and institutional trust have mutually supportive effects on a country's innovation (the mutual support hypothesis).

Our analysis helps to clarify the relationship of institutional support, institutional trust, and innovation performance. First, there is no evidence for the mutual support hypothesis. This hypothesis predicts that institutional support and institutional trust will have a positive interaction effect on innovation performance. However, although the interaction of institutional support and institutional trust was significant on both innovation performance and short-term improvement in innovation, this interaction was a negative rather than a positive interaction.

The significant negative interaction supports the compensation hypothesis. According to this hypothesis, lack of institutional support can dampen a country's innovation performance. However, institutional trust can compensate for this dampening effect. The results reported in the section "The Role of Institutional Trust" consistently show that countries with strong institutional support have high and stable innovation performance irrespective of whether institutional trust was high. However, countries that lack institutional support are able to achieve high and stable levels of innovation performance if people in these countries trust the emerging institutions.

The evidence for the mediation hypothesis is mixed. Institutional trust partially mediates the association between institutional support and innovation performance. However, after controlling for institutional trust, the association between institutional support and innovation performance remained highly significant. In short, the evidence does not support the strong argument that institutional trust fully mediates the effect of institutional support on innovation performance.

Types of Innovations

Our analysis highlights the importance of differentiating different types of innovation. Having a good supply of quality talents may be enough for generating incremental knowledge and technology outputs (Chiu et al., in press). The presence of formal institutions that protect freedom of expression and intellectual property rights is also needed for generating transformational knowledge and technology outputs (Kwan & Chiu, 2015). However, strict institutional regulations may stifle production of creative outputs (Bendapudi et al., in press). Instead, creative industries, including online creative industries, tend to flower in a loose culture, where talented creators encounter few regulations that may suppress self-expansive values.

Policy Implications

Finally, our analysis has important implications for national policies in innovation development. At the beginning of the chapter, we underscored the strategic importance of innovation for sustaining the economic growth of both developed and transforming economies. Most developed economies have already established strong legal, democratic, and political institutions to protect freedom of expression and the innovators' proprietary rights to their intellectual and financial properties. They have also been relatively successful in attracting and nurturing talents. The major challenge in these economies is to be able to maintain an open culture to harness the creative benefits of cultural diversity from their global talents (Zhan et al., 2015).

In contrast, many transforming economies are trying to improve its global competitiveness in innovation. Some of these countries (e.g., China) have invested heavily in its tertiary education and R&D infrastructures. They have also set up aggressive global talent attraction schemes. Our analysis shows that these investments are likely to yield good returns if these countries will build up institutional support for innovation (Chiu et al., in press). However, institution building takes time. Before strong institutions are established, these countries need to build up their citizens' trust in the countries' emerging institutions.

In conclusion, building an innovation economy is a national priority in both developed and developing countries. In this chapter, we review the existing and new evidence pertinent to the institutional, cultural, historical, and psychological factors that predict the overall level of innovation performance in a country, as well as short-term and long-term temporal changes in a country's innovation performance. This analysis underscores the utility of including both macro and micro factors in an explanatory model of innovation performance at the country level.

ACKNOWLEDGMENTS

Preparation of this chapter is supported by a research grant to the authors by the Center for Positive Social Science, the Chinese University of Hong Kong, and a grant to the first author by the Global China Research Program, the Chinese University of Hong Kong.

REFERENCES

Beck, T., & Webb, I. (2003). Economic, demographic and institutional determinants of life insurance consumption across countries. *World Bank Review*, *17*, 51–88.

Bendapudi, N., Zhan, S., & Hong, Y-y. (in press). Quality education does not always guarantee creative output: The moderating role of cultural values. *Journal of Cross-Cultural Psychology*.

Chen, X., Leung, A. K-y., Yang, D. Y-J., Chiu, C-y., Li, Z-q, & Cheng, S. Y. Y. (2016). Cultural threats in culturally mixed encounters hamper creative performance for individuals with lower openness to experience. *Journal of Cross-Cultural Psychology*.

Cheng, C-y., & Leung A. K.-y. (2013). Revisiting the multicultural experience-creativity link: The effects of cultural distance and comparison mindset. *Social Psychological and Personality Science*, *4*, 475–482.

Cheng, C-y., Leung, A. K.-y., & Wu, T. Y. + (2011). Going beyond the multicultural experience–creativity link: The emotional pathway underlying dual-cultural activation and creativity. *Journal of Social Issues*, *67*, 806–824.

Chiu, C-y., & Kim, Y-h. (2011). Rethinking culture and the self: Some basic principles and their implications. In S. Breugelmans, A. Chasiotis, & van de Vijver (Eds.), *Fundamental questions in cross-cultural psychology* (pp. 518–541). New York, NY: Cambridge University Press.

Chiu, C-Y., & Kwan, L. (2010). Culture and creativity: A process model. *Management and Organization Review*, *6*, 447–461.

Chiu, C-y., & Kwan, L. y-y. (2015). Coevolution of market integration and fairness norms. *PsycCRITIQUES*, *60*(4).

Chiu, C-y., Kwan, L. Y-y., & Liou, S. (2013). Culturally motivated challenges to innovations in integrative research: Theory and solutions. *Social Issues and Policy Review*, *7*, 149–172.

Chiu, C-y., Liou, S., & Kwan, L. Y-y. (2016). The institutional and cultural contexts of creativity and innovation in China. In A. Lewin, M. Kenny, & J. P. Murmann (Eds.), *China's innvovation challenge: Overcoming the middle income trap* (pp. 368–393). New York, NY: Cambridge University Press.

Cook, K. S., Hardin, R., & Levi, M. (2005). *Cooperation without risk?* New York, NY: Russell Sage Foundation.

Dixit, A. K. (2004). *Lawlessness and economics: Alternate modes of governance*. Princeton, NJ: Princeton University Press.

Dutta, S. (2011, Ed.). *The Global Innovation Index 2011: Accelerating growth and development*. Fontainebleau: INSEAD.

Dutta, S. (2012, Ed.). *The Global Innovation Index 2012: Stronger innovation linkages for global growth*. Ithaca, NY: Fontainebleau.

Dutta, S., & Lanvin, B. (2013, Eds.). *The Global Innovation Index 2013: The local dynamics of innovation*. Ithaca, NY: Cornell University, INSEAD, & WIPO.

Dutta, S., Lanvin, B., & Wunsch-Vincent (2014, Eds.). *The Global Innovation Index 2014: The Human factor in innovation*. Ithaca, NY: Cornell University, INSEAD, & WIPO.

Erez, M. (in press). From local to cross-cultural to global work motivation and innovation. In M. Gelfand, C-y. Chiu, & Y-y. Hong (Eds.). *Handbook of advances in culture and psychology: Volume 7*. New York, NY: Oxford University Press.

Erez, M., Lisak, A., Harush, R., Glikson, E., Nouri, R., & Shokef, E. (2013). Going global: Developing management students' global characteristics through a multicultural team project. *Academy of Management Learning & Education, 12*, 330–355.

Granovetter, M. S. (1985). Economic action and social structure: The problem of embeddedness. *American Journal of Sociology, 91*, 481–510.

Han, J., Peng, S-q., Chiu, C-y., & Leung, A. K.-y. (2010). Workforce diversity and creativity: A multilevel analysis. In A. K.-y. Leung, C-y. Chiu, & Y-y. Hong (Eds.), *Cultural processes: A social psychological perspective* (pp. 286–311). New York, NY: Cambridge University Press.

Kwan, L. Y-y., & Chiu, C-y. (2015). Country variations in different innovation outputs: The interactive effects of institutional support and human capital. *Journal of Organizational Behavior, 36*, 1050–1070.

Leung, A. K.-y. & Chiu, C-y. (2008). Interactive effects of multicultural experiences and openness to experience on creativity. *Creativity Research Journal, 20*, 376–382.

Leung, A. K.-y. & Chiu, C-y. (2010). Multicultural experience, idea receptiveness, and creativity. *Journal of Cross-Cultural Psychology, 41*, 723–741.

Leung, A. K.-y., Maddux, W., Galinsky, A., & Chiu, C-y. (2008). Multicultural experience enhances creativity: The when and how. *American Psychologist, 63*, 169–181.

Li, C., Kwan, L. Y-Y., Liou, S., & Chiu, C-y. (2013). Culture, group processes and creativity (pp. 143). In M. Yuki & M. Brewer (Eds.), *Culture and group processes*. New York, NY: Oxford University Press.

Liou, S., Kwan, Y-Y. L., & Chiu, C-y. (2016). Historical and cultural obstacles to frame-breaking innovations in China. *Management and Organization Review, 12*(1), 35–39.

Liou, S., & Lan, X. (in press). Cultural differences in team creativity process. *Journal of Cross-Cultural Psychology*.

Loewenstein, J., & Mueller, J. (2016). Implicit theories of creative ideas: How culture guides creativity assessments. *Academy of Management Discovery, 2*(4), 320–348.

Luhmann, N. (1979). *Trust and power*. Chichester, UK: John Wiley & Sons.

Mayer, R. C., Davis, J. H., & Schoorman, F. D. (1995). An integrative model of organizational trust. *Academy of Management Review, 20*, 709–734.

Morris, M. W., & Leung, K. (2010). Creativity east and west: Perspectives and parallels. *Management and Organization Review, 6*, 313–327.

Murmann, J. P., Aldrich, H. E., Levinthal, D., & Winter, S. G. (2003). Evolutionary thought in management and organization theory at the beginning of the new millennium: A symposium of the state of the art and opportunities for future research. *Journal of Management Inquiry, 12*, 22–40.

North, D. C. (1990). *Institutions, institutional change, and economic performance*. Cambridge, UK: Cambridge University Press.

Nouri, R., Erez, M., Lee, C., Liang, J., Banister, B. D., & Chiu, W. (2015). Keeping the supervisor and peers out of sight: The effect of culture and the social work context on creativity. *Journal of Organizational Behavior, 36*(7), 899–918.

Office of Science and Technology Policy, the White House. (May 2010). *National security and international affairs*. Retrieved from https://www.whitehouse.gov/administration/eop/ostp/divisions/natsecintaff.

Peng, M. W. (2003). Institutional transitions and strategic choices. *Academy of Management Review, 28*, 275–296.

Simonton, D. K., & Ting, S-S. (2010). Creativity in Eastern and Western civilizations: The lessons of historimetry. *Management and Organization Review, 6*, 329–350.

Singh, J. V., & Lumsden, C. J. (1990). Theory and research in organizational ecology. *Annual Review of Sociology, 16*, 161–195.

Stupples, P. (2014). Creative contributions: The role of the arts and the cultural sector in development. *Progress in Development Studies, 14*, 115–130.

Tan, J., Yang, J., & Veliyath, R. (2009). Particularistic and system trust among small and medium enterprises: A comparative study in China's transition economy. *Journal of Business Venturing, 24*, 544–557.

Zhan, S., Bendapudi, N., & Hong, Y-y. (2015). Re-examining diversity as a double-edged sword for innovation process. *Journal of Organizational Behavior, 36*, 1026–1049.

5

Cultural Diversity (Fractionalization) and Economic Complexity

Effects on Innovation Performance and Human Development

LETTY Y.-Y. KWAN AND CHI-YUE CHIU ■

A living culture is not static or isolated. To the extent that its members are free to think, a culture grows and develops in response to other cultures and changes in its environment . . . UNESCO's World Commission on Culture and Development, in its 1995 report, Our Creative Diversity, stated that any national policy of "nation-building" that seeks to make all groups homogeneous—or to allow one to dominate—is neither desirable nor feasible.

—CANADIAN CENTER FOR TEACHING PEACE,
http://www.peace.ca/sheet10.htm

Like the UNESCO and the Canadian Center for Teaching Peace, some scholars (e.g., Page, 2007) believe that cultural diversity is essential to the promotion of creativity and human development. This belief has been referred to as the diversity dividend hypothesis (Gerring, Thacker, Lu, & Huang, 2015). However, contrary to this hypothesis, research has shown that the level of a country's cultural diversity is negatively associated with the country's innovation performance and human development. This is because countries with severe ethnic and linguistic fractionalization are vulnerable to civil strife and internal conflicts, which in turn will harm economic, social, and technological development. For example, ethnic and linguistic divisions within a country can create barriers to communication and increase factions, rivalries, and internal conflicts (Easterly, 2001; Easterly & Levine, 1997). In contrast, cultural homogeneity can foster interpersonal trust (Zak & Knack, 2001). The negative effect of cultural diversity on a country's human development has been referred to as the *diversity debit hypothesis* (Gerring et al., 2015).

In the next section, we will review the evidence pertinent to the effects of cultural diversity on innovation and human development. We propose that to understand the linkages between cultural diversity, on the one hand, and innovation and human development, on the other, we need to consider the multidimensional nature of cultural diversity and distinguish between cultural fractionalization and cultural complexity. Specifically, we will argue with evidence from a multinational study that although the extent of ethnolinguistic fractionalization of a country is negatively related to its innovation performance and progress in human development, cultural complexity is positively related to innovation performance, and it can attenuate the negative association between ethnolinguistic fractionalization and progress in human development.

CULTURAL DIVERSITY, CREATIVITY, AND INNOVATION

Creativity refers to the capability to generate new and useful ideas that can be implemented in a certain production, whereas innovation refers to the successful implementation of creative ideas. The relationship of cultural diversity with creativity and innovation varies across levels of analysis (Han, Peng, Chiu, & Leung, 2010). At the individual level, correlational and experimental evidence shows that individuals living in culturally diverse environments tend to have higher performance in standard tests of creativity (Leung & Chiu, 2010; Leung, Maddux, Galinsky, & Chiu, 2008). This is because exposure to multiple cultures destabilizes normative ways of thinking, leads to the experience of cognitive dysfluency (Mourey, Lam, & Oyserman, 2015), and motivates effortful integration of seemingly conflicting information and creative extension of conceptual boundaries, which in turn promotes creative problem solving (Cheng & Leung, 2013; Cheng, Leung, & Wu, 2011). The creative effects of multicultural experiences are particularly pronounced among individuals who are open to experiences (Chen et al., 2016; Leung & Chiu, 2008).

At the group and organizational levels, the relationship between cultural diversity and innovation is less clear. In 2004, eight Central European countries joined the European Union, leading to an unprecedented influx of immigrants in the United Kingdom. Nathan and Lee (2013) analyzed the innovation performance of 7,600 London-based firms between 2005 and 2007 and found that firms with higher levels of immigrant diversity among its owners and partners were more likely to develop innovative products or services, modify existing products, introduce new equipment into their operations, and invent and implement new ways of working. Based on data from a comprehensive survey of 1,800 professionals, 40 case studies, and numerous focus groups and interviews in the United States, Hewlett, Marshall, and Sherbin (2013) also concluded that firms with culturally diverse leadership are more likely to report growth in market share and success in capturing a new market. Analysis of data from a 1940–2000 state panel in the United States further reveals that a 1 percentage point increase in immigrant college graduates' population share is accompanied by a 9%–18% increase in number of patents per capita (Hunt & Gauthier-Loiselle, 2010). Data from Germany also showed that the level of cultural diversity of knowledge workers in R&D firms is positively related to the firms' innovation performance (Niebuhr, 2010).

However, based on their analysis of a dataset of 4,582 firms in the Netherlands, Ozgen, Nijkamp, and Poot (2013) found that although firms that employ a more diverse foreign workforce tend to be more innovative, firms that employ relatively more immigrants are *less* innovative. This result suggests that in companies that employ only a small percentage of foreign workers who come from many different countries, the local employees do not experience the threat of potential outgroup domination or competition and are therefore more prepared to seek inspirations from the "novel" ideas of the foreign workers. However, in companies that employ a large percentage of foreign employees from the same cultural group, the local employees may experience the threat of outgroup domination and competition, leading to clashes between the local and foreign cultural groups. In addition, cultural fault lines may develop between the opposing cultural traditions, which tend to retard innovation performance (see Chiu, Kwan, & Liou, 2013; Li, Kwan, Liou & Chiu, 2013).

The relationship between cultural diversity and innovation at the country level is even more ambiguous. For example, research has shown that the amount of ethnic diversity of a country is *negatively* associated with its investments in innovation and innovation output (Zhan, Bendapudi, & Hong, 2015). However, the amount of ideological diversity (diversity in terms of cultural values) in a country is positively associated with its innovation performance as long as the level of ethnic polarization in the country is low (Zhan et al., 2015).

In summary, although cultural diversity facilitates creative and innovation performance of individuals (particularly those who are open to experience) and organizations (particularly those that employ a smaller percentage of foreign workers), ethnic diversity has a negative relationship with innovation performance at the country level. We will return to the negative effect of cultural diversity on a country's innovation after we have reviewed the findings pertaining to the relationship between cultural diversity and human development.

CULTURAL DIVERSITY AND HUMAN DEVELOPMENT

In the field of international development, human development refers to the progress in enlarging people's choices that allow people to lead a long and healthy life, to be educated, and to have a decent standard of living (United Nations Development Program, 1997). The Human Development Index (United Nations Development Program, 1997), a widely used measure of the level of human development of a country, is a composite measure of a country's life expectancy, education, and per capita income. Other widely used measures of human development are measures of social stability, life expectancy at birth, infant mortality per 1,000 new births, percentage of population with access to improved sanitary facilities, and percentage of population with access to clean water. Consistent with the diversity debit hypothesis, using data drawn from the Demographic and Health Survey, which covers a large number of developing countries, Gerring et al. (2015) found that the amount of cultural diversity in a country has negative relationships with its child mortality, fertility, education, and wealth.

However, it is worth noting that the relationship between the amount of cultural diversity in a country and its progress in human development depends on how cultural diversity is measured. For example, the amount of linguistic diversity in a country is negatively related to its economic performance and social stability (Desmet, Ortuno-Ortin, & Wacziarg, 2016). In contrast, the amount of religious diversity in a country is positively associated with social stability (Nettle et al., 2007). In addition, Hlepas (2013) found that in European countries, cultural diversity is not always associated with lower levels of human development. A critical moderator is the extent to which the countries are open to diversity.

In summary, having more ideological diversity (e.g., religious diversity) in a country may confer opportunities for intercultural learning and hence promote creativity, innovation, and human development, particularly in countries that are open to and accept diversity. However, ethnic and linguistic diversity may accentuate ethnolinguistic fractionalization in the country, lead to destabilizing internal conflicts, and hinder economic and human development.

TYPES OF CULTURAL DIVERSITY

The findings from Zhan et al. (2015) and Nettle et al. (2007) underscore the importance of differentiating ethnolinguistic fractionalization from ideological/religious diversity. In Zhan et al.'s (2015) study, ethnic diversity is negatively related to innovation output, whereas ideological diversity (diversity in cultural values) is positively related to innovation input among countries with lower levels of ethnic polarization. In the Nettle et al. (2007) study, linguistic diversity predicts lower levels of social stability, but religious diversity predicts higher levels of social stability.

Although earlier measures of cultural diversity have focused on ethnolinguistic diversity (e.g., Roeder, 2001), several attempts have been made to differentiate different types of cultural diversity. For example, Fearson (2003) has created separate measures of ethnic and linguistic fractionalization of 159 countries or regions, whereas Alesina, Devleeschauwer, Easterly, Kurlat, and Wacziarg (2003) have constructed separate measures of ethnic, linguistic, and religious fractionalization for 215 countries or regions. Likewise, separate measures of linguistic, religious, and ethnic fractionalization are available from the Organization of Economic Co-operation and Development (OECD; Patsiurko, Campbell, & Hall, 2012).

We collated the Roeder measure of ethnolinguistic fractionalization measured in 1961 and 1985, the Fearson (2003) measures of ethnic and linguistic fractionalization, Alesina et al.'s measures of ethnic, linguistic, and religious fractionalization, and the OECD measures of ethnic, linguistic, and religious fractionalization. Next, we normalized each measure and performed principal component analysis on the 10 measures. This analysis allows us to identify the principal components that underline the different measures of cultural diversity.

Analysis revealed a two-factor model that accounted for 75.0% of the total matrix variance, with the first and second factor explaining 60.2% and 14.8% of the variance, respectively. The two factors were rotated to an orthogonal structure using varimax rotation. As shown in Table 5.1, all measures of ethnic and linguistic fractionalization had large loadings (>.50) on Factor 1 only, and the two measures of religious diversity had large loadings (>.50) on Factor 2 only. Thus, we collapsed the eight normalized ethnic and linguistic fractionalization measures to form a measure of ethnolinguistic fractionalization and the two normalized religious diversity measures to form a measure of religious diversity. The correlation between ethnolinguistic fractionalization and religious diversity was small ($r = .26$, $p < .0001$). This result confirms the importance of separating ethnolinguistic fractionalization from religious diversity.

Table 5.1. ROTATED FACTOR STRUCTURE OF MEASURES OF ETHNIC, LINGUISTIC, AND RELIGIOUS DIVERSITY

	Factor 1 Ethnolinguistic Fractionalization	Factor 2 Religious Diversity
Ethnic (Alesina et al.)	**0.86**	0.03
Linguistic (Alesina et al.)	**0.74**	0.21
Religious (Alesina et al.)	0.10	**0.60**
Ethnic (Fearson)	**0.90**	0.06
Linguistic (Fearson)	**0.78**	0.00
Ethnolinguistic 61 (Roeder)	**0.90**	0.34
Ethnolinguistic 85 (Roeder)	**0.90**	0.35
Linguistic (OECD)	**0.73**	0.24
Religious (OECD)	0.09	**0.63**
Ethnic (OECD)	**0.64**	0.12

The bolded numbers indicate items for the corresponding Factor 1 or Factor 2.

RELATIONSHIP OF CULTURAL DIVERSITY WITH
INNOVATION AND HUMAN DEVELOPMENT

Next, we examined the relationship of the two types of cultural diversity with innovation performance and human development. The Global Innovation Index (GII) provided data on the innovation performance of 141 countries or regions in 2013. The innovation output subindex of the GII covers a comprehensive list of innovation outputs, which are grouped into two broad categories: knowledge and technology outputs (e.g., number of patent applications, utility model applications, scientific publications, new business density, high-tech outputs) and creative outputs (e.g., information and communication technology, number of national feature films produced, amount of creative goods exported). Table 5.2 shows that only ethnolinguistic fractionalization is negatively related to the innovation output subindex.

The Human Development Index provides summary information on the levels of human development of 179 countries or regions in 2012. We also obtained from the OECD data from 185 to 208 countries or regions on life expectancy at birth, infant mortality rate, percentage of population with access to improved sanitary facilities, and percentage of population with access to clean water in 2012. Again, as shown in Table 5.2, only ethnolinguistic fractionalization was negatively related to all measures of human development. These findings again confirm the utility of differentiating ethnolinguistic fractionalization from religious diversity, and they support the diversity debit hypothesis: higher levels of ethnolinguistic

Table 5.2. CORRELATIONS OF CULTURAL DIVERSITY (ETHNOLINGUISTIC FRACTIONALIZATION AND RELIGIOUS DIVERSITY) AND ECONOMIC COMPLEXITY WITH INNOVATION PERFORMANCE (INNOVATION OUTPUT) AND HUMAN DEVELOPMENT (HUMAN DEVELOPMENT INDEX)

	Ethnolinguistic Fractionalization	Religious Diversity	Economic Complexity
Total Innovation Output	$-.35\ (p < .0001)$	$.04\ (p = .62)$	$.79\ (p < .0001)$
Knowledge and technology outputs	$-.26\ (p = .002)$	$.13\ (p = .12)$	$.67\ (p < .0001)$
Creative outputs	$-.34\ (p < .0001)$	$-.03\ (p = .72)$	$.70\ (p < .0001)$
Human development index 2012	$-.45\ (p < .0001)$	$-.03\ (p = .70)$	$.76\ (p < .0001)$
Life expectancy at birth	$-.48\ (p < .0001)$	$-.15\ (p < .04)$	$.71\ (p < .0001)$
Infant mortality rate (per 1000 live births)	$.48\ (p < .0001)$	$.08\ (p = .25)$	$-.72\ (p < .0001)$
Population with access to improved sanitary facilities	$-.43\ (p < .0001)$	$-.10\ (p = .17)$	$.64\ (p < .0001)$
Population with access to clean water	$-.36\ (p < .0001)$	$-.02\ (p = .76)$	$.68\ (p < .0001)$

fractionalization are accompanied by interethnic instability that may hurt a country's innovation performance and human development.

INNOVATION AND ECONOMIC COMPLEXITY MITIGATE THE EFFECTS OF ETHNOLINGUISTIC FRACTIONALIZATION ON HUMAN DEVELOPMENT

How can we explain the negative relationship between ethnolinguistic fractionalization and human development? An assumption behind the prediction that cultural diversity enhances human development (the diversity dividend hypothesis) is that in countries with relatively high levels of cultural diversity, their cultures can learn from and grow and develop in response to other cultures. However, the mere presence of cultural heterogeneity within a country is not sufficient for the promotion of intercultural learning, because cultural heterogeneity may also lead to cultural frictions and conflicts. Thus, we need to identify mechanisms that will enable a country to create opportunities of intercultural learning. In cultural psychology, a distinction has been made between culturalism and polyculturalism (Morris, Chiu, & Liu, 2015). Culturalism recognizes and celebrates the positive distinctiveness of every cultural group and advocates preservation of the purity of heritage cultures. Although culturalism respects cultural differences, it also discourages intercultural learning and may even encourage tribalistic narrowing of in-group identification and reactionary movements seeking purity. Like culturalism, polyculturalism recognizes and respects the distinctiveness of different heritage cultures. Polyculturalism posits that cultures are not homogenous monoliths. Instead, because different cultures are connected by individuals, their activities and productions constantly affect each other. Thus, cultures constantly interact with and borrow ideas from other cultures (Morris et al., 2015).

Take international trade as an example. Countries are connected to other cultures through the products and services imported from and exported to other countries. Through the production of exported goods and consumption of imported products and services, individuals in a country will learn about different cultures and become the agents of cultural exchange and culture mixing. International trades will have a particularly large impact on intercultural learning in countries that make goods that require a large amount of capabilities or know-how from different countries to manufacture, and in countries that sell their products to everywhere in the world. The Economic Complexity Indicator (ECI; Hausmann et al., 2014) captures the extent of cultural lending and borrowing through international trade. The ECI measures the amount of international interactions of a country through the country's exports. Countries that have higher levels of economic complexity are those that export a large number of different products to different countries and make *complex products* that require a large amount of capabilities or know-how from different countries to manufacture (Hidalgo & Hausmann, 2009).

How are innovation, economic complexity, and human development related to one another? As mentioned in the previous section, human development refers to the process of enlarging people's choices and enhancing the range of things people can do so that they are freer to make decisions that would enable them to live a long and healthy life, to have access to knowledge, to enjoy a decent standard of living, and to participate in community life (United Nations Development Programme, 1990). Innovation allows countries to grow by producing high value-added and complex products that are marketable globally. As such, innovation will increase the level of economic complexity in a country. Increased economic complexity gives people more occupational and consumption choices and consequently promotes their well-being (Hartmann & Pyka, 2013).[1] In short, innovation can increase a country's economic complexity, which in turn fosters human development.

Does innovation also mitigate the negative impact of ethnolinguistic fractionalization on human development? As mentioned in the previous paragraph, innovation increases the level of economic complexity in a country. An economic complex society nurtures cosmopolitan orientations and tastes (Leung, Koh, & Tam, 2015). Individuals in these societies readily accept cultural lending and borrowing, as well as combination of ideas and practices from different cultures. The enhanced creative diversity in these societies creates a virtuous circle of productive and human capability expansion (Hartmann & Pyka, 2013) that can promote human development even in societies with high levels of ethnolinguistic diversity. Thus, we contend that the benefits of innovation through enhanced economic complexity on human development may be able to mitigate the negative effects of ethnolinguistic fractionalization in countries with high levels of ethnic and linguistic diversity. This contention is illustrated in Figure 5.1. We tested this contention with multinational data.

As the first step to test the proposed model depicted in Figure 5.1, we evaluated the correlations between economic complexity, on the one hand, and innovation output and the indicators of human development, on the other. The levels

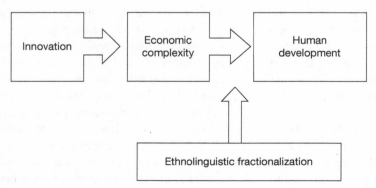

Figure 5.1. Innovation and economic complexity mitigate the negative effects of ethnolinguistic fractionalization on human development.

of economic complexity of 128 countries in 2013 were used in the current study. As shown in Table 5.2, a country's economic complexity is positively related to its levels of innovation output and human development.

Next, we tested the predicted interaction of innovation and ethnolinguistic fractionalization on human development. To facilitate interpretation, we standardized both predictors. In addition, we controlled for the effects of GDP per capita, total health expenditure per capita, gross expenditure on R&D, and population size. As shown in Table 5.3, human development was positively related to innovation output and negatively associated with ethnolinguistic fractionalization. More important, the interaction of innovation output and ethnolinguistic fractionalization was significant. As shown in Figure 5.2, a country's human development was significantly poorer when its innovation output was low *and* ethnolinguistic fractionalization was high. Countries with little ethnolinguistic fractionalization had relatively good performance in human development regardless of the levels of innovation output. However, among countries with a lot of ethnolinguistic fractionalization, innovation made a difference. Those with relatively low levels of innovation performed significantly more poorly in human development, as the diversity debit hypothesis predicts. However, those with relatively high levels of innovation output had comparable levels of human development as those with little ethnolinguistic fractionalization. This result indicates that innovation can mitigate the negative impact of ethnolinguistic fractionalization on human development.

Finally, we included the main effect of economic complexity and its interaction with ethnolinguistic fractionalization in the regression analysis. Our model predicts that the interaction of innovation output and ethnolinguistic fractionalization would become nonsignificant, whereas the interaction of economic complexity and ethnolinguistic fractionalization would be significant (Muller, Judd, & Yzerbyt, 2005). This is because the interaction of innovation output and ethnolinguistic fractionalization was fully mediated by the interaction of economic complexity and ethnolinguistic fractionalization.

Table 5.4 shows that this was indeed the case. For all five measures of human development, after controlling for the effects of economic complexity and its interaction with ethnolinguistic fractionalization, the interaction of innovation output and ethnolinguistic fractionalization became nonsignificant. For the human development index, the infant mortality rate, and life expectancy, the interaction of economic complexity and ethnolinguistic fractionalization was significant. Figure 5.3 illustrates the nature of these significant interactions. Again, countries with little ethnolinguistic fractionalization had relatively good performance in human development regardless of the levels of economic complexity. However, among countries with a lot of ethnolinguistic fractionalization, those that were relatively low in economic complexity performed significantly more poorly in human development. However, those that were economically complex had comparable levels of human development as those with little ethnolinguistic fractionalization. This result is consistent with the theoretical model depicted in Figure 5.1.

Table 5.3. THE ROLE OF ETHNOLINGUISTIC FRACTIONALIZATION AND INNOVATION PERFORMANCE IN HUMAN AND SOCIAL DEVELOPMENT: REGRESSION ANALYSIS

	Human Development Index	Life Expectancy	Infant Mortality Rate	Access to Sanitary Facilities	Access to Clean Water
Predictors					
Ethnolinguistic fractionalization (EF)	-0.04***	-2.81***	7.84***	-7.44**	-3.80**
Innovation output (IO)	0.06***	4.42***	-12.13***	14.97***	7.16***
EF x IO	**0.03****	**1.30***	**-6.34****	**6.88*****	**4.62*****
Control Variables					
GDP/capita	0.0001	0.05	0.01	-0.15	-0.01
Total health expenditure/capita	$2.01e^{-5}$	0.0006	-0.001	0.003	0.0004
Population size	$-1.16e^{-7}$	$-3.14e^{-6}$	$1.74e^{-5}$*	$-3.45e^{-5}$***	$-5.72e^{-6}$
Gross expenditure on R&D	0.0007	-0.03	0.04	-0.04	-0.002
Intercept	0.67	72.21	19.21	82.18	91.84
N	102	106	107	102	105
R²-adj	72.7%	60.0%	58.4%	57.2%	52.1%

*** $p \leq .0001$; ** $p \leq .01$; * $p < .05$.

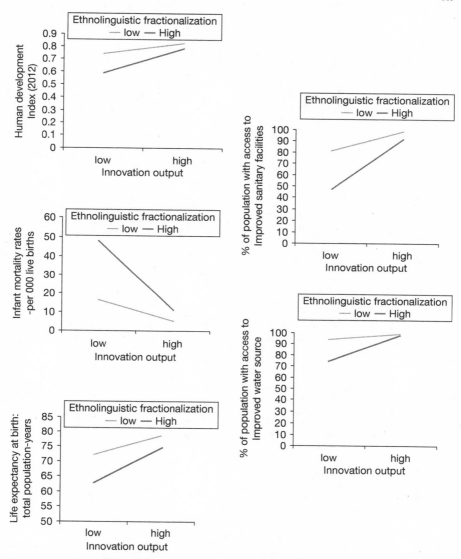

Figure 5.2. The interaction of innovation output and ethnolinguistic fractionalization on human development.

CONCLUSIONS

Although some writers believe that cultural diversity can create better societies (Page, 2007), there is a dearth of evidence for the diversity dividend hypothesis. Instead, there is consistent evidence from several multinational studies for the more pessimistic diversity debit hypothesis (Desmet et al., 2016; Gerring et al., 2015; Zhan et al., 2015), which states that cultural diversity could lead to internal conflicts that hinder technological and human development.

Table 5.4. THE MEDIATING ROLE OF ECONOMIC COMPLEXITY: REGRESSION ANALYSIS

	Human Development Index	Life Expectancy	Infant Mortality Rate	Access to Sanitary Facilities	Access to Clean Water
Predictors					
Ethnolinguistic fractionalization (EF)	−0.03**	−2.70***	7.34***	−7.05**	−3.45**
Innovation output (IO)	0.04**	2.57**	−7.41**	10.16**	5.82**
EF x IO	0.009	0.30	−0.74	5.04	3.30
Economic complexity (EC)	0.02	2.11*	−8.06**	6.76*	3.05
EF x EC	0.03*	1.90*	−7.35**	2.76	1.72
Control Variables					
GDP/capita	0.001	0.11	−0.07	0.01	0.0008
Total health expenditure/capita	$1.23e^{-5}$	0.0003	−0.0002	0.001	−0.00001
Population size	$-9.96e^{-8}$*	$-2.05e^{-5}$	0.00002*	$-3.25e^{-5}$**	$-5.21e^{-6}$
Gross expenditure on R&D	0.0003	−0.06*	0.13	−0.14	−0.02
Intercept	0.69	73.78	13.29	87.40	92.75
N	94	98	98	94	96
R²-adj	75.3%	67.6%	69.6%	59.5%	53.1%

*** $p \leq .0001$; ** $p \leq .01$; * $p < .05$.

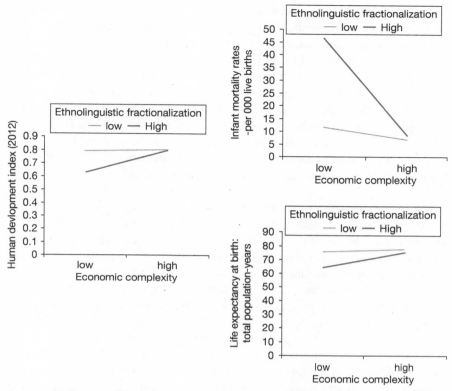

Figure 5.3. The interaction of economic complexity and ethnolinguistic fractionalization on human development.

The results of the multinational study presented in this chapter (see also Zhan et al., 2015) suggest that the negative effect of cultural diversity is limited to ethnolinguistic fractionalization. The effects of religious or other forms of deep diversity on technological and human development are either positive (as in Nettle et al., 2007; Zhan et al., 2015) or nonsignificant (as in the current study). This result highlights the importance of differentiating surface diversity based on ethnolinguistic characteristics and deep diversity based on values and beliefs (Han et al., 2010).

Ethnolinguistic fractionalization should also be differentiated from cultural complexity. Ethnolinguistic fractionalization is often measured by the extent of ethnolinguistic heterogeneity within a country. Cultural complexity reflects the frequency and intensity of intercultural interactions. Whereas ethnolinguistic heterogeneity can sometimes lead to cultural clashes, frequent positive intercultural interactions within a country and between countries can promote intercultural learning. Whereas ethnolinguistic fractionalization within a country is negatively related to technological and human development, a country's level of economic complexity (cultural complexity in the economic domain) is positively associated with its innovation output and human development.

Innovation leads to increased economic diversification and economic complexity. Economic complexity, in turn, gives people more occupational and consumption choices, and consequently promotes their well-being (Hartmann & Pyka, 2013). As mentioned in the previous paragraph, economic complexity has a direct effect on human development. In addition, the results of the multinational study reviewed in the present chapter suggest that economic complexity also mitigates the negative impacts of ethnolinguistic fractionalization on human development. The double benefits of economic complexity highlight the fact that the mere presence of cultural heterogeneity does not always benefit a country's development. Ethnolinguistic diversity will create developmental benefits only in countries that promote intercultural exchange and culture mixing (Morris et al., 2015).

Across countries, the correlation between economic complexity and innovation output was .78, suggesting that countries with better innovation performance have more complex economies; these countries tend to produce complex products that are sold globally. However, the strength of positive association between innovation output and economic complexity varies with the type of innovation outputs. The GII measures six types of innovation outputs: knowledge creation (e.g., number of patents, publications, and H-index), knowledge impact (e.g., new business density), knowledge diffusion (e.g., high-tech exports), intangible assets (trademark registrations, business model creation), creative goods and services (e.g., national feature films produced, creative goods exported), and online creativity (e.g., Wikipedia monthly edits, YouTube uploads). The correlations between innovation output and economic complexity range from .25 (intangible assets) to .70 (creative goods and services), .72 (knowledge creation), and .78 (online creativity). This result is consistent with the idea that innovations that build on global exchange of ideas and knowledge (e.g., globally cited scientific knowledge or applications, knowledge published in global online platforms, globally marketable creative goods) are most strongly related to economic complexity.

In the current study, we have focused on the effect of economic complexity at the country level. Recent studies have started to examine the effects of cultural complexity in other domains (e.g., in the domains of intercultural interaction) at the individual and group levels. These studies show that at the individual level, taking a polyculturalist perspective to culture (the view that cultures coevolve through intercultural interactions) can reduce stereotyping and improve intercultural relations (Bernardo, Rosenthal, & Levy, 2013; Rosenthal & Levy, 2012, 2013; Torelli, Chiu, Tam, Au, & Keh, 2011). At the group level, taking a polyculturalist perspective to culture can improve the quality of collaboration in multicultural teams (Chiu et al., 2013).

In summary, the presence of severe ethnic and linguistic fractionalization can increase a country's vulnerability to civil strife and internal conflicts and slow down the country's economic, social, and technological developments. Nonetheless, cultural complexity supports innovation and can weaken the negative impacts of ethnolinguistic fractionalization on human development.

NOTE

1. Economic diversification may also have negative effects on human development. It can lead to the obsolescence of some old sectors, and individuals who have become specialized in the old sectors will suffer. It may also have adverse effects on ecological sustainability. Finally, the marginal return of economic diversification may diminish with higher levels of economic diversification (Hartmann & Pyka, 2013).

REFERENCES

Alesina, A., Devleeschauwer, A., Easterly, W., Kurlat, S., & Wacziarg, R. (2003). Fractionalization. *Journal of Economic Growth, 8*, 155–194.

Bernardo, A. B. I., Rosenthal, L., & Levy, S. R. (2013). Polyculturalism and attitudes toward people from other countries. *International Journal of Intercultural Relations, 37*, 335–344.

Chen, X., Leung, A. K-y., Yang, D. Y-J., Chiu, C-y., Li, Z-q, & Cheng, S. Y. Y. (2016). Cultural threats in culturally mixed encounters hamper creative performance for individuals with lower openness to experience. *Journal of Cross-Cultural Psychology, 47*, 1321–1334.

Cheng, C-y., & Leung, A. K.-y. (2013). Revisiting the multicultural experience-creativity link: The effects of cultural distance and comparison mindset. *Social Psychological and Personality Science, 4*, 475–482.

Cheng, C-y., Leung, A. K.-y., & Wu, T. Y. (2011). Going beyond the multicultural experience –creativity link: The emotional pathway underlying dual-cultural activation and creativity. *Journal of Social Issues, 67*, 806–824.

Chiu, C-y., Kwan, L. Y-y., & Liou, S. (2013). Culturally motivated challenges to innovations in integrative research: Theory and solutions. *Social Issues and Policy Review, 7*, 149–172.

Desmet, K., Ortuno-Ortin, I., & Wacziarg, R. (2016). Linguistic cleavages and economic development. In V. Ginsburgh & S. Weber (Eds.), *The Palgrave handbook of economics and language* (pp. 425–446). New York, NY: Palgrave Macmillan.

Easterly, W. (2001) Can institutions resolve ethnic conflict? *Economic Development and Cultural Change, 49*, 687–706.

Easterly, W., & Levine, R. (1997) Africa's growth tragedy: Policies and ethnic divisions. *Quarterly Journal of Economics, 112*, 1203–50.

Fearson, J. D. (2003). Ethnic and cultural diversity by country. *Journal of Economic Growth, 8*, 195–222.

Gerring, J., Thacker, S. C., Lu, Y., & Huang, W. (2015). Does diversity impair human development? A multi-level test of the diversity debit hypothesis. *World Development, 66*, 166–188.

Han, J., Peng, S., Chiu, C-y., & Leung, A. K-y. (2010). Workforce diversity and creativity: A multilevel analysis. In A. K-y. Leung, C-y. Chiu, & Y-y. Hong, (Eds.), *Cultural processes: A social psychological perspective* (pp. 286–311). New York, NY: Cambridge University Press.

Hartmann, D., & Pyka, A. (2013). *Innovation, economic diversification and human development*. FZID Discussion Papers, No. 65-2013, Center for Research on Innovation and Services, University of Hohenheim.

Hausmann, R., Hidalgo, C. A., Bustos, S., Coscia, M., Chung, S., Jimenez, J., Simoes, A., & Yıldırım, M. A. (2014). *The atlas of economic complexity*. Cambridge, MA: MIT Press.

Hewlett, S. A., Marshall, M., & Sherbin, L. (2013, December). How diversity can drive innovation. *Harvard Business Review*. Retrieved December 22, 2017, from https://hbr.org/2013/12/how-diversity-can-drive-innovation

Hidalgo, C. A., & Hausmann, R. (2009). The building blocks of economic complexity. *Proceedings of the National Academy of Sciences of the United States of America, 106,* 10570–10575.

Hlepas, N. (2013). *Cultural diversity and national performance*. SEARCH Working Paper. University of Barcelona.

Hunt, J. H., & Gauthier-Loiselle, M. (2010). How much does immigration boost innovation? *American Economic Journal: Macroeconomics, 2,* 31–56.

Leung, A. K.-y., & Chiu, C-y. (2008). Interactive effects of multicultural experiences and openness to experience on creativity. *Creativity Research Journal, 20,* 376–382.

Leung, A. K.-y., & Chiu, C-y. (2010). Multicultural experience, idea receptiveness, and creativity. *Journal of Cross-Cultural Psychology, 41,* 723–741.

Leung, A. K-y., Koh, K., & Tam, K-P. (2015). Being environmentally responsible: Cosmopolitan orientation predicts pro-environmental behaviors. *Journal of Environmental Psychology, 43,* 79–94.

Leung, A. K.-y., Maddux, W., Galinsky, A., & Chiu, C-y. (2008). Multicultural experience enhances creativity: The when and how. *American Psychologist, 63,* 169–181.

Li, C., Kwan, L. Y-Y., Liou, S., & Chiu, C-y. (2013). Culture, group processes and creativity. In M. Yuki & M. Brewer (Eds.), *Culture and group processes* (pp. 143–165). New York, NY: Oxford University Press.

Mourey, J. A., Lam, B. C. P., & Oyserman, D. (2015). Consequences of cultural fluency. *Social Cognition, 33,* 308–344.

Morris, M. W., Chiu, C-y., & Liu, Z. (2015). Polycultural psychology. *Annual Review of Psychology, 66,* 631–659.

Muller, D., Judd, C. M., & Yzerbyt, V. Y. (2005). When moderation is mediated and mediation is moderated. *Journal of Personality and Social Psychology, 89,* 852–863.

Nathan, M., & Lee, N. (2013). Cultural diversity, innovation, and entrepreneurship: Firm-level evidence from London. *Economic Geography, 89,* 367–394.

Nettle, D., Grace, J. B., Choisy, M., Cornell, H. V., Guégan, J-F., & Hochberg, M. E. (2007). Cultural diversity, economic development and societal instability. *PLOS One, 2*(9), PMID: 17895970.

Niebuhr, A. (2010). Migration and innovation: Does cultural diversity matter for regional R&D activity? *Regional Science, 89,* 563–585.

Ozgen, C., Nijkamp, P., & Poot, J. (2013). The impact of cultural diversity on firm innovation: Evidence from Dutch micro-data. *IZA Journal of Migration*, doi:10.1186/2193-9039-2-18

Page, S. (2007). *The difference: How the power of diversity creates better groups, firms, schools, and societies*. Princeton, NJ: Princeton University Press, 2007.

Patsiurko, N., Campbell, J. L., & Hall, J. A. (2012). Measuring cultural diversity: Ethnic, linguistic and religious fractionalization in the OECD. *Ethnic and Racial Studies, 35,* 195–217.

Roeder, P. G. (2001). *Ethnolinguistic Fractionalization (ELF) Indices, 1961 and 1985.* Available at http://weber.ucsd.edu/~proeder/elf.htm.

Rosenthal, L., & Levy, S. R. (2012). The relation between polyculturalism and intergroup attitudes among racially and ethnically diverse adults. *Cultural Diversity and Ethnic Minority Psychology, 18,* 1–16.

Rosenthal, L., & Levy, S. R. (2013). Thinking about mutual influences and connections across cultures relates to more positive intergroup attitudes: An examination of polyculturalism. *Social and Personality Psychology Compass, 7,* 547–558.

Torelli, C. J., Chiu, C-y., Tam, K-P., Au, A. K. C., & Keh, H. T. (2011). Exclusionary reactions to foreign cultures: Effects of simultaneous exposure to cultures in globalized space. *Journal of Social Issues, 67,* 716–742.

United Nations Development Programme. (1997). *Human Development Report 1990. Concept and measurement of human development.* New York, NY: Oxford University Press.

Zak, P. J., & Knack, S. (2001). Trust and growth. *The Economic Journal, 111,* 295–321.

Zhan, S., Bendapudi, N., & Hong, Y-y. (2015). Re-examining diversity as a double-edged sword for innovation process. *Journal of Organizational Behavior, 36,* 1026–1049.

6

Cultural Differences in Creative Professional Domains

VLAD PETRE GLĂVEANU AND TODD LUBART ■

The relationship between creativity and culture is, at once, both central to our understanding of creative expression and rarely addressed in the existing literature. It is essential for theorizing and researching creativity for a number of reasons. First and foremost, creativity "uses" culture to "produce" culture (Glăveanu, 2011) or, in other words, it employs and transforms existing cultural artifacts (objects, ideas, scripts, etc.) in a continuous process of revitalizing the material and symbolic environment of individuals, groups, and entire societies. Second, the expression of creativity appears to be culturally specific (Bhawuk, 2003; Weiner, 2000), as cultural norms channel the creative energies of people, constantly delineating the space of the "possible" and "thinkable" within specific contexts. When creative outcomes—particularly what is known as historical or Big-C creativity (Boden, 1994)—push further the boundaries of this space, they do so by engaging with culture and not disconnecting from it (since even recognizing the "new" requires knowledge of the "old"; the "already there"). Finally, not only are representations and experiences of creativity different in different cultural contexts (Lubart, 1999a), but the very processes of creation might be shaped by culture. This remains an open question, given that virtually no research has considered the ways in which the creative process and its temporal unfolding in creative acts vary depending on cultural setting.

The present chapter aims to make a contribution in this regard. To begin with, it will offer a new conceptualization of culture, drawing on cultural psychology, which allows us to theorize this phenomenon beyond national or ethnic units. In this chapter, culture is understood as a dynamic system integrating material, symbolic, and social elements and describing the context of human action. From this perspective, culture exists not only between nations but also, and especially so, within nations, at the level of different groups and communities (Cole, 1996;

Rogoff, 2003). Professional groups are a good example of cultural units. They bring together people who share a number of norms and values, work within a given set of material constraints, and co-construct a common identity. Artists, scientists, and designers represent distinctive professional groups associated with recognized forms of creative activity. This creativity, however, both in terms of outcomes and processes, is expected to show similarities and differences across the three groups. We will present here research that explores precisely (a) the factors involved in creative expression in art, science, and design, and (b) the creative processes specific for different stages of creative work within each of these domains. The findings will be interpreted in light of cultural and contextual influences.

CONCEPTUALIZING CULTURE

In the words of Jahoda (1992, p. 1), "the relationship between 'mind' and 'culture' has emerged as a prominent issue during the last quarter of the twentieth century." And yet, despite extensive interest from psychologists (and, of course, anthropologists), the exact definition of culture still eludes us. Famously, in 1952, Kroeber and Kluckhohn listed no fewer than 164 definitions of this concept. More recently, Markus and Hamedani (2007) summarized five approaches to culture—dimensional, sociocultural, cognitive toolkit, ecocultural, and dynamic constructivist—each one defined by a different empirical goal and set of mechanisms. Psychologists utilize frequently the dimensional approach in an effort to specify the various dimensions of culture and relate them to differences in people's attitudes, values, and behaviors. This quest for a universal classifying structure for cultural systems is at the core of cross-cultural psychology. One cannot help but reflect here on Hofstede's (2001) model of cultural dimensions, including power distance (low and high), individualism (vs. collectivism), uncertainty (low and high), and masculinity (vs. femininity).

Although useful for practice and research, cross-cultural frameworks also came under criticism in the past decades from a new branch of psychology, identified as cultural (Cole, 1996) or sociocultural psychology (Valsiner & Rosa, 2007). This orientation is both recent and old in the discipline. Its roots can be found in Wundt's (1921) interest in language, mythology, and religion (his "Völkerpsychologie") and supported by developments in different areas of psychology, most notably social and developmental, from Piaget's (1954) constructivism to Vygotsky's (1997) theory of mediation. Although cross-cultural approaches usually assume that culture can be represented by a set of external variables (or dimensions) that come into play in human cognition and action, cultural psychological theories start from the premise of the *interdependence* (not simply interaction) between person and sociocultural context (Rogoff, 2003; Shweder, 1990). This has profound implications for how we understand and study cultural phenomena. As observed by Triandis (2007), cross-cultural psychologists tend to emphasize content, whereas cultural psychologists emphasize context; the former are also interested in the stable and "universal" attributes of culture, whereas the latter concern themselves with dynamic processes. At a methodological level, cross-cultural researchers typically use large surveys in different national cultures (especially within organizational and political psychology), whereas sociocultural psychologists prefer ethnographic or experimental work performed in few cultures, and often only in one culture (so as to capture the intricacies of a cultural system; usually these investigations are social, educational, and developmental). However, as Triandis (2007) rightfully observes, such dichotomies are more blurred nowadays with cross-cultural research expanding from its initial theoretical focus.

In this chapter, we will advocate for a conceptualization of culture that both cross-cultural and sociocultural scholars could agree with. As summarized by Markus and Hamedani (2007, p. 11), culture designates "patterns of representations, actions, and artifacts that are distributed or spread by social interaction." This definition captures three essential elements about the content and processes of culture. First of all, it considers it a *pattern or a configuration.* Culture is therefore not a monolithic, homogenous entity but an organized (and organizing) system with increased internal variability. Second, the "contents" of culture are simultaneously psychological, behavioral, and material. Culture includes *representations or meaning.* This aspect is clearly emphasized by authors like Geertz (1973, p. 5), for whom cultures are "webs of significance" and humans, "unfinished" animals suspended in these webs that they themselves have spun. Culture is also *action* and, when socially organized, a *social practice.* This is very obvious in the Russian cultural-historical approach. For its representatives (including Vygotsky and Leontiev), "the structure and development of human psychological processes emerge through culturally mediated, historically developing, practical activities" (Cole, 1996, p. 108; also Ratner, 1996). Culture has as well a material aspect and incorporates a variety of *artifacts or cultural objects.* It is to be noted, however, that artifacts are both physical and symbolic, both material and ideal (Cole, 1996). Take a chair, for instance. It has a physicality defined by its structure and fabric, but it also has a meaning, a shared representation (that of a sitting tool), that relates to other representations and engenders new meanings (think about the difference between a kitchen chair and a throne). The same can be said about language—a classic example of a cultural artifact—including both expression (verbal or written) and significance. Finally, Markus and Hamedani note the importance of *social interaction* for the distribution of culture and, indeed, the emergence and circulation of symbols, actions, and artifacts requires self–other relations and various channels of communication.

Unlike the dimensional approach specific for mainstream cross-cultural research, cultural psychology advances our understanding of culture by considering the interrelation between representations, actions, and artifacts both within and between cultural systems. From this perspective, culture exists not only at the level of national units but also at the very basic level of interpersonal relations, of groups and communities within nations. To capture the essence of the cultural approach, we need to refer to the basic *mediation triangle* (Cole, 1996; Zittoun, Gillespie, Cornish, & Psaltis, 2007) comprising self, other, and object. This elementary unit of culture is, according to a sociocultural model, found in the most mundane interactions between people and between people and their material environment. The idea of mediation, drawing on Vygotsky's (1997) scholarship, argues that cultural phenomena are mediated phenomena; the relation between self and other is mediated by "objects" (for example, think about language as a cultural artifact), the relation between self and object is mediated by others (in our example, language acquisition and expression as social in origin), and finally, the relation between other and object is mediated by the self (who is not a passive recipient, but an active agent of cultural exchanges). In summary, cultural psychologists remind us that "cultural processes are not the same as membership in national or ethnic groups, and that individuals are often participants in more than one community's cultural practices, traditions, and institutions" (Rogoff, 2003, p. 52).

This last observation raises an important issue for the *theory of creativity*. As people participate in more groups and communities, each one characterized by a number of unique practices, traditions, and institutions, there is potential for creative expression in both the use and mixture of cultural resources (see the hypothesis of group contact and creativity formulated by Bartlett, 1923). This brings to the foreground the relation between creativity and culture, most commonly understood in the past from a cross-cultural perspective. When cultures are described in dimensional terms as modes of representation or sets of shared value, the main question becomes that of the "relationship between different values and value dimensions of creativity" (Westwood & Law, 2003, p. 247). For example, nowadays we encounter many descriptions of "Western" and "Eastern" views of creativity, emphasizing mainly what sets them apart. Niu and Sternberg (2006) point to the philosophical roots of these conceptions and describe the Western glorification of the individual creator. Indeed, in the West, creativity is often associated with the image of the genius and the revolutionary product, whereas Eastern traditions relate creativity more consistently to ideas of process and social relations (Lubart, 1999a). Although informative about conceptions of creativity in different cultures, these observations tell us little about how culture actually shapes creative processes. Simonton (1999) carried out in this regard a substantial program of research that looked into the connections between creative production and the zeitgeist of entire societies at particular moments in time. His historiometric method, however, can only capture the high ends of the creativity continuum and tells us little about the psychological processes involved in creative action. In the following section, we propose a cultural psychology approach and multivariate framework in order to address these shortcomings.

CONCEPTUALIZING CREATIVITY

The cultural psychology of creativity (Glăveanu, 2010; Moran & John-Steiner, 2003; Sawyer, 1995) conceptualizes this phenomenon with the help of the mediation triangle briefly described earlier. According to this perspective, the creation of new and meaningful artifacts takes place in the relation between creators and different audiences (collaborators, peers, critics, etc.), mediated by an existing system of cultural resources (both material and ideal: objects, images, procedures, norms, etc.). This formulation *relocates* creativity from within the individual to a cultural space of social and material relations. It proposes a model of distributed creation that takes the unit of individual and environment as a starting point (for details see Glăveanu, 2014). Several important implications can be abstracted from here in relation to the connection between creativity and culture. To begin with, the cultural psychology of creativity opposes a view of creators working from outside of culture and society, struggling to change established norms and routines. This latter vision, quite common for the paradigm of the genius (Montuori & Purser, 1995), is based on isolating creativity only in its historical forms and misrepresenting culture as an institutionalized and static reality. On the contrary, creators exist as cultured individuals who effectively exploit the transformative potential inherent to any cultural system. Moreover, the status of "creator" is not only reserved to those individuals legitimized by society (as suggested by the systemic view of Csikszentmihalyi, 1999, a view we will return to later on) but is present in the everyday and specific for any person and type of activity. This resonates with the tenets of the creative cognition approach (Finke, Ward, & Smith, 1992), which stresses the fact that creativity is widely distributed and supported by "normal" cognitive processes. However, the cultural psychology of creativity looks beyond cognition in its understanding of creativity and is concerned with the interaction between multiple psychological and social elements reunited by the creative act. This view is also central to what became known as the multivariate approach to creativity.

In agreement with the sociocultural perspective on creativity outlined earlier, Sternberg and Lubart (1995) proposed an *investment model* depicting creative people in terms of a set of resources they use to "buy low" (pursue ideas that are new and disregarded by others) and, after developing their contribution, to "sell high" (meaning to persuade others of the value of the creative outcome). This approach therefore emphasizes the social and cultural dynamic of creative production: exploiting cultural resources that the vast majority of others ignore and then presenting the novel products to broader audiences at just the right time. Afterward, creators can move further to invest in other ideas. Although this process reflects the activity of recognized innovators very nicely, it can also be applied to more mundane levels of creativity. In fact, Sternberg and Lubart postulated a number of resources required by creative acts, all of them present (to different degrees) in the case of each and every individual. The general categories for these resources are intelligence, knowledge, cognitive styles, personality, motivation, and environmental context. Most important, Sternberg and Lubart considered a person's creativity as more than the simple sum of his or her level on any of these components. They argued that there might be thresholds for some of the resources (for instance, knowledge or intelligence), below which creative expression might be difficult to achieve, regardless of one's level on the other components. Also, partial compensation might be possible (i.e., the development of one aspect, for example a strong motivation to create, could balance weaknesses in other components, for example, knowledge). Third, and most important from a cultural psychological perspective, these different types of resources act together and their coactivation leads to multiplicative effects. This integrated, systemic view is fundamental for the multivariate approach.

The multivariate approach, as further developed by Lubart and colleagues (Lubart, 1999b; Lubart, Mouchiroud, Tordjman, & Zenasni, 2003), groups factors necessary for creativity into four main categories: cognitive, conative, emotional, and environmental. From a *cognitive* perspective, intelligence and knowledge are the main resources creators draw on in their activity. At a more micro-level, the processes involved relate to (a) identifying, defining, and redefining problems; (b) selectively encoding different aspects of the environment relevant for the creative task; (c) using analogies, metaphors, and selective comparisons to establish links between different domains; (d) selectively combining elements to come up with new ideas; (e) generating multiple solutions with the help of divergent thinking; (f) auto-evaluating or monitoring one's progress; and (g) abandoning, if needed, an initial idea to explore new directions (flexibility). These cognitive processes are complemented by *conative* aspects related to personality traits, cognitive styles, and types of motivation. For example, it has often been noted that creative individuals are described by traits such as perseverance, tolerance to ambiguity, openness to new experiences, individuality, risk taking, and even psychoticism. Although often disregarded in creativity research, emotional factors are another important category of personal resources. Affective states seem to play several roles in creative action; they can serve as sources of motivation, as contextual variables, or have a functional role when activating idiosyncratic ideas conducive for creative work. Last but not least, the *environment* and its characteristics need to be taken into account as cognitive, conative, and emotional resources find their ultimate expression in relation to particular settings. We can identify a multitude of environments important for creativity, from familial, educational, and professional to the broader social and cultural milieu creators belong to. Formative, symbolic, and material aspects of the environment are all captured by the multivariate approach.

This general framework is in dialogue with other componential models, such as the one proposed by Amabile (1996). She suggested that creativity requires the interaction between motivation (in particular, intrinsic motivation), domain-relevant skills, and creativity-relevant processes. These intraindividual attributes, in turn, are related to characteristics of the social environment. However, the environment is somewhat exterior to the person and thus can "condition," "facilitate," or "constrain" creativity by acting particularly on task motivation. The cultural psychology of creativity perspective adopted here considers environment and individual as codependent and, indeed, the multivariate approach focuses on the interrelation between all its four components or resources for creative expression. What both these models bring to the fore nonetheless is an understanding of creativity as *both* domain general and domain specific. There has been an ongoing debate in the field of creativity trying to determine whether creativity depends primarily on skills required across domains (Plucker, 2005), or whether creative processes are different within each domain (Baer, 1998). The multivariate approach, based on its multilayered structure, invites us in this regard "to examine the similarities and differences between work in varying fields, or between different tasks within a given field" (Lubart & Guignard, 2004, p. 47). This means that, even within a domain, we must always consider the "matching" between the resources of the individual (cognitive, conative, emotional, etc.) and the requirements of particular tasks. In agreement with the cultural psychological approach to creativity, the multivariate model defines creativity in relational terms and "locates" it between the individual and the task at hand, between individual and (social and material) context. This is why it becomes increasingly important when we study creativity to ask ourselves what characterizes different domains and activities within them or, in other words, to understand the sociocultural constitution of different areas of creative expression. The arts, sciences, sports, design, music, and so on all represent particular cultural systems marked by specific social relations, tasks, and task requirements. Exploring the profiles of creative individuals, the resources necessary for working in each domain and the way they come into play in the creative process represent major concerns for a cultural approach to creativity grounded in the multivariate approach.

CREATIVITY AND PROFESSIONAL CULTURES

To summarize, we argued earlier that culture can be defined as an integrated and dynamic system of representations, actions, and artifacts shared through social interaction. Creativity is the process that engages with these three types of resources in order to generate new ones, and its expression at an individual level requires the interaction between cognitive, conative, emotional, and environmental factors. From the perspective of cultural psychology, the cultural system is uniquely shaped not only between but also within national units. Culture is thus associated with the existence and functioning of human communities (Jovchelovitch, 2007), and these communities vary in size and forms of organization. Professional domains bring together a community of people who share common forms of training, engage in similar activities, and integrate their participation at an identity level. Professional domains are also socially recognized and benefit from different degrees of institutionalization. They represent *meso-cultural universes* situated "in between" the micro-level of institutional cultures (specific for each organization) and the macro-level of national cultures (that incorporates both organizations and professional domains). Creative expression is socially and culturally constituted at each of these levels. If we accept that creativity involves a "community of people" with shared thinking, acting and learning (Hennessey, 2003), professional domains appear as primary contexts for the expression of one's creative potential. Within them, creative expression is regulated by certain types of normativity, and this criterion can be used to distinguish between professional cultures.

To understand the types of normativity that characterize a professional domain (or any cultural domain for this matter) and their relation to creativity, we need to consider the literature on *systemic models of creativity* (Feldman, Csikszentmihalyi, & Gardner, 1994). Its proponents, in particular, Csikszentmihalyi, assert that "creativity is a phenomenon that is constructed through an interaction between producer and audience" and therefore, "creativity is not the product of single individuals, but of social systems making judgments about individuals' products" (Csikszentmihalyi, 1999, p. 314). From this perspective, the "equation" of creativity includes three key elements: creators (individuals characterized by a certain genetic pool and set of personal experiences), domains (symbolic systems of culture), and fields (the social organization of the domain). The emergence and recognition of creative achievements requires the interrelation of each one of these elements. Individuals, in order to express and assert their creativity, need to develop a set of skills and abilities and integrate a body of knowledge specific for the domain. Having mastered (at least part of) the contents of this symbolic cultural system, they also have to interact with other members involved in the domain. In the systemic model, the field is usually made up a group of experts entitled to judge what is to be included in the domain or, in other words, what can be considered a valuable contribution to a domain of knowledge. As noted by Gardner (1994, p. 152), "an important feature of the field is the extent to which it is hierarchical: that is, the extent to which a few powerful individuals can render influential judgments about the quality of the work." Let's take the example of the cultural domain of the arts. Artists (creators) need to engage with the knowledge and norms specific for the domain of the arts (work techniques, composition, knowledge about the historical trajectory of the arts, etc.) and interact in their work with various "gatekeepers" (the social field made up of teachers, critics, museum curators, etc.). This triangular model of person–domain–field bears a clear resemblance to the cultural psychological approach outlined earlier and its basic meditational triangle of self–other–object (however, the systems model's emphasis on institutionalization restricts its potential to address everyday life creativity; Jones, 2009).

In this chapter, we are considering the expression of creativity in three different professional domains—*art, design, and science*—within the French society. It is therefore important to understand, before presenting the factors and process of creativity in these three domains, what characterizes the professional culture in each sector. A study based on interviews with recognized creators in five domains (including art, science, and design) highlighted qualitative differences in the way creators engage in their work and relate to their environment depending on their profession. The analysis of these interviews, reported elsewhere (Glăveanu et al., 2013), explored the motivations, actions, obstacles, and social and material relations specific for creative work in each of the five domains. For the purposes of this chapter, we will summarize some of the differences noted in the interviews and relate them to the dominant type of normativity specific for the professional culture in art, science, and design.

Two observations are needed in this regard. First, descriptions of each domain are based on interview material and not actual observation of practices; they therefore primarily reflect how artists, designers, and scientists talk about their work and its context. However, this discursive element, we can argue, is part and parcel of what actually constitutes the culture of a domain and can describe but also regulate actual practices within the profession (as conventional reflections on "how things work"). Second, the typology proposed later draws on the distinction between creator–domain–field and focuses on the kinds of normativity associated with each of them. By connecting a professional culture to one central type of normative relations, we are not implying the reduced importance of the other components (particularly since they all operate in a systemic manner) but try to capture a dominant feature for every domain, one that needs to be interpreted contextually.

Creator Normativity and the Professional Culture of the Artistic Domain

The creative activity of artists is, on the whole, normatively regulated primarily by constraints imposed by the creator himself or herself. The experience, preferences, emotions, and vision of the artist are elements that come to the fore in the discussion of their creative work and the general domain of the arts. This is evident from the kinds of motivations considered by recognized creators to be at the origin of their expression: a need to experiment, to "incarnate," "a physical desire" to work, a kind of "internal pressure," curiosity and rebellion, a "narrative desire," and the need to find new sensations. These personal types of motivation are captured in the seminal research on creativity and art by Getzels and Csikszentmihalyi (1976), who identified internal tensions as a common source for creative expression. Since an artist's work relates closely to his or her quest for personal meaning, the main type of obstacle one encounters—such as a creative block—relates to frustration and a feeling of uncertainty regarding one's own capacity to "create."

We conducted a series of interviews of 12 French professional artists engaged in art as their professional activity (Glăveanu et al., 2013; see also Botella et al., 2013). This sample included seven men and five women with an average age of 47 and extensive professional experience in various art domains such as painting, digital art, sculpture, and installation art. Our qualitative analysis of French artists' interviews revealed several stages in artistic work. Preparing for the creative activity, artists stress the importance of personal contact with the world around them. "The first stage [of work] is life," said one of the respondents who compared herself with a "sponge" that absorbs things from the environment. A preliminary stage of "impregnation" or "sensibilization" is required, facilitated by taking long walks, reading, going to the theatre or to different exhibitions, seeing a movie, all of them without a clear purpose in mind. Being always receptive and "someone who looks a lot" is part of an artist's identity. The creative process starts, for the vast majority, from a general vision, an image or form that triggers a series of other thoughts and emotions and matures when the artist starts interacting with the material support. It is in the dialogue among the action of the artist and the reactions of the material and of the emerging work of art, that initial visions are perfected, at times even completely transformed (see also Mace & Ward, 2002).

The actual work routines vary widely across artists. Some enjoy the mechanical aspects of repetitive gestures, others start working only when they have a clear idea in mind, and still others want to preclude any intentionality by seeking only to respond to the first sensations in relation to their work. The physicality of the creative process is emphasized by all the participants, who discussed at length the tactile, embodied presence of materials and their need for "contact" and acts of "observing through the hand."

Social relations refer to frequently interacted significant others, mostly partners and close collaborators, as well as the general public. Knowing how another looks at the work makes the artist "see" it differently, opens a symbolic "third eye" for him or her. Relations with spectators, buyers, and critics are ambivalent. On the one hand, artists admit that they enjoy recognition and positive feedback, while stressing also that they "don't want to make works of art to seduce other people." Criteria for success are (at least at a declarative level) as internal as they are external: feeling satisfied with one's outcomes.

One of the most important questions in this regard, and one that points once more to a self-imposed type of normativity, arises when the work of art is finished. For many of the interviewed artists, a piece can be finished when it needs to be exhibited but, at a more fundamental level, the processes that generated it are always ongoing. For Mace and Ward (2002), this chronic state of incompleteness comes from an artist's difficulty of evaluating the work while emotionally engaged with it. Cawelti, Rappaport, and Wood (1992, p. 92) note that artists often think of their creative lives "as an unfolding vision," in which each work contributes to "the enlargement and expansion of that vision." This is why most constraints or norms present in their work are actually self-imposed. In our research, artists commented on how they set up their own demands, for instance not having the outcome too easily described by language or too "decorative," and so on. Stokes (2001) captures this creator normativity clearly when discussing the artistic success of Claude Monet. For Monet, a high level of variability was a self-imposed constraint that forced him to preclude habitual and previously successful solutions to a problem. This doesn't mean, however, that artists are outside the normativity of the field and domain. It is certainly the case that personal "norms" in creation emerge in reaction to accumulated knowledge in the domain and the preferences of the field. However, this response is often one of rejection on the part of the artist and a constant attempt to find one's own "call" and form of expression. For Getzels and Csikszentmihalyi (1976, p. 77), "the creative process in art appears to be inspired by personally felt problems of an existential nature which the artist tries to confront on his own terms."

Field Normativity and the Professional Culture of the Design Domain

The conclusions earlier can be contrasted with those coming from interviewing 12 designers, eight men and four women, with a mean age of 41 and extensive professional experience in various areas, from interior design to visual communication, logos, and packaging (see Glăveanu et al., 2013). These interviews revealed that designers share many similarities with artists in terms of motivations for work and processes involved in creating. However, designers emphasize some distinctive features having mostly to do with the presence of clients and users, an element particular to this field (by comparison to both art and science). Different groups of others—people who evaluate, buy, or use the creation—generate for designers an "external," field-related normativity that regulates creative action and personal forms of expression. Like artists, designers commented on the motivation to create as the need to make or touch, to build or transform, and to be original. However, the starting point of creative work for designers was much more often connected to the practicalities of solving a problem, responding to a certain demand, and wanting to make clients (and oneself) feel satisfied with the outcome. The types of obstacles designers encounter in their work reflect this practical focus. Obstacles can involve technical difficulties (i.e., missing the technology) or money and time constraints, very often imposed by clients who want designers to work with certain materials and deliver the outcome by a certain date.

When it comes to the actual processes involved in the design of new and creative artifacts, the existing literature is cognitively oriented in its focus (see Arnellos, Spyrou, & Darzentas, 2005; Howard, Culley, & Dekoninck, 2008). It considers mainly the mental processes required by design and disregards their (social and cultural) context. Our interviews with French designers offer a broader perspective by situating creative work and considering both its antecedents and subsequent stages. The first phase of creation in design resembles the "impregnation" moments discussed by artists. Designers acknowledge the fact that "inspiration comes from everywhere," and they need to always be open to everyday life and constantly "collect" things. There is a better specified time and place of creation for members of this professional domain, especially when they work on a client order. Similar to art, creative work starts from a general idea, an image, that becomes gradually refined, explored, and "channeled." The same interplay between action and perception made authors like Tan and Melles (2010, p. 474) note that, in design, "activities were observed to be for the most part dynamic, iterative, and opportunistic."

And yet, in this case, both the initial idea and its realization are often marked by working together with a client (or discussing the evolving project with the client). Every paid project starts from a set of guidelines, which constrains one's freedom; however, these constraints can have a positive effect, as having too much freedom could lead someone "astray." The work in design usually progresses by making an initial set of sketches, then a prototype, and finally, the finished product. This transition (which is often not as linear as depicted earlier), requires constant interactions with different people (clients, technicians, users, etc.) and material support. The physicality of the work makes respondents consider that "a designer is in the concrete." Similar to artists, designers typically engage in their work with a variety of materials, from paper, wood, clay, and cardboard, to metal, glass, or textiles. If working on a commissioned project, it is again the client who normally needs to agree to the types of materials used depending on price and quality.

Constraints are commonplace in a designer's activity. Many of these are imposed by the medium itself: the physical and structural properties of the materials used. Another defining category of constraints relates to the requests and feedback received from the client. Designers often commented in their interviews on how, in their line of work, people need to "conform" to the wishes of others, to adapt to their vision and their aims. Considering that a designer "needs to eat as well," the client (part of the social field of creation) has extensive power over the work; and yet there is clearly agency on the part of designers, particularly in shaping the initial demand, giving a particular "form" to an imposed "content." As one of the respondents emphasized, even with more clear specifications, there is always room for creativity because "there are potentially millions of responses to a task." Creative work in this professional domain is actually shaped by the exchange between designers and clients, where the latter propose materials and alternatives to the former. Moreover, this exchange is very fruitful because an "intelligent request" can make one's work easy and pleasant. This is not to deny that some designers also complain about the mediocrity of certain requests or the fact that they might actually be contradictory and full of unnecessary information. In the end, it is again the client who usually decides when the work is finished.

In summary, the field imposes itself and its own normativity within this professional culture. Outside of clients, there are also engineers and users (the general public) that designers have to consider in their work (constraints from clients and users are considered differently depending on level of expertise and nature of the task; Chevalier & Bonnardel, 2007). However, this is not to imply that design projects cannot be self-initiated but, even in that case, they are eventually presented to potential clients and users because in the end, design is oriented toward to the public rather than a personal expression to be "consumed" only by the designer himself or herself. This need to share or communicate with others is also characteristic of scientists' work, as we shall see next.

Domain Normativity and the Professional Culture of the Scientific Domain

Unlike the self-selected norms common for artists or the client requirements that designers need to consider, the domain of knowledge itself imposes a specific normativity on the creative process in science. The highly specialized and formalized knowledge that makes up scientific domains—such as mathematics, physics, chemistry, astronomy, and so on—guides the work of scientists at all levels of their career. Indeed, the long process of acquiring this knowledge and learning its procedural aspects sets this domain apart from others, including the arts (Piirto, 1998). Also, unlike the arts (but closer to design), the motivation to engage in scientific work revolves around the need to answer certain questions or solve certain problems. The conclusions that follow come from interviews with 12 scientists, 11 men and one woman, with an average age of 42; this group included six physicists, three mathematicians, two information and technology specialists, and one chemist (see Glăveanu et al., 2013). Based on these interviews, curiosity, the pleasure of working in their field, and the desire of always learning something new are characteristics often mentioned as sources of motivation by scientists. Considering the high degree of specialization, obstacles in science often relate to missing certain technical possibilities, and also the fundamental state of "incomprehension," of being unable to understand or decipher something.

Usually, a long period of formation is needed before scientists produce creative work. This formal type of apprenticeship, lasting typically around a decade, gives them "an intellectual basis that is solid and rigorous" and "a scientific general culture." This culture is certainly complemented, on a daily basis, by another more informal process of learning. Keeping oneself up to date with the progress in the domain is a fundamental requirement for a scientist, and this involves reading books and articles, attending conferences, and having discussions with colleagues. Many scientists start their day by surveying what is new in their field. Although the time for working is not necessarily fixed (some do have a strict daily routine), the place tends to be stable and is usually represented by the office, a symbolic "cocoon" that protects from many outside distractions. In contrast, the thinking process is continuous and one can think about a problem at any time of the day—at waking, when going to sleep, during deliberate work time, or during extraprofessional activities and leisure.

Scientific work starts usually with a question, and the first stages of activity focus on defining it and reflecting on whether it is the right question to ask. Questions arise from a close knowledge of the domain and its developments, acquired through reading and discussions with peers. An existing consensus in the domain gives valuable points of reference and can help frame a problem. The phases of work after this stage are domain specific (they depend on whether the scientist is a mathematician or a chemist, etc.), but most scientists tend to start from defining a series of answers, testing them, and, in this process, reaching the best solution (in a typical moment of "illumination"). Multiple psychological processes are involved in these phases: making interconnections, simplifying models, using analogies, analytically deconstructing a whole, and so on. The end is invariably represented by a report of the findings, again following strict sets of guidelines specified by the domain. In a brief summary by one of our respondents, work in science progresses in three main stages: there is an "obsessional" period (searching for answers), a "luminous" phase (finding the solution), and a tedious "perspiration" stage of formalizing and communicating the results.

Scientists did not mention the material support in their interviews as often as artists and designers. However, they discussed at length their relations to their peers. Discussions with colleagues are crucial for getting ideas and starting projects; they can orient work in progress and guide one's creative expression. Working within the same domain, scientists know that "what attracts the interest of colleagues tends to attract one as well." There is an inherent dimension of teamwork in science and the activity progresses through meetings and constant exchanges (for a study of lab meetings among molecular biologists, see Dunbar, 1997). Finally, the larger scientific community needs to be considered as well, especially because creative outcomes are always scrutinized and judged according to criteria specified by each domain. Scientists need to learn to communicate but also promote their results in an increasingly competitive environment. In summary, others are part and parcel of the creative process. Even when a scientist works in solitude, "one is never alone" because one "never learns anything alone, completely alone."

Science presents a domain-normative culture because it relies heavily on acquiring and respecting norms and procedures inscribed into the process of producing new scientific knowledge. This is obvious in other studies as well, for instance, Gruber's (1981) analysis of the work of Darwin. In science, creators add to the established domain and, occasionally, get to transform it through their activity. This implies that the field (i.e., gatekeepers of the domain) is also important when it comes to recognizing what is a valuable contribution and what should be communicated and "preserved." But, ultimately, the gatekeepers in science form a widely distributed network and all participants get, in different forms, to assess the work of their peers according to the normativity of the general domain.

CONCLUSION

The concept of professional culture has been the focus of this chapter. The relationship between creativity, culture, and professional domains is, at once, both central to our understanding of creative expression and rarely addressed in the existing literature. In this context, culture is understood as a dynamic system integrating material, symbolic, and social elements and describing the context of human action. As such, culture exists not only between nations but also, and especially, within nations, at the level of different groups and communities. Professional groups are a good example of cultural units; they bring together people who share a number of norms and values, work within a given set of material constraints, and co-construct a common social identity. This chapter focused on the examples of artists, scientists, and designers, representing distinctive professional groups associated with recognized forms of creative activity. Cultural differences in the creative process within the three creative professional domains of art, design, and science were explored. It was suggested that creative work in the three domains bears similarities and differences based on the main factors required by professional activities in these "creative" jobs and the processes involved at different stages of work. In the end, it is hoped that the present approach to creativity, at the professional culture level, will shed new light on the contextual aspects of creative expression. Creativity is a strongly embedded practice, taking form somewhat differently in each professional domain of activity, a key characteristic that contributes to its rich and complex nature.

REFERENCES

Amabile, T. M. (1996). *Creativity in context*. Boulder, CO: Westview Press.

Arnellos, A., Spyrou, T., & Darzentas, J. (2005). Exploring creativity in the design process: A systems-semiotic perspective. *Cybernetics and Human Knowing, 14*(1), 37–64.

Baer, J. (1998). The case for domain specificity of creativity. *Creativity Research Journal, 11*(2), 173–177.

Bartlett, F. C. (1923). *Psychology and primitive culture*. Cambridge, UK: Cambridge University Press.

Bhawuk, D. (2003). Culture's influence on creativity: The case of Indian spirituality. *International Journal of Intercultural Relations, 27*, 1–22.

Boden, M. (1994). What is creativity? In M. Boden (Ed.), *Dimensions of creativity* (pp. 75–117). London, UK: MIT Press/Badford Books.

Botella, M., Glăveanu, V., Zenasni, F., Storme, M., Myszkowski, N., Wolff, M., & Lubart, T. (2013). How artists create: The creative process and multivariate factors. *Learning and Individual Differences, 26*, 161–170.

Cawelti, S., Rappaport, A., & Wood, B. (1992). Modeling artistic creativity: An empirical study. *Journal of Creative Behavior, 26*(2), 83–94.

Chevalier, A., & Bonnardel, N. (2007). Articulation of web site design constraints: Effects of the task and designers' expertise. *Computers in Human Behavior, 23*(5), 2455–2472.

Cole, M. (1996). *Cultural psychology: A once and future discipline*. Cambridge, UK: Belknap Press.

Csikszentmihalyi, M. (1999). Implications of a systems perspective for the study of creativity. In R. Sternberg (Ed.), *Handbook of creativity* (pp. 313–335). Cambridge, UK: Cambridge University Press.

Dunbar, K. (1997). How scientists think: On-line creativity and conceptual change in science. In T. B. Ward, S. M. Smith, & J. Vaid (Eds.), *Creative thought: An investigation of conceptual structures and processes* (pp. 461–493). Washington, DC: American Psychological Association.

Feldman, D. H., Csikszentmihalyi, M., & Gardner, H. (1994). *Changing the world: A framework for the study of creativity*. Westport, CT: Praeger.

Finke, R. A., Ward, T. B., & Smith, S. S. (1992). *Creative cognition: Theory, research, and applications*. Cambridge, MA: MIT Press.

Gardner, H. (1994). The creators' patters. In M. Boden (Ed.), *Dimensions of creativity* (pp. 143–158). London, UK: MIT Press/Badford Books.

Geertz, C. (1973). *The interpretation of cultures*. New York, NY: Basic Books.

Getzels, J. W., & Csikszentmihalyi, M. (1976). *The creative vision: A longitudinal study of problem finding in art*. New York, NY: John Wiley & Sons.

Glăveanu, V. P. (2010). Principles for a cultural psychology of creativity. *Culture & Psychology, 16*(2), 147–163.

Glăveanu, V. P. (2011). Creativity as cultural participation. *Journal for the Theory of Social Behaviour, 41*(1), 48–67.

Glăveanu, V. P. (2014). *Distributed creativity: Thinking outside the box of the creative individual*. Cham, UK: Springer.

Glăveanu, V., Lubart, T., Bonnardel, N., Botella, M., Desainthe-Catherine, M., Georgsdottir, A., . . . Zenasni, F. (2013). Creativity as action: Findings from five creative domains. *Frontiers in Educational Psychology, 4*, 1–14.

Gruber, H. E. (1981). *Darwin on man: A psychological study of scientific creativity* (2nd ed.). Chicago, IL: The University of Chicago Press.

Howard, T. J., Culley, S. J., & Dekoninck, E. (2008). Describing the creative design process by the integration of engineering design and cognitive psychology literature. *Design Studies, 29*, 160–180.

Jahoda, G. (1992). *Crossroads between culture and mind: Continuities and change in theories of human nature*. New York, NY: Harvester Wheatsheaf.

Jones, K. (2009). Culture and creative learning: A literature review. *Creativity, Culture and Education Series*. Retrieved from https://www.creativitycultureeducation.org/

Jovchelovitch, S. (2007). *Knowledge in context: Representations, community and culture*. London, UK: Routledge.

Hennessey, B. (2003). Is the social psychology of creativity really social? Moving beyond a focus on the individual. In P. Paulus & B. Nijstad (Eds.), *Group creativity: Innovation through collaboration* (pp. 181–201). New York, NY: Oxford University Press.

Hofstede, G. (2001). Culture's consequences: Comparing values, behaviors, institutions and organizations across nations (2nd ed.). Thousand Oaks, CA: Sage.

Kroeber, A. L., & Kluckhohn, C. (1952). *Culture: A critical review of concepts and definitions*. New York, NY: Vintage Books.

Lubart, T. (1999a). Creativity across cultures. In R. Sternberg (Ed.), *Handbook of creativity* (pp. 339–350). Cambridge, UK: Cambridge University Press.

Lubart, T. (1999b). Componential models. In M. A. Runco & S. R. Pritsker (Eds.), *Encyclopaedia of creativity* (vol. I, pp. 295–300). New York, NY: Academic Press.

Lubart, T., & Guignard, J. (2004). The generality-specificity of creativity: A multivariate approach. In R. J. Sternberg, E. L. Grigorenko, & J. L. Singer (Eds.), *Creativity: From potential to realization* (pp. 43–56). Washington, DC: American Psychological Association.

Lubart, T., Mouchiroud, C., Tordjman, S., & Zenasni, F. (2003). *Psychologie de la créativité*. Paris, France: Armand Colin.

Mace, M.-A., & Ward, T. (2002). Modeling the creative process: A grounded theory analysis of creativity in the domain of art making. *Creativity Research Journal, 14*(2), 179–192.

Markus, H. R., & Hamedani, M. (2007). Sociocultural psychology: The dynamic interdependence among self systems and social systems. In S. Kitayama & D. Cohen (Ed.), *Handbook of cultural psychology* (pp. 3–39). New York, NY: Guilford.

Montuori, A., & Purser, R. (1995). Deconstructing the lone genius myth: Toward a contextual view of creativity. *Journal of Humanistic Psychology, 35*(3), 69–112.

Moran, S., & John-Steiner, V. (2003). Creativity in the making: Vygotsky's contemporary contribution to the dialectic of development and creativity. In R. K. Sawyer et al. (Eds.), *Creativity and development* (pp. 61–90). Oxford, UK: Oxford University Press.

Niu, W., & Sternberg, R. J. (2006). The philosophical roots of Western and Eastern conceptions of creativity. *Journal of Theoretical and Philosophical Psychology, 26*(1-2), 18–38.

Piaget, J. (1954). *The construction of reality in the child*. New York, NY: Basic Books.

Piirto, J. (1998). *Understanding those who create* (2nd ed.). Scottsdale, AZ: Gifted Psychology Press.

Plucker, J. A. (2005). The (relatively) generalist view of creativity. In J. C. Kaufman & J. Baer (Eds.), *Creativity across domains: Faces of the muse* (pp. 307–312). Mahwah, NJ: Lawrence Erlbaum Associates.

Ratner, C. (1996). Activity as a key concept for cultural psychology. *Culture & Psychology*, 2, 407–434.

Rogoff, B. (2003). *The cultural nature of human development*. Oxford, UK: Oxford University Press.

Sawyer, R. K. (1995). Creativity as mediated action: A comparison of improvisational performance and product creativity. *Mind, Culture, and Activity, 2*(3), 172–191.

Shweder, R. (1990). Cultural psychology—What is it? In J. Stigler, R. Shweder, & G. Herdt (Eds.), *Cultural psychology: Essays on comparative human development* (pp. 1–43). Cambridge, UK: Cambridge University Press.

Simonton, D. K. (1999). Historiometry. In M. Runco & S. Pritzker (Eds.), *Encyclopaedia of creativity*, vol. I (pp. 815–822). San Diego, CA: Academic Press.

Sternberg, R. J., & Lubart, T. (1995). *Defying the crowd: Cultivating creativity in a culture of conformity*. New York, NY: Free Press.

Stokes, P. D. (2001). Variability, constraints, and creativity: Shedding light of Claude Monet. *American Psychologist, 56*(4), 355–359.

Tan, S., & Melles, G. (2010). An activity theory focused case study of graphic designers' tool-mediated activities during the conceptual design phase. *Design Studies, 31*, 461–478.

Triandis, H. (2007). Culture and psychology: A history of the study of their relationship. In S. Kitayama & D. Cohen (Eds.), *Handbook of cultural psychology* (pp. 59–76). New York, NY: Guilford.

Valsiner, J., & Rosa, A. (2007). Contemporary socio-cultural research: Uniting culture, society, and psychology. In J. Valsiner & A. Rosa (Eds.), *The Cambridge handbook of sociocultural psychology* (pp. 1–20). Cambridge, UK: Cambridge University Press.

Vygotsky, L. S. (1997). The history of the development of higher mental functions. In R. W. Rieber (Ed.), *The collected works of L. S. Vygotsky*, vol. IV (pp. 1–251). New York, NY: Plenum Press.

Weiner, R. P. (2000). *Creativity and beyond: cultures, values, and change*. Albany, NY: State University of New York Press.

Westwood, R., & Low D. (2003). The multicultural muse: Culture, creativity and innovation. *International Management of Cross-Cultural Management, 3*(2), 235–259.

Wundt, W. (1921). *Elements of folk psychology*. London, UK: Allen and Unwin.

Zittoun, T., Gillespie, A., Cornish, F., & Psaltis, C. (2007). The metaphor of the triangle in theories of human development. *Human Development, 50*(4), 208–229.

Diversifying Experiences and Creativity

7

Culture, Language, and Creativity

BAOGUO SHI AND JING LUO ■

Since the groundbreaking work on divergent thinking done by Guilford (1950) 67 years ago, there is now a multitude of approaches and perspectives for the investigation of creativity. For example, creativity has been studied in the fields of personality psychology, social psychology, cognitive psychology, biological psychology, and neuroscience. One important trend is an increase in research on creativity and culture. Generally, creativity is viewed as a process or the product of creative thoughts (Amabile, 1983; Eysenck, 1994; Woodman, Sawyer, & Griffin, 1993). Scholars also studied creativity as an interaction between personal and contextual characteristics (e.g., Amabile, 1997). As Csikszentmihalyi (1999) noted, creativity is a culturally bound phenomenon, not simply a mental process.

As for the meaning of culture, people have different understandings. Tylor (1871) put forward the view that culture consists of knowledge, beliefs, art, morals, laws, customs, and any other capabilities and habits acquired by humans as members of society, so we can regard culture as a complex whole. Geertz (1973, p. 89) defined culture as "a historically transmitted pattern of meanings embodied in symbols, a system of inherited conceptions expressed in symbolic forms by means of which men communicate, perpetuate, and develop their knowledge about and attitudes toward life." Hofstede and Bond (1988) proposed that culture is a collective programming of the mind, which can distinguish members of one group or a category of people from another. Recently, Chiu and Hong (2007) regarded culture as a set of loosely organized ideas and practices produced and reproduced by a network of interconnected individuals. Together, culture can be generally viewed as a complicated system that is shared by a relatively large group of people and can be transferred largely unchanged from generation to generation. As prior studies showed, culture can influence the definition, expression, and evaluation of creativity, and even how frequently it occurs (Niu & Sternberg, 2001; Simonton, 1994; Sternberg & Lubart, 1996).

In this chapter, we first discuss some differences in the conceptualization of creativity from the East–West perspective. Does "creativity" mean the same thing in the Western and East Asian cultural settings? Recent research based on lay people's definitions of creativity, including implicit and explicit theories of creativity, descriptions of creative people, and evaluations of creative products, will be highlighted. Second, as a key component of culture, language has very important implications for understanding creativity. We will review recent research on this topic, including the relationship between bilingualism and creativity and empirical discoveries from groundbreaking behavioral and neuroimaging studies on insight problem solving that involve Chinese characters.

THE INFLUENCE OF CULTURE ON CREATIVITY

The Conceptualization of Creativity

According to Sternberg and Lubart's (1999) investment theory, creativity requires a confluence of six distinct but interrelated resources: intellectual abilities, knowledge, thinking styles, personality, motivation, and environment. All of these resources can be divided into two categories. One concerns the internal or individual aspects such as intelligence, personality, motivation, thinking styles, and knowledge, and the other concerns the external or environmental aspects. Most studies on creativity focused on personal characteristics, such as personality and cognitive ability, and on analyzing the few creative individuals (Ebert, 1994; Feldhusen, 1995; Hayes, 1989). Research on the impact of contextual characteristics on creativity has been increasing since the late 1980s (e.g., Amabile, 1983; George & Zhou, 2001; Zhou & Shalley, 2003). These studies suggest that environment, including the culture people live in, can be a core resource for creativity.

More recently, Leung and Morris (2010) have proposed that although creative performance is influenced by individual difference variables, it is useful to consider a normative account of creativity that acknowledges the shaping of creative activities through social norms that are prevalent in the cultural context. Relatedly, Lubart (1999) distinguished a series of contexts (e.g., physical environment, family, school, workplace, culture) of which these contexts and creativity can mutually influence each other in the ways of how people conceive of creativity and the criteria that are employed to evaluate whether ideas or behaviors are creative. Based on this logic, creativity can be viewed as a culturally embedded concept (Chiu & Kwan, 2010).

Prior research indicated that the Western cultural model stresses invention, novelty, rejection of tradition, and self-actualization, as well as a celebration of individual accomplishment (Sawyer, 2012). The judgment of creativity depends very much on the acceptance by a proper group or experts, with the evaluation criteria usually emphasizing the degrees of novelty and appropriateness of the creations (Amabile, 1983). Although these evaluation criteria also apply to the Eastern culture, East Asians may also emphasize other evaluation domains. For example, researchers and educators studying creativity in the Chinese culture tend to link creativity to ethical and moral standards more than those in the

Western culture (Rudowicz, 2004). Unlike Westerners, Chinese show a preference for creative activities that can contribute to the progress of society and can inspire people (Rudowicz & Hui, 1997). In fact, in Chinese philosophy, creativity is viewed as an inspired imitation of nature, stressing the importance of showing respect for the past and keeping harmony with nature (Rudowicz, 2004). Whereas Westerners tend to emphasize the rejection of tradition in order to instigate creativity, the Chinese tend to emphasize the inheritance of tradition. Just as the famous ancient philosopher Lao Tze (about 571–471 B.C.) said, "Man takes his law from the Earth, the Earth takes its law from Heaven, Heaven takes its law from the Tao, and the Tao takes its law from nature" (quoted from Taodejing, sixth century B.C.). In traditional Chinese culture, individuals are always following nature and discovering truth, regardless of whether they seek to make something new. In many cases, inventions do not belong to a single person because they are derived from nature, with nature being the source of power of the emperor and the emperor offering the ultimate support for all things under his rule, including creative inventions. Many classic works and world-famous inventions (e.g., compass and gunpowder) were not the result of creative efforts of a single inventor but were collaboratively generated (Rudowicz, 2004). Next, we discuss how these cultural differences in people's understanding of creativity are reflected in both explicit and implicit conceptualizations of creativity.

Explicit and Implicit Concepts of Creativity in Western and Chinese Cultures

Explicit theories are propositions theorized by psychologists or other scientists based on the data collected from people performing various psychological tasks (Sternberg, 1985). Some of the explicit theories focus on the process of creative thinking, such as Guilford's structure of intellect theory (1967) and the Geneplore model (Finke, Ward, & Smith, 1992), whereas some explicit theories focus on the interactive process between the creative person and the environment, such as Csikszentmihalyi's (1999) systems model. Others highlight the sources necessary for creativity, such as Amabile's (1996) componential model, Eysenck's (1995) creativity model, and Sternberg and Lubart's (1996) investment theory. It is common that explicit theories construe the concept of creativity as measurable, multidimensional (e.g., the novelty and appropriateness dimensions), and adaptive within specific sociocultural contexts (Amabile, 1996; Rudowicz, 2003; Sawyer, 2012; Sternberg & Lubart, 1995).

Notably, explicit conceptualization of creativity varies between Western and Eastern cultures. As Weiner (2000) argued, "creativity in the Western sense might be seen as absurd from common Hindu and Buddhist perspectives" (p. 160). According to the Western conceptions, being creative implies rejection of convention or tradition (Sawyer, 2012). Yet this conception might not be highly endorsed in the Chinese culture, since the traditional Chinese understanding of creativity puts much emphasis on respecting the past and maintaining harmony with nature

(Lubart, 1999; Rudowicz, 2004). As mentioned earlier, according to traditional Chinese Taoism, creativity pertains to the quality of discovering the nature or following "the Way" (the Tao). The most important goal of creative activities is to attain harmony with forces that are far stronger than humans, and this leads to inventions such as silk weaving and china that are aimed to honor "the eternal ways of heaven and nature, the ancestors, and the ancient texts" (Weiner, 2000, p. 178).

To illustrate, we can refer to the legend about the invention of the carpenter's saw by Lu Ban. Lu Ban or Gong Shu Ban (507–444 B.C.), a very famous ancient Chinese inventor and engineer, had invented many tools, such as the saw, drill, and ink maker. As the legend says, when he found sharp teeth on the side of a blade of wild grass in the mountains, Lu Ban was inspired to invent the saw. The explicit concept of creativity in Chinese culture places high importance on the ethical and moral requirement of coming up with inventions that can serve other people(Cheng, 1999; Rudowicz, 2004). As described in the book of *Mo-tze*, Mo Di (birth and death year unknown), the ancient Chinese distinguished thinker, philosopher, and politician, said to Lu Ban: "anything you made can be said to be beautiful only when it is beneficial to man, and anything not beneficial to man is said to be stupid" (quoted from Lu's Question, Mo-tze, Warring States Period, 475–221 B.C.). This relation between creativity and the ethical and moral standards of contributing to humankind might have its roots in the value of collectivism in Chinese culture. Even in contemporary China, schools usually combine innovation education with moral education. The science and art curricula are not only knowledge and skills oriented but also aim to cultivate proper moral and ethical values and attitudes among students.

Complementing explicit theories, different psychological concepts, including intelligence, wisdom, and creativity, can also be described through implicit theories (Sternberg, 1985), which are beliefs and anticipations held by lay persons or people other than scientists and researchers. Implicit concepts reflect a kind of tacit knowledge commonly acquired among lay people (Runco, 1999). Generally, researchers use questionnaire and interview methods to investigate lay people's implicit understanding of creativity (e.g., Sen & Sharma, 2011), probing them to define creativity, to describe the characteristics of creators or products, and so on, and conducting content analyses on their answers.

Although there is an increase in the number of studies on implicit theories, cross-cultural studies on implicit theories of creativity are scarce (Lim & Plucker, 2001). These limited studies have started to uncover some important cross-cultural differences in implicit creativity theories (Rudowicz, 2003). For example, when describing a creative person in Western culture, people tend to emphasize his or her (a) motivational characteristics such as being active, excited, and impulsive; (b) personality characteristics such as being self-confident, curious, and ambitious (Runco & Bahleda, 1986; Runco et al., 1993; Sternberg, 1985; Westby & Dawson, 1995); or (c) cognitive characteristics such as having a high IQ score, being capable of making connections and distinguishing between ideas (Sternberg, 1985), and being adept at problem solving (Runco & Bahleda, 1986) and critical questioning (Runco et al., 1993). In contrast, Chinese culture is more likely to relate creativity with moral traits, such as showing qualities of moral goodness, societal contributions, appreciating connections between traditions and new creations, and authenticity (Averill, Chon, & Hahn, 2001; Kaufman & Beghetto, 2013; Lubar, 1999; Niu & Sternberg, 2002; Rudowicz & Yue, 2000).

Despite between-culture variations in implicit creativity theories, different cultures share some common understanding of what constitutes creativity. In one recent study, Zhou and colleagues (2013) investigated the implicit concept of creativity of 515 teachers from China, Germany, and Japan. They found that teachers from all of these countries perceived creativity as a divergent thinking ability that supports the generation of novel ideas. In another study, Paletz and Peng (2008) surveyed 412 students from Japan, China, and the United States and had participants rate some products on creativity. Unexpectedly, the results showed that the Chinese were more influenced by novelty and less by appropriateness than the Japanese and Americans. It is reasonable to argue that the Chinese participants might have paid more attention to the aspect of creativity that is lacking in their culture (i.e., novelty).

LANGUAGE AND CREATIVITY

Bilingualism and Creativity

Language is an integral part of human survival. With the increasing need to engage in cross-cultural communication, more and more people have become bilingual or multilingual individuals who are proficient in two or more languages. Specifically, bilingualism can be considered as the ability of being "like a native speaker to master two or more languages" (Bloomfield, 1933, p. 56). However, it might be difficult to acquire proficiency of a second language like a native speaker. A broader definition of bilingualism concerns the "practice of alternately using two languages" (Weinrich, 1968, p. 1) or "regularly using two or more languages" (Grosjean, 2008, p. 10). Bilingual individuals can be categorized into (a) early bilingual or late bilingual depending on their age of learning the second language; (b) natural bilingual or achieved bilingual depending on the environment of language acquisition; (c) balanced bilingual or unbalanced bilingual depending on whether they are equally proficient in both languages; and (d) bicultural bilingual or monocultural bilingual depending on whether they identify with one or two cultures (Baker, 2001; Hoffmann, 1991).

Prior studies suggested that bilingualism influences the development of high-order cognitive function, such as creativity (Bialystok, 2009; Ricciardelli, 1992a; Simonton, 2008). Srivastava (1991) compared the differences in creative performance among trilingual, bilingual, and monolingual individuals, and results revealed that trilinguals' creativity was higher than that of bilinguals and monolinguals. Lee and Kim (2010) found that bilinguals achieved higher novelty scores than monolinguals. Divergent thinking, an important ability that supports creative activities, was found to be more superior among bilingual than monolingual individuals (Kharkhurin, 2008; Ricciardelli, 1992b). Further looking at different facets of creativity, Kharkhurin (2007, 2008) showed that bilinguals scored higher in fluency and flexibility, but lower in originality than monolinguals. In another study, Kharkhurin (2010a) found that bilinguals performed significantly better in verbal creativity, but significantly worse in non-verbal creativity than monolinguals. There is also evidence suggesting that early bilinguals who acquire the second language earlier are more creative (Cushen & Wiley, 2011; Kharkhurin, 2007, 2008, 2010a, 2010b; Kharkhurin & Motalleebi, 2008). Nevertheless, some contradictory results demonstrated that bilingualism had no significant influence on creativity (Adesope et al., 2010; Rosenblum & Pinker, 1983; Simonton, 2008) or even a negative influence on creativity (Genesee, 2009). Taken together, extant research generally supports the creative benefits of bilingualism (Kharkhurin, 2007, 2008, 2010a, 2010b; Lee & Kim, 2010, 2011; Ricciardelli, 1992; Srivastava, 1991).

Bilingualism is a complex phenomenon and some factors have been identified that modulate the relationship between bilingualism and creativity. Leikin and Tovli (2014) confirmed the hypothesis that bilingual children have higher creative ability than monolingual children. However, the effect differs according to the domain of creativity. There were significant differences between bilinguals and monolinguals on the flexibility and originality of mathematical creativity, but no differences between them on general creativity, which suggested that bilingualism influences different types of creativity differently. Hommel, Colzato, Fischer, and Christoffels (2011) predicted that the level of language proficiency is important for the relationship between bilingualism and creativity. Using experimental method, their results revealed that high-proficient bilinguals outperformed low-proficient bilinguals in the Remote Association Task (measuring convergent thinking), while low-proficient bilinguals performed better in the Alternative Uses Test (measuring divergent thinking), especially for the score of fluency. Moreover, some prior research found that gender plays an important role in the relationship between bilingualism and creativity. For example, Mendonca and Fleith (2005) revealed that bilingual males performed better than bilingual females on verbal originality. Kim (2006) showed that bilingual females performed better than bilingual males on precision and abstraction of headline. However, Lee and Kim (2011) found that gender has no effect on the relationship between the degree of bilingualism (measured by the Word Association Test) and elaboration and abstractness of titles in a title generation creativity task, although girls outperformed boys on the scores of bilingualism, elaboration, and abstractness of titles.

There are two major mechanisms underlying the creative advantages of bilingualism. One mechanism attests to the notion of bilingual learning based on the model of language-mediated concept activation (LMCA) (Kharkhurin, 2008). According to this model, the specific architecture of bilingual memory may promote greater spreading activation between concepts. In other words, one could activate disassociated concepts in bilingual memory by LMCA. Another mechanism pertains to explaining bilingual individuals' creative advantages through more adept functioning of their executive control system (Bialystok & Martin, 2004), attention focus (Bialystok & Shapero, 2005), and inhibitory control (Costa et al., 2009). (未找到) For example, Bialystok and Martin (2004) demonstrated that bilingual children have better inhibitory control for ignoring perceptual information than their monolingual peers do. Here, as part of conceptual inhibition, inhibitory control is good for avoiding attention to the obsolete feature and may facilitate creativity.

Language and Creativity: Implications From Behavioral and Neuroimaging Studies on Insight Problem Solving

Although the relationship between language and thinking is generally recognized, the one between language and creativity is, at least, less consistent. Instead, the reverse tendency that the employment of linguistic processing may inhibit rather than promote one's creativity has received some empirical support. For example, there is evidence that suggests a specific type of creative thinking, insight problem solving, is realized through a nonsentential process wherein one does not use verbal forms to label his or her process of thinking that may reinforce and anchor on the ordinary way of problem solving, as summarized by Schooler, Ohlsson, and Brooks (1993): First, anecdotes from scientists and other creative individuals indicated that their discoveries occurred as wordless thoughts. William James (1890) noted that many important insights were reported to have occurred in the absence of words: "Great thinkers have vast premonitory glimpses of schemes of relations between terms, which hardly even as verbal images enter the mind, so rapid is the whole process" (p. 255). Albert Einstein (cited in Schlipp, 1949) later provided eloquent support for James's claim that creative insights often precede their translation into language, noting that "these thoughts did not come in any verbal formulation. I very rarely think in words at all. A thought comes, and I may try to express it in words afterwards" (p. 288).

Second, similar types of experiences have also been observed with the more mundane discoveries of solutions to laboratory insight problems. For example, Durkin (1937) observed that problem solvers typically become silent immediately before an insight. She asked participants to verbalize their thought processes while attempting to solve insight problems and observed that the solutions to these problems involved "sudden reorganization" (p. 80). Durkin further noted that these sudden reorganizations were typically preceded by an inability to verbalize thoughts, as she put it: "Usually a rather short very quiet pause occurs just preceding the sudden reorganization" (p. 80). More recent discussions of protocols associated with insight problem solving have also noted the degree to which the critical steps in the insight solution are not reported (e.g., Ericsson & Simon, 1984; Kaplan & Simon, 1990).

Third, participants usually know, by their feeling-of-knowing (FOK) judgments, when they are on the verge of solving analytic problems (such as those found in a standardized test). However, participants had little ability to rate their closeness to solutions to insight problems, supporting the hypothesis that the processes that prepare for insights are nonreportable (Metcalfe, 1986a, 1986b; Metcalfe & Weibe, 1987).

Fourth, Maier (1931) asked participants to retrospectively report their solutions to an insight problem for which they had been given a (seemingly accidental) hint by the experimenter. Participants who could report the stepwise construction of the solution also reported the hint and its effects on their problem solution, but those who reported the solutions as having arrived in a flash of insight gave no evidence of being aware of the hint.

Fifth and finally, Schooler and colleagues (1993) confirmed in their own study that verbalization could even interfere with insight problem solving. In that study, participants were interrupted during problem solving and asked either to verbalize their strategies (retrospective verbalization) or engage in an unrelated activity (control). Participants in the retrospective verbalization condition were significantly less successful than control participants on insight problems.

In contrast to these early behavioral observations, recent studies, especially the cognitive neuroscience ones on insight problem solving, nicely demonstrated the participation of the brain areas whose function was well known to be related to semantic or linguistic processing (Luo & Niki, 2003; Luo et al., 2004; Mai et al., 2004). Although this could be partially attributable to the fact that most of neuroimaging studies on creative insight have adopted the tasks which were semantic in their nature and so it was not surprising that many semantic activities were found in the brain at the moment of creative thinking, the participation of language in creative thinking is undeniable. A way to understand the inconsistent roles of language in creativity is to take the form of problem into consideration: If the task were visuospatial in nature (as this is true for most of the traditional creative insight tasks such as the nine-dot problem, the two-string problem, and the profound physical questions pondered by Einstein), then the linguistic process could be disturbing. However, if the tasks were semantic in nature such as logogriph, a form of word puzzle to identify the component letters of a key word, then the linguistic process should be necessary.

The Relationship Between Language and Creativity From the Perspective of Culture

From the cultural perspective, the question on how language can promote or hinder creativity becomes whether or not a specific type of language can be more creativity-friendly than others. Taking the field of mathematics, for example, people who use Arabic numerals are much more productive than other people who use other numeral systems such as those used in ancient Rome or China. However, it is difficult for this argument to stand when it comes to the real world. For example, it is hard, if not impossible, to test the hypothesis that people who use an alphabetic writing system (such as English) could be more creative than those who use the more ideographical ones (such as Chinese) or the opposite. To

clarify this, one would need to take all of the sociocultural, educational, econom-
ical, and political factors, which could also be reciprocally interacted with the
form of language, into consideration.

A fundamental difference between English and Chinese lies in the most basic
units or chunks that make up the words. In English, the most basic units are
meaningless letters—there are only 26 letters in English. However, in Chinese,
the most basic units are meaningful radicals or simple characters that cannot be
further separated into meaningful radicals—there are about 6,500 frequently used
Chinese characters in modern Chinese. Although it is still unknown whether or
not the complexity and meaningfulness of the most basic units in a language
system can influence its speakers' thinking style and creativity, there are some
theoretical clues for us to understand this. For example, in L. Ledderose's famous work *Ten Thousand Things: Module and Mass Production in Chinese Art*, he
attributed the tremendous productivity of Chinese artists in producing bronzes,
terra-cotta figurines, lacquer, porcelain, architecture, printing, and painting to the
production systems for assembling objects from standardized parts in modules.
These parts could be massively produced and quickly recombined to create a variety of objects from a limited number of components. This associates the way of
modular production with the character-based word formation of Chinese language because the characters could be regarded as typical modules.

According to cognitive science studies on creative insight problem solving, there
is one creative thinking process that could be closely related to the functioning of
modular or chunks: the process of chunk decomposition (Knoblich et al., 1999;
Ohlsson, 1984). However, contrary to L. Ledderose's viewpoint that regarded the
recombination or reorganization of the familiar chunks as the ways for creation,
from a psychological point of view the decomposition of the familiar chunks
into their meaningless elements and the novel and meaningful recombination of
these elements constitute ideal examples of true creation. In the next section, we
will mainly focus on the cognitive and neurological processes underlying chunk
decomposition, especially the ones involved in the decomposing of Chinese
characters, and discuss the implications of these studies on the relationship between the form of language and creativity.

Chunk Decomposition

In contrast to the ordinary, noncreative problem solving in which the initial
problem situation could progress toward attainment of a solution in a stepwise
manner (Newell & Simon, 1972), the process of creative thinking could be dis-
continuous. For example, in creative insight problem solving, the ordinary way
of thinking usually leads the problem solver into an impasse state wherein he or
she cannot move further; only when he or she breaks the initial mental set and
finds a new suitable interpretation of the problem can the problem solver successfully find a way to achieve the goal state. To account for such a key process,
cognitive theorist Ohlsson extended Newell and Simon (1972)'s problem space

theory and established the *representational change theory* of insight and creative thinking (Ohlsson, 1984, 1992). According to this theory, past experience can lead to a biased goal representation of the problem that is overly constrained, thus preventing realization of the solution to the problem. To solve the problem, one needs to relax these constraints, thereby extending the space of possible solutions. In other words, the problem solver has to change his or her initial mental representation of the problem and form a novel but useful one in order to make an efficient solution possible.

Critically, based on the fact that one's inappropriate mental representations of the problem can be either formed when one makes predictions on the goal state or even when one encodes the component elements of the problem, the representational change theory proposes two ways for the problem solver to achieve a successful representational change: *constraint relaxation* and *chunk decomposition*. Theoretically, only through one of these two processes can people alter their initial, unsuitable mental representation about the problem or its goals to successfully achieve a creative breakthrough. In particular, the process of constraint relaxation is useful when the goal state of the problem has to be readjusted. For example, to the creative insight problem "How can four equilateral triangles be formed using only six matchsticks?" most problem solvers unknowingly impose the unnecessary constraint that the solution has to be achieved in a two-dimensional space. However, the problem can only be solved when solvers also consider solutions in a three-dimensional space (the solution is to form a pyramid).

In contrast to the process of constraint relaxation that is essential for reinterpreting the goal state, the process of chunk decomposition is useful when the problem itself is not encoded in a way that is suitable for solving the representation question. For example, if you were given the word "BIT" and were required to make another new word by moving one letter away, it should be easy for you to think about the way to move away the letter "B" and to form the new word "IT." The reason is that the letters "B," "I," and "T" remain meaningful chunks. However, if you were required to form another new word by moving away one part of a letter (not the whole letter) from "BIT," it could be relatively hard for you to think about the way to transform the word "BIT" to "PIT" by removing the lower part of the letter "B." This is because the letter "B" is a perceptual chunk wherein all pieces of the component are tightly bound together. Therefore, as the process to decompose familiar patterns into their component elements so that they can be regrouped in another meaningful manner, chunk decomposition plays a key role in creative thinking, in particular, in insight problem solving.

It was argued that if during initial encoding the problem elements become automatically grouped into familiar chunks, then this may prohibit the chance of finding a novel or efficient solution to the problem (Luo et al., 2006). Take, for example, the matchsticks arithmetic task that was first developed by Knoblich and colleagues (1999) to investigate the mental process of chunk decomposition. Participants were given a false arithmetic statement (such as "VI = VII + I"), written using roman numerals (e.g., "I," "II," and "IV"), operations ("+" and "−"), and an equal sign ("="), and were required to transform the statement into a correct equation by moving only one stick from one position to another within the pattern. In the aforementioned equation of "VI = VII + I," the solution is to decompose the "VII" into "VI" and "I," and then move the "I" to the left side of the equal sign to result in a correct equation of "VII = VI + I." However, other problems could be more difficult (Knoblich et al., 1999, 2001), such as the one that requires transforming the equation from "XI = III + III" to "VI = III + III." The nature of chunk decomposition can explain why these problems differ in their difficulty level. "VII" is a relatively loose chunk that is composed of meaningful small chunks (i.e., "V" and "I"); in contrast, "X" and "V" are much tighter chunks. To reform "XI" to "VI," the "X" should be decomposed into its meaningless components (i.e., "\" and "/") and regrouped as "V."

The validity of chunk decomposition as a specific form of insight problem solving has been widely demonstrated by various kinds of behavioral evidences such as solution rate, reaction time (RTs), and eye movement (Knoblich et al., 2001; Ollinger et al., 2008). For example, combined behavioral and eye movement evidence found three facts on chunk decomposition. First, it produces mental impasses as the typical insight problem does, because people tended to sit and stare at the problem, accompanied by fewer eye movements (i.e., longer fixation times). Second, the impasses could be caused by inappropriate initial representations. In the case of matchstick arithmetic, this was embodied by participants' persistent visual fixation on the problem components, which are usually valid for the solving of ordinary problems but indeed invalid for the solving of the present insight one. Third, impasses could be resolved by relaxing inappropriate constraints and decomposing unhelpful perceptual chunks, which was associated with the sudden onset of visual attentive shifting from the invalid problem component to the valid ones (Knoblich et al., 2001).

Follow-up lesion studies found that focal damage to the lateral frontal cortex, the brain area known to be crucial for defining a set of ordinary responses that are usually suitable for solving the typical problems (but indeed invalid for the present insight problem), could promote one's ability to solve chunk decomposition task, implying the weakening of top-down control and related ordinary strategies for problem solving to help promote creative chunk decomposition (Reverberi et al., 2005). In addition, transcranial direct current stimulation (tDCS) studies on insightful chunk decomposition also found that the cathodal stimulation (decreasing excitability) of the left anterior temporal lobe (ATL) together with anodal stimulation (increasing excitability) of the right ATL could facilitate performance on insight creativity task (Chi & Snyder, 2011). This observation was not only consistent with the general hypothesis that the left hemisphere is involved in the maintenance of existing hypotheses and representations, while the right hemisphere is associated with novelty and with updating hypotheses and representations, but also specifically consistent with studies that found that the right ATL participates in insight problem solving (Jung-Beeman, 2004) and the inhibition of the left ATL is associated with emergence of certain cognitive skills and a less top-down or hypothesis-driven cognitive style (Miller et al., 1998).

Insightful Decomposition of Chinese Characters

To overcome the issue that the matchstick arithmetic problem cannot provide a sufficient variety of trials to allow reliable neuroimaging analyses, Luo and Knoblich (2007) proposed a new chunk decomposition task using Chinese characters as materials. Chinese characters are ideal examples of perceptual chunks that are composed of radicals, which, in turn, are composed of strokes. Strokes are the most simple and basic components of a Chinese character. Usually, isolated strokes do not carry meaning. In contrast, radicals convey information about the meaning and pronunciation of the character. They usually consist of several strokes and can be thought of as the most basic chunk in the Chinese writing system (Figure 7.1). According to the theory of chunk decomposition (Öllinger, Knoblich, 2009), it should be much easier to separate a character by its radicals than to separate a character by its strokes, because particular strokes are tightly embedded in a perceptual chunk. In other words, the decomposition of characters into strokes should require a specific process that breaks the tight bond among strokes created by the perceptual chunk. Therefore, we could study the cognitive and neurological processes of chunk decomposition by contrasting the radical-level and stroke-level chunk decomposition of Chinese characters.

Based on the approach of using Chinese characters as materials to study the cognitive mechanism of chunk decomposition (Luo, Niki& Knoblich, 2006), researchers could further systematically investigate the fundamental issues on insight chunk decomposition in the strictly controlled experimental settings. We will discuss these fundamental issues next, which include the contribution of the perceptual process on insightful chunk decomposition (Luo et al., 2006; Wu et al., 2009, 2010), the role of the right hemisphere in chunk decomposition (Tang et al., 2009), and the "nonlinear" way of thinking in insightful chunk decomposition (Wu et al., 2013), as well as the separable cognitive-neurological basis for processing the "novel" and "appropriate" features in insightful chunk decomposition (Huang et al., 2015).

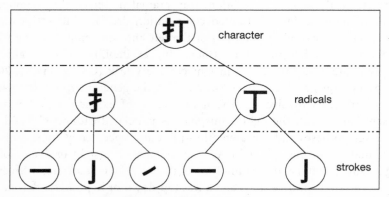

Figure 7.1. The construction principle of Chinese characters.

It should be noted that these issues are not only important in the case of chunk decomposition but also very basic and critical in almost all kinds of creative thinking. For example, "novelty" and "appropriateness" are the two key features that have been most widely recognized as the components of creativity. However, there is still not much empirical evidence to illustrate the cognitive and neurological basis that supports the processing of these two fundamental features. As we will demonstrate later, by using the task of chunk decomposition, we can manage to separate the cognitive-neurological basis mediating the processing of the "novelty" and the "appropriateness" features. These investigations could provide important clues for us to understand the nature of insight and creative thinking. Another point we want to clarify is that although the process of chunk decomposition, as well as that of constraint relaxation, plays a key role in supporting the representational change for insight and creative problem solving, there is still no empirical evidence indicating cultural differences in these processes. However, given that Chinese language system contains more basic chunks or characters than the alphabetic writing system, it is reasonable to predict that individuals in Chinese culture may resort more to the process of chunk decomposition in their creation than individuals in Western culture do. (We will return to this topic in the final discussion of this part.)

THE ATTENUATION OF EARLY VISUAL INFORMATION IN INSIGHTFUL CHUNK DECOMPOSITION

The neuroimaging approach provided us a window to observe directly how visual information processing is reorganized during creative chunk (e.g., Chinese character) decomposition. The way our visual cortex identifies a target such as a Chinese character somewhat resembles a well-organized workshop that divides the whole procedure of work into different steps or levels. The early visual cortex is responsible for the processing of the basic visual features, whereas the higher visual cortex functions to integrate these features. As to the perception of Chinese characters, the division of labor is that the early visual cortex processes individual stroke-level features, whereas the higher visual cortex joins these features together. (It should be noted that this processing, though precisely divided, can also be highly rapid and automatic.) However, to decompose a chunk successfully, the higher visual areas must at least partially be "disconnected" from the input provided by early visual processing in order to allow simple features to be rearranged into a different perceptual chunk. That is, the exact original features embedded in a character might be temporally neglected to get rid of the restriction of the perceptual chunk, and this process might be accompanied by negative activations in early visual cortex and positive activations in higher visual cortex (Figure 7.2). Through comparing the stroke-level chunk/character decomposition at the component or subchunk level (which requires insightful chunk decomposition) and the radical-level character decomposition at the chunk level (which merely requires noncreative, ordinary way of thinking), we can detect

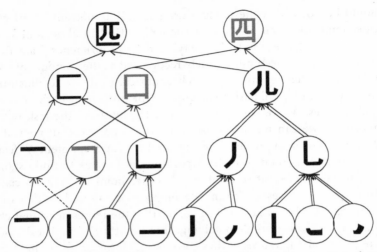

Figure 7.2. The assumed hierarchical processing of a Chinese character. Note that, when native speakers perceive a character, such as the top-right character in gray that means "four," the processing of basic components leads to an automatic activation of a perceptual chunk representing that character on a higher level of visual processing (as demonstrated by the arrows). However, in order to successfully decompose a chunk, the higher visual areas must at least partly be "disconnected" from the input provided by early visual processing (as demonstrated by the arrows and character) in order to allow simple features to be rearranged into a different perceptual chunk, such as the top-left character in black that means "match."

and analyze brain activities in the early and late visual cortex during chunk decomposition (see section on "Insightful Decomposition of Chinese Characters" for more discussion about the key differences between stroke- and radical-level decomposition).

Our neuroimaging experiment confirmed our prediction about the reorganization of visual information processing during chunk decomposition (Figure 7.3; Luo et al., 2006). That is, relative to noninsight chunk decomposition, the insight ones demonstrated more negative activation in the early visual cortex and more positive ones in the higher visual cortex. Furthermore, it was found in electroencephalogram (EEG) study that the condition of insight chunk decomposition exhibited a stronger alpha activation, which could reflect an idle state of the brain in the primary visual cortex as compared to performing noninsight chunk decomposition (Wu et al., 2009). This observation, together with the functional magnetic resonance imaging (fMRI) results, provides convincing evidence that attenuation of early visual information is required to generate new meanings (Wu et al., 2009). The stroke-level information is automatically processed by the early visual cortex, and the attenuation of this early visual information may help people get rid of the restriction allocated by the perceptual chunk and promote creative reorganization of these visual components.

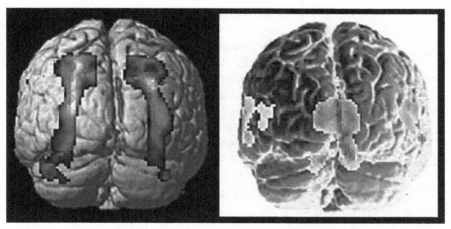

Figure 7.3. Negative activation in early visual cortex (right) and positive ones (left) in higher visual cortex during the moment of insightful chunk decomposition.

THE CONTRIBUTION OF THE RIGHT HEMISPHERE FOR INSIGHTFUL CHUNK DECOMPOSITION

The role of the right hemisphere in creative chunk decomposition was also observed by using Chinese characters as materials to detect the hemispheric differences following successful or unsuccessful problem solving and during hint presentation. Previous studies using hemi-visual field presentation technology found that the keynotes (i.e., the solution) for the insight puzzle that participants have failed to find could be more quickly perceived and understood when these keynotes were presented to the left visual field (i.e., the right hemisphere) than to the right visual field, especially when the keynotes were presented several seconds after the unsolved puzzle had disappeared from one's view (Bowden & Jung-Beeman, 2003). This observation implied that the right hemisphere, relative to the left one, might play a more important role in keeping the information of the unsolved problem in one's mind and might be more ready in processing the related clue for that problem.

To testify the hypothesis about participation of the right hemisphere in insightful chunk decomposition, we compared the event-related potentials (ERPs) between the solved and unsolved insightful Chinese chunk decomposition problems during (a) the moment when the participants pressed a key to indicate whether or not they could solve the problem by themselves before seeing any external hint, and (b) the moment when participants were given the hint. The ERP results showed that, during the moment of participants' confirmation of their successful or unsuccessful problem solving, the unsolved problems were accompanied with a more positive P150 over the right frontal cortex, whereas the solved ones exhibited a more positive P150 over the left side. Consistently, during the moment of hints presentation, the hints to the unsolved problems also elicited a more positive P2 over the right hemisphere, whereas the hints to the solved problems elicited a more positive P2 over the left side. These results confirmed the hypothesis that, after the failure in insight problem solving, the right hemisphere might be more positive in preserving the unsolved problem in mind and be more responsive to the external hint for problem solving (Tang et al., 2009). This observation demonstrated that, even for a chunk/character decomposition task that is apparently linguistic, the right hemisphere still plays a more dominant role in preserving the unsolved problem and in directing more attention for finding possible solutions. This result implies that the right hemisphere participates more in some stages of insightful problem solving for the verbal task, though it is the left hemisphere that is generally thought to be mainly involved in processing semantic or linguistic information.

THE "NONLINEAR" WAY OF THINKING IN INSIGHTFUL CHUNK DECOMPOSITION

In contrast to the standard theory of problem solving in which problem solving is conceived as taking a stepwise route through a well-defined problem space (Newell & Simon, 1972), recent theory proposed that in insight problem solving, people usually have to overcome multiple difficulty factors in a single thinking step (Kershaw & Ohlsson, 2004). For example, it has been claimed that the nine-dot problem (connecting nine dots arranged in a 3 x 3 square with exactly four straight lines without lifting the pen from the paper) is difficult to solve because it poses multiple obstacles to the solution, including constraints from interfering prior knowledge (Weisberg & Alba, 1981), perceptual factors (e.g., the way the problem and hint are presented; Chronicle et al., 2001), and processing factors (e.g., the adoption of the maximization heuristic and the progress-monitoring heuristic in solving the problem; MacGregor et al., 2001) during solution generation. Therefore, removing one obstacle or overcoming one type of difficulty is not enough to enable the problem solvers to reach a solution to insight problems. Rather, overcoming two or more obstacles or difficulties constitutes the "nonlinear" feature of insight problem solving. For chunk decomposition, there are at least two kinds of obstacles or difficulty factors that need to be overcome. Through studying the distinct cognitive effects of these two types of difficulty factors on chunk decomposition, we could reveal the "nonlinear" feature (i.e., overcoming multiple difficulties in one single thinking step) of creative insight. The first source of difficulty for chunk decomposition is chunk tightness, which varies as a function of whether the components in a chunk are loosely or tightly grouped. In "loose chunks," the perceptual subcomponents of the chunk are meaningful themselves (like the letters "T" and "O" in the string "TO"). In contrast, the components in "tight chunks" are not meaningful themselves (like the strokes "/" and "\" in the letter "X").

The second difficulty factor in chunk decomposition is chunk familiarity caused by more or less intimate knowledge of chunks. High familiarity with the mapping between particular perceptual patterns and particular meanings is likely to increase the difficulty of the chunk decomposition process because the components of highly familiar chunks are more closely associated with each other than the components of less familiar chunks. Accordingly, chunk tightness can be manipulated by setting stroke-level (tight) or radical-level (loose) character decomposition, whereas chunk familiarity can be manipulated by performing the decomposition on those real, meaningful characters (familiar) or on those meaningless, pseudo-Chinese characters (unfamiliar). Research showed that chunk familiarity could be overcome through an inhibition of familiar meanings that is mediated by brain activities in the left prefrontal cortex and anterior cingulate cortex (ACC) that are specifically responsible for semantic inhibition (Wu et al., 2013), whereas overcoming chunk tightness requires visual-spatial processing, which is mediated by bilateral superior and inferior parietal areas (BA7/40), middle occipital gyrus (BA19), left superior frontal gyrus (BA8), and the right medial and superior frontal gyrus (BA6/8) (Wu et al., 2013). Furthermore, the interaction between chunk familiarity and chunk tightness led to the discovery of an ACC area whose activation can only be observed when both kinds of difficulties are encountered at the same time. This result demonstrates that the sources of difficulty in a problem do not always simply add up. Rather, the difficulty of a problem can reside in the interaction of multiple sources of difficulty (Figure 7.4) (Wu et al., 2013).

Additionally, this "1 + 1 > 2" effect was also demonstrated by dynamic causal modeling (DCM), which detects effective connectivity of the dorsal ("where") and ventral ("what") visual pathways in the performing of chunk decomposition that is systematically varied in chunk tightness and familiarity (Wu et al., 2010). Results showed that (a) when the structure was loose, increased familiarity

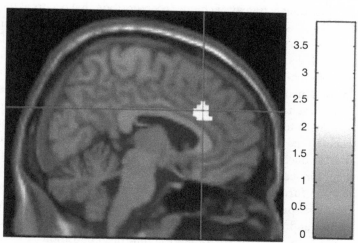

Figure 7.4. In insight problem solving, people usually have to overcome multiple difficulty factors in a single thinking step. Through using the insightful Chinese character chunk decomposition task, results found an area in anterior cingulate cortex (ACC), which could not be activated by the difficulty of chunk familiarity or that of chunk tightness alone, exhibited activation when both types of difficulty were met at the same time, suggesting that in insight problem solving, the two difficulty sources do not always simply add up but interact together to enlarge the entire task difficulty.

caused an increase in the effective connectivity of the "where" pathway; (b) when the familiarity was low, increased structural tightness caused an increase in both the "what" and the "where" pathways; and (c) when familiarity and structural tightness both increased, not only would the effective connectivity of the "what" and the "where" pathways increase, but also the effective connectivity between the terminal of the "what" pathway and that of the "where" pathway.

THE SEPARABLE COGNITIVE-NEUROLOGICAL BASIS FOR PROCESSING THE "NOVEL" AND "APPROPRIATE" FEATURES IN INSIGHTFUL CHUNK DECOMPOSITION

Creativity has been widely recognized as the ability to generate thoughts that are both original (new, unusual, novel, unexpected) and valuable (useful, good, adaptive, appropriate). In other words, originality and appropriateness have been considered the two basic features of creative thinking (Barron, 1955; Hennessey & Amabile, 2010; Runco & Jaeger, 2012; Stein, 1953; Sternberg & Lubart, 1996, 1999). However, the neural basis of novelty and appropriateness of creative thinking remains basically unknown. The chunk decomposition task permits the systematic manipulation of both novelty and appropriateness in an experimental setting. For example, in the Matchstick Arithmetic Task, the novelty of chunk decomposition could be manipulated by asking participants to perform the familiar, chunk- (or subchunk-) level decomposition or the unfamiliar, elemental-level decomposition (for details of this task, read the section "Chunk Decomposition"). For example, to reorganize the number "IV" to "VI" by moving the "I" from the left side to the right involves a familiar strategy of chunk decomposition that occurs at the chunk ("I" and "V") level, whereas to reorganize the number "IX" to "IV" by removing the "/" from "X" and rejoining it with the remaining "\" involves an unfamiliar strategy of chunk decomposition that occurs at the elemental level.

The appropriateness of chunk decomposition, however, is determined by whether the obtained result is reasonable. Decomposition that leads to a suitable or meaningful result would be regarded as an appropriate solution, and decomposition that leads to an unsuitable or meaningless result would be considered inappropriate. In the aforementioned example, we can define the chunk decomposition that produces a true Roman numerical figure as an appropriate solution and one that produces an unrecognized figure as inappropriate.

To elaborate further with examples, radical-level chunk decomposition represents familiar processing, such as decomposing the character "泠" into "令" (real character) and the character "决" into "夬" (false character) by removing the radical " 冫." In contrast, stroke-level chunk decomposition is novel, such as decomposing the character "汗" into "汁" (real character) and the character "汪" into "汢" (false character) by removing the stroke "一." The appropriateness (or usefulness) of chunk decomposition depends on whether the decomposition results in real characters. It is natural for individuals to evaluate a decomposition that leads to another real character as appropriate, such as the decomposition of the character "泠" into "令" and "汗" into "汁", and to evaluate a decomposition that leads to a false or unreal character as inappropriate, such as the decomposition of the character "决" into "夬" and "汪" into "汢.."

The results of an fMRI experiment found that novelty processing generally involves functional areas for procedural memory (caudate), mental rewarding (substantia nigra, SN), and visuospatial processing, whereas appropriateness processing is mediated by areas for declarative memory (hippocampus), emotional arousal (amygdala), and orthography recognition (Huang et al., 2015). These results update people's typical understanding about the nature of insight problem solving. The insight, because of its capability of evoking insightful "Aha!" reaction and vivid long-term memories, is typically proposed to be episodic memory or hippocampus dependent. However, based on the aforementioned study, we argued that the key neural structure for nondeclarative, procedural memory, say the caudate, could also take part in processing the "novelty" feature of chunk decomposition. This implies that nondeclarative and declarative memory systems may jointly contribute to the two fundamental features of creative thinking, and the nondeclarative memorizing process could also be necessary for the achievement of insight (Huang et al., 2015).

Implications of Insightful Chunk Decomposition for Cultural Differences in Creativity

We suppose that the distinctive cognitive-neurological mechanism of chunk decomposition could be applied to other cultures rather than being specific to the Chinese culture. Notably, we discuss in this paper the general mechanism of the chunk decomposition process. Although this mechanism was found by using the stroke- and radical-level Chinese character decomposition task, it could also be applied to other linguistic systems. For example, one could transfer the Roman numerals "X" to "V," or transfer the English letter "B" to "P" by removing the lower hemicycle part of "B." In fact, the process of chunk decomposition could also be found in the technical field. For example, Henry Ford's invention of the assembly line may require the decomposition of the holistic construction procedure of a car (in a sense we could also regard this holistic procedure as a chunk) into its basic components or steps and then the reorganization of these components in a highly efficient manner: the modern assembly line. It is in this sense that we think the process of chunk decomposition is culture or language general.

Nevertheless, we argue that the process of chunk decomposition is more inclined to happen in the Chinese culture. For example, in China, a traditional way of fortune telling is to analyze the component parts of a Chinese character that is freely or randomly thought of by the person who wants to know about his or her future. For example, the last Emperor Chongzhen of the Ming Dynasty repeatedly dreamed of the character "有" (read as "you" meaning "have") being written in his hand by someone, and he wanted to know the implication of this dream. The eunuch who served him thought that this indicated the nation would be destroyed because the Empire of Ming was written as a two-character word "大明" (read as "da ming" meaning "the Great Ming [Empire]") in Chinese. The dreamed character, "有", is the result of recombining some parts of the two-character word by breaking the characters into pieces and rejoining some of these pieces together. This way of fortune telling, known as Chai-Zi (拆字; character decomposition and reinterpretation) in China, essentially contains the process of creative chunk decomposition. This specific way of thinking was so novel that the ancient Chinese believed it was able to predict the future.

Another example of chunk decomposition comes from Buddhism. Qing-Yuan Wei-Xin is an ancient Chinese senior Buddhism master, and he had a very famous description about his experiences in Buddhism practicing and enlightenment: The first stage is "seeing a hill is just a hill," the second stage is "seeing a hill is not a hill," and the third stage is "seeing a hill is not just a hill." Here, "hill" could be regarded as a type of perceptual chunk, and "seeing a hill is not just a hill" means creative decomposition of these typical chunks. Theoretically, we might even conjecture that the invention of movable type printing in the eleventh century of China could also be related to the process of chunk decomposition, because it is natural for people to perceive a page of a book or a stone tablet as a whole (a chunk). Only by getting rid of the restriction of chunking and decomposing the perceptual chunk into its components could the Chinese conceive of movable type printing. All in all, chunk functions as a double-edged sword. It greatly increases the efficiency of information processing, on the one hand, but may also hinder cognitive flexibility and creativity, on the other hand. It is the dual nature of the cognitive chunk that makes the Chinese who rely heavily on the modular way of cognition to be highly productive in making use of various kinds of chunks to create new things (Ledderose, 2001). However, the downside is that they also seem to be more easily restricted by established knowledge and skills, so the deconstruction of the established chunks is always encouraged and sought by traditional philosophy such as the Taoist school.

REFERENCES

Adesope, O. O., Lavin, T., Thompson, T., & Ungerleider, C. (2010). A systematic review and meta-analysis of the cognitive correlates of bilingualism. *Review of Educational Research, 80*, 207–245.

Amabile, T. M. (1983). The social psychology of creativity: A componential conceptualization. *Journal of Personality and Social Psychology, 45*, 357–376.

Amabile, T. M. (1996). *Creativity in context: Update to the social psychology of creativity.* Boulder, CO: Westview Press.

Amabile, T. M. (1997). Entrepreneurial creativity through motivational synergy. *Journal of Creative Behavior, 31*, 18–31.

Averill, J. R., Chon, K. K., & Hahn, D. W. (2001). Emotions and creativity, East and West. *Asian Journal of Social Psychology, 4*, 165–183.

Baker, M. C. (2001). *The atoms of language.* New York: Basic Books.

Barron, F. (1955). The disposition towards originality. *Journal of Abnormal and Social Psychology, 51*, 478–485.

Bialystok, E. (2009). Bilingualism: The good, the bad, and the indifferent. *Bilingualism: Language and Cognition, 12*, 3–11.

Bialystok, E., & Martin, M. M. (2004). Attention and inhibition in bilingual children: evidence from the dimensional change card sort task. *Developmental Science, 7*(3), 325–339.

Bialystok, E., & Shapero, D. (2005). Ambiguous benefits: the effect of bilingualism on reversing ambiguous figures. *Developmental Science, 8*(6), 595–604.

Bloomfield, L. (1933). *Language*. New York: Holt, Rinehart, & Winston.

Bowden, E. M., & Jung-Beeman, M. (2003). Aha! Insight experience correlates with solution activation in the right hemisphere. *Psychonomic Bulletin & Review, 10*, 730–737.

Cheng, S. K. (1999). East–West differences in views on creativity: Is Howard Gardener correct? Yes, and no. *Journal of Creative Behavior, 33*, 112–123.

Chi, R. P., & Snyder, A. W. (2011). Facilitate insight by non-invasive brain stimulation. *Plos One, 6* (e166552).

Chiu, C. Y., & Kwan, L. Y. Y. (2010). Culture and creativity: A process model. *Management and Organization Review, 6*, 447–461.

Chiu, C., & Hong, Y.-Y. (2007). Cultural processes: Basic principles. In E. T. Higgins & A. E. Kruglanski (Eds.), *Social psychology: Handbook of basic principles* (pp.785–806). New York, NY: Guilford.

Chronicle, E. P., Ormerod, T. C., & MacGregor, J. N. (2001). When insight just won't come: The failure of visual cues in the nine-dot problem. *Quarterly Journal of Experimental Psychology, 54*, 903–919.

Costa, A., Hernández, M., Costa-Faidella, J., & Sebastián-Gallés, N. (2009). On the bilingual advantage in conflict processing: Now you see it, now you don't. *Cognition, 113*(2), 135–149.

Csikszentmihalyi, M. (1999). Implications of a systems perspective for the study of creativity. In R. J. Sternberg (Ed.), *Handbook of creativity* (pp. 313–335). New York, NY: Cambridge University Press.

Cushen, P. J., & Wiley, J. (2011). Aha! voila! eureka! bilingualism and insightful problem solving. *Learning and Individual Differences, 21*(4), 458–462.

Durkin, H. E. (1937). Trial-and-error, gradual analysis and sudden reorganization. An experimental study of problem solving. *Archives of Psychology, 30*, 1–85.

Ebert, E. S. (1994). The cognitive spiral: Creative thinking and cognitive processing. *Journal of Creative Behavior, 28*, 275–290.

Ericsson, K. A., & Simon, H. A. (1984). *Protocol analysis*. Cambridge, MA: MIT Press.

Eysenck, H. (1995). *Genius: The natural history of creativity*. Cambridge, UK: Cambridge University Press.

Eysenck, H. J. (1994). Creativity and personality: Word association, origence, and psychoticism. *Creativity Research Journal, 7*, 209–216.

Feldhusen, J. F. (1995). Creativity: A knowledge base, meta cognitive skills, and personality factors. *Journal of Creative Behavior, 29*, 255–268.

Finke, R. A., Ward, T. B., & Smith, S. M. (1992). *Creative cognition: Theory, research, and applications*. Cambridge, MA: MIT Press.

Geertz, C. (1973). Thick description: Toward an interpretive theory of culture. In *The interpretation of cultures* (pp. 1–30). New York, NY: Basic Books.

Genesee, F. H. (2009). Early bilingualism: Perils and possibilities. *Journal of Applied Research on Learning*, 2, 1–20.

George, J. M., & Zhou, J. (2001). When openness to experience and conscientiousness are related to creative behavior: An interactional approach. *Journal of Applied Psychology*, 86, 513–524.

Grosjean, F. (2008). *Studying bilinguals*. New York, NY: Oxford University Press.

Guilford, J. (1950). Creativity. *American Psychologist*, 5, 444–454.

Guilford, J. P. (1967). *The nature of human intelligence*. New York, NY: McGraw-Hill.

Hayes, J. R. (1989). Cognitive processes in creativity. In J. A. Glover, R. R. Ronning, & C. R. Reynolds (Eds.), *Handbook of creativity* (pp. 135–145). New York, NY: Plenum.

Hennessey, B. A., & Amabile, T. M. (2010). Creativity. *Annual Review of Psychology*, 61, 569–598.

Hoffmann, C. (1991). *An introduction to bilingualism*. New York, NY: Longman.

Hofstede, G., & Bond, M. H. (1988). The Confucius connection: From cultural roots to economic growth. *Organizational Dynamics*, 15, 4–21.

Hommel, B., Colzato, L. S., Fischer, R., & Christoffels, I. K. (2011). Bilingualism and creativity: Benefits in convergent thinking come with losses in divergent thinking. *Frontiers in Psychology*, 2, 273.

Huang, F., Fan, J., & Luo, J. (2015). Neural basis of novelty and appropriateness in processing of creative chunk decomposition. *NeuroImage*, in press.

James, W. (1890). *Principles of Psychology*, Volumes I and II. New York: Henry Holt and Co.

Jung-Beeman, M., Bowden, E., M., Haberman, J., Frymiare, J. L., Arambel-Liu, S., Greenblatt, R., ... Kounios, J. (2004). Neural activity when people solve verbal problems with insight. *Plos Biology*, 2, 500–510.

Kaplan, C. A., & Simon, H. A. (1990). In search of insight. *Cognitive Psychology*, 22, 374–419.

Kaufman, J. C., & Beghetto, R. A. (2013). Do people recognize the four Cs? Examining layperson conceptions of creativity. *Psychology of Aesthetics, Creativity, and the Arts*, 7, 229.

Kershaw, T. C., & Ohlsson, S. (2004). Multiple causes of difficulty in insight: The case of the nine-dot problem. *Journal of Experimental Psychology Learning Memory & Cognition*, 30(1), 3–13.

Kharkhurin, A. V. (2007). The role of cross-linguistic and cross-cultural experiences in bilinguals' divergent thinking. In *Cognitive aspects of bilingualism* (pp. 175–210). Amsterdam, the Netherlands: Springer.

Kharkhurin, A. V. (2008). The effect of linguistic proficiency, age of second language acquisition, and length of exposure to a new cultural environment on bilinguals' divergent thinking. *Bilingualism: Language and Cognition*, 11, 225–243.

Kharkhurin, A. V. (2010a). Bilingual verbal and nonverbal creative behavior. *International Journal of Bilingualism*, 14, 211–226.

Kharkhurin, A. V. (2010b). Sociocultural differences in the relationship between bilingualism and creativity potential. *Journal of Cross-Cultural Psychology*, 41, 776–783.

Kharkhurin, A. V. & Motalleebi, S. V. S. (2008). The impact of culture on the creative potential of american, russian, and iranian college students. *Creativity Research Journal*, 20(4), 404–411.

Kim, K. H. (2006). Is creativity unidimensional or multidimensional? analyses of the torrance tests of creative thinking. *Creativity Research Journal, 18*(3), 251–259.

Knoblich, G., Ohlsson, S., Haider, H.,& Rhenius, D. (1999). Constraint relaxation and chunk decomposition in insight problem solving. *Journal of Experimental Psychology: Learning, Memory and Cognition, 25*, 1534–1556.

Knoblich, G., Ohlsson, S., & Raney, G. E. (2001). An eye movement study of insight problem solving. *Memory & Cognition, 29*(7), 1000–1009.

Ledderose, L. (2001). *Ten thousand things: Module and mass production in Chinese art.* Princeton, NJ: Princeton University Press.

Lee, H., & Kim, K. H. (2010). Relationships between bilingualism and adaptive creative style, innovative creative style, and creative strengths among korean american students. *Creativity Research Journal, 22*(4), 402–407.

Lee, H., & Kim, K. H. (2011). Can speaking more languages enhance your creativity? Relationship between bilingualism and creative potential among Korean American students with multicultural link. *Personality and Individual Differences, 50*, 1186–1190.

Leikin, M., & Tovli, E. (2014). Bilingualism and creativity in early childhood. *Creativity Research Journal, 26*, 411–417.

Leung, A. K.-y., & Morris, M. V. (2010). Culture and creativity: A social psychological analysis. In D. D. Cramer, J. K. Murnighan & R. van Dick (Eds.), *Social psychology and organizations* (pp. 371–395). New York: Routledge.

Lim, W., & Plucker, J. A. (2001). Creativity through a lens of social responsibility: Implicit theories of creativity with Korean samples. *Journal of Creative Behavior, 35*, 115–130.

Lin, C., Hu, W., Adey, P., & Shen, J. (2003). The influence of CASE on scientific creativity. *Research in Science Education, 33*, 143–162.

Lubart, T. I. (1999). *Creativity across cultures.* In R. J. Sternberg (Ed.), *Handbook of creativity* (pp. 339–350). Cambridge, UK: Cambridge University Press.

Luo, J., & Knoblich, G. (2007). Studying insight problem solving with neuroscientific methods. *Methods, 42*, 77–86.

Luo, J., & Niki, K. (2003). The function of hippocampus in "insight" of problem solving. *Hippocampus, 13*, 274–781.

Luo, J., Niki, K., & Knoblich, G. (2006). Perceptual contributions to problem solving: Chunk decomposition of Chinese characters. *Brain Research Bulletin, 70*(4–6), 430–443.

Macgregor, J. N., Ormerod, T. C., & Chronicle, E. P. (2001). Information processing and insight: a process model of performance on the nine-dot and related problems. *Journal of Experimental Psychology Learning Memory & Cognition, 27*(1), 176–201.

Mai, X. Q., Luo, J., Wu, J. H., & Luo, Y. J. (2010). "aha!" effects in a guessing riddle task: an event-related potential study. *Human Brain Mapping, 22*(4), 261–270.

Maier, N. R. F. (1931). Reasoning in humans. ii. The solution of a problem and its appearance in consciousness. *Journal of Comparative Psychology, 12*(2), 181–194.

Mendonça, P. V. D. C. F., & Fleith, D. D. S. (2005). Relationship between monoliguals and bilinguals' creativity, inteligence, and self-concept. *Psicologia Escolar e Educacional, 9*(1), 37–46.

Metcalfe, J. (1986a). Feeling of knowing in memory and problem solving. *Journal of Experimental Psychology: Learning, Memory, and Cognition, 12*, 288–294.

Metcalfe, J. (1986b). Premonitions of insight predict impending error. *Journal of Experimental Psychology: Learning, Memory, and Cognition, 12*, 623–634.

Metcalfe, J., & Wiebe, D. (1987). Intuition in insight and noninsight problem solving. *Memory & Cognition, 15*, 238–246.

Miller, B. L., Cummings, J., Mishkin, F., Boone, K., Prince, F., Ponton, M., & Cotman, C. (1998). Emergence of artistic talent in frontotemporal dementia. *Neurology, 51*, 978–982.

Newell, A., & Simon, H. A. (1972). *Human problem solving.* Englewood Cliffs, NJ: Prentice Hall.

Niu, W., & Sternberg, R. J. (2001). Cultural influences on artistic creativity and its evaluation. *International Journal of Psychology, 36*, 225–241.

Niu, W., & Sternberg, R. J. (2003). Societal and school influences on student creativity: The case of China. *Psychology in the Schools, 40*, 103–114.

Ohlsson, S. (1984). Restructuring revisited: An information processing theory of restructuring and insight. *Scandinavian Journal of Psychology, 25*, 117–129.

Ohlsson, S. (1992). Information-processing explanations of insight and related phenomena. In K. J. Gilhooley (Ed.), *Advances in the psychology of thinking* (pp. 1–44). London, UK: Harvester-Wheatsheaf.

Ollinger, M., Jones, G., & Knoblich, G. (2008). Investigating the effect of mental set on insight problem solving. *Experimental Psychology, 55*(4), 269.

Öllinger, M., & Knoblich, G. (2009). *Psychological research on insight problem solving* (pp. 275–300). Berlin-Heidelberg, Germany: Springer.

Paletz, S. B. F., & Peng, K. (2008). Implicit theories of creativity across cultures novelty and appropriateness in two product domains. *Journal of Cross-Cultural Psychology, 39*(3), 286–302.

Reverberi, C., Toraldo, A., D'Agostini, S., & Skrap, M. (2005). Better without (lateral) frontal cortex? Insight problems solved by frontal patients. *Brain, 128*, 2882–2890.

Ricciardelli, L. A. (1992a). Creativity and bilingualism. *The Journal of Creative Behavior, 26*, 242–254.

Ricciardelli, L. A. (1992b). Bilingualism and cognitive development in relation to threshold theory. *Journal of Psycholinguistic Research, 21*, 301–316.

Ricciardelli, L. A. (1992c). Bilingualism and cognitive development: A review of past and recent findings. *Journal of Creative Behavior, 26*, 242–254.

Rosenblum, T., & Pinker, S. A. (1983). Word magic revisited: Monolingual and bilingual children's understanding of the word-object relationship. *Child Development, 54*, 773–780.

Rudowicz, E. (2003). Creativity and culture: A two way interaction. *Scandinavian Journal of Educational Research, 47*, 273–290.

Rudowicz, E. (2004). Applicability of the test of creative thinking-drawing production for assessing creative potential of Hong Kong adolescents. *The Gifted Child Quarterly, 48*, 202–218.

Rudowicz, E. (2004). Creativity among Chinese People: Beyond Western Perspective. In Lau, S., Hui, A, N.N., &Ng, G. Y.C. (Eds.), *Creativity:When East Meets West* (pp. 55–86). World Scientific Publishing.

Rudowicz, E., & Hui, A. (1997). The creative personality: Hong Kong perspective. *Journal of Social Behavior & Personality, 12*, 139–157.

Rudowicz, E., & Yue, X. D. (2000). Concepts of creativity: Similarities and differences among Mainland, Hong Kong, and Taiwanese Chinese. *The Journal of Creative Behavior, 34*, 175–192.

Runco, M. A. (1999). Tension, adaptability and creativity. In S. W. Russ (Ed.), *Affect, creative experience, and psychological adjustment* (pp. 165–194). Philadelphia, PA: Taylor & Francis.

Runco, M. A., & Bahleda, M. D. (1986). Implicit theories of artistic, scientific, and everyday creativity. *The Journal of Creative Behavior, 20*, 93–98.

Runco, M. A., & Jaeger, G. J. (2012). The standard definition of creativity. *Creativity Research Journal, 24*, 92–96.

Runco, M. A., Johnson, D. J., & Bear, P. K. (1993). Parents' and teachers' implicit theories of children's creativity. *Child Study Journal, 23*, 91–113.

Sawyer, R. K. (2012). *Explaining creativity: The science of human innovation* (2nd ed.). New York, NY: Oxford.

Schlipp, P. A. (1949). *Albert Einstein: Philosopher-scientist.* Cambridge, England: Cambridge University Press.

Schooler, J. W., Ohlsson, S., & Brooks, K. (1993). Thoughts beyond words: When language overshadows insight. *Journal of Experimental Psychology, General, 122*, 166–183.

Sen, R. S., & Sharma, N. (2011). Through multiple lenses: Implicit theories of creativity among Indian children and adults. *The Journal of Creative Behavior, 45*, 273–302.

Shin, S. J., & Zhou, J. (2003). Transformational leadership, conservation, and creativity: Evidence from Korea. *Academy of Management Journal, 46*, 703–714.

Simonton, D. K. (1994). *Greatness: Who makes history and why.* New York, NY: Guilford.

Simonton, D. K. (2008). Bilingualism and creativity. In J. Altarriba & R. R. Heredia (Eds.), *An introduction to bilingualism: Principles and processes* (pp. 147–166). Mahwah, NJ: Lawrence Erlbaum.

Srivastava, B. (1991). Creativity and linguistic proficiency. Psycho-Lingua.acquisition, and length of exposure to a new cultural environment on bilinguals' divergent thinking. *Bilingualism: Language and Cognition, 11*, 225–243.

Stein, M. I. (1953). Creativity and culture. *Journal of Psychology, 36*(2), 311–322.

Sternberg, R. J. (1988.) *The nature of creativity.* Cambridge, UK: Cambridge University Press.

Sternberg, R. J. (1985). Implicit theories of intelligence, creativity and wisdom. *Journal of Personality and Social Psychology, 49*, 607–627.

Sternberg, R. J., & Lubart, T. I. (1996). Investing in creativity. *American Psychologist, 51*, 677–688.

Sternberg, R. J., & Lubart, T. I. (1999). The concept of creativity: Prospects and paradigms. In R. J. Sternberg, *Creativity handbook* (pp. 3–15). New York, NY: Cambridge University Press.

Sternberg, R. J., & Zhang, L. (1995). What do we mean by giftedness? A pentagonal implicit theory. *Gifted Child Quarterly, 39*, 88–94.

Tang, X. C., Pang, J. Y., & Luo, J. (2009). Zeigarnik effect in Insight problem solving: Hemispheric difference in brain activities following problem solving and during hint presentation (in Chinese). *Chinese Science Bulletin (Chinese Version), 54*, 3464–3474.

Tylor, E. B. (1920[1871]). *Primitive culture.* New York, NY: J. P. Putnam's Sons.

Weiner, B. (2000). Attributional thoughts about consumer behavior. *Journal of Consumer Research, 27*, 382–387.

Weinrich, U. (1968). *Languages in contact.* The Hague, the Netherlands: Mouton.

Weisberg, R. W., & Alba, J. W. (1981). An examination of the alleged role of "fixation" in the solution of several "insight" problems. *Journal of Experimental Psychology General, 110*(2), 169–192.

Westby, E. L., & Dawson, V. L. (1995). Creativity: Asset or burden in the classroom? *Creativity Research Journal, 8*, 1–10.

Woodman, R. W., Sawyer, J. E., & Griffin, R. M. (1993). Toward a theory of organizational creativity. *Academy of Management Review, 18*, 293–321.

Wu, L., Knoblich, G., & Luo, J. (2013). The role of chunk tightness and chunk familiarity in problem solving: Evidence from ERPs and fMRI. *Human Brain Mapping, 34*, 1173–1186.

Wu, L., Knoblich, G., Wei, G., & Luo, J. (2009). How perceptual processes help to generate new meaning: An EEG study of chunk decomposition in Chinese characters. *Brain Research, 1296*, 104–112.

Wu, Q. Y., Wu, L. L., & Luo, J. (2010). Effective connectivity of dorsal and ventral visual pathways in chunk decomposition. *Science China-life Sciences, 53*, 1474–1482.

Zhou, J., & Shalley, C. E. (2003). Research on employee creativity: A critical review and directions for future research. *Research in Personnel and Human Resources Management, 22*, 165–217.

Zhou, J., Shen, J., Wang, X., Neber, H., & Johji, I. (2013). A cross-cultural comparison: Teachers' conceptualizations of creativity. *Creativity Research Journal, 25*, 239–247.

8

Diversity in Creative Teams

Reaching Across Cultures and Disciplines

SUSANNAH B. F. PALETZ, IVICA PAVISIC,
ELLA MIRON-SPEKTOR, AND CHUN-CHI LIN ■

Today's hardest problems are being tackled by culturally and/or disciplinarily diverse teams: Poverty, global health, and international crisis management all require individuals working across nations and disciplines (Derry & Schunn, 2005; Kidwell & Langholtz, 1998). Even the study of teamwork itself is benefitted by methodological and disciplinary diversity (Beck, 2013). Numerous books, chapters, and articles have been published on creative and innovative teams (e.g., Hackman, 2011; John-Steiner, 2000; Paulus & Nijstad, 2003; Salas, Sims, & Burke, 2005; Thompson & Choi, 2006), with many focusing on team diversity in particular (e.g., Chatman, Polzer, Barsade, & Neale, 1998; Derry, Schunn, & Gernsbacher, 2005; Jackson & Ruderman, 1996; Mannix & Neale, 2005; Stahl, Maznevski, Voigt, & Jonsen, 2010; van Knippenberg & Schippers, 2007; Williams & O'Reilly, 1998). This literature paints a mixed picture of the success of multidisciplinary and/or multicultural teams (e.g., Cady & Valentine, 1999; Haas, 2010; Timmerman, 2000). On the one hand, diverse teams are both increasing in prevalence and are found to be superior in terms of scientific innovation and impact (e.g., Adams, 2013; Freeman & Huang, 2014; Wuchty, Jones, & Uzzi, 2007). On the other hand, multicultural teams are likely to have more interpersonal conflict than single-culture teams (Ayub & Jehn, 2010; Stahl et al., 2010), and multidisciplinary teams are often plagued with coordination and communication problems, particularly involving methodological norms and disciplinary foci (e.g., Beck, 2013; Derry et al., 2005).

The goal of this chapter is to synthesize a broad literature on multidisciplinary and/or multicultural creative teams. Furthermore, this chapter will cover both cultural and disciplinary diversity, as these teams face many of the same challenges and opportunities (e.g., Dahlin, Weingart, & Hinds, 2005). This chapter covers

(1) definitions and issues surrounding key constructs; (2) the main similarities and differences between cultural and disciplinary diversity; (3) theoretical background; (4) a summary on the relationship between these diverse teams and creativity, conflict, information sharing, and some additional factors; and (5) gaps in the literature and potential future work.

This chapter utilizes two overarching frameworks: the input-mediator (process)-output-input model (IMOI; Ilgen, Hollenbeck, Johnson, & Jundt, 2005) and the acknowledgment that teams act across multiple levels: individual, team, higher contextual levels (e.g., organization, culture), and time (see Figure 8.1). Figure 8.1 organizes this complex problem space via a two-dimensional table, with the input-process-output (and then linking to inputs again) model as the top row and the multiple levels of teamwork on the left column. Diversity itself thus falls into the cell that has *inputs* as a header and is in the row of *team-level* factors. Issues of diversity in teams are inherently multilevel (Brodbeck, Guillaume, & Lee, 2011; Joshi, Liao, & Roh, 2011). These different levels interact with each other via top-down and bottom-up processes (Erez & Gati, 2004). Individuals act within teams that are within organizational departments, organizations, industries, nations, and so on (Joshi & Roh, 2009). In the IMOI model, inputs lead to processes (mediators), which lead to outputs, which feed back into inputs (Ilgen et al., 2005). For instance, a team with intense conflict may result in some members quitting (an output), thus changing the team's composition (an input). Although the team-level inputs and outputs tend to involve the entire team (e.g.,

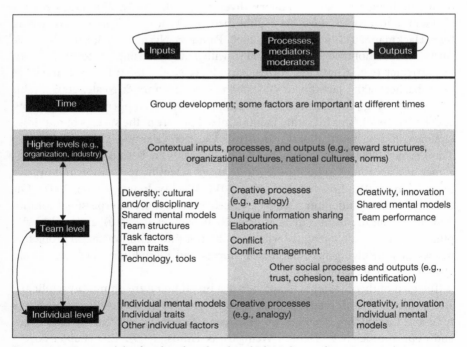

Figure 8.1. Framework of multicultural and multidisciplinary diversity in creative teams.

team composition, team creative outputs), team processes may only involve some of the team members (e.g., conflict). Processes can be mediators but can also be moderators of each other and inputs.

DEFINITIONS OF KEY CONSTRUCTS

In this section, we lay out the psychological definitions of creativity, types of team diversity, and mental models.

Creativity

Creativity (and innovation, see later) is one of many potential team perfor-mance outcomes. Creativity has been applied to products, processes, people, and environments, and generally requires (1) novelty or originality and (2) usefulness or appropriateness (Amabile, 1983, 1996; Mayer, 1999). Creativity can be generated from an everyday process, as part of normal learning, by professional experts, and by eminent people (Beghetto & Kaufman, 2007; Kaufman & Beghetto, 2009). It can entail (1) divergent processes that involve broadening options or ideas (e.g., elaboration, fluency of ideas, flexibility, and originality; Torrance, 1988), and/or (2) convergent processes that involve narrowing options or ideas (e.g., evaluation, recognition of excellence, the choice of the "best" creative ideas; Cropley, 2006).

This chapter focuses on creativity as an everyday process ("little-c") and/ or generated by professional experts ("pro-c," Kaufman & Beghetto, 2009). Innovation is creativity plus implementation with the goal of societal, group, or individual benefit (West & Farr, 1990). This chapter does not delve into the differences between creativity and innovation. Teams of professionals or lay-people can be creative and/or innovative, and creativity can be observed at either the individual or team level (Figure 8.1).

Team Diversity

Teams are a type of group (although we will use those terms interchangeably) that is interdependent, a bounded social entity, and comprised of differentiated member roles (Guzzo & Dickson, 1996; Hackman, 2012). Teams can be diverse on many dimensions, including cognitive styles, abilities, ethnicity, personality, job seniority, and so on (e.g., Aggarwal & Woolley, 2013; Brophy, 2006; Dahlin et al., 2005; Mannix & Neale, 2005; Mohammed & Angell, 2004). *Diversity* has been operationalized in (at least) three different ways: as separation, or differences along a continuum (e.g., a bimodal distribution of opinions on the death pen-alty); as variety, or differences in categories (e.g., gender diversity in a team); and as disparity, where the focus is on the unequal distribution of a resource within the group (Harrison & Klein, 2007). When examining cultural and disciplinary diversity, variety is usually the type of diversity studied. For instance, most discussions of cultural or disciplinary diversity examine heterogeneous versus homogeneous groups (e.g., Mannix & Neale, 2005; Williams & O'Reilly, 1998).

Multidisciplinary and Multicultural Diversity

Disciplines are different domains of academic study (e.g., geology) or practical fields (e.g., marketing versus information systems). Disciplines can be distinguished by segmentation processes between professions (Gerson, 1983), such as separate conferences, newsletters, journals, and books (Schunn, Crowley, & Okada, 1998). Individuals are unlikely to encounter the more nuanced work arising from other disciplines, and people from different disciplines typically obtain different training and keep abreast of their fields by drawing on different information sources. Even closely related subdisciplines may use the same language to mean subtly different concepts, such as "theory." Cross-disciplinary teams assemble when something is to be achieved by collaboration (e.g., Derry & Schunn, 2005; Schunn et al., 1998).

Disciplines can vary so widely that they become different subcultures (Chiu, Kwan, & Liou, 2014; Paletz, Miron-Spektor, & Lin, 2014). Beyond disciplines, team members may also differ in terms of their national or ethnic cultures. *Culture*, in general is a shared system of learned and communicated meanings (Rohner, 1984) that exists within individuals' minds (Peng, Ames, & Knowles, 2001), as well as the shared practices, institutions, and artifacts that are produced in part by this system (Kroeber & Kluckhohn, 1952; Morling & Lamoreaux, 2008). Cultural differences can be present wherever there are differences in shared mental models between subgroups (Hong, Morris, Chiu, & Benet-Martinez, 2000). *Mental models* are representations in the mind of almost any construct—people, objects, actions, or situations—and include both the content of the knowledge and the relationships between constructs (Johnson-Laird, 1980). Mental models, which exist at the individual level, are often conceptualized as preexisting inputs, but they can also change and be developed based on team interactions (Figure 8.1). Although mental models are dynamic in the sense that they change, at any one point they are static. Mental models can be made explicit, but more often are studied as unspoken assumptions. When mental models overlap, such that multiple people have similar constructs and networks of constructs in their minds, they form *shared mental models* (Klimoski & Mohammed, 1994; Mohammed, Ferzandi, & Hamilton, 2010). Although culture is represented in the mind as shared mental models (Hong et al., 2000), differences between shared mental models can be greater (as between dramatically different national cultures) or smaller (as between subdisciplines; see more later).

Team shared mental models can include both the details of the task the team is doing as well as team members' roles and responsibilities (Mohammed & Dumville, 2001). Achieving shared mental models is important for team effectiveness (DeChurch & Mesmer-Magnus, 2010; Kozlowski & Ilgen, 2006; Mathieu et al., 2000; Rentsch & Hall, 1994; Salas et al., 2005; Turner, Chen, & Danks, 2014). Shared mental models are used to interpret and integrate new information, affecting how individuals perceive their environment and what they consider to be appropriate reactions (Burke et al., 2006; Salas, Stagl, & Burke, 2004). Shared mental models can support problem solving in ad hoc, short-term teams doing complex tasks, such as when a pilot and co-pilot are flying (e.g., Nokes-Malach, Meade, & Morrow, 2012). Shared mental models are particularly helpful if they are accurate (Edwards, Day, Arthur, & Bell, 2006). It is not enough for a team to have a shared idea of who does what work; they should also have an accurate view of each person's capabilities and role within the team (e.g., DuRussel & Derry, 2005). For instance, the statistician on a multidisciplinary team is best utilized doing statistics, rather than data entry. Because members of different disciplines and cultures may have different mental models, promoting shared mental models may be more difficult in diverse groups.

Of importance, mental models are not necessarily categorically different: A team may share some aspects of some mental models, or only some mental models (Cronin & Weingart, 2007). The average size of the difference between mental models may be less important than the general heterogeneity of the mental models (Weingart, Todorova, & Cronin, 2010). Given the importance of shared mental models to teamwork, and the differences between individual mental models, the issue of shared and unshared mental models is key to understanding the issues and opportunities present for diverse teams (Figure 8.1; Paletz & Schunn, 2010; Weingart et al., 2010).

As constructs, disciplines and "cultures" (nation-states, tribes, ethnic groups) each represent different types and combinations of very different factors. That noted, they share some important abstract similarities, such as boundaries with different groups; learning processes of culture; and shared norms, history, and values. Importantly, these two types of diversity may reside in the same team. For example, multidisciplinary teams can be culturally homogeneous or diverse. Similarly, multicultural teams can belong to the same discipline (as in the case of our authorship team) or to different disciplines. Most research focuses on one type of diversity only. We see value in distinguishing between cultural and disciplinary diversity and, drawing on faultline research (e.g., Lau & Murninghan, 1998; Thatcher & Patel, 2011, 2012), considering their isolated and joint effects on creativity. We elaborate in the next section on likely differences and similarities between groups heterogeneous on national culture and discipline.

SIMILARITIES AND DIFFERENCES BETWEEN DIVERSITY OF DISCIPLINES AND CULTURES

This section deals with some of the similarities and differences between cultural and disciplinary diversity (Table 8.1). When researchers discuss multicultural diversity, they generally are referring to ethnic or subcultural diversity within nations, national diversity (with or without ethnic diversity), and/or other types

Table 8.1. SIMILARITIES AND DIFFERENCES BETWEEN *DIVERSITY* OF DISCIPLINES
AND CULTURES AND COMPLICATING FACTORS

Similarities	Differences
1. Differences in shared mental models	1. Language and communication
2. Language and meaning differences	differences are greater between people
3. Different social identities	who speak different languages.
4. Power and status differences may fall	2. Cultural differences are deeper between
along disciplinary or cultural lines	cultures and nations versus disciplines.
5. Possible preexisting intergroup	3. Disciplinary differences are more
conflicts	likely to be task relevant than cultural
6. Potential for creativity	differences.

of visible/audible diversity of cultural groups (e.g., American Southerners versus Midwesterners).

Similarities

Teams diverse on either culture or discipline will have similar challenges in terms of potential differences in their (1) mental models, (2) language and meaning, (3) social identities, (4) power and status that fall along disciplinary or cultural lines, (5) preexisting intergroup conflicts, and (6) creativity. These differences (i.e., mental models, meaning, social identity, power) are all "deep-level" underlying psychological characteristics, even though it would seem as though national/ethnic differences would be more apparent and less task here relevant than disciplinary differences (Bell, 2007; Harrison, Price, & Bell, 1998; Hulsheger, Anderson & Salgao, 2009).

First, individuals within heterogeneous disciplinary or cultural groups may rely on different mental models for describing the same phenomena and/or may simply deal with different issues so as to have unshared mental models about those issues. Hong et al. (2000), in their dynamic constructivist theory of culture, contend that culture and cultural assumptions can be a type of shared mental model. Bicultural individuals can switch mental model frameworks when primed by cues reminding them of the relevant culture (Hong et al., 2000; Hong, Benet-Martinez, Chiu, & Morris, 2003). Culture and other shared mental models are co-created and transmitted between individuals, learned, activated by relevant information, and put into use when they are applicable in the situation (Hong et al., 2000, 2003; Oyserman, 2011). Thus, members of any subgroup may have shared mental models different from other subgroups, causing cultural differences between members of different regions, disciplines, occupations, religions, and so on. For instance, a molecular biologist will have a different, richer, and more complex understanding of cell walls than a software designer.

Second, tied deeply with mental model differences are language and meaning differences. For both types of heterogeneous groups, the same word might actually have different meanings. To a social psychologist, the word "model" might mean a diagram indicating individual constructs and directional relationships between them; to a hardware engineer, a model is a physical prototype; and to a layperson, a model is a good-looking person who is paid to display clothes (Paletz, 2014). The use of the same word that has different meanings can cause confusion at best and disdain at worst. Similarly, language differences within multicultural teams can cause translation problems, even between individuals who ostensibly speak the same language (e.g., "pissed" means angry and drunk in American and British English, respectively). An acronym used by one discipline may be unknown to others, and, of course, words can be completely unknown between members of different national cultures.

Third, members of different disciplines and cultures may have different social identities (Haslam, 2001; Hogg, 1992). Social identities exist when an individual categorizes himself or herself as part of one social group versus another. These social categories may include multiple categories at once, are dynamic, and contingent on context, but nonetheless have great power over self- and other-perception and behavior (e.g., Turner, Oakes, Haslam, & McGarty, 1994). Welsh, English, and Scottish are all different social identities, as are electrical, mechanical, and computer engineers, despite fluidity and melding between each set of groups and ignorance of differences between them by outsiders. Social identities are derived from group membership and culture, even as intragroup processes may in turn create and influence group identity (Postmes, Haslam, & Swaab, 2005).

Fourth, different social identities often have histories of power and status differences. The social valuation of quantitative fields over qualitative ones (Gerson, 1983) and the domination of certain cultural, ethnic, and/or national groups over others means that interactions between members of different groups of both types may be fraught with replaying of historical power differentials and/ or struggles to overcome them (DiTomaso et al., 2007). Fifth, the combination of mental model differences (Bearman, Paletz, Orasanu, & Thomas, 2010; Cronin & Weingart, 2007) and historical power differences makes intergroup conflict more likely, both historically between social identity groups and presently within teams. Finally, both types of heterogeneous groups have the potential for more creativity. This last point is a focus of this chapter.

Differences

Despite all the similarities noted, there are also important differences between teams that are diverse on culture and those that are diverse by discipline. These differences can be either *categorical* ("qualitative") or a matter of *degree* (where the gaps are on a continuum), depending on the team composition, languages, and cultures being examined. First, language differences may be much greater in culturally heterogeneous teams. Multidisciplinary language differences regarding particular words is minor compared to *actual* language differences, which can make mutual comprehension impossible. Not all multicultural groups draw from different language families or have no languages in common, although some countries have substantial internal language diversity. Still, the potential for different native languages is greater in multicultural teams from across the globe than in a multidisciplinary same-nation team.

Similarly, a second difference between multidisciplinary and multicultural teams is the depth of the cultural differences involved. National and regional cultures, in particular, have many documented differences in terms of values, conceptions of the self, what types of relationship structures are apt for what situations, lay theories of various topics, and even how powerful and constraining norms are (e.g., Fiske, 1992; Gelfand et al., 2011; Hofstede, 2001; Markus & Kitayama, 1991; Peng et al., 2001; Salazar & Salas, 2013; Schwartz et al., 2011; Smith, Bond, & Kagitcibasi, 2006; Triandis, 1989). Regional cultures can shape how people respond to a loss of social reputation (e.g., Kim & Cohen, 2010), their conceptions of joint work (Salazar & Salas, 2013), and even how they respond to Likert scale questionnaires (Chen, Lee, & Stevenson, 1995; Johnson, Kulesa, Cho, & Shavitt, 2005). The breadth and depth of differences between prominent cultural groups is undoubtedly greater than between disciplinary groups. All of these differences may accentuate the effects described in subsequent sections for some groups versus others and/or may require other factors (moderators) to manage.

Third, multidisciplinary teams may be more likely to have job- and task-relevant diversity than multicultural teams. This difference between diverse groups is by type rather than degree. Task-relevant diversity is thought to involve education and functional expertise compared to visible, but less relevant diversity such as gender or ethnicity (Horwitz & Horwitz, 2007). One meta-analysis found that task-relevant diversity is more related to team performance than visible, superficial diversity (Horwitz & Horwitz, 2007), but two other meta-analyses found no consistent, significant effect of job-related diversity on innovation (Hulsheger, Anderson, & Salgado, 2009) or team performance (Webber & Donahue, 2001). These mixed findings may be because demographic differences are sometimes job relevant and some expertise/education differences are job irrelevant, such that the background information that should improve performance is not always identifiable in these studies along the superficial/deep distinction. For instance, when an engineering team is designing a computer for the global market, national and socioeconomic differences will become task relevant for determining design requirements and marketing strategies. Moreover, multicultural teams can also be multidisciplinary, with members from different cultures representing different disciplines. This potential overlap makes it difficult to isolate the effect of cultural and disciplinary diversity on team performance. Further, there are numerous moderators to any relationship between diversity and performance (see later sections). Although the job relevance of the type of diversity may depend on the task, the task-relevance dimension may still help to distinguish these types of diverse teams.

Although this section has described similarities and differences between multidisciplinary and multicultural teams, many teams simultaneously experience both types of diversity. Multiple types of diversity may cross or overlap within and between individuals, such as when a single Chinese American is also the only marketing professional in a team of mostly European American software engineers. Distinctions within groups on diversity lines are called faultlines, and "faultline strength" is greater when these differences align at the same time on multiple characteristics, such as gender, ethnicity, functional background, educational background, and so on (Homan, van Knippenberg, van Kleef, & De Dreu, 2007; Lau & Murninghan, 1998; Meyer, Glenz, Antino, Rico, & González-Romá, 2014; Thatcher & Patel, 2011, 2012). The faultline literature suggests that researchers should consider the potential additive and interactive effects of diversity as a whole, rather than to try to study each type of diversity separately. For example, a faultline exists within a group of five that consists of three men and two women, and that faultline is stronger if the three men are Caucasians while the two women are South Asians. Stronger faultlines have negative effects on group performance and team satisfaction above and beyond the effects of group diversity (Thatcher & Patel, 2012). Informational diversity is more likely to improve performance when the information is not divided up according to demographic and other differences at the same time: when team informational diversity falls along demographic lines (such as with the Chinese American example), conflict is more likely (Homan et al., 2007). Further, faultlines may be dormant (underlying) or active (perceived by team members based on a set of attributes). The negative effects of faultlines are stronger for active than for dormant faultlines, but even dormant faultlines have negative effects on team satisfaction and performance (Meyer et al., 2014; Thatcher & Patel, 2012). Thus, we consider that the possible negative effects for diversity may be more pronounced in multidisciplinary, multicultural teams.

In addition to faultlines, further issues may complicate the experience of diversity. The higher level context (e.g., organization, nation) may influence some types of diversity differently than others, such as when multicultural diversity is viewed as an opportunity or a threat, depending on an organization's climate (Li, Lin, Tien, & Chen, 2015). Finally, language and mental models can converge over time, changing the degree of differences in teams over time (e.g., Tuckman & Jensen, 1997; see Figure 8.1).

THEORETICAL BACKGROUND

Historically, two theoretical traditions have dominated the team diversity literature: information processing and social categorization (van Knippenberg & Schippers, 2007; Williams & O'Reilly, 1998). The information processing tradition contends that backgrounds of almost any type (e.g., ethnic, age, disciplinary) bring a variety of experiential information (McLeod, Lobel, & Cox, 1996; Shaw & Barrett-Power, 1998; van Knippenberg & Schippers, 2007). Cultural diversity, for instance, can entail deeper schema differences (e.g., Bell, 2007; Harrison et al., 1998; Shaw & Barrett-Power, 1998). The focus of the information processing approach is on the cognitive benefits of diversity. In general, idea generation is considered a process of retrieving and producing ideas from memory (known as the search for ideas in an associative memory model or SIAM; Nijstad & Stroebe, 2006). Almost any kind of diversity, but most specifically background information diversity, is assumed to bring with it the potential for greater creativity, as a broader knowledge base can result in more combinations and more *creative* combinations (e.g., Nijstad & Stroebe, 2006; Paletz & Schunn, 2010; Reiter-Palmon, Wigert, & de Vreede, 2011; Shaw & Barrett-Power, 1998). These claims are essentially supported by the literature, given some moderators such as task complexity (needs to be high; van Dijk, van Engen, & van Knippenberg, 2012); task interdependence and goal interdependence (need to be high; Van der Vegt & Janssen, 2003); task structure (needs to be weak) and specificity (needs to be low; Nouri et al., 2013); and the use of constructive confrontation strategies, such as encouraging open expression and avoiding negative affect (Kellermanns, Floyd, Pearson, & Spencer, 2008). Indeed, multidisciplinary teams specifically draw not just from their own individual knowledge to come up with creative ideas but also cross boundaries via their broader networks (Ratcheva, 2009).

In contrast, research derived from the social categorization tradition, which draws on social identity, social categorization, and similarity/attraction theories, focuses on how differences will spark intergroup processes, such as subgrouping, generally to the detriment of social team outcomes such as cohesion, conflict, and social integration (e.g., Chatman, Polzer, Barsade, & Neale, 1998; Haas, 2010; Mannix & Neale, 2005; O'Reilly, Williams, & Barsade, 1998; Thatcher & Patel, 2011; Williams & O'Reilly, 1998). This theory generally focuses on the negative affective and social outcomes associated with differences based on social identity. Social identities bring with them the baggage of shared history, languages/dialects, power differentials, and so on, which often, in turn, bring slightly different shared mental models. Thus, groups that are diverse across many categories may also have a harder time achieving shared mental models (Cronin & Weingart, 2007; Paletz & Schunn, 2010).

These different theories have different ostensible implications for multicultural and multidisciplinary teams. Superficially, these theories suggest that multidisciplinary teams, with their expected greater task-related knowledge diversity, are more likely to be creative, whereas multicultural teams, with their deeper cultural and social identity differences, are more prone to social problems. But multicultural teams can be more creative than homogeneous teams (e.g., Freeman & Huang, 2014) and have a less clearly negative relationship with information integration compared to multidisciplinary teams (Dahlin et al., 2005). Indeed, multidisciplinary teams may also suffer from difficulties in their social processes (e.g., Derry et al., 2005). Further, it is often the *perceptions* of differences that are important, with perceptions potentially changing over time (Shemla, Meyer, Greer, & Jehn, 2014; Zellmer-Bruhn, Maloney, Bhappu, & Salvador, 2008). In particular, perceived work style similarity may decrease over time due to conflict, as individuals get to know each other and realize they have less in common than they thought when they first met (Zellmer-Bruhn et al., 2008). Social category diversity perceptions, on the other hand, seem somewhat stable (Zellmer-Bruhn et al., 2008). Thus, as individuals learn about each other after joining a group, their perceptions of deep diversity may change, revealing similarities and differences.

Recent research and theoretical models often combine both approaches, examining the interaction between social identity and idea generation, or examining both social and cognitive outcomes simultaneously (e.g., Dahlin et al., 2005; Homan et al., 2007; Jehn, Northcraft, & Neale, 1999; Pelled, Eisenhardt, & Xin, 1999; van Knippenberg, De Dreu, & Homan, 2004; Weingart et al., 2010; Zellmer-Bruhn et al., 2008). For instance, van Knippenberg and colleagues (2004) combined the two traditional approaches to create the categorization-elaboration model (CEM). They propose that diversity enhances team creativity and decision quality via the possibility of the elaboration of task-relevant information and perspectives, but that this process is moderated both by task-relevant factors (e.g., task-related motivation and ability) and by intergroup biases. These intergroup biases do not inevitably result from social categorization processes: Social categorization is contingent on the cognitive accessibility of the social categories and whether the social categories are sensible, meaningful, and applicable to the team members. In other words, the simple existence of social category differences does not lead to social categorization psychological processes, which are dependent on perceptions and cognition. Furthermore, they contend that identity threat is an important moderator, affecting whether social categorization processes lead to negative affective reactions and poor team processes.

Effective team creativity is thought to be supported by four principles: the creative potential of the group, the effective sharing of relevant ideas and information, the accessibility of additional ideas and information relevant to what has previously been shared, and effective convergence on high-quality ideas (Nijstad, Rietzschel, & Stroebe, 2006). Two recent models of multidisciplinary team creativity and innovation reemphasize, combine, and elaborate upon these four principles (Paletz & Schunn, 2010; Reiter-Palmon, de Vreede, & de Vreede, 2013). Individual creativity (Reiter-Palmon et al., 2013) and a variety of background knowledge (e.g., information from disciplinary backgrounds) provide ways in which a group may have great creative potential (Paletz & Schunn, 2010). Both models add the caveat that information needs to be effectively shared, especially unique information (Mesmer-Magnus & DeChurch, 2009). Finally, effective convergence toward what are considered high-quality ideas generally requires acquiring shared mental models (e.g., Paletz & Schunn, 2010; Reiter-Palmon et al., 2013). Other elements of these theories, such as conflict, will be discussed in later sections.

Last, the self-verification literature provides an important extension and caveat to social categorization theories (Swann, Polzer, Seyle, & Ko, 2004). If individuals within a diverse team can perceive each other both as they perceive themselves (high self-verification) and as individuals rather than as representatives of groups (individuation, or viewing team members as unique individuals), the negative effects of social categorization can be minimized. Teams with high self-verification and diversity had better social integration and group identification, lower relationship conflict, and improved creative task performance compared to when self-verification was low (Polzer, Milton, & Swann, 2002). In a separate study, when team members had positive early impressions of each other, higher diversity predicted greater individuation of impression targets (Swann, Kwan, Polzer, & Milton, 2003). Individuation then predicted self-verification weeks later, which subsequently predicted both positive group identification and team performance (Swann et al., 2003). Consequently, a potentially effective way of harnessing diversity involves encouraging initial positive views of others, which leads to a perception of team members as unique individuals and the team as being genuinely diverse, which in turn leads to team members viewing others as they would view themselves.

In sum, even with the extensions of self-verification and other theories, the social categorization and information processing theories continue to have a strong impact on the literature, even as models become more complex and moderators and mediators are discovered.

DIVERSE MENTAL MODELS, CREATIVITY, AND TWO TEAM PROCESSES

In this section, we present research about the effects of multidisciplinary and/ or multicultural groups on creativity, conflict, participation, and information sharing, as well as some important additional factors. Although there is research on additional team processes (e.g., social integration, cohesion; Stahl et al., 2010), we focus on conflict and information sharing/elaboration as two key factors because of their importance to the accessibility, sharing, and choice of ideas, which are subsequently relevant to creativity, as noted in previous reviews and models (Hoever, van Knippenberg, van Ginkel, & Barkema, 2012; Nijstad et al., 2006; Paletz & Schunn, 2010; Reiter-Palmon et al., 2013).

Creativity

FINDINGS OF THE DIVERSITY–CREATIVITY RELATIONSHIP
Teams in general are less creative than individuals in traditional brainstorming settings (Mullen, Johnson, & Salas, 1991), but they may be more creative when tasks are multifaceted and solutions require a variety of background knowledge (Brophy, 1998; Nokes-Malach et al., 2012). One of the promises of both multicultural and multidisciplinary teams is that they provide a broader set of unique background experiences and expertise that can, if the social processes are managed properly, result in greater creativity than homogeneous groups—a finding often supported by the literature, including recent meta-analyses of both types of diverse teams (e.g., Adams, 2013; Freeman & Huang, 2014; Mannix & Neale, 2005; Stahl et al., 2010; van Dijk et al., 2012; Williams & O'Reilly, 1998; Wuchty et al., 2007).

These meta-analyses typically deal with creative outcomes. One specific creative *process*, analogy, can be generated by an individual and/or a team, but it is often neglected in social/organizational psychological meta-analyses because it is studied mostly by cognitive and design psychologists. Analogy is a fundamental cognitive (and creative) process (e.g., Gentner, 1983), where an individual accesses past knowledge to assist with a current problem (e.g., Ball & Christensen, 2009). Applying past information to the current issue is termed mapping (Gentner, 1983). Analogies can be used to predict and solve problems (e.g., Ball & Christensen, 2009; Bearman, Ball, & Ormerod, 2007; Christensen & Schunn, 2007). For example, a scientist working on a Mars mission drew an analogy between a chess game and potential rover instrument readings, drawing the connection that each required a specific order and planning to achieve (Paletz, Schunn, & Kim, 2013). Analogies can be positively associated with originality in engineering designs when multiple and/or different disciplines are considered (e.g., Chan et al., 2011; Dahl & Moreau, 2002). Similarly, multidisciplinary biology labs outperformed more homogeneous labs, in part because they were able to create a broader set of analogies from their more diverse knowledge bases (Dunbar, 1995, 1997). Researchers could investigate whether multicultural teams similarly act as analogy generators.

GREATER VARIETY OF MEASURES OF CREATIVITY NEEDED

Analogy is just one type of divergent creative process that may be used by diverse teams. It is worth examining what other kinds of creativity are promoted (or negatively affected) by diversity, and if there is a difference for multidisciplinary versus multicultural diversity. Creativity can entail divergent or convergent aspects, processes, or outcomes; be at the individual or team level; and be operationalized by a variety of different measures (Figure 8.1). As noted by Reiter-Palmon and colleagues (2011), most social psychological research on team creativity focuses on brainstorming and idea generation, which emphasize the divergent aspects of creativity (e.g., fluency, originality; Stroebe, Nijstad, & Rietzschel, 2010). The convergent aspect of creativity (e.g., choosing the best idea, accumulating knowledge) may require shared mental models (Cropley, 2006). At first blush, divergent creativity should be benefitted by diversity (Stroebe et al., 2010), but convergent creativity should not (Paletz & Schunn, 2010). Compared to homogenous teams, diverse teams may have a wider pool of information available from which to generate a greater number of, and more novel, ideas. However, convergent creativity requires focusing on an agreed-upon set of criteria for success and narrowing down options (Paletz & Schunn, 2010). Without a shared mental model, these criteria may differ from person to person within a diverse team, resulting in disagreements and counterproductive conflict (Paletz & Schunn, 2010). Indeed, a study of teams analyzing case studies (writing up and defending solutions, a convergent task) found that nationally homogeneous groups outperformed the culturally heterogeneous ones (Thomas, 1999).

Many creativity studies test creative outcomes rather than processes directly, such as supervisor and peer ratings of employee creativity (e.g., Taggar, 2002), overall team creativity (Gilson, Mathieu, Shalley, & Ruddy, 2005; Miron-Spektor, Erez, & Naveh, 2011), experimental creative task outcomes (e.g., Gino, Argote, Miron-Spektor, & Todorova, 2010; Goncalo & Staw, 2006), and citation and publication rates (e.g., Freeman & Huang, 2014; Wuchty et al., 2007). These measures each have pros and cons. Citation and publication rates have the benefit of combining both convergent and divergent creative processes (e.g., knowing how to write for a specific disciplinary audience). Real-world teams do not usually separate convergent and divergent aspects of creativity, such as when evaluation occurs in different configurations within team creativity (Harvey & Kou, 2013). However, citation rates and publications have several limitations, including that they neither uncover nor question the motivations behind citation behaviors, nor do they enable the unpacking of social processes (Wagner et al., 2011). Also, supervisor ratings of employee creativity are moderated by perceptions of how successful employees are at bringing creative ideas to their supervisors' attention (Randel, Jaussi, & Wu, 2011). Thus, the effects of diversity should be tested explicitly on different types of creativity, including using process measures (Reiter-Palmon et al., 2011).

ADDITIONAL VARIABLES IMPACTING THE RELATIONSHIP BETWEEN CULTURE AND CREATIVITY

Given that the diversity–creativity link is well established but difficult to achieve, additional literature focuses on possible moderators. We recently formulated a dynamic constructivist model of culture, creativity, and conflict (Paletz et al., 2014). We contend that multicultural environments are more likely to involve conflict (e.g., Stahl et al., 2010), but whether this conflict leads to enhanced creativity depends on whether the conflict is perceived as a threat or not. Further, whether this conflict is perceived as a threat is moderated by many cultural factors, including culturally appropriate responses to conflict, interpretations of the same disagreement behavior, tolerance for conflict, reactions and interpretations of face threat, and so on—in other words, culture as it exists within the mind as individual mental models. When a behavior is viewed as a threat, a prevention focus, rather than a promotion focus, may be activated. A prevention focus is generally shown to be negatively related to originality and creativity, whereas a promotion focus may enhance it. Thus, when a team member presents a behavior, various team members may respond quite differently—responses that have implications for their individual and team creativity via whether they feel threat. In multicultural teams, individual traits (Figure 8.1) such as cultural competence, or the use of appropriate behaviors in different cultural settings, and cultural meta-knowledge, or the knowledge of what members of another culture prefer or know, are related to improved communication (Leung, Lee, & Chiu, 2013) and more nuanced conflict management (Sieck, Smith, & Rasmussen, 2013). Thus, multicultural teams made up of culturally competent members may mitigate the degree to which disagreements are viewed as threats. This model can easily be extended to multidisciplinary teams, although the differences between the relevant norms regarding threat may not be as great.

Additional variables add complexity to the diversity–creativity link, specifically, the distance between mental models and the different topics of the mental models at play. Indeed, when a person is faced with a greater cultural difference, having a comparison mindset that focuses on differences, rather than similarities, may increase creative insights (Cheng & Leung, 2013). Similarity in different types of mental models may also have dissimilar influences. Although shared mental models of the task may be necessary for multidisciplinary teams to be innovative (Reiter-Palmon et al., 2011), shared mental models of other teamwork issues may simply make social interactions easier. Whether these better social interactions enhance or hinder team creativity depends on the nature of the shared norms. For example, diverse teams that share constructive confrontation norms ("open expression, disagreement, and the avoidance of negative affect") tend to experience more beneficial conflict and make higher quality decisions than diverse teams that do not (Kellermanns et al., 2008, p. 120). Similarly, the positive relationship between cultural (ethnic and national) diversity and team and individual creativity was stronger when a climate for inclusion was present (Li, Lin, Tien, & Chen, 2015). The inclusive climate consisted of equitable and inclusive employment practices in decision making, thereby establishing shared norms of including diverse perspectives.

Finally, additional factors complicate the relationships between creativity, prevention focus, promotion focus, and their associated emotions. Generally, a promotion focus and/or approach behaviors are thought to increase creativity, and a prevention focus and/or avoidance heuristics are thought to stifle it (Friedman & Forster, 2000, 2001, 2002, 2005), but even those relationships are dependent on other factors. A prevention focus can enhance creativity when creativity helps to achieve a desired goal (Roskes, De Dreu, & Nijstad, 2012) and when the desired goal is unfulfilled (Baas, De Dreu, & Nijstad, 2011).

In summary, although diverse teams of both types will be more creative, (1) team processes have to be managed and optimized, (2) the particular definitions and measurements of creativity have so far driven what is considered to be "more creative," and (3) moderating and mediating factors further complicate the issue. Additional research is necessary to tease apart the degree to which each of these issues is important for multicultural versus multidisciplinary teams. The next sections deal with two team processes key to team creativity.

Conflict

EFFECTS OF DIVERSITY ON CONFLICT

Generally, both multicultural and multidisciplinary teams are thought to have worse social outcomes than homogenous teams by experiencing more conflict (Figure 8.1; Cronin & Weingart, 2007; Lovelace, Shapiro, & Weingart, 2001; Stahl et al., 2010; Zellmer-Bruhn et al., 2008), less cohesion (Staples & Zhao, 2006; Thomas, Ravlin, & Wallace, 1996), and lower social integration (Stahl et al., 2010). Conflict is often considered to be "perceived incompatibilities or discrepant views among the parties involved" (Jehn & Bendersky, 2003, p. 189). Past research indicates that when properly managed, constructive conflict can enable dissimilar mental models to be harnessed for better decision making (e.g., Kellermanns et al., 2008; Tjosvold, Wong, & Chen, 2014). Gaps in shared mental models may cause more conflict, and such conflict may be more difficult to overcome than simpler conflicts over specific facts or information (Bearman et al., 2010). Gaps in mental models do not *have* to cause conflict, but differences regarding goals are particularly likely to do so (Cronin & Weingart, 2007). In addition, differences in mental models regarding problem construction and solution evaluation may be more likely to generate conflict or disagreement.

TYPES OF CONFLICT AND THE DIVERSITY–CONFLICT LINK

One question is, what type of conflict is most likely to be related to diversity? The main typology of conflict breaks it down into task conflict, or conflict about the work the team is doing; process conflict, or how they go about doing the work (scheduling, delegation, etc.); and relationship conflict, or conflict about interpersonal incompatibility (Jehn, 1995, 1997; Jehn & Bendersky, 2003). Conflict may also have negative affect or be neutral, with affective conflict focusing more on interpersonal issues (Amason, 1996). Compared to teams with members from the same discipline, multidisciplinary teams are more likely to suffer from both task conflict (Lovelace et al., 2001) and relationship conflict (Todorova et al., 2013). Surprisingly, a meta-analysis revealed that cultural (national and ethnic) diversity was positively related to task conflict, but *unrelated* to process and relationship conflict (Stahl et al., 2010). Indeed, recent meta-analyses of demographic faultlines found that faultline strength—when subgroups are divided on multiple categories—is positively related to both task and relationship conflict (Thatcher & Patel, 2011), and that these effects are above and beyond team diversity effects on conflict (Thatcher & Patel, 2012). These meta-analytic findings suggest that cultural diversity alone is not necessarily related to relationship conflict, but when multiple types of diversity are embodied in the same people (particularly race and gender diversity), then relationship conflict is more likely to occur.

Although the task, process, and relationship distinctions have dominated the literature, other dimensions of conflict may have powerful effects on creativity and team performance (Barki & Hartwick, 2004; DeChurch, Mesmer-Magnus, & Doty, 2013) and may also be associated more with diversity. One distinction is between mild and intense conflict. Mild task conflict includes debate and disagreement, whereas intense conflict involves more rigidity in positions (Todorova, Bear, & Weingart, 2013). Indeed, mild task conflict may be positively related to information acquisition, whereas intense task conflict may hinder it (Todorova et al., 2013). The brevity of a conflict (moments versus minutes versus hours) may be related to its intensity (Paletz, Schunn, & Kim, 2011). Conflict management processes (*how* the team disagrees) are also important and have a separate impact from conflict type on the experience and severity of conflict, such that collectivistic conflict processes (e.g., cooperation, reliance on others within the team, collaborative conflict resolution styles) are associated with better outcomes (DeChurch et al., 2013).

Even more insidious are differences in norms surrounding conflict itself. In general, shared mental models regarding conflict in a group facilitate smoother social interactions. That noted, even culturally homogeneous teams manage and experience conflict differently from each other. Different homogeneous teams may have more or less conflict, depending on their prevailing cultural values (e.g., individualistic versus collectivistic values affecting cooperation; Wagner, 1995), conflict management styles (e.g., competing, avoidant, collaborative), and whether it is even appropriate to talk during emotional conflict situations (von Glinow, Shapiro, & Brett, 2004). If the team's shared norm is to avoid conflict, there may be less conflict. Similarly, team values can influence the type of conflict resolution strategies employed. For instance, the mean level of vertical individualism is positively related to avoidant conflict resolution (Boros, Meslec, Curseu, & Emons, 2010). In the case of heterogeneous teams, if the team does not have shared norms about conflict, then *asymmetrical* perceptions of conflict may result. Teams where members perceive and report different levels of conflict from each other are likely to have lower performance and creativity, mediated through social processes, such as communication and cooperation (e.g., Jehn, Rispens, & Thatcher, 2010).

There are several moderators to the diversity–conflict link. Cultural diversity is more likely to be positively related to conflict when task complexity is high (versus low), when a team is collocated (versus distributed across space), and in longer tenure teams (versus ones with shorter tenure; Stahl et al., 2010). This last finding is surprising, given that other research suggested that the negative effects of gender diversity may decrease over time (Harrison et al., 1998). Although not studied, there may be similar moderators for the effects of disciplinary diversity on conflict. In addition, this meta-analysis showed that there were no differences regarding whether the cultural diversity was within or between nations (Stahl et al., 2010). In other words, diversity within cultures between subgroups (e.g., ethnic or subnational diversity) was just as likely to spark task conflict as diversity between national cultural members. Further, as noted previously, stronger faultlines are more likely to result in more conflict, and different types of conflict, above and beyond effects for cultural and demographic diversity (Thatcher & Patel, 2012). This finding is particularly salient for mixed multidisciplinary-multicultural teams.

EFFECTS OF CONFLICT ON CREATIVITY

Another question is about the effects of conflict on creativity in diverse teams (Paletz et al., 2014). In teams that enable open-minded, constructive argumentation and disagreement, unique insights may be shared (Kellermanns et al., 2008; Tjosvold et al., 2014). If the team can share productive communication norms, the conflict generated from diversity can be useful, or at least not destructive. In a study of cross-functional product teams, while there was a significant positive relationship between diversity and task conflict, the relationship between task conflict and innovation was dependent on communication norms: When communication was collaborative, with workers feeling free to express doubts, the relationship between task conflict and innovation was nonsignificant rather than negative (Lovelace, Shapiro, & Weingart, 2001). Indeed, avoiding conflict may stifle unique perspectives (e.g., Nemeth, 1986; Oldham & Cummings, 1996).

Whether conflict can be beneficial for teams generally is both under debate and dependent on many factors. Achieving open-minded disagreement can be difficult. The negative effects of conflict are thought to occur in affective, process, and relationship conflict, compared to cognitive and task conflict (e.g., Amason, 1996; Jehn, 1997; de Wit et al., 2012). Conflict management can minimize relationship conflict: Collaborating conflict management strategies (and to a lesser degree, other strategies such as accommodation) help to minimize relationship conflict, whereas competitive conflict management strategies increase it (DeChurch, Hamilton, & Haas, 2007). Contempt within conflict can be especially poisonous (Gottman & Notarius, 2000). Although some researchers have argued that task conflict can be beneficial, particularly for creativity and innovation (e.g., De Dreu & West, 2001; Jehn, 1997; Jehn & Mannix, 2001; Kurtzberg & Mueller, 2005; Nemeth, 1986; Pelled, Eisenhardt, & Xin, 1999), a famous meta-analysis found that even task conflict was negatively related to team performance (De Dreu & Weingart, 2003; see also Langfred & Moye, 2014). A more recent meta-analysis replicated the stable, negative relationships between process or relationship conflict and performance but also presented *no* significant association between task conflict and team performance (de Wit, Greer, & Jehn, 2012; also, for innovation, see Hulsheger et al., 2009). The latter relationship depends on moderators. If task and relationship conflict were unrelated, task conflict was positively related to performance.

Additional moderators may affect the relationship between conflict and creativity (De Dreu & Nijstad, 2008). For example, conflict, as it occurs in a larger context, can impact creativity (Figure 8.1). Ambient cultural disharmony was found to negatively impact individual creativity on tasks that required combining multicultural knowledge and elements (Chua, 2013). This effect was mediated by beliefs about cultural incompatibility. The greater context of intergroup conflict hurt individual creativity unless the individual herself believed that the different cultures could be compatible.

Summary

In brief, diverse teams are more likely to have conflict than homogeneous teams, although this depends in part on shared norms regarding the expression of conflict and the type of conflict. Multicultural teams are no more likely to have process or relationship conflict than culturally homogeneous teams, although they have more task conflict (Stahl et al., 2010). On the other hand, multidisciplinary teams are more likely to suffer from both task and relationship conflict (Lovelace et al., 2001; Todorova et al., 2013). Faultlines increase conflict above and beyond these diversity effects, suggesting that mixed multidisciplinary-multicultural teams where the cultural and disciplinary identities overlap will experience greater negative effects (e.g., Thatcher & Patel, 2012). This research needs to be further refined by examining different dimensions and types of conflict (e.g., intensity, length of time) and conflict management processes. Conflict, under very particular conditions and when properly managed, may be beneficial for creativity in diverse teams.

Information Sharing, Elaboration, and Participation

Participation and information sharing are essential to success in teams in general (Turner et al., 2014), including diverse teams (Maznevski, 1994). If the main benefit of diverse teams is their variety of background knowledge, then it is necessary for such information to be communicated for new ideas and idea combinations to arise. In addition to requiring shared mental models about both the task and communication norms, effective diverse team communication may require perspective taking, motivation to communicate, and trust (Maznevski, 1994). For a diverse team to have success, not only does information need to be shared in general, but unique information sharing and elaboration are particularly important (Figure 8.1; Hoever et al., 2012; Mesmer-Magnus & DeChurch, 2009). The literature on "hidden profiles" suggests that groups that do not share unique information suffer from poorer decision making, particularly when the information necessary for the task is unshared across the team (e.g., Greitemeyer & Schulz-Hardt, 2003; Greitemeyer, Schulz-Hardt, Brodbeck, & Frey, 2006; Schulz-Hardt, Brodbeck, Mojzisch, Kerscheiter, & Frey, 2006; Stasser & Titus, 1985). When individuals within teams have unique information, discussion within the teams generally enlarges prediscussion preferences rather than correcting for them.

Diverse teams *can* capitalize on their unique information, however (e.g., Hoever et al., 2012; Zellmer-Bruhn et al., 2008). One study found a generally increasing linear relationship between disciplinary diversity and the range and depth of information use (Dahlin et al., 2005). Assigning experts (Stewart & Stasser, 1995) and making sure that experts are identified (Stasser, Stewart, & Wittenbaum, 1995) are important techniques for overcoming the tendency to discuss mostly shared information. More than half of the team may be required to know of each other's' areas of expertise for the team to take advantage of it and facilitate the sharing of unique information (Baumann & Bonner, 2013). Taking others' perspectives within a diverse team is more likely to lead to elaborating those different perspectives and subsequent team creativity, compared to teams that do not take each other's perspectives (Hoever et al., 2012). The distribution of information across heterogeneous teams may also be a factor. Phillips and colleagues (2004) found that groups with an "odd person out"—the person with both social and knowledge minority status—repeatedly discussed task-relevant knowledge in general and unique task-relevant knowledge in particular more often than groups in which the team member with the rare information was socially tied to another group member. This finding suggests a complex relationship between faultlines and opinion/numeric minority status.

Although a meta-analysis showed no overall relationship between cultural diversity and communication effectiveness, there are significant moderators (Stahl et al., 2010). When cultural diversity was measured using deep-level attributes (e.g., personal values, attitudes, and shared history), it was positively associated with communication effectiveness, but when cultural diversity was measured using surface-level attributes (e.g., ethnicity, nationality), the relationship was negative (Stahl et al., 2010). This finding suggests that the nature of the diversity has different effects on communication, aligned with the information processing and social categorization theories. Team size and team tenure were also significant moderators, such that cultural diversity is associated with less effective communication for culturally diverse teams that are either large in size or long in tenure, compared to those that are either small or short in tenure (Stahl et al., 2010). Thus, team managers could emphasize deep-level diversity attributions (e.g., differences in cultural background), use a small team, and have a shorter lasting team (Stahl et al., 2010).

In summary, both multicultural and multidisciplinary teams are likely to have access to a broader range of information than homogenous teams. Information sharing and participation are important to team performance generally (Mesmer-Magnus & DeChurch, 2009), and teams with diverse background knowledge may have difficulty in sharing that information. However, it is entirely possible for such teams to share their unique information, given the right structures, such as having a small team and having more than half the team know of each other's expertise.

Additional Factors for Diversity in Creative Teams

This section will touch on some of the major mediating and moderating factors associated with the relationship between diversity in teams and creativity, conflict, information sharing, and/or performance. In broad strokes, these factors are (1) task factors, (2) team structural factors, (3) social factors (4) team trait factors, (5) team tool use, (6) the greater organizational and national context, and (7) the influence of time passing over all the factors (Figure 8.1).

TASK FACTORS
First, task factors such as complexity, structure, and specificity may be moderators (Erez & Nouri, 2010). Separate meta-analyses found that when task complexity is high rather than low, diverse teams are more likely to result in better performance (van Dijk et al., 2012), as well as experience more task conflict (Stahl et al., 2010). Nouri et al. (2013) found that high task specificity (clear instructions, requirements, and direction) mitigated the negative effects of cultural heterogeneity on convergent performance in dyads. Additional task features may be important, underscoring the importance of testing different types of creativity.

TEAM STRUCTURE
Second, team structural factors may make a difference. Many multinational teams are also virtual, working via email and video conferencing software (Connaughton & Shuffler, 2007; Gibson, Huang, Kirkman, & Shapiro, 2014). Although there are anecdotal reports that communication delays may slow the progress of distributed

multinational, multicultural teams (e.g., Connaughton & Shuffler, 2007), it is possible to use the time delay as a benefit when engaging in interdependent, but serial tasks. For instance, although simultaneous work is difficult, research often involves writing and editing drafts: The time zone differences can enable, as in the case of this chapter, one author to edit a paper while the others are sleeping, and so can minimize the problem of multiple people editing the same draft.

Even within diverse, virtual teams, the team structure can make a difference to team processes and outcomes via emphasizing faultlines. Polzer and colleagues (2006) conducted a study of virtual teams where some teams were fully distributed (an individual in each location), and other teams were composed of two or three subgroups of collocated individuals. They found that fully distributed, nationally heterogeneous groups have more team trust than teams with subgroups of collocated people, and more conflict in teams with two equally sized subgroups than in teams with three subgroups or in teams that were fully distributed (Polzer, Crisp, Jarvenpaa, & Kim, 2006). Participants reported less conflict within their subgroups than with teammates who were distributed, but nationally heterogeneous subgroups reported more conflict than homogeneous subgroups. This research suggests that subgroup processes are highlighted in virtual teams, and that research needs to distinguish between subgroup processes and other processes tied to whether a team is geographically distributed. Indeed, another study found that problems with cohesion and conflict in short-term culturally heterogeneous teams could be improved using virtual rather than face-to-face teams (Staples & Zhao, 2006).

Another structural factor is team size. A longitudinal study of research groups and disciplinary and institutional heterogeneity found that larger groups had more trouble managing diversity (Cummings, Kiesler, Zadeh, & Balakrishnan, 2013). Although the larger groups had more publications and citations, marginal productivity declined as heterogeneity increased.

SOCIAL FACTORS

Third, the social relationships between the individuals in a team should not be ignored. These social factors have been studied as both outcomes and processes (Figure 8.1). Psychological safety and trust are important for effective teamwork in general (Salas et al., 2005) and are likely to be important for diverse teams and their innovation (Connaughton & Shuffler, 2007; Nishii & Goncalo, 2008; Post, 2012). Similarly, collective team identification may moderate the relationship between multidisciplinarity and team performance/team learning (Van der Vegt & Bunderson, 2005), and be directly related to diverse team performance in general (Kearney, Gerbert, & Voelpel, 2009; Swann et al., 2003). The ability for a team to get along and have a higher level identity is not simply a separate issue from task success but may be related to other aspects of teamwork. As noted, perspective taking seems to be a necessary condition for harnessing diversity (Hoever et al., 2012).

TEAM TRAITS

Fourth, like individuals, teams may be characterized as having traits (Figure 8.1). For instance, Kearney, Gerbert, and Voelpel (2009) found that team need for cognition was an important moderator in a study of 83 teams across eight German organizations. When team level need for cognition was high, disciplinary diversity was positively related to the elaboration of task-relevant information, collective team identification, and subsequent team performance (with elaboration of information and collective team identification as mediators). Similarly, team collective intelligence is positively related to participation equality (low variance in the number of speaking turns across team members; Woolley, Chabris, Pentland, Hashmi, & Malone, 2010). It is possible that team need for cognition, or team intelligence, can thereby lead to the development of shared mental models. Other team traits may include team aggregated personality (e.g., team average conscientiousness, team minimum agreeableness; Bell, 2007) or variance in personality traits (e.g., breadth of individual neuroticism). These aggregated individual differences may be mediators or moderators of team diversity, even as they represent a different set of inputs (Figure 8.1).

TECHNOLOGY AND TOOLS
Another set of factors is the types of tools and technology used (Figure 8.1). Multicultural teams are often also distributed across space and time, so the technology they use may influence team processes and outcomes (Gibson et al., 2014). The norms regarding the use of technology and whether the tools support conflict management, communication, and so on may also be important (McGrath, 1998).

GREATER CULTURAL AND ORGANIZATIONAL CONTEXTS
Sixth, the applicable culture and organizational contexts are likely multilayered and multifaceted, further affecting the relationship between diversity and creativity. Importantly, the greater context may impact that team's processes differently depending on the type of diversity it has (e.g., Brodbeck et al., 2011). For instance, a reward structure may favor or disfavor members from different disciplines or cultures, or it may favor individuals over teams in general (or vice versa). Diversity at the occupation level can have a moderating effect, such that ethnic diversity has a stronger negative effect on performance in occupations dominated by Whites (Joshi & Roh, 2009). The culture of the overarching organization may favor members of some groups over others, or there may be multiple organizations with competing interests overlapping with the diverse team. Interteam and intergroup processes may affect intrateam functioning. Alternately, the organization may strive for a global identity (e.g., Erez & Gati, 2004), or the organization can put processes in place that encourage a climate of inclusion (Li et al., 2015).

TEMPORALITY
Seventh, the temporal aspect should be examined in more detail (Figure 8.1; Connaughton & Shuffler, 2007; Langfred & Moye, 2014). Is the relationship between diversity and other factors (e.g., creativity) the same over time? Early research on ethnic diversity suggested that higher initial levels of performance and process by homogeneous (European American) groups compared

to very heterogeneous groups decreased temporally, such that there were no differences in process or overall performance by the end of 17 weeks (Watson, Kumar, & Michaelsen, 1993). One exception was with divergent creativity tasks (measuring range of perspectives and creative alternatives), where heterogeneous groups scored higher at the fourth wave of data collection (Watson et al., 1993). Given that cultural diversity is associated with higher levels of conflict in longer tenure teams versus shorter tenure teams (Stahl et al., 2010), the relationships between diversity and other factors may also change over time.

Just as the relationship between diversity and other factors may change over time, some factors may be important early or later in a team's development (Mathieu, Tannenbaum, Donsbach, & Alliger, 2014; Stahl et al., 2010; Taylor & Greve, 2006). For example, both the mean and the variance of cultural values within a team may be related to team performance, but different cultural values may be important at different times (e.g., uncertainty avoidance may be positively related to performance early in a team's life but not later; Cheng, Chua, Morris, & Lee, 2012). Although the passage of time enables team members to get to know each other better (e.g., Swann et al., 2003), team membership may change (Mathieu et al., 2014). It is possible that different aspects of diversity impact different elements of the group development process (i.e., forming, storming, norming, performing; Shaw & Barrett-Power, 1998).

In short, these seven factors (i.e., task, team structure, social, trait, tool, context, and time) may all impact the relationship between multicultural and/or multidisciplinary diversity and creativity, information sharing, and conflict. And these factors can interact with each other. These seven broad factors, along with diversity, creativity (in its various incarnations), conflict, and information sharing and elaboration are organized according to whether they are inputs, processes, and/or outputs, as well as their levels of analysis (individual, team, etc.; Figure 8.1). Just as inputs influence processes, so too do top-down and bottom-up processes occur, with the potential relationships (arrows) between individual factors too numerous to document cleanly. Still, our framework provides a conceptual organization to an extremely broad field.

GAPS, FUTURE RESEARCH, AND CONCLUSION

The literature reviewed in this chapter is broad, varied, and often innovative. However, gaps still remain.

Gaps and Future Research

Some of the gaps in the literature that are ripe for future research include studying a greater variety of types and operationalizations of the relevant variables; broadening the methodologies used; teasing apart different aspects of context within which the team exists, including leadership; and creating an appropriate, comprehensive theoretical model.

Many of the meta-analyses noted here examine either cultural diversity or disciplinary diversity, but not both. Additional studies can examine what occurs in multidisciplinary and multicultural teams—not just where information falls, as in the faultline literature (e.g., Homan et al., 2007), but explicitly comparing multicultural, multidisciplinary, mixed multicultural/multidisciplinary, and homogeneous teams. For instance, there is research on analogy in multidisciplinary teams, but we are unaware of research on analogy use in multicultural teams. More research is also needed to examine whether cultural and disciplinary diversity affect creativity in an additive or interactive manner. It could be, for example, that on average teams that are both disciplinary and culturally diverse are less creative than culturally homogeneous yet multidisciplinary teams. Although both teams benefit from having diverse knowledge, the latter teams are less likely to suffer from social categorization processes that impede creativity. Additional research can examine and compare preexisting background knowledge better to assess which aspects are truly job relevant or not, and whether this dimension could drive possible differences between multicultural and multidisciplinary teams. This chapter discussed some of the similarities and differences between multicultural and multidisciplinary groups (Table 8.1). These differences can be manipulated and tested for their effects on creativity and team processes. For instance, regardless of whether multicultural teams are within or between country, measures of the depth of shared mental model differences could help illuminate their role in different types of diverse teams simultaneously.

Studying a greater variety of operationalizations of all the main constructs would be useful. Creativity, team processes, and even diversity could all be examined differently. Creativity can be divergent, convergent, or both. Creativity can also entail any number of specific processes, such as fluency, elaboration, creative recombination, analogy, problem finding, and evaluation (Mumford, Reiter-Palmon, & Redmond, 1994; Paletz & Schunn, 2010; Reiter-Palmon et al., 2011). It may be useful to distinguish between subcomponents of creativity as well, such as novelty from usefulness, as well as differentiating between everyday versus expert creativity (Beghetto & Kaufman, 2007; Kaufman & Beghetto, 2009). Just as divergent creativity may benefit more from diversity than convergent creativity (Paletz & Schunn, 2010), so too may novelty be benefitted from diversity more than usefulness.

Although most research on diversity examines differences based on categorization (the variety type of diversity), for some variables, the separation element (differences on a continuum) may be more appropriate. The degree (Earley & Mosakowski, 2000) and the type of heterogeneity may matter (Paletz, Peng, Erez, & Maslach, 2004; Paletz et al., 2014). Although there are differences between sociologists and psychologists, for example, they share assumptions on the utility of survey methodology more than, say, either anthropologists or astrophysicists. The degree of overlap of mental models may require a noncategorical way to examine certain types of diversity. Furthermore, studying different types of heterogeneity (and homogeneity) may prove fruitful. Not all heterogeneous teams have the same team composition, and not all countries have the same dominant ethnic groups. An ethnically diverse team in Malaysia would be composed of different ethnic groups with different histories of status than in the United Kingdom. Diverse teams are also embedded within a greater societal context of demographic numbers, power, and status (Brodbeck et al., 2011; DiTomaso, Post, & Parks-Yancy, 2007; Paletz et al., 2004).

This research could also be benefitted by more methodological breadth. Conflict has been primarily studied in this literature as self-report, global, retrospective assessments, even when studied as a longitudinal process (e.g., Langfred & Moye, 2014), but it could be measured as behavioral micro-processes (e.g., Paletz et al., 2011). Both types of operationalizations can be compared directly. No methodology is without its problems, so a diversity of methods could triangulate phenomena. Indeed, a recent meta-analysis suggests that a negative relationship between performance and demographic diversity may be due in large part to rater biases when assessing performance, as the relationship does not hold when performance is measured more objectively (van Dijk et al., 2012).

Furthermore, the greater context needs to be quantified, recorded, and tested. For instance, Paletz and colleagues (2004) found that even Caucasians enjoyed working in minority-dominated groups more than in homogeneous groups, but this finding may be due to a broader context that valued diversity (Joshi & Roh, 2009). Leadership may be particularly important to multicultural and multidisciplinary teams (Reiter-Palmon et al., 2013; Salas, Burke, Wilson-Donnelly, & Fowlkes, 2004). In teams in Korean companies, transformational leadership interacted with disciplinary heterogeneity such that when inspirational and motivational leadership (i.e., transformational leadership) was high, multidisciplinary teams had higher creativity than homogeneous teams, whereas multidisciplinary teams had relatively lower creativity when transformational leadership was low (Shin & Zhou, 2007). The success of creative teams requires supportive leadership, as well as supportive organizational contexts and systems (e.g., reward systems, resources, the right preconditions; Brophy, 1998). Thus, higher level factors, such as leadership, can be examined in combination with organizational values and other contextual factors in studying diverse teams.

Finally, most research is inspired by the information processing and social categorization literature traditions, but it has moved beyond it to detail specific relationships and important additional specific variables, such as self-verification. The typical ball-and-arrow model is becoming insufficient to represent the complexity and proliferation of relevant variables, and existing models that tease out key factors already overlap (e.g., Paletz & Schunn, 2010; Reiter-Palmon et al., 2011). Taking a broader theoretical perspective may be of use here. Lewin's (1936, 1938, 1997) original field theory has undergirded a great deal of social psychological theorizing. Drawing from metaphors based on physics (i.e., Newtonian physics and electromagnetic field theory), Lewin's theory has provided a valuable way to think about dynamic psychological forces. However, given the multilayered, probabilistic, and ever-changing nature of teamwork, a more complex metaphor may be necessary to drive theory forward. A better metaphor for teamwork research may be the search for a unified field theory, which attempts to combine multiple physics theories into a greater whole, attempting to explain phenomena from the scale of subatomic particles to the scale of far larger systems.

CONCLUSION

To be creative, groups need to have creative potential, effectively share ideas and information, have those ideas and information be relevant to what has been shared, and then effectively converge on high-quality ideas (Nijstad et al., 2006). Each of these steps may be influenced by a variety of factors that are dynamic, have different strengths and directions, and may interact with each other (Lewin, 1948/ 1997). This review, drawing on numerous recent meta-analyses and individual studies, summarized the most recent findings and issues for multicultural and multidisciplinary creative teams. Scholars can appreciate the complexity of diverse creative teams and move the field forward both theoretically and empirically.

REFERENCES

Adams, J. (2013). The fourth age of research. *Nature, 497,* 557–560.

Aggarwal, I., & Woolley, A. W. (2013). Do you see what I see? The effect of members' cognitive styles on team processes and errors in task execution. *Organizational Behavior and Human Decision Processes, 122,* 92–99.

Amabile, T. M. (1983). The social psychology of creativity: A componential conceptualization. *Journal of Personality and Social Psychology, 45,* 357–376.

Amabile, T. M. (1996). *Creativity in context: Update to the social psychology of creativity.* Boulder, CO: WestviewPress.

Amason, A. (1996). Distinguishing the effects of functional and dysfunctional conflict on strategic decision making: Resolving a paradox for top management teams. *Academy of Management Journal, 39,* 123–143.

Ayub, N., & Jehn, K. A. (2010). The moderating influence of nationalism and the relationship between national diversity and conflict. *Negotiation and Conflict Management Research, 3,* 249–275.

Baas, M., De Dreu, C. K. W., & Nijstad, B. A. (2011). When prevention promotes creativity: The role of mood, regulatory focus, and regulatory closure. *Journal of Personality and Social Psychology, 100,* 794–809.

Ball, L. J., & Christensen, B. T. (2009). Analogical reasoning and mental simulation in design: Two strategies linked to uncertainty resolution. *Design Studies, 30*(2), 169–186.

Barki, H., & Hartwick, J. (2004). Conceptualizing the construct of interpersonal conflict. *International Journal of Conflict Management, 15,* 216–244.

Baumann, M. R., & Bonner, B. L. (2013). Member awareness of expertise, information sharing, information weighting, and group decision making. *Small Group Research, 44*, 532–562.

Bearman, C. R., Ball, L. J., & Ormerod, T. C. (2007). The structure and function of spontaneous analogising in domain-based problem solving. *Thinking & Reasoning, 13*(3), 273–294.

Bearman, C. R., Paletz, S. B. F., Orasanu, J., & Thomas, M. J. W. (2010). The breakdown of coordinated decision making in distributed systems. *Human Factors, 52*, 173–188.

Beck, S. J. (2013). Moving beyond disciplinary differences in group research. *Small Group Research, 44*, 195–199.

Beghetto, R. A., & Kaufman, J. C. (2007). Toward a broader conception of creativity: A case for "mini-c" creativity. *Psychology of Aesthetics, Creativity, and the Arts, 1*, 73–79.

Bell, S. T. (2007). Deep-level composition variables as predictors of team performance: A meta-analysis. *Journal of Applied Psychology, 92*, 595–615.

Boroş, S., Meslec, N., Curşeu, P. L., & Emons, W. (2010). Struggles for cooperation: Conflict resolution strategies in multicultural groups. *Journal of Managerial Psychology, 25*(5), 539–554.

Brodbeck, F. C., Guillaume, Y. R. F., & Lee, N. J. (2011). Ethnic diversity as a multilevel construct: The combined effects of dissimilarity, group diversity, and societal status on learning performance in work groups. *Journal of Cross-Cultural Psychology, 42*, 1198–1218.

Brophy, D. R. (1998). Understanding, measuring, and enhancing collective creative problem-solving efforts. *Creativity Research Journal, 11*, 199–229.

Brophy, D. R. (2006). A comparison of individual and group efforts to creatively solve contrasting types of problems. *Creativity Research Journal, 18*(3), 293–315.

Burke, C. S., Stagl, K. C., Salas, E., Peirce, L., & Kendall, D. (2006). Understanding team adaptation: A conceptual analysis and model. *Journal of Applied Psychology, 91*, 1189–1207.

Cady, S. H., & Valentine, J. (1999). Team innovation and perceptions of consideration: What difference does diversity make? *Small Group Research, 30*, 730–750.

Chan, J., Fu, K., Schunn, C. D., Cagan, J., Wood, K., & Kotovsky, K. (2011). On the benefits and pitfalls of analogies for innovative design: Ideation performance based on analogical distance, commonness, and modality of examples. *Journal of Mechanical Design, 133*, 081004.

Chatman, J. A., Polzer, J. T., Barsade, S. G., & Neale, M. A. (1998). Being different yet feeling similar: The influence of demographic composition and organizational culture on work processes and outcomes. *Administrative Science Quarterly, 43*, 749–780.

Chen, C., Lee, S., & Stevenson, H. (1995). Response style and cross-cultural comparisons. *Psychological Science, 6*, 170–175.

Cheng, C.-Y., Chua, R. Y. J., Morris, M. W., & Lee, L. (2012). Finding the right mix: How the composition of self-managing multicultural teams' cultural value orientation influences performance over time. *Journal of Organizational Behavior, 33*(3), 389–411.

Cheng C.-Y., & Leung, A. K.-Y. (2013). Revisiting the multicultural experience-creativity link: The effects of perceived cultural distance and comparison mind-set. *Social Psychological and Personality Science, 4*, 475–482.

Chiu, C.-Y., Kwan, L. Y.-Y., & Liou, S. (2014). Professional and disciplinary cultures. In A. B. Cohen (Ed.), *Culture reexamined: Broadening our understanding of social and evolutionary influences* (pp. 11–30). Washington, DC: American Psychological Association. http://dx.doi.org/10.1037/14274-001

Christensen, B. T., & Schunn, C. D. (2007). The relationship of analogical distance to analogical function and pre-inventive structure: The case of engineering design. *Memory & Cognition, 35*(1), 29–38.

Chua, R. Y. J. (2013). The costs of ambient cultural disharmony: Indirect intercultural conflicts in social environment undermine creativity. *Academy of Management Journal, 56*, 1545–1577.

Connaughton, S. L., & Shuffler, M. (2007). Multinational and multicultural distributed teams: A review and future agenda. *Small Group Research, 38*, 387–412.

Cronin, M. A., & Weingart, L. R. (2007). Representational gaps, information processing, and conflict in functionally diverse teams. *Academy of Management Review, 32*, 761–773.

Cropley, A. (2006). In praise of convergent thinking. *Creativity Research Journal, 18*, 391–404.

Cummings, J. N., Kiesler, S., Zadeh, R. B., & Balakrishnan, A. D. (2013). Group heterogeneity increases the risks of large group size: A longitudinal study of productivity in research groups. *Psychological Science, 24*(6), 880–890.

Dahl, D. W., & Moreau, P. (2002). The influence and value of analogical thinking during new product ideation. *Journal of Marketing Research, 39*, 47–60.

Dahlin, K. B., Weingart, L. R., & Hinds, P. J. (2005). Team diversity and information use. *Academy of Management Journal, 48*, 1107–1123.

De Dreu, C. K. W., & Nijstad., B. A. (2008). Mental set and creative thought in social conflict; Threat rigidity versus motivated focus. *Journal of Personality and Social Psychology, 95*, 648–661.

De Dreu, C. K. W., & Weingart, L. R. (2003). Task versus relationship conflict, team performance, and team member satisfaction: A meta-analysis. *Journal of Applied Psychology, 88*, 741–749.

De Dreu, C. K. W., & West, M. A. (2001). Minority dissent and team innovation: The importance of participation in decision making. *Journal of Applied Psychology, 86*, 1191–1201.

De Wit, F. R. C., Greer, L. L., & Jehn, K. A. (2012). The paradox of intragroup conflict: A meta-analysis. *Journal of Applied Psychology, 97*, 360–390.

DeChurch, L. A., Hamilton, K. L., & Haas, C. (2007). Effects of conflict management strategies on perceptions of intergroup conflict. *Group Dynamics: Theory, Research, and Practice, 11*, 66–78.

DeChurch, L. A., & Mesmer-Magnus, J. R. (2010). The cognitive underpinnings of effective teamwork: A meta-analysis. *Journal of Applied Psychology, 95*, 32–53.

DeChurch, L. A., Mesmer-Magnus, J. R., & Doty, D. (2013). Moving beyond relationship and task conflict: Toward a process-state perspective. *Journal of Applied Psychology, 98*, 559–578.

Derry, S. J., & Schunn, C. D. (2005). Introduction to the study of interdisciplinarity: A beautiful but dangerous beast. In S. J. Derry, C. D. Schunn, & M. A. Gernsbacher (Eds.), *Interdisciplinary collaboration: An emerging cognitive science* (pp. xiii–xx). Mahwah, NJ: Erlbaum.

Derry, S. J., Schunn, C. D., & Gernsbacher, M. A. (Eds.) (2005). *Interdisciplinary collaboration: An emerging cognitive science*. Mahwah, NJ: Erlbaum.

DiTomaso, N., Post, C., & Parks-Yancy, R. (2007). Workforce diversity and ine-quality: Power, status, and numbers. *Annual Review of Sociology, 33*, 473–501.

Dunbar, K. (1995). How scientists really reason: Scientific reasoning in real-world laboratories. In R. J. Sternberg & J. E. Davidson (Eds.), *The nature of insight* (pp. 365–395). Cambridge, MA: The MIT Press.

Dunbar, K. (1997). How scientists think: On-line creativity and conceptual change in science. In T. B. Ward, S. M. Smith, & J. Vaid (Eds.), *Creative thought: An investigation of conceptual structures and processes* (pp. 461–493). Washington, DC: American Psychological Association.

DuRussel, L. A., & Derry, S. (2005). Schema alignment in interdisciplinary teamwork. In S. J. Derry, C. D. Schunn, & M. A. Gernsbacher (Eds.), *Interdisciplinary collaboration: An emerging cognitive science* (pp. 187–219). Mahwah, NJ: Erlbaum.

Earley, P. C., & Mosakowski, E. (2000). Creating hybrid team cultures: An empirical test of transnational team functioning. *Academy of Management Journal, 43*, 26–49.

Edwards, B. D., Day, E. A., Arthur, W., & Bell, S. T. (2006). Relationships among team ability composition, team mental models, and team performance. *Journal of Applied Psychology, 91*, 727–736.

Erez, M., & Gati, E. (2004). A dynamic, multi-level model of culture: From the micro level of the individual to the macro level of a global culture. *Applied Psychology: An International Review, 53*, 583–598.

Erez, M., & Nouri, R. (2010). Creativity: The influence of cultural, social and work contexts. *Management and Organizational Review, 6*(3), 351–370.

Fiske, A. P. (1992). The four elementary forms of sociality: Framework for a unified theory of social relations. *Psychological Review, 99*, 689–723.

Freeman, R. B., & Huang, W. (2014). Collaborating with people like me: Ethnic co-authorship in the US. National Bureau of Economic Research Working Paper 19905. Retrieved from http://www.nber.org/papers/w19905.

Friedman, R. S., & Forster, J. (2000). The effects of approach and avoidance motor actions on the elements of creative insight. *Journal of Personality and Social Psychology, 79*, 477–492.

Friedman, R. S., & Forster, J. (2001). The effects of promotion and prevention cues on creativity. *Journal of Personality and Social Psychology, 81*, 1001–1013.

Friedman, R. S., & Forster, J. (2002). The influence of approach and avoidance motor actions on creative cognition. *Journal of Experimental Social Psychology, 38*, 41–55.

Friedman, R. S., & Forster, J. (2005). Effects of motivational cues on perceptual asymmetry: Implications for creativity and analytical problem solving. *Journal of Personality and Social Psychology, 88*, 263–275.

Gelfand, M. J., Raver, J. L., Nishii, L., Leslie, L. M., Lun, J., Lim, B. C., . . . Yamaguchi, S. (2011). Differences between tight and loose cultures: A 33-nation study. *Science, 332*, 1100–1104.

Gentner, D. (1983). Structure-mapping: A theoretical framework for analogy. *Cognitive Science, 7*, 155–170.

Gerson, E. M. (1983). Scientific work and social worlds. *Knowledge, 4*, 357–377.

Gibson, C. B., Huang, L., Kirkman, B. L., & Shapiro, D. L. (2014). Where global and virtual meet: The value of examining the intersection of these elements in twenty-first-century teams. *Annual Review of Organizational Psychology and Organizational Behavior, 1*, 217–244.

Gilson, L. L., Mathieu, J. E., Shalley, C. E., & Ruddy, T. M. (2005). Creativity and standardization: Complementary or conflicting drivers of team effectiveness? *Academy of Management Journal*, 48(3), 521–531.

Gino, F., Argote, L., Miron-Spektor, E., & Todorova G. (2010). First get your feet wet: When and why prior experience fosters team creativity. *Organizational Behavior and Human Decision Processes*, 111(2), 93–101.

Goncalo, J. A., & Staw, B.A. (2006). Individualism-collectivism and group creativity. *Organization Behavior and Human Decision Processes*, 100, 96–109.

Gottman, J. M., & Notarius, C. I. (2000). Decade review: Observing marital interaction. *Journal of Marriage and the Family*, 62, 927–947.

Greitemeyer, T., & Schulz-Hardt, S. (2003). Preference-consistent evaluation of information in the hidden profile paradigm: Beyond group-level explanations for the dominance of shared information in group decisions. *Journal of Personality and Social Psychology*, 84, 322–339.

Greitemeyer, T., Schulz-Hardt, S., Brodbeck, F. C., & Frey, D. (2006). Information sampling and group decision making: The effects of an advocacy decision procedure and task experience. *Journal of Experimental Psychology: Applied*, 12, 31–42.

Guzzo, R. A., & Dickson, M. W. (1996). Teams in organizations: Recent research on performance and effectiveness. *Annual Review of Psychology*, 47, 307–338.

Haas, H. (2010). How can we explain mixed effects of diversity on team performance? A review with emphasis on context. *Equality, Diversity, and Inclusion*, 29, 458–490.

Hackman, J. R. (2011). *Collaborative intelligence: Using teams to solve hard problems: Lessons learned from and for intelligence professionals*. San Francisco, CA: Berrett-Koehler.

Hackman, J. R. (2012). From causes to conditions in group research. *Journal of Organizational Behavior*, 3, 428–444.

Harrison, D. A., & Klein, K. J. (2007). What's the difference? Diversity constructs as separation, variety, or disparity in organizations. *Academy of Management Review*, 32, 1199–1228.

Harrison, D. A., Price, K. H., & Bell, M. P. (1998). Beyond relational demography: Time and the effects of surface- and deep-level diversity on work group cohesion. *Academy of Management Journal*, 41, 96–107.

Harvey, S., & Kou, C.-Y. (2013). Collective engagement in creative tasks: The role of evaluation in the creative process in groups. *Administrative Science Quarterly*, 58, 346–386.

Haslam, S. A. (2001). *Psychology in organizations: The social identity approach*. London, England: Sage.

Hoever, I. J., van Knippenberg, D., van Ginkel, W. P., & Barkema, H. G. (2012). Fostering team creativity: Perspective taking as key to unlocking diversity's potential. *Journal of Applied Psychology*, 97, 982–996.

Hofstede, G. (2001). *Culture's consequences: Comparing values, behaviors, institutions, and organizations across nations*. Thousand Oaks, CA: Sage.

Hogg, M. A. (1992). *The social psychology of group cohesiveness: From attraction to social identity*. London, England: Harvester Wheatsleaf.

Homan, A. C., van Knippenberg, D., van Kleef, G. A., & De Dreu, C. K. W. (2007). Interacting dimensions of diversity: Cross-categorization and the functioning of diverse work groups. *Group Dynamics: Theory, Research, and Practice*, 11, 79–94.

Hong, Y.-Y., Benet-Martinez, V., Chiu, C.-Y., & Morris, M. (2003). Boundaries of cultural influence: Construct activation as a mechanism for cultural differences in social perception. *Journal of Cross-Cultural Psychology, 34,* 453–464.

Hong, Y.-Y., Morris, M. W., Chiu, C.-Y., & Benet-Martinez, V. (2000). Multicultural minds: A dynamic constructivist approach to culture and cognition. *American Psychologist, 55,* 709–720.

Horwitz, S. K., & Horwitz, I. B. (2007). The effects of team diversity on team outcomes: A meta-analytic review of team demography. *Journal of Management, 33,* 987–1015.

Hulsheger, U. R., Anderson, N., & Salgado, J. F. (2009). Team-level predictors of innovation at work: A comprehensive meta-analysis spanning three decades of research. *Journal of Applied Psychology, 94,* 1128–1145.

Ilgen, D., R., Hollenbeck, J. R., Johnson, M., & Jundt, D. (2005). Teams in organizations: From input-process-output models to IMOI models. *Annual Review of Psychology, 56,* 517–543.

Jackson, S. E., & Ruderman, M. N. (Eds.) (1996). *Diversity in work teams: Research paradigms for a changing workplace.* Washington, DC: American Psychological Association.

Jehn, K. A. (1995). A mulitmethod examination of the benefits and detriments of intragroup conflict. *Administrative Science Quarterly, 40,* 256–282.

Jehn, K. A. (1997). A qualitative analysis of conflict types and dimensions in organizational groups. *Administrative Science Quarterly, 42,* 530–557.

Jehn, K. A., & Bendersky, C. (2003). Intragroup conflict in organizations: A contingency perspective on the conflict-outcome relationship. *Research in Organizational Behavior, 25,* 187–242.

Jehn, K. A., & Mannix, E. A. (2001). The dynamic nature of conflict: A longitudinal study of intragroup conflict and group performance. *Academy of Management Journal, 44,* 238–251.

Jehn, K. A., Northcraft, G. B., & Neale, M. A. (1999). Why differences make a difference: A field study of diversity, conflict, and performance in workgroups. *Administrative Science Quarterly, 44,* 741–763.

Jehn, K. A., Rispens, S., & Thatcher, S. M. B. (2010). The effects of conflict asymmetry on work group and individual outcomes. *Academy of Management Journal, 53,* 596–616.

John-Steiner, V. (2000). *Creative collaboration.* Oxford, UK: Oxford University Press.

Johnson-Laird, P. N. (1980). Mental models in cognitive science. *Cognitive Science, 4,* 71–115.

Johnson, T., Kulesa, P., Cho, Y. K., & Shavitt, S. (2005). The relation between culture and response styles: Evidence from 19 countries. *Journal of Cross-Cultural Psychology, 36,* 264–277.

Joshi, A., Liao, H., & Roh, H. (2011). Bridging domains in workplace demography research: A review and reconceptualization. *Journal of Management, 37,* 531–552.

Joshi, A., & Roh, H. (2009). The role of context in work team diversity research: A meta-analytic review. *Academy of Management Journal, 52,* 599–627.

Kaufman, J. C., & Beghetto, R. A. (2009). Beyond big and little: The four C model of creativity. *Review of General Psychology, 13,* 1–12.

Kearney, E., Gebert, D., & Voelpel, S. C. (2009). When and how diversity benefits teams: The importance of team members' need for cognition. *Academy of Management Journal, 52,* 581–598.

Kellermanns, F. W., Floyd, S. W., Pearson, A. W., & Spencer, B. (2008). The contingent effect of constructive confrontation on the relationship between shared mental models and decision quality. *Journal of Organizational Behavior, 29,* 119–137.

Kidwell, B., & Langholtz, H. J. (1998). Personnel selection, preparation, and training for U. N. peacekeeping missions. In H. J. Langholtz (Ed.), *The psychology of peacekeeping* (pp. 89–100). Westport, CT: Praeger.

Kim, Y.-H., & Cohen, D. (2010). Information, perspective, and judgments about the self in face and dignity cultures. *Personality and Social Psychology Bulletin, 36*(4), 537–550.

Klimoski, R., & Mohammed, S. (1994). Team mental model: Construct or metaphor? *Journal of Management, 20,* 403–437.

Kozlowski, S. W. J., & Ilgen, D. R. (2006). Enhancing the effectiveness of work groups and teams. *Psychological Science in the Public Interest, 7,* 77–124.

Kroeber, A. L., & Kluckhohn, C. (1952). *Culture: A critical review of concepts and definitions.* New York, NY: Random House.

Kurtzberg, T. R., & Mueller, J. S. (2005). The influence of daily conflict on perceptions of creativity: A longitudinal study. *International Journal of Conflict Management, 16,* 335–353.

Langfred, C. W., & Moye, N. (2014). Does conflict help or hinder creativity in teams? An examination of conflict's effects on creative processes and creative outcomes. *International Journal of Business and Management, 9,* 30–42.

Lau, D. C., & Murnighan, J. K. (1998). Demographic diversity and faultlines: The compositional dynamics of organizational groups. *Academy of Management Review, 23,* 325–340.

Leung, A. K.-Y., Lee, S-L., & Chiu, C.-Y. (2013). Meta-knowledge of culture promotes cultural competence. *Journal of Cross-Cultural Psychology, 44*(6), 992–1006.

Lewin, K. (1936). *Principles of topological psychology.* New York, NY: McGraw-Hill.

Lewin, K. (1938). *The conceptual representation and the measurement of psychological forces.* Durham, NC: Duke University Press.

Lewin, K. (1997). *Resolving social conflicts and field theory in social science.* Washington, DC: American Psychological Association. (Original work published 1948).

Li, C.-R., Lin, C.-J., Tien, Y.-H., & Chen, C.-M. (2015). A multilevel model of team cultural diversity and creativity: The role of climate for inclusion. *Journal of Creative Behavior,* doi: 10.1002/jocb.93

Lovelace, K., Shapiro, D. L., & Weingart, L. R. (2001). Maximizing cross-functional new product teams' innovativeness and constraint adherence: A conflict communications perspective. *Academy of Management Journal, 44,* 779–793.

Mannix, E., & Neale, M. A. (2005). What differences make a difference? The promise and reality of diverse teams in organizations. *Psychological Science in the Public Interest, 6,* 2.

Markus, H., & Kitayama, S. (1991). Culture and the self: Implications for cognition, emotion, and motivation. *Psychological Review, 98,* 224–253.

Mathieu, J. E., Heffner, T. S., Goodwin, G. F., Salas, E., & Cannon-Bowers, J. A. (2000). The influence of shared mental models on team process and performance. *Journal of Applied Psychology, 85,* 273–283.

Mathieu, J. E., Tannenbaum, S. I., Donsbach, J. S., & Alliger, G. M. (2014). A review and integration of team composition models: Moving toward a dynamic and temporal framework. *Journal of Management, 40,* 130–160.

Mayer, R. E. (1999). Fifty years of creativity research. In R. J. Sternberg (Ed.), *Handbook of creativity* (pp. 449–460). Cambridge, UK: Cambridge University Press.

Maznevski, M. L. (1994). Understanding our differences; Performance in decision-making groups with diverse members. *Human Relations, 47*, 531–552.

McGrath, J. E. (1998). A view of group composition through a group-theoretic lens. In D. H. Gruenfeld, (Ed.), *Research on managing groups and teams* (Vol. 1, pp. 255–272). Stamford, CT: JAI Press.

McLeod, P. L., Lobel, S. A., & Cox, T. H. (1996). Ethnic diversity and creativity in small groups. *Small Group Research, 27*, 248–264.

Mesmer-Magnus, J. R., & DeChurch, L. A. (2009). Information sharing and team performance: A meta-analysis. *Journal of Applied Psychology, 94*, 535–546.

Meyer, B., Glenz, A., Antino, M., Rico, R., & González-Romá, V. (2014). Faultlines and subgroups: A meta-review and measurement guide. *Small Group Research, 45*, 633–670.

Miron-Spektor, E. Erez, M., & Naveh, E. (2011). The effect of conformists and attentive-to-detail members on team innovation: Reconciling the innovation paradox. *Academy of Management Journal, 54*(4), 740–760.

Mohammed, S., & Angell, L. C. (2004). Surface-and deep-level diversity in workgroups: Examining the moderating effects of team orientation and team process on relationship conflict. *Journal of Organizational Behavior, 25*, 1015–1039.

Mohammed, S., & Dumville, B. C. (2001). Team mental models in a team knowledge framework: Expanding theory and measurement across disciplinary boundaries. *Journal of Organizational Behavior, 22*(2), 89–106.

Mohammed, S., Ferzandi, L., & Hamilton, K. (2010). Metaphor no more: A 15-year review of the team mental model construct. *Journal of Management, 36*, 876–910.

Morling, B., & Lamoreaux, M. (2008). Measuring culture outside the head: A meta-analysis of individualism collectivism in cultural products. *Personality and Social Psychology Review, 12*, 199–221.

Mullen, B., Johnson, C., & Salas, E. (1991). Productivity loss in brainstorming groups: A meta-analytic integration. *Basic and Applied Social Psychology, 12*(1), 3–23.

Mumford, M. D., Reiter-Palmon, R., & Redmond, M. R. (1994). Problem construction and cognition: Applying problem representations in ill-defined domains. In M. A. Runco (Ed.), *Problem finding, problem solving, and creativity* (pp. 3–39). Norwood, NJ: Ablex.

Nemeth, C. J. (1986). Differential contributions of majority and minority influence. *Psychological Review, 93*, 23–32.

Nijstad, B. A., & Stroebe, W. (2006). How the group affects the mind: A cognitive model of idea generation in groups. *Personality and Social Psychology Review, 10*, 186–213.

Nijstad, B. A., Rietzschel, E. F., & Stroebe, W. (2006). Four principles of group creativity. In L. Thompson, & H. S. Choi (Eds.), *Creativity and innovation in organizational teams* (pp. 161–179). Mahwah, NJ: Lawrence Erlbaum.

Nishii, L. H., & Goncalo, J. A. (2008). Demographic faultlines and creativity in diverse groups. *Research on Managing Groups and Teams, 11*, 1–26.

Nokes-Malach, T. J., Meade, M. L., & Morrow, D. G. (2012). The effect of expertise on collaborative problem solving. *Thinking & Reasoning, 18*(1), 32–58.

Nouri, R., Erez, M., Rockstuhl, T., Ang, S., Leshem-Calif, L., & Rafaeli, A. (2013). Taking the bite out of culture: The impact of task structure and task type on overcoming impediments to cross-cultural team performance. *Journal of Organizational Behavior,* *34*(6), 739–763.

Oldham, G. R., & Cummings, A. (1996). Employee creativity: Personal and contextual factors at work. *Academy of Management Journal, 39*(3), 607–634.

O'Reilly, C. A., Williams, K. Y., & Barsade, S. (1998). Group demography and innovation: Does diversity help? In D. H. Gruenfeld (Ed.), *Research on managing groups and teams* (Vol., 1, pp. 183–207). Stamford, CT: JAI Press.

Oyserman, D. (2011). Culture as situated cognition: Cultural mindsets, cultural fluency, and meaning making. *European Review of Social Psychology, 22,* 164–214.

Paletz, S. B. F. (2014, April). *Multidisciplinary teamwork and big data.* Paper presented at the Human Centered Big Data Research Workshop, Laboratory for Analytic Sciences and NC State University, Raleigh, NC.

Paletz, S. B. F., Miron-Spektor, E., & Lin, C.-C. (2014). A cultural lens on interpersonal conflict and creativity in multicultural environments. *Psychology of Aesthetics, Creativity, and the Arts, 8*(2), 237–252.

Paletz, S. B. F., Peng, K., Erez, M., & Maslach, C. (2004). Ethnic composition and its differential impact on group processes in diverse teams. *Small Group Research, 35,* 128–157.

Paletz, S. B. F., & Schunn, C. D. (2010). A social-cognitive framework of multidisciplinary team innovation. *Topics in Cognitive Science, 2*(1), 73–95.

Paletz, S. B. F., Schunn, C. D., & Kim, K. (2011). Intragroup conflict under the microscope: Micro-conflicts in naturalistic team discussions. *Negotiation and Conflict Management Research, 4,* 314–351.

Paletz, S. B. F., Schunn, C. D., & Kim, K. H. (2013). The interplay of conflict and analogy in multidisciplinary teams. *Cognition, 126*(1), 1–19.

Paulus, P. B., & Nijstad, B. A. (2003). *Group creativity: Innovation through collaboration.* Oxford, UK: Oxford University Press.

Pelled, L. H., Eisenhardt, K. M., & Xin, K. R. (1999). Exploring the black box: An analysis of work group diversity, conflict, and performance. *Administrative Science Quarterly, 44,* 1–28.

Peng, K., Ames, D., & Knowles, E. (2001). Culture and human inference: Perspectives from three traditions. In D. Masumoto (Ed). *Handbook of culture and psychology* (pp. 243–263). New York, NY: Oxford University Press.

Phillips, K. W., Mannix, E. A., Neale, M. A., & Gruenfeld, D. H. (2004). Diverse groups and information sharing: The effects of congruent ties. *Journal of Experimental Social Psychology, 40,* 497–510.

Polzer, J. T., Crisp, C. B., Jarvenpaa, S. L., & Kim, J. W. (2006). Extending the faultline model to geographically dispersed teams: How colocated subgroups can impair group functioning. *Academy of Management Journal, 49*(4), 679–692.

Polzer, J. T., Milton, L. P., & Swann, W. B. (2002). Capitalizing on diversity; Interpersonal congruence in small work groups. *Administrative Science Quarterly, 47,* 296–324.

Post, C. (2012). Deep-level team composition and innovation: The mediating roles of psychological safety and cooperative learning. *Group & Organization Management, 37,* 555–588.

Postmes, T., Haslam, S. A., & Swaab, R. I. (2005). Social influence in small groups: An interactive model of social identity formation. *European Review of Social Psychology, 16,* 1–42.

Randel, A., Jaussi, K. S., & Wu, A. (2011). Does being creative lead to being rated as creative? The moderating role of perceived probability of successfully bringing ideas to a supervisor's attention. *Creativity Research Journal, 23,* 1–8.

Ratcheva, V. (2009). Integrating diverse knowledge through boundary spanning processes—The case of multidisciplinary project teams. *International Journal of Project Management, 27,* 206–215.

Reiter-Palmon, R., de Vreede, T., & de Vreede, G. J. (2013). Leading creative interdisciplinary teams: Challenges and solutions. In S. Hemlin, C. M. Allwood, B. Martin, and M. D. Mumford (Eds.), *Creativity and leadership in science, technology and innovation* (pp. 240–267). New York, NY: Routledge.

Reiter-Palmon, R., Wigert, B., & de Vreede, T. (2011). Team creativity and innovation: The effect of team composition, social processes and cognition. In D. M. Michael (Ed.), *Handbook of organizational creativity* (pp. 295–326). San Diego, CA: Academic Press.

Rentsch, J. R., & Hall, R. J. (1994). Members of great teams think alike: A model of team effectiveness and schema similarity among team members. *Advances in Interdisciplinary Studies of Work Teams, 1,* 223–261.

Rohner, R. P. (1984). Toward a conception of culture for cross-cultural psychology. *Journal of Cross-Cultural Psychology, 15,* 111–138.

Roskes, M., De Dreu, C., K. W., Nijstad, B. A. (2012). Necessity is the mother of invention: Avoidance motivation stimulates creativity through cognitive effort. *Journal of Personality and Social Psychology, 103,* 242–256.

Salas, E., Burke, C. S., Wilson-Donnelly, K. A., & Fowlkes, J. E. (2004). Promoting effective leadership within multicultural teams: An event-based approach. In D. V. Day, S. J. Zaccaro, & S. M. Halpin (Eds.), *Leaders development for transforming organizations: Growing leaders for tomorrow* (pp. 293–323). Mahwah, NJ: Lawrence Erlbaum.

Salas, E., Sims, D. E., & Burke, C. S. (2005). Is there a "big five" in teamwork? *Small Group Research, 36,* 555–599.

Salas, E., Stagl, K. C., & Burke, C. S. (2004). 25 years of team effectiveness in organizations: Research themes and emerging needs. In C. L. Cooper & E. T. Robertson (Eds.), *International review of industrial and organizational psychology* (Vol. 19, pp. 47–91). Chichester, England: John Wiley & Sons.

Salazar, M., & Salas, E. (2013). Reflections of cross-cultural collaboration science. *Journal of Organizational Behavior, 34,* 910–917.

Schulz-Hardt, S., Brodbeck, F. C., Mojzisch, A., Kerschreiter, R., & Frey, D. (2006). Group decision making in hidden profile situations: Dissent as a facilitator for decision quality. *Journal of Personality and Social Psychology, 91,* 1080–1093.

Schunn, C. D., Crowley, K., & Okada, T. (1998). The growth of multidisciplinarity in the cognitive science society. *Cognitive Science, 22,* 107–130.

Schwartz, S. H., Melech, G., Lehmann, A., Burgess, S., Harris, M., & Owens, V. (2001). Extending the cross-cultural validity of the theory of basic human values with a different method of measurement. *Journal of Cross-Cultural Psychology, 32,* 519–542.

Shaw, J. B., & Barrett-Power, E. (1998). The effects of diversity on small work group processes and performance. *Human Relations, 51,* 1307–1325.

Shemla, M., Meyer, B., Greer, L., & Jehn, K. A. (2014). A review of perceived diversity in teams: Does how members perceive their team's composition affect team processes and outcomes? *Journal of Organizational Behavior,* doi: 10.1002/job.1957.

Shin, S. J., & Zhou, J. (2007). When is educational specialization heterogeneity related to creativity in research and development teams? *Journal of Applied Psychology, 92,* 1709–1721.

Sieck, W. R., Smith, J. L., & Rasmussen, L. J. (2013). Metacognitive strategies for making sense of cross-cultural encounters. *Journal of Cross-Cultural Psychology, 44*(6), 1007–1023.

Smith, P. B., Bond, M. H., & Kagitcibasi, C. (2006). *Understanding social psychology across cultures: Living and working in a changing world.* London, UK: Sage.

Stahl, G. K., Maznevski, M. L., Voigt, A., & Jonsen, K. (2010). Unraveling the effects of cultural diversity in teams: A meta-analysis of research on multicultural work groups. *Journal of International Business Studies, 41,* 690–709.

Staples, D. S., & Zhao, L. (2006). The effects of cultural diversity in teams versus face-to-face teams. *Group Decisions and Negotiation, 15,* 389–406.

Stasser, G., Stewart, D. D., & Wittenbaum, G. M. (1995). Expert roles and information exchange during discussion: The importance of knowing who knows what. *Journal of Experimental Social Psychology, 31,* 244–265.

Stasser, G., & Titus, W. (1985). Pooling of unshared information in group decision making: Biased information sampling during group discussion. *Journal of Personality and Social Psychology, 48,* 1467–1478.

Stewart, D. D., & Stasser, G. (1995). Expert role assignment and information sampling during collective recall and decision making. *Journal of Personality and Social Psychology, 69,* 619–628.

Stroebe, W., Nijstad, B. A., & Rietzschel, E. F. (2010). Beyond productivity loss in brainstorming groups: The evolution of a question. *Advances in Experimental Social Psychology, 43,* 157–203.

Swann, W. B., Kwan, V. S. Y., Polzer, J. T., & Milton, L. P. (2003). Fostering group identification and creativity in diverse groups: The role of individuation and self-verification. *Personality and Social Psychology Bulletin, 29,* 1396–1406.

Swann, W. B., Polzer, J. T., Seyle, D. C., & Ko, S. J. (2004). Finding value in diversity: Verification of personal and social self-views in diverse groups. *Academy of Management Review, 29,* 9–27.

Taggar, S. (2002). Individual creativity and group ability to utilize individual creative resources: A multilevel model. *Academy of Management Journal, 45*(2), 315–330.

Taylor, A., & Greve, H. R. (2006). Superman or the Fantastic Four? Knowledge combination and experience in innovative teams. *Academy of Management Journal, 49*(4), 723–740.

Thatcher, S. M. B., & Patel, P. C. (2011). Demographic faultlines: A meta-analysis of the literature. *Journal of Applied Psychology, 96,* 1119–1139.

Thatcher, S. M. B., & Patel, P. C. (2012). Group faultlines: A review, integration, and guide to future research. *Journal of Management, 38,* 969–1009.

Thomas, D. C. (1999). Cultural diversity and work group effectiveness: An experimental study. *Journal of Cross-Cultural Psychology, 30*(2), 242–263.

Thomas, D. C., Ravlin, E. C., & Wallace, A. W. (1996). Effect of cultural diversity in work groups. *Research in the Sociology of Organizations, 14,* 1–33.

Thompson, L., & Choi, H. S. (Eds.) (2006). *Creativity and innovation in organizational teams.* Mahwah, NJ: Lawrence Erlbaum.

Timmerman, T. (2000). Racial diversity, age diversity, interdependence, and team performance. *Small Group Research, 31*, 592–606.

Tjosvold, D., Wong, A. S. H., & Chen, N. Y. F. (2014). Constructively managing conflicts in organizations. *Annual Review of Organizational Psychology and Organizational Behavior, 1*, 545–568.

Todorova, G., Bear, J. B., & Weingart, L. R. (2013, December 2). Can conflict be energizing? A study of task conflict, positive emotions, and job satisfaction. *Journal of Applied Psychology*, doi: 10.1037/a0035134

Torrance, E. P. (1988). The nature of creativity as manifest in its testing. In R. J. Sternberg (Ed.), *The nature of creativity: Contemporary psychological perspectives* (pp. 43–75). Cambridge: Cambridge University Press.

Triandis, H. C. (1989). The self and social behavior in differing cultural contexts. *Psychological Review, 96*, 506–520.

Tuckman, B. W., & Jensen, M. A. C. (1977). Stages of small-group development revisited. *Group Organization Management, 2*, 419–427.

Turner, J. C., Oakes, P. J., Haslam, S. A., & McGarty, C. (1994). Self and collective: Cognition and social context. Special issue: The self and the collective. *Personality & Social Psychology Bulletin, 20*, 454–463.

Turner, J. R., Chen, Q., & Danks, S. (2014). Team shared cognitive constructs: A meta-analysis exploring the effects of shared cognitive constructs on team performance. *Performance Improvement Quarterly, 27*, 83–117.

Van der Vegt, G. S., & Bunderson, J. S. (2005). Learning and performance in multidisciplinary teams: The importance of collective team identification. *Academy of Management Journal, 48*(3), 532–547.

Van der Vegt, G. S., & Janssen, O. (2003). Joint impact of interdependence and group diversity on innovation. *Journal of Management, 29*(5), 729–751.

van Dijk, H., van Engen, M. L., & van Knippenberg, D. (2012). Defying conventional wisdom: A meta-analytic examination of the difference between demographic and job-related diversity relationships with performance. *Organizational Behavior and Human Decision Processes, 119*, 38–53.

van Knippenberg, D., De Dreu, C. K. W., & Homan, A. C. (2004). Work group diversity and group performance: An integrative model and research agenda. *Journal of Applied Psychology, 89*, 1008–1022.

van Knippenberg, D., & Schippers, M. (2007). Work group diversity. *Annual Review of Psychology, 58*, 515–541.

Von Glinow, M. A., Shapiro, D. L., & Brett, J. M. (2004). Can we talk, and should we? Managing emotional conflict in multicultural teams. *Academy of Management Review, 29*, 578–592.

Wagner, C. S., Roessner, J. D., Bobb, K., Klein, J. T., Boyack, K. W., Keyton, J., Rafols, I., & Borner, K. (2011). Approaches to understanding and measuring interdisciplinary scientific research (IDR): A review of the literature. *Journal of Informetrics, 165*, 14–26.

Wagner, J. A. (1995). Studies of individualism-collectivism: Effects on cooperation in groups. *Academy of Management Journal, 38*(1), 152–172.

Watson, W. E., Kumar, K., & Michaelsen, L. K. (1993). Cultural diversity's impact on interaction process and performance: Comparing homogeneous and diverse task groups. *Academy of Management Journal, 36*, 590–602.

Webber, S. S., & Donahue, L. M. (2001). Impact of highly and less job-related diversity on work group cohesion and performance: A meta-analysis. *Journal of Management, 27*, 141–162.

Weingart, L. R., Todorova, G., & Cronin, M. A. (2010). Task conflict, problem-solving, and yielding: Effects on cognition and performance in functionally diverse innovative teams. *Negotiation and Conflict Management Research, 3*, 312–337.

West, M. A., & Farr, J. L. (1990). Innovation at work. In M. A. West & J. L. Farr (Eds.), *Innovation and creativity at work: Psychological and organizational strategies* (pp. 3–13). Chichester, UK: John Wiley & Sons.

Williams, K. Y., & O'Reilly, C. A. (1998). Demography and diversity in organizations: A review of 40 years of research. In B. Staw & R. Sutton (Eds.), *Research in organizational behavior, Vol. 20* (pp. 77–140). Greenwich, CT: JAI Press.

Woolley, A. W., Chabris, C. F., Pentland, A., Hashmi, N., & Malone, T. W. (2010). Evidence for a collective intelligence factor in the performance of human groups. *Science, 330*, 686–688.

Wuchty, S., Jones, B. F., & Uzzi, B. (2007). The increasing dominance of teams in production of knowledge. *Science, 316*(5827), 1036–1039.

Zellmer-Bruhn, M. E., Maloney, M. M., Bhappu, A. D., & Salvador, R. B. (2008). When and how do differences matter? An exploration of perceived similarity in teams. *Organizational Behavior and Human Decision Processes, 107*, 41–59.

9

Intercultural Relationships and Creativity

Current Research and Future Directions

FON WIRUCHNIPAWAN AND ROY Y. J. CHUA ■

Globalization, the economic interdependence among countries stemming from cross-national flows of products and resources, spurs individuals, teams, and organizations to operate in multicultural contexts (Chua, 2014; Tsui, Nifadkar, & Ou, 2007). Competing on a global scale, businesses capitalize on global resources to innovate so as to stay competitive (Brimm, 2010). Firms export not only goods and services but also intermediate work and best practices across the globe. Physical distance and time differences are no longer insurmountable barriers to collaboration, thanks to advancements in communication technology. Modern-day employees are therefore increasingly embedded in a culturally diverse social environment if not themselves part of a multicultural work team.

Globalization prompts intercultural relationships across levels of interaction, meanwhile altering the dynamics of creative endeavors. There are multiple ways in which individuals can be exposed to cultural diversity that could impact creativity. This chapter focuses on a specific form of cultural exposure—intercultural relationships in a culturally diverse social environment—and its effects on creativity. Other forms of cultural exposure may include multicultural experiences stemming from biculturalism (e.g., Cheng, Sanchez-Burks, & Lee, 2008), living abroad (e.g., Maddux & Galinsky, 2009), or exposure to multicultural priming (e.g., Leung & Chiu, 2010). These topics are covered in other chapters in this handbook.

Creativity, the production of novel and useful ideas (Amabile, 1983), predicates all innovations, because the invention of new practices, products, or services requires first and foremost the development of creative ideas (Amabile, Conti, Coon, Lazenby, & Herron, 1996). Creative thinking at the individual level is thus a sine qua non for any form of organizational innovation. How do creative ideas arise? Recent research on the antecedents of creativity posits that creative ideas arise from a recombination of existing ideas (Baughman & Mumford, 1995; Chua & Iyengar, 2008; Guilford, 1950; Rietzschel, Nijstad, & Stroebe, 2007) and/or exposure to unfamiliar environmental stimuli that stimulate new thinking (Leung & Chiu, 2010; Sternberg, 1985; Ward, Smith, & Finke, 1999). The widely studied creative cognition perspective suggests that creative ideas arise from the generative (acquiring, assessing, and combining ideas) and exploratory (mining ideas for novel combinations and testing their viability) creative processes (Finke, Ward, & Smith, 1992; Ward, 2001). These two processes might operate cyclically and simultaneously. Individuals acquire ideas from experiences and exposures to environmental stimuli, combine the acquired ideas, and fine-tune the combined ideas to arrive at creative solutions.

Having access to global ideas and resources enhances the creative processes and, hence, innovation. Specifically, a heightened magnitude and variety of ideas and resources derived from diverse cultural knowledge serve as useful raw ingredients for creative endeavors (Chua, 2013). Culture has been defined in different ways— "as the collective programming of the mind (Hofstede, 1991); as a shared meaning system (Shweder & LeVine, 1984); as patterned ways of thinking (Kluckhohn, 1954); and as unstated standard operating procedures or ways of doing things (Triandis, 1994)" (Gelfand, Erez, & Aycan, 2007, p. 481). Regardless of the precise definition, culture has largely been emphasized as a distinguisher between one group of people from the other (Hofstede, Hofstede, & Minkov, 2010), the kind that is shared, adaptive, and transmittable across time and generations (Triandis, 1994). Indeed, cultural differences are a source of disparities in the knowledge of the world (Chua, Morris, & Mor, 2012). Specifically, individuals of different cultures internalize and adhere to different shared social norms, knowledge bases, values, assumptions, and traditions, yielding divergent ideas and intellectual resources for creative endeavors (Chua, 2013).

Various studies have linked cultural diversity (e.g., Cheng, Chua, Morris, & Lee, 2012; Cox, Lobel, & McLeod, 1991; Giambatista & Bhappu, 2010; McLeod, Lobel, & Cox, 1996; Stahl, Maznevski, Voigt, & Jonsen, 2009; Watson, Kumar, & Michaelsen, 1993) to creative performance. Intercultural relationships in a social network or multicultural teams spur an influx of varied ideas, perspectives, and knowledge, which facilitates association of existing ideas and stimulation of new thinking, thereby potentiating creativity. For example, in multicultural teams, individuals from varying cultural backgrounds build up a large knowledge repertoire (Blau, 1977; Cox, 1994; Cox & Blake, 1991; Govindarajan & Gupta, 2001), as each individual member provides access to different ideas that others can build on to achieve creativity (Paulus & Brown, 2003; Paulus, Larey, & Dzindolet, 2001).

Intercultural relationships, nonetheless, do not always beget creativity (e.g., Giambatista & Bhappu, 2010; Hackman, 1990; O'Reilly, Williams, & Barsade, 1998; Swann, Kwan, Polzer, & Milton, 2003; see Williams & O'Reilly, 1998). Intercultural anxiety, tensions, and conflicts in cross-cultural encounters (Jehn & Mannix, 2001; Jehn, Northcraft, & Neale, 1999; Pelled, Eisenhardt, & Xin, 1999;

Stephan & Stephan, 1985) may result from varied and sometimes incompatible assumptions, values, and norms specific to the different cultures (Hall, 1976; Harris, 1968; Triandis, 1994). In addition, negative stereotypes and biases against outgroup members could engender intergroup tensions and conflicts (Allport, 1954; Stephan & Stephan, 1985), causing difficulties in cross-cultural collaboration. Such differences and disagreements, if not overcome, are detrimental to creative performance.

Given these intercultural dynamics, when do intercultural relationships enhance creativity? Scholars have addressed this question by investigating multiple moderators of the relationship (cf. Stahl et al., 2009). Some point to team members' cultural value orientations (Cheng et al., 2012) and cultural metacognition (Crotty & Brett, 2012), whereas others focus on team-level factors such as self-verification (Polzer, Milton, & Swann, 2002) and diversity perspectives (Ely & Thomas, 2001). The answer is likely a combination of these factors.

Cross-cultural encounters, as noted, occur at multiple levels of interaction. Individuals interact with one another, exchange information, and oftentimes collaborate toward a common goal of creativity. It is thus imperative to examine the effects of intercultural relationships on creativity at different levels of analysis to fully understand the boundary conditions and underlying mechanisms of the relationship.

In this chapter, we discuss when and how intercultural relationships implicate individual-, dyadic-, and team-level creativity. In doing so, we examine the mediators of the intercultural relationships–creativity link to explain the mechanisms by which cultural diversity impacts creativity. We also investigate the boundary conditions of the focal relationship to understand when culturally diverse relationships enhance creativity and when they may not. We conclude by connecting and integrating existing research on intercultural relationships and creativity and proposing future research directions.

INDIVIDUAL-LEVEL CREATIVITY

Individuals need not be part of a multicultural work team to be influenced by intercultural relationships. Due to forces of globalization, individuals are increasingly embedded in multicultural social networks in both daily lives and at work; their exposure to intercultural ties, directly or indirectly, has been found to impact their individual-level creativity. In this section, we discuss how exposure to intercultural ties both helps and hurts individuals' creativity.

How Networks Stimulate Individual-Level Creativity

The idea that interpersonal ties in one's social environment can enhance individual-level creativity has been investigated in the network literature (Burt, 2004; Perry-Smith, 2006; Rodan & Galunic, 2004). The main arguments for the creativity-enhancing effects of social networks, as articulated by Chua, Morris, and Ingram (2010), include (1) an increased flow of divergent ideas and perspectives between contacts that stimulates association of seemingly unrelated ideas; (2) more efficient discussion of novel ideas through various stages of development that helps test, improve, and refine ideas to meet specific needs; and (3) higher levels of social support and encouragement throughout the idea development process. Put differently, having many different ideas being flowed and discussed in social networks is a form of cognitive diversity, which stimulates creative thinking (Paulus, 2000). Individuals' creative idea generation has been found to improve with exposure to others' ideas that are related to the tasks at hand (Fink et al., 2010, 2012). Further, as individuals go through each arduous step of idea gathering, combining, and testing, having a network of support and encouragement may help them see ideas through to fruition. Indeed, the confluence of these interpersonal factors improves creativity.

In the same vein, being part of a culturally diverse social network likely facilitates the flow and discussion of culturally diverse ideas and perspectives, thus spurring creative thinking. The exposure to cultural diversity in a social network is distinct from other types of cultural experience (e.g., living abroad) such that individuals may draw on a multitude of valuable resources offered by ongoing interpersonal relationships within the network (Coleman, 1990). Chua (in press) showed in a field experiment and a laboratory experiment, using Blau's (1977) heterogeneity index to capture network cultural heterogeneity,[1] that cultural heterogeneity in social networks enhances individuals' creativity exclusively on tasks that require multicultural knowledge. Both studies showed that the creativity-enhancing effects of network cultural heterogeneity are domain specific. In particular, participants performed better on *global* tasks (which called for diverse cultural knowledge), but not *local* tasks (which mainly called for local cultural knowledge) or *imagination* tasks (which assessed creativity in general and did not require cultural knowledge).

The main findings resonate with the line of creativity research asserting that creativity requires domain-specific knowledge and relevant skills (Amabile, 1983; Baer, 1993), and that bicultural experience enhances creativity only in tasks related to the cultural domains specific to the bicultural experience (Cheng et al., 2008). Contrarily, a previous study by Maddux and Galinsky (2009) found that living abroad contributes to creative performance in general. Chua et al. (2010) reconcile the discrepancies by reasoning that the effects of multicultural experiences on creativity likely depend on the type of exposure. Indeed, having a multicultural network and living abroad are two different types of multicultural experiences. A prolonged and intense immersion in a foreign culture could permanently broaden individuals' worldviews, thus promoting general creativity. On the other hand, a relatively short and less intense exposure to multiple foreign cultures within a social network may provide multicultural knowledge for relevant tasks, but the weak exposure is unlikely to have a broad implication on creative performance.

In addition, the experimental results shed light on the interpersonal pathway linking network cultural heterogeneity to creativity. Specifically, network cultural heterogeneity was associated with the receipt of more culture-related ideas,[2] but not other types of ideas, from people in the social networks whether or not they were from a different culture. This pattern of results suggests that cultural heterogeneity in individuals' social networks may signal to all others in the networks that the individuals are open to diverse cultures, thus inviting the exchange and discussion of varied ideas related to cultures. In other words, the findings suggest that by forging intercultural ties, individuals improve their chances of receiving novel culture-related ideas from those with the same as well as different cultural ties.

Sharing new ideas, culture related or not, runs risks of being ridiculed (Nemeth, Personnaz, Personnaz, & Goncalo, 2004) or the ideas being stolen (Chua et al., 2010). Although being embedded in a social network (having ties to common third parties) is empirically linked to increased transfer of ideas and knowledge (Ingram & Roberts, 2000; Reagan & McEvily, 2003; Reagans & Żuckerman, 2001; Uzzi, 1997, 1999; Uzzi & Lancaster, 2003), interpersonal trust—the willingness to be vulnerable to others' motives, intentions, and actions (Kramer, 1999; Mayer, Davis, & Schoorman, 1995)—has been acknowledged as central to the link (Burt, 2005; Coleman, 1988; Ferrin, Dirks, & Shah, 2006; Walker, Kogut, & Shan, 1997). Trust is intensified the more embedded individuals are in the social network (Burt, 2005; Coleman, 1988; Ferrin et al., 2006; Walker et al., 1997), and heightened trust renders individuals more willing to share new ideas and knowledge with one another (Andrew & Dalahay, 2000; Chua, 2014; Penley & Hawkins, 1985; Tsai & Goshal, 1998). Using an egocentric network survey of midlevel executives, Chua and colleagues (2010) found that affective trust (trust based on a socioemotional base), as opposed to cognitive trust (trust based on a calculative basis) (McAllister, 1995), mediates the relationship between network embeddedness and idea sharing.

To elaborate, affective trust develops out of the care and concern about others' welfare (Lewis & Weigert, 1985; Rempel, Holmes, & Zanna, 1985), whereas cognitive trust springs from instrumental calculation of others' competence and reliability (Butler, 1991; Cook & Wall, 1980; Zucker, 1986). Embeddedness in a social network increases a sense of social support (House, Landis, & Umberson, 1988; Kadushin, 1982; Polister, 1980) and solidarity (Kadushin, 1982; Wellman, 1988), which enhances affective trust. In addition, affective, but not cognitive, trust has been found to relate positively to embeddedness (Chua et al., 2010). These distinctions between affective and cognitive trust have an important implication on the relationship between network cultural heterogeneity and individuals' creativity. Specifically, the increased flow and discussion of diverse cultural ideas resulting from network cultural heterogeneity are likely to be explained by the level of affective trust in the intercultural relationships. The denser the multicultural social networks, the more likely individuals are to affectively trust one another. Affective trust creates a safe environment for individuals to share and discuss novel cultural ideas without fear of being ridiculed or the ideas being stolen, thus stimulating creativity.

Pitfalls of Multicultural Social Environment

As much as intercultural relationships in a social environment enable creative thinking, there are potential pitfalls. Specifically, individuals' creativity, similar to other types of performance, could suffer from what goes wrong in the larger environment (Frost, 2003; Porath & Erez, 2009; Schneider & Reichers, 1983; Scott, 1992). For example, Frost (2003) suggests that an unpleasant work environment caused by insensitive attitudes and behaviors of managers and employees imposes a negative impact on work performance of people around them. Indeed, based on three laboratory experiments, Porath and Erez (2007) found that witnessing rudeness enacted by an authoritative figure or a peer may increase negative affect, which in turn reduces performance on routine and creative tasks.

Related to a multicultural social environment, recent research by Chua (2013) demonstrates in a network survey and two laboratory experiments that ambient cultural disharmony—indirect experience of multicultural tensions and conflicts in the immediate social environment—compromises creativity that requires multicultural knowledge by promoting the belief that ideas from different cultures are incompatible. Importantly, this research confirms the findings that the effects of intercultural relationships on creativity are domain specific (Chua, in press), as the negative effects of ambient cultural disharmony on creativity were significant for multicultural, but not general, creativity tasks. Importantly, this research shows that the creativity-dampening impacts of intercultural tensions and conflicts may spill over onto observers who are aware of but are not directly involved in the tensions and conflicts. This finding suggests that individuals' creative performance can be easily undermined by disharmonious intercultural relationships surrounding them.

This research also identifies individuals' implicit belief that ideas from different cultural sources are incompatible as the mediator of the ambient disharmony–creativity relationship. Specifically, the intercultural disharmony individuals observe in their social environment activates or increases their implicit belief that ideas from disparate cultures are incompatible. Once such implicit belief is developed, individuals are less likely to simultaneously access knowledge from different cultures and draw nonobvious connections among them, thus compromising creativity (Cheng et al., 2008; Mok & Morris, 2010).

Chua (2013) explains that individuals' implicit belief about the incompatibility of ideas from different cultural sources is related to their belief in cultural essentialism—that cultural characteristics are innate and fixed (Chao, Chen, Roisman, & Hong, 2007; Chao, Okazai, & Hong, 2011; Hong, Chao, & No, 2009). Indeed, the belief about multicultural compatibility could be affected by environmental stimuli (No et al., 2008). For example, bicultural individuals who have experienced difficulties navigating between the two cultures likely view the cultures in question as incompatible (Benet-Martínez, Leu, Lee, & Morris, 2002; Vivero & Jenkins, 1999). Similar to individuals holding an implicit belief about ambient cultural disharmony, believers of cultural essentialism would also perceive that ideas from diverse cultures are incompatible and are difficult to be morphed or combined, rendering a lower willingness to explore creative associations between these ideas.

The Cultural Alignment Model of Global Creativity

Not all forms of cross-cultural creative endeavors are fruitful. Another type of pitfall resulting from a multicultural social environment occurs when the culture of the innovator is not aligned with that of the audience. Recent research has proposed a cultural alignment model of global creativity, which explains the effect of culture on creativity in a global context (Chua, Roth, & Lemoine, 2015). This theoretical model extends the previous work on cross-cultural creativity to look at the impact of cultural norms of the innovator and the audience on the innovator's creative engagement as well as success.

Using data from a global online crowdsourcing platform, Chua and colleagues (2015) demonstrate that cultural tightness—the strength of social norms and the level of sanctioning within a given society (Gelfand, Nishii, & Raver, 2006)— lowers the odds that individuals would engage and succeed in foreign creative tasks. Tight local norms, they argue, decrease individuals' creative self-efficacy, or the confidence in the ability to be creative (Tierney & Farmer, 2002), which in turn lessens their willingness to attempt creative endeavors in a culture that is unfamiliar to them. Moreover, being restricted by tight cultural norms that sanction deviant mindsets and behaviors makes it harder for these individuals to be successful in their cross-cultural creative attempts.

Individuals embedded in tight cultures tend to falter not only at breaking away from prescribed ways of thinking and doing but also at accumulating the domain knowledge outside of their local cultures, the two critical ingredients that boost creative self-efficacy and encourage creative engagement. In fact, working in an unfamiliar cultural context poses a psychological challenge (Earley & Ang, 2003) for individuals who come from tight cultures where deviation and change are discouraged. These individuals are not prepared to think out of their comfort zone or to internalize the critical knowledge about the foreign cultural context which helps them navigate and learn an unfamiliar culture. Such lack of preparation drains the confidence that they would excel in cross-cultural creative tasks, rendering them less likely to initiate any creative endeavors abroad.

Even when individuals from tight cultures go against the odds and venture in foreign creative tasks, their chance of success is slim compared to those from loose cultures. Chua and colleagues (2015) explained that the former are worse at combining existing ideas to produce new ideas and at judging the viability of potential creative solutions due to their prevention focus, self-regulation, and low tolerance for deviation from currently known solutions. When optimal creative solutions require the cultural knowledge outside of one's own cultural domain, it is even more difficult for these individuals to understand the needs and preferences of foreign audiences. Taken together, these individuals' preventive mindset forged by their adherence to restrictive cultural norms and their lack of cultural knowledge jointly undermine their development of creative ideas, particularly those that will be effective in a foreign culture.

Further, the less aligned the innovator's and the audience's culture, the stronger the negative effects of cultural tightness. Put differently, cultural distance— the degree to which two cultures differ in their value systems (Shenkar, 2001; Tihanyi, Griffith, & Russell, 2005)—accentuates the negative relationship between cultural tightness and creative engagement and success in a foreign culture. When differences in various aspects (e.g., traditions, norms, customs, business environments) between one's own culture and an audience's culture are wide, individuals from tight cultures feel less able to deliver novel and workable solutions, slashing their creative self-efficacy and thereby the likelihood that they would attempt the task. Even when they do go for it, these individuals are less likely to succeed, considering that their cultural restrictions discourage them to think out of the box or to take risks.

Tight cultural norms are, nonetheless, not always detrimental to creativity. When creative endeavors are done locally as opposed to abroad, individuals who are local to tight cultures are more likely to attempt and succeed in these endeavors. Chua and colleagues (2015) argue that these individuals, compared to their counterparts from loose cultures, should experience higher creative self-efficacy because they are familiar with the clearly defined local cultures, thus increasing their likelihood of creative engagement and success. Specifically, norms in tight cultures are widely shared among the locals, so local innovators should be able to cater to the local audiences' needs and preferences. Indeed, these local innovators enjoy their home field advantage of knowing the audiences, facing less competition due to the restrictive norms that are unfriendly to foreign innovators, and being able to effectively navigate the idea space in which they search for insights and evaluate possible ideas that will fit the local cultural context. On the contrary, local norms are neither firmly defined nor widely shared in loose cultures, making the local audiences' preferences less predictable (Au, 1999; Triandis, 1989). Because new ideas must be acceptable to the audience to be successful, individuals from tight cultures are hence more likely than those from loose cultures to succeed in their creative attempts.

In sum, individuals' creativity could benefit as well as suffer from exposure to the different types of intercultural relationships embedded in their social networks. The benefits arise chiefly from individuals' exposure to cognitive diversity from the flow and discussion of culture-related ideas with others in the network. How well individuals can harness the creativity benefits depends in part on the level of trust they have with these social contacts. Conversely, intercultural tensions and conflicts in the social environment, although merely observed, could backfire. Finally, the cultural alignment between the innovator and the audience can also affect the likelihood of engagement in and success for creative endeavors.

DYADIC-LEVEL CREATIVITY

Beyond individual-level creativity, intercultural relationships could affect dyadic-level creative collaboration. When two people of different cultural backgrounds collaborate on a creative task, the nature of their interactions has been shown to directly impact their collaborative potential and joint creativity. Indeed, different cultural knowledge (influenced by disparate cultural experiences and identities) may cause anxiety, misunderstandings, and gaps in problem representation that compromise effectiveness and efficiency in intercultural collaborations (Adler, 2002; Gelfand et al., 2001; Lievens, Harris, Van Keer, & Bisqueret, 2003; Takeuchi, Yun, & Tesluk, 2002), especially when the interactions are less structured and more open to idea experimentation, such as in creative collaboration. Interpersonal trust between the two people, however, may mitigate these negative effects of cultural diversity on creativity within the dyad. Specifically, interpersonal trust facilitates the forming of an effective intercultural relationship, which in turn creates an environment where the two people feel ascertained that their ideas would not be corrupted or stolen, and thus safe to share information and feedback.

A recent research by Chua and colleagues (2012) investigated the relationship between intercultural relationships and creativity at the dyadic level by examining affective trust and cultural metacognition as two key variables. In three studies, individuals with higher cultural metacognition were found to be more likely to develop affective trust toward people of different cultures, which in turn enhanced creative collaboration of the intercultural dyads.

Cultural metacognition, the ability to reflect on, adapt, and update cultural assumptions before, during, and after intercultural interactions (Ang, Van Dyne, & Tan, 2011; Earley & Ang, 2003; Earley, Ang, & Tan, 2006; Klafehn, Banerjee, & Chiu, 2008; Thomas, 2006) is crucial for effective dyadic creative collaboration. The concept of cultural metacognition is one of the key dimensions of cultural intelligence (CQ), defined as an individual's capability in effectively dealing with intercultural interactions (Ang, Van Dyne, & Koh, 2006). Scholars have identified CQ as including various dimensions—motivation, behavior, cognition (knowledge), and metacognition (metacognitive awareness). In particular, cultural metacognition, as a regulator of other dimensions of CQ (Thomas et al., 2008), attests to some higher order cognitive processes that manage the use of cultural knowledge.

To elaborate, cultural metacognition promotes "contextualized thinking," or the understanding that cultural contexts shape individuals' motivations and behaviors, and "cognitive flexibility" or the ability to discriminatively use mental maps and behavioral patterns during intercultural interactions (Chua et al., 2012, p. 117). Contextualized thinking and cognitive flexibility help individuals make use of diverse cultural knowledge by overcoming associated challenges such as misunderstandings, tensions, and conflicts caused by gaps in problem representation (Cronin & Weingart, 2007). Therefore, these cognitive mechanisms lubricate the processes of combining and experimenting on disparate cultural ideas to enhance intercultural creative collaboration via effective communication, which cultivates affective trust (Ang et al., 2007).

How does affective trust function as the central mechanism linking cultural metacognition to effective creative collaboration? First, cultural metacognition engenders affective trust via feelings of being on the "same wavelength" resulting from appropriately adjusted conversation and behavioral styles during intercultural interactions (Chua et al., 2012, p. 118). Individuals of high cultural metacognition are adept at adjusting their cultural assumptions and behaviors to audiences of specific cultural backgrounds, thus building the foundation for developing affective trust. Second, affective trust facilitates intercultural creative collaboration. Affective trust ameliorates risks of creative collaboration that involve experimentation and sharing of time-sensitive, new ideas, making the involved parties especially vulnerable to various uncertainties (Diehl & Stroebe, 1987, 1991; Rubenson & Runco, 1995). As noted earlier, a study by Chua et al. (2010) showed that affective trust was positively correlated with new idea sharing among managers' professional networks. Not only does affective trust increase safe and secure feelings in exposing ideas to others, it may relieve intercultural anxiety in intercultural collaboration as it motivates individuals to take the time to understand and appreciate others' alternative perspectives. The resulting understanding and appreciation enable the process of managing culture-related differences to generate creative solutions to the problem at hand. In sum, cultural metacognition represents the mental processes that make sense of intercultural experiences, plan intercultural encounters, and adjust intercultural assumptions, thus promoting interpersonal trust and enhancing creative collaboration.

Three studies by Chua, Morris and Mor (2012) provide empirical evidence for the arguments earlier. Using a multirater assessment, the first study showed that managers' self-reported cultural metacognition was positively correlated with other-culture associates' assessments of the effectiveness of their intercultural creative collaboration. This positive correlation persisted after controlling for various measures of multicultural experiences—the number of languages spoken, the number of countries lived in (for at least 6 months), the number of countries visited last year, and past interactions with people of different cultures and countries. Therefore, this study also supports the claim that cultural metacognition is different from multicultural experiences, which have been found to influence creativity (Leung, Maddux, Galinsky, & Chiu, 2008; Maddux & Galinsky, 2009).

The second study employed an egocentric network survey to investigate the mediating role of affective versus cognitive trust in the relationship between cultural metacognition and dyadic creative collaboration in the form of new idea sharing. Managers listed up to 24 contacts whom they considered important in their professional networks, assessed the likelihood that they discussed new ideas with each contact, rated how much they affectively and cognitively trusted each contact, and answered some questions about the nature of their dyadic relationships (e.g., length of relationships, frequency of interactions). Controlling for factors that could influence new idea sharing either directly or through interpersonal trust (e.g., the degree of cultural diversity in managers' networks, the number of contacts, the job function of that manager), results of moderated mediation analysis indicate that cultural metacognition positively predicted the amount of affective trust (not cognitive trust) and the likelihood of sharing new ideas with contacts of different cultural backgrounds, but not those of the same cultural background. Thus, the study confirmed that cultural metacognition and the affective trust mechanism impact new idea sharing only in the specific context of intercultural, as opposed to intracultural, encounters.

The third study showed similar results across three different dependent variables—third-party ratings of joint creative products (creative fusion dishes), perception of the other person as an effective partner, and assessment of idea exchange during the joint task. The results revealed that higher cultural metacognition in an intercultural dyad (which involved strangers) led to more effective creative collaboration (Study 3), greater idea sharing (Studies 2 and 3), and higher creative performance (Study 3), as long as the participants engaged in a personal conversation before the task. In this study, personal conversation was an experimental manipulation used to induce affective trust. Mediational analyses further confirmed that affective trust (but not cognitive trust) explains the pathway linking cultural metacognition to the different dependent measures in dyadic collaboration.

Based on these studies, Chua and colleagues (2012) identify two insights that address the challenges of intercultural creative collaboration in dyads. First, the dyad requires at least one interaction partner to have higher levels of cultural metacognition to consider the other's perspective, to take the initiative to avoid cross-cultural misunderstanding, and to build effective intercultural rapport in order to facilitate successful creative collaboration. Second, affective trust can be built among new acquaintances by engaging in personal conversations. Once affective trust is established, the dyad is likely to achieve higher creativity outcomes.

Whereas the research we reviewed thus far focuses on the impact of cultural metacognition on creative collaboration, the overall CQ has also been shown to enhance intercultural negotiation processes and outcomes, which often require integrative solutions to arrive at creative problem solving. Imai and Gelfand (2010), using transcripts of 124 American and East Asian negotiators, demonstrated that CQ measured a week prior to negotiations predicted negotiators' complementary integrative information behaviors (i.e., the dyad exchanged integrative information on disparate topics), which in turn predicted joint profit. Note that this effect was over and beyond other types of intelligence, including cognitive ability (Barry & Friedman, 1998; Kurtzberg, 1998) and emotional intelligence (Elfenbein, Foo, White, Tan, & Aik, 2007), and personality traits including openness to experience (Ma & Jaeger, 2005). The researchers reasoned that CQ provides negotiators with cooperative and epistemic motives to promote cooperation and sense making during negotiation, which jointly enable them to invest more cognitive effort into accurately understanding their culturally different counterparts and adopt more integrative negotiation strategies. Notably, the negotiator with the lower levels of CQ in the dyad is the one determining the dyad's engagement in effective negotiation sequences. This is unsurprising, given that it takes both sides to engage in integrative behaviors in order to improve joint profit.

In sum, we reviewed evidence on the relations between cultural metacognition and intercultural creative collaboration and between CQ and creative negotiation outcomes at the dyadic level. One may as well assume a similar process at the intrateam level, which could be viewed as a collection of dyadic relationships that simultaneously influence the multicultural team's creative outcomes. Nonetheless, the whole may not merely be the sum of its parts. In the next section, we discuss existing research on multicultural teams wherein team members' intercultural relationships influence the team's creative outcomes.

TEAM-LEVEL CREATIVITY

A multicultural team is a team consisting of individuals from at least three different national cultures working together toward a common goal (Crotty & Brett, 2012). As the business environments become increasingly globalized, organizations rely on multicultural teams to capitalize on their diverse knowledge, expertise, and experience to achieve creativity and innovation (Behfar, Kern, & Brett, 2006). Mounting evidence, however, suggests that many multicultural teams fail to utilize their available multicultural resources toward producing creative outcomes.

How members of a multicultural team relate to, interact, and communicate with others plays an especially critical role in determining whether or not the team as a whole would be creative. A multicultural team comprises numerous intercultural dyadic relationships working alongside. Although a team member may engage multiple other members simultaneously, the quality and nature of the individual dyadic relationship matter. The effectiveness of the team's intercultural relationships therefore depends on how well different dyads bond together and how well these dyads interact.

Possible explanations for a multicultural team's failure to achieve higher levels of creativity include a lack of a common understanding (Earley & Gibson, 2002; Maznevski, 1994), poor-quality communication (Giambatista & Bhappu, 2010), low attachment or commitment (Tsui, Egan, & O'Reilly, 1992), low social integration (Smith et al., 1994), differences in norms and assumptions (Behfar et al., 2006; Gelfand et al., 2011; Gibson & Zellmer-Bruhn, 2001, 2002; Watson, Kumar, & Michaelson, 1993), and lack of language proficiencies (Beyene, Hinds, & Cramton, 2009). Demographic cues can also prompt negative stereotypes among team members of different ethnic backgrounds (Allport, 1954; Dovidio, Evans, & Tyler, 1986; Duncan, 1976), causing intrateam conflicts and tensions. Taken together, this array of factors are likely to trouble intercultural relationships, giving rise to a team climate that is unaccommodating of idea exchange and experimentation, thus undermining team collaboration and performance (Cramton & Hinds, 2004; Lau & Murnighan, 1998).

To understand the implications of intercultural relationships on creativity in multicultural teams, we discuss four related issues. First, we address intercultural evaluation apprehension, a main challenge members of multicultural teams face as a result of their cultural differences. Second, we discuss intercultural perceptions, which are influenced by cultural differences but could be enhanced to promote team creativity. Third, we describe the process of building intercultural relationships and how it may affect team creative performance over time. Fourth, we review the concept of intercultural brokerage, which explains the different roles individual team members with distinct cultural knowledge play in facilitating creative collaboration.

Intercultural Evaluation Apprehension

A team's creative outcomes should not be equated with the sum of its individual members' creative endeavors. This notion is supported by evidence in studies of group brainstorming, a process which facilitates idea generation and consequently creative problem solving (Parnes, 1992; Treffinger, Isaksen, & Dorval, 1994). Because production gains in group brainstorming derive mostly from the diverse ideas exchanged among group members (see Paulus, Putman, Dugosh, Dzindolet, & Coskun, 2002, for a review on production gains and losses in group brainstorming), a multicultural team consisting of members from varied cultures should reap the highest benefits from group brainstorming. Yet the group brainstorming literature finds that interactive groups are usually less productive in terms of idea generation than the same number of individuals in nominal groups irrespective of race or ethnicity of group members (Diehl & Stroebe, 1987; Lamm & Trommsdorff, 1973; Mullen, Johnson, & Salas, 1991). Nominal groups are groups of individuals who brainstorm ideas in isolation and their generated ideas are pooled together to form the group product. A key reason for production losses in group brainstorming is evaluation apprehension.

A main driver of evaluation apprehension is that individuals tend to implicitly or explicitly evaluate themselves by comparing performance with one another using different and, sometimes, incompatible norms, values, and assumptions (Cottrell, 1972; Sanna, 1992). In the context of multicultural teams, team members' norms, values and assumptions are heavily shaped by their cultural backgrounds (Behfar et al., 2006; Gibson & Zellmer-Bruhn, 2001, 2002; Watson et al., 1993). For instance, those from a collectivistic culture may yield to social pressures, whereas those from an individualistic culture tend to adhere to their own beliefs. Individual members of a multicultural team are thus more prone to feeling anxious about their own performance than those of a culturally homogenous team because it is unclear against which norms, values, and assumptions the team assesses performance. Further, these individuals may not feel psychologically safe to experiment with new ideas (Edmondson, 1999) or to undertake initiatives to enhance their work for fear of negative judgment.

Nonetheless, certain work practices could reconcile evaluation apprehension arising from the differences in norms, values, and assumptions to enable creativity. Recent research by Crotty and Brett (2012) showed that fusion teamwork—teamwork that recognizes and respects cultural differences among team members in their work practices and approaches—promotes team creativity, and team members with higher cultural metacognition tend to describe their teamwork as fusion. Next, we discuss the relationships among fusion teamwork, cultural metacognition, and creativity in the context of multicultural teams.

How does fusion teamwork promote creativity? Fusion teamwork consists of two interdependent, creativity-enhancing norms: the coexistence of culturally different approaches to manage teamwork and meaningful participation (Janssens & Brett, 2006). Individual members of a fusion team should feel less apprehensive about their differences in norms, values, and assumptions, because the team acknowledges and manages instead of condemning or suppressing these differences. Further, meaningful participation, a practice where team members readily speak up when they have unique information to contribute to the team, encourages team members with different perspectives to express their ideas. Taken together, fusion teamwork supports the building of intrateam relationships that are based on an understanding of differences among team members, and it provides a channel through which team members can capitalize on their diverse cultural knowledge. For example, team members from the United States and China can build a better creative collaborative relationship because they learn to embrace appropriate norms specific to the situation. Specifically, the Chinese could learn to be proactive when pitching their ideas to the Americans, while the Americans could learn to be mindful of the face-saving culture when dealing with the Chinese. This type of understanding is likely to maximize the contribution of both the Americans and the Chinese to the team. Fusion teamwork thus creates a team environment that eases evaluation apprehension with dynamic team norms and embraces multicultural resources as inputs for creativity via the practice of meaningful participation.

Why are team members with high (vs. low) cultural metacognition more likely to engage in fusion teamwork? Team members with high cultural metacognition constantly check and update their cultural assumptions to arrive at appropriate behaviors during intercultural interactions. These individuals are likely to develop effective relationships with other team members of different cultural backgrounds because they are knowledgeable about, adaptive to, and comfortable with intercultural interactions. Therefore, they are less frustrated by cultural dissimilarities and more effective in finding optimal ways to resolve these dissimilarities.

Besides evaluation apprehension, another significant factor that prompts multicultural teams to fail at achieving creativity is team members' inability to foster effective communication (Carlile, 2004; Dougherty, 1992; Hackman, 1990; Wiersema & Bantel, 1992). Low-quality communication perpetuates misunderstanding and misinterpretation, which harm creative performance within intercultural relationships. Conversely, high-quality communication exerts the opposite effects. A study on national diversity of virtual teams by Gibson and Gibbs (2006) supports this argument. Using interview data from teams across industries and survey data from aerospace design teams that worked together with varying degrees of "virtuality," Gibson and Gibbs (2006) found that a psychologically safe communication climate moderated the negative relationship between national diversity and team innovation. Specifically, national diversity creates different communication preferences and undermines team identification, thus compromising the forming of a shared vision, a sine qua non for innovation. However, a psychologically safe communication climate, defined as a team environment that is supportive of open communication and risk taking (Baer & Frese, 2003; Edmondson, 1999, 2003; Gibb, 1961), may help bridge in-group and out-group differences and resolve conflict, misinterpretation, and misunderstanding by easing evaluation apprehension. In sum, although national diversity in multicultural teams may inhibit effective communication, a team context that provides a safety net for team members to share and experiment on ideas with one another should alleviate the creativity-dampening effects of national diversity.

Furthermore, different communication methods may affect the relative saliency of the advantages versus the disadvantages of diversity in multicultural teams. A study by Giambatista and Bhappu (2010) showed the interaction effects between communication styles (nominal group technique [NGT] vs. computer-mediated communication [CMC]) and impacts of ethnic diversity (positive variety properties that make use of nonredundant categories of knowledge and experience versus negative separation properties that focus on perception of team members' differences) on team creative performance.[3] The results revealed that ethnically diverse teams benefitted from the process of NGT that involves a strict order of nominal idea generation, discussion of ideas, and nominal voting (Van de Ven & Delbecq, 1971), as well as the process of CMC that involves parallel processing and reductive characteristics (as the absence of visual or verbal cues promotes anonymity). In addition, whereas NGT might accentuate the positive variety properties of ethnic diversity because it separates idea generation from idea evaluation, allowing team members to share unique ideas and perspectives without evaluation apprehension, CMC helps minimize the negative separation properties of ethnic diversity by reducing in-group bias and facilitating efficient and effective participation of diverse team members. With these communication methods in place, the positive variety properties should outweigh the negative separation properties, creating a team context where team members are empowered to make the most use of their multicultural resources to enhance team creative performance.

Intercultural Perceptions

Oftentimes, individuals of different cultures might have a biased perception of each other because they use their own worldview to make judgments. Their ability to look past their differences in norms, values, and assumptions associated with their cultural backgrounds could be conducive for establishing mutual understanding and building effective intercultural relationships, which enhance team creativity.

A study by Polzer, Milton, and Swann (2002) showed that self-verification, the degree to which team members see the other team members as the other team members see themselves, moderates the team diversity–creativity relationship. Specifically, longitudinal data on various work teams indicated that diversity improved creative performance once teams had established high self-verification. Indeed, teams with high self-verification are less likely to experience disagreement and misunderstanding because team members have taken the time to understand the other team members for who they are or, more precisely, for who they see themselves to be. In addition, high self-verification may generate a sense of validation, which encourages the sharing of unique knowledge among team members and promotes higher creative performance.

Using longitudinal data from small teams of MBA students, Swann, Kwan, Polzer, and Milton (2003) identified the antecedents of self-verification within multicultural teams. They found that team members' impressions of the others (targets) when teams started to form influenced the level of individuation of the targets at a later time—the process by which the targets are identified as distinguished from one another. Target individuation predicted the targets' self-verification, which in turn predicted team creative performance. The researchers reasoned that positive (as opposed to neutral or negative) impressions of the targets might motivate perceivers to spend more time with them and learn more about them personally (e.g., Dabbs & Ruback, 1987); thus, they are likely to individuate the target's idiosyncratic characteristics rather than lumping them with all others. Indeed, individuation serves as a necessary (although not sufficient) condition for self-verification because forming individuated appraisals of the targets increases the chance of those appraisals to align with the targets' self-views. Notably, the importance of individuation is pronounced in intercultural relations because members of a multicultural team need to acknowledge their cultural differences and see others for who they are in order to capitalize on the multicultural resources toward creativity.

The Process of Building Intercultural Relationships

It is common that members of a multicultural team overcome different challenges across different stages of team formation in order to build intercultural relationships over time and to optimize the creative benefits of multicultural resources. Two studies illustrated how different stages of team formation interact with certain aspects of multicultural teams—ethnic diversity (Giambatista & Bhappu, 2010) and value orientations (Cheng et al., 2012)—to impact creative performance. In one study, Giambatista and Bhappu (2010) demonstrated that ethnic diversity attests to both negative separation and positive variety properties (defined earlier), but the negative separation properties only showed in newly formed teams, whereas the positive variety properties were evident only in mature teams. This finding is consistent with some previous research (e.g., Harrison, Price, Gavin, & Florey, 2002; Zellmer-Bruhn, Maloney, Bhappu, & Salvador, 2008), suggesting that the positive variety properties become more salient as a team matures, outweighing perceptions of differences among team members. Indeed, in forging effective intercultural relationships, team members face a difficult period of reconciling and adapting to one another's differences before coming to a common understanding. Over time, team members may build a common identity around their work and become more accepting of one another's differences. They are then more likely to welcome and build on one another's unique contribution to the team's creative performance.

In another study on multicultural team development, Cheng and colleagues (2012) found that uncertainty avoidance and relationship orientation—two of Hofstede's (1980) four cultural dimensions—exerted different effects on team creative performance, depending on the stage of team formation. Using longitudinal data from self-managing multicultural teams, the researchers showed that at the initial stage of team formation, multicultural teams with a low level of uncertainty avoidance (i.e., a tolerance for ambiguity) and a moderate degree of variance among team members' uncertainty avoidance were more likely to excel in creative performance. It is because as a multicultural team starts to form, team members with lower levels of uncertainty avoidance can cope better with the interpersonal anxiety associated with working with unknown individuals from different cultures, and thereby make better use of the multicultural resources. Further, a moderate level of variance in team members' uncertainty avoidance means that there are not too many different relationships resulting from this cultural value orientation within the team, allowing members to better capitalize on the diverse cultural resources to achieve creativity.

At later stages of team development, a high level of team relationship orientation (i.e., an emphasis on relationships and not competitiveness) and a moderate degree of variance among team members' relationship orientation enhanced creative performance. It is because at later stages team members are likely to have overcome the initial challenges prompted by cultural differences, putting a greater emphasis on relationships could foster an interpersonal understanding and effectively actualize the benefits of cultural diversity. In addition, a moderate level of variance in relationship orientation and a high level of average relationship orientation should be the best combination to enhance creative performance. With high variance in relationship orientation, team members may feel disconnected from the team, thus shunning themselves from effective collaboration. Low variance in relationship orientation, on the other hand, may render team members to feel overly comfortable with their interpersonal relationships and reduce their readiness to dissent, if needed. This type of team dynamic increases the likelihood of team members falling into the trap of groupthink, whereby team decisions are made without critical evaluation of alternatives (Turner & Pratkanis, 1998).

In fact, these findings from Cheng and colleagues (2012) are consistent with those from the study by Giambatista and Bhappu (2010). Both research studies demonstrate that team members' intercultural differences are most apparent during the initial phase of team formation due to the experience of uncertainty and ambiguity from working with unfamiliar individuals. However, these differences may become less apparent over time. When team members gradually have learned about, bonded, accepted, and validated one another, they could take more advantage of the multicultural diversity to benefit the team's creative outcomes.

Intercultural Brokerage

Because there is a general assumption that team members who possess knowledge of multiple cultures should have a higher chance of bridging cultural differences, existing research tends to examine how certain characteristics of these individuals affect team outcomes (e.g., DiMarco, Taylor, & Alin, 2010; Haas, 2006). Emerging research, however, has begun to investigate the different roles team members engage in to facilitate cross-cultural creative collaboration.

Recently, Jang (2014) introduced the concept of cultural brokerage, the act of facilitating cross-cultural interaction. Using both inductive and deductive methods, her research demonstrated that members of a multicultural team could help cross-cultural creative collaboration in different ways, depending on their prior knowledge of the relevant cultures. Jang categorizes these members as cultural insiders (those with deep knowledge of the cultures of other team members) and cultural outsiders (those with little knowledge of the cultures of other team members) and identifies the different styles of brokerage they engage in to facilitate team creative collaboration. Specifically, cultural insiders engage in the act of *compensating*—managing cultural differences on behalf of the team; conversely, cultural outsiders engage in the act of *empowering*—enabling other members to address cultural issues. For example, cultural insiders would directly translate what a team member says in one language to another language that other team members can understand. Cultural outsiders, on the other hand, would motivate other team members to work through their differences by, for instance, advancing their cultural knowledge or complimenting them for behaving in a culturally appropriate way. Despite the different styles, Jang found that cultural insiders and cultural outsiders are equally effective at enhancing team creative performance. Potentially, the emergent theory of cultural brokerage opens the door to future research on how different styles of member interactions may impact creative performance of multicultural teams.

In sum, the effects of intercultural relationships on team-level creativity are not straightforward but mixed and oftentimes moderated. The ultimate impact on creativity may depend on the tradeoff between the positives and the negatives, as well as other critical determining factors that range from team members' characteristics to team-level factors such as norms and communication methods. The positive variety properties stem mostly from the fact that team members could capitalize on the available multicultural resources—ideas, perspectives, and knowledge associated with different cultures—to enhance the creative process. An effective intercultural relationship creates a team climate where members feel safe to share and test their unique ideas and perspectives in order to promote higher team creativity. The negative separation properties derive mainly from team members' different and sometimes incompatible norms, values, and assumptions due to their different cultural backgrounds. These differences, if not properly handled, could drive a wedge between team members, plaguing their relationships with misunderstandings, conflicts, and tensions, thus undermining team creative performance. Taken together, if the goal is to enable multicultural teams to achieve higher levels of creativity, putting in place factors or conditions that allow team members to build effective intercultural relationships that reconcile cultural differences and reap the intellectual resources presented by cultural diversity is a must.

DISCUSSION

Summary

This chapter outlines how relationships between individuals of different cultural backgrounds may influence creativity at three different levels—individual, dyadic, and team. Two elements appear to be key for harnessing intercultural relationships toward creative outcomes: (a) a deep understanding of intercultural dynamics and (b) the establishment of working behaviors that enable effective intercultural ties. Personal characteristics or social conditions that support these two elements would enable a positive intercultural relationships–creativity link. We next interpret the major concepts we have discussed in this chapter with regard to these two elements.

Fusion teamwork, for example, enables the building of team dynamics that enhance creativity via two norms. The first norm promotes team members' understanding of their cultural differences, whereas the second norm establishes a working behavior that facilitates cross-cultural creative collaboration. These two fusion workteam norms, therefore, work hand in hand to enable effective intercultural relationships, subsequently enhancing team creativity.

Affective trust, self-verification, and cultural metacognition also contribute to the two key elements, thus enabling the intercultural relationships–creativity link. First, affective trust between two individuals ensures that they could share their unique ideas without fear of being criticized despite their cultural differences. Once developed, affective trust reinforces a mutual understanding that surpasses cultural differences and creates a sense of security that the shared ideas would not be judged negatively due to the different criteria the other person holds based on his or her cultural lens. Second, high self-verification indicates that individuals see others as others see themselves irrespective of their differences in cultural identities. High self-verification generates a sense of validation, which encourages the sharing of knowledge and cultural resources, enhancing creative collaboration. Third, cultural metacognition allows for an update of cultural assumptions before, during, and after cultural interactions. As noted, cultural metacognition stimulates contextualized thinking and cognitive flexibility. These two aspects of cultural metacognition match with the two key elements for harnessing intercultural relationships toward creativity. Specifically, contextualized thinking creates an understanding that cultural contexts shapes individuals' motivations and behaviors, supporting an understanding of intercultural dynamics. Cognitive flexibility cultivates the ability to behave in culturally appropriate ways, contributing to the establishment of work behaviors that enable effective intercultural ties.

On the other hand, factors that undermine a deep understanding of intercultural dynamics and the establishment of working behaviors that enable effective intercultural ties may reverse the creativity-enhancing effects of intercultural relationships. First, ambient cultural disharmony exemplifies an environmental disabler of the intercultural relationships–creativity link. Second, intercultural evaluation apprehension accentuates concerns that those from different cultural backgrounds would negatively judge performance because of the different performance criteria associated with their cultural identities. As a result, individuals with evaluation apprehension tend not to take risks in accepting or experimenting with new ideas, likely hurting their creative performance. Third, the cultural misalignment between the innovator and the audience can pose a barrier to creative engagement and success. When individuals come from tight cultures that confine them to strict and clearly defined norms that sanction deviant mindsets or behaviors, they are relatively less adaptive to think divergently or experiment with ideas out of the box. These missing qualities undermine cross-cultural creative endeavors.

Future Research Directions

Despite recent growth in research that aims to investigate when and how multicultural relationships promote creativity, our understanding of the whole story is still developing. One important area that future research may look into is how mandating a primary language in a cross-cultural context may impact creative collaboration and outcomes. Cross-cultural dyads or teams usually have a primary language that individuals use to communicate their ideas and perspectives to others. Having a common language is necessary for individuals to understand one another, but it may, however, dilute the contribution of those who are not native speakers of the primary language for three main reasons. First, it is difficult to express oneself in a foreign language, especially if the ideas are new and underdeveloped. Nonnative speakers may struggle to find the right words or timing to explain their ideas, and therefore reserve their opinions or only propose ideas that are simple to explain but not necessarily new or relevant. Second, nonnative speakers may constantly be under evaluation apprehension when speaking the second language and their tensions may disrupt effective collaborations with native speakers (Beyene et al., 2009). Third, the ability to use the primary language may be viewed as a status characteristic—the desirable skill against which individuals compare themselves and others (Berger, Cohen, & Zelditch, 1972)—which prompts less favorable evaluations for those without the relevant skill

(Tajfel & Turner, 1979). Unequal status evaluations widen status gaps and produce differential performance expectations such that nonnative speakers may choose to withhold their contributions when they are attributed a lower status. Future research could examine the different mechanisms that explain how having a primary language may compromise creative outcomes of cross-cultural dyads or teams. For example, researchers could test whether or not mandating a primary language in a multicultural team will lower perceived status and contribution of nonnative speakers of the primary language, thus undermining team creativity.

Second, although cultural diversity brings diverse ideas to the table, cultural differences in norms, values, and assumptions can come along as distractions. As individuals grapple with these distractions, they may have limited cognitive capacity to process diverse and sometimes conflicting information at any given time (Baddeley, 1999; Duncan, 1999) and experience cognitive overload—the cognitive state that arises when required cognitive resources surpass available cognitive resources (Lang, 2000). Once cognitive overload occurs, more inputs will undermine rather than stimulate performance (Fox, Park, & Lang, 2007). For example, members of a multicultural team may be so overloaded by the different and conflicting ideas that they could not reach any agreed-upon solution to a problem at hand. Relatedly, research on asymmetric perceptions of conflict in teams indicated that members who perceive more conflict than others will be more distracted and become less effective in their work performance (Jehn, Rispens, & Thatcher, 2010). We also speculate that these individuals are likely to exhaust their cognitive resources because they overspend their mental capacity to process differences and do not have enough for engaging in the creative process.

Relatedly, we theorize that cultural distance could moderate the relationship between cultural diversity and creativity. Previous research has shown that inputs from diverse sources are more cognitively taxing and prone to prompt cognitive overload than inputs from similar sources (Fox et al., 2007; Lang, 2000). As such, the less similar any two cultures are, the more cognitive resources individuals need to process ideas from the two cultures and the more likely their creative performance will suffer from cognitive overload. Future research could investigate the different types of distractions cultural diversity begets that may hurt creativity and how the degree of dissimilarities between the relevant cultures could moderate the impact.

Third, we see an important contribution for future research to investigate what leaders could do to facilitate creative collaboration in cross-cultural dyads and teams. In a cross-cultural context, leadership is the culmination of cultural metacognition and intercultural brokerage—leaders should be able to manage their cultural knowledge to effectively connect individuals of different cultural backgrounds to work together. For example, how could leaders help individuals with different norms, values, and assumptions deal with intercultural anxiety and evaluation apprehension? Especially in newly formed dyads or teams, intercultural encounters create a feeling of uncertainty around unfamiliar interpersonal relationships (Cheng et al., 2012). Team members are likely uncertain of what others think and against what criteria they judge performance. Future research may examine if the leader's role in putting in place norms or practices such as organizing ice-breaking sessions or clarifying performance criteria helps ease these negative emotions.

Additionally, leaders have the authority and responsibility to assign individuals to work together. To match any two individuals for creative collaboration, leaders need to understand their differences in cultures and associated views of the world. Future studies may ask what kind of cultural knowledge is needed for leaders to be effective in intercultural brokerage. For example, a leader should not put individuals with a history of cultural tension into a dyad to avoid interpersonal conflict that may interfere with their work. Future research can also look at how leadership styles impact intercultural relationships in creative teams. For example, participative leadership, defined as joint decision making by a leader and his or her subordinates (Koopman & Wierdsma, 1998), is likely to amplify the effectiveness of the fusion practice of meaningful participation to enhance the creative process. Specifically, leaders who value a joint decision-making process tend to encourage team members to share their ideas and stimulate creative thoughts.

It is also worth noting that an investigation into any single level of creativity as the dependent variable can only give an incomplete understanding of the impact of intercultural relationships on creativity. Creativity is, in fact, a multifaceted construct, and the unleashing of team members' creative potentiality depends very much on the implicated context (Zhou & Hoever, 2013). The impacts of multiculturalism on creativity may spill over or interact across different levels. For example, cultural harmony or tension in the social network may interact with individuals' characteristics to affect their creativity, which in turn influences the quality of their intercultural relationships with others. Conversely, multicultural team dynamics may result from the interaction between the various dyadic intercultural relationships of team members. Because cross-cultural collaboration occurs across levels of social interactions, researchers should examine its impact on creativity across different levels to gain a nuanced understanding of the phenomenon.

NOTES

1. Network cultural heterogeneity = $1 - \Sigma\, p_i^{\,2}$, where p_i is the proportion of the group in the ith category. In Chua (in press), the categories were eight different cultural groups—European American, African American, Asian American, European, East Asian, Middle Eastern, Latino, and other.
2. Chua et al. (2011) coded an idea as culture related if it contained elements of cultures, race, or countries outside of the United States.
3. The nominal group technique is a structured decision-making process that encourages all members of a team to contribute their opinions and ideas. Members typically take turns voicing their point of view after an individual brainstorming session.

REFERENCES

Adler, N. J. (2002). Global managers: No longer men alone. *International Journal of Human Resource Management, 13*(5), 743–760.

Allport, G. W. (1954). *The nature of prejudice*. Reading, MA: Addison-Wesley.

Amabile, T. M. (1983). The social psychology of creativity: A componential conceptualization. *Journal of Personality and Social Psychology, 45*(2), 357–376.

Amabile, T. M., Conti, R., Coon, H., Lazenby, J., & Herron, M. (1996). Assessing the work environment for creativity. *Academy of Management Journal, 39*(5), 1154–1184.

Andrews, K. M., & Delahaye, B. L. (2000). Influences on knowledge processes in organizational learning: The psychosocial filter. *Journal of Management Studies, 37*(6), 797–810.

Ang, S., Van Dyne, L., & Koh, C. (2006). Personality correlates of the four-factor model of cultural intelligence. *Group & Organization Management, 31*(1), 100–123.

Ang, S., Van Dyne, L., Koh, C., Ng, K. Y., Templer, K. J., Tay, C., & Chandrasekar, N. A. (2007). Cultural intelligence: Its measurement and effects on cultural judgment and decision making, cultural adaptation and task performance. *Management and Organization Review, 3*(3), 335–371.

Ang, S., Van Dyne, L., & Tan, M. L. (2011). Cultural intelligence. In R. J. Sternberg & S. B. Kaufman (Eds.), *Cambridge handbook on intelligence* (p. 582–602). New York, NY: Cambridge University Press.

Au, K. Y. (1999). Intra-cultural variation: Evidence and implications for international business. *Journal of International Business Studies, 30*, 799–812.

Baddeley, A. (1999). Memory. In R. Wilson & F. Keil (Eds.), *The MIT encyclopedia of the cognitive sciences* (pp. 514–517). Cambridge, MA: MIT Press.

Baer, J. (1993). *Divergent thinking and creativity: A task specific approach*. Hillsdale, NJ: Lawrence Erlbaum.

Baer, M., & Frese, M. (2003). Innovation is not enough: Climates for initiative and psychological safety, process innovations, and firm performance. *Journal of Organizational Behavior, 24*(1), 45–68.

Barry, B., & Friedman, R. A. (1998). Bargainer characteristics in distributive and integrative negotiation. *Journal of Personality and Social Psychology, 74*(2), 345–359.

Baughman, W. A., & Mumford, M. D. (1995). Process-analytic models of creative capacities: Operations influencing the combination-and-reorganization process. *Creativity Research Journal, 8*(1), 37–62.

Behfar, K., Kern, M., & Brett, J. (2006). Managing challenges in multicultural teams. *Research on Managing Groups and Teams, 9*, 233–262.

Benet-Martínez, V., Leu, J., Lee, F., & Morris, M. W. (2002). Negotiating biculturalism: Cultural frame switching in biculturals with oppositional versus compatible cultural identities. *Journal of Cross-Cultural Psychology, 33*(5), 492–516.

Berger, J., Cohen, B. P., & Zelditch Jr, M. (1972). Status characteristics and social interaction. *American Sociological Review, 37*, 241–255.

Beyene, T., Hinds, P., & Cramton, C. D. (2009). *Walking through jelly: Language proficiency, emotions, and disrupted collaboration in global work* (No. 09-138). Cambridge, MA: Harvard Business School.

Blau, P. M. (1977). *Inequality and heterogeneity: A primitive theory of social structure* (Vol. 7). New York, NY: Free Press.

Brimm, L. (2010). *Global cosmopolitans: The creative edge of difference*. New York, NY: Palgrave Macmillan.

Burt, R. S. (2004). Structural holes and good ideas. *The American Journal of Sociology, 110*(2), 349–399.

Burt, R. S. (2005). *Brokerage and closure: An introduction to social capital*. New York, NY: Oxford University Press.

Butler, J. K. (1991). Toward understanding and measuring conditions of trust: Evolution of a conditions of trust inventory. *Journal of Management, 17*(3), 643–663.

Carlile, P. R. (2004). Transferring, translating, and transforming: An integrative framework for managing knowledge across boundaries. *Organization Science, 15*(5), 555–568.

Chao, M. M., Chen, J., Roisman, G. I., & Hong, Y. Y. (2007). Essentializing race: Implications for bicultural individuals' cognition and physiological reactivity. *Psychological Science, 18*(4), 341–348.

Chao, M. M., Okazaki, S., & Hong, Y. Y. (2011). The quest for multicultural competence: Challenges and lessons learned from clinical and organizational research. *Social and Personality Psychology Compass, 5*(5), 263–274.

Cheng, C. Y., Chua, R. Y., Morris, M. W., & Lee, L. (2012). Finding the right mix: How the composition of self-managing multicultural teams' cultural value orientation influences performance over time. *Journal of Organizational Behavior, 33*(3), 389–411.

Cheng, C. Y., Sanchez-Burks, J., & Lee, F. (2008). Connecting the dots within creative performance and identity integration. *Psychological Science, 19*(11), 1178–1184.

Chua, R. Y. (2013). The costs of ambient cultural disharmony: Indirect intercultural conflicts in social environment undermine creativity. *Academy of Management Journal, 56*(6), 1545–1577.

Chua, R. Y. (2014). Unleashing creativity across cultural borders. *Asian Management Insights, 1*, 1–7.

Chua, R. Y., Roth, Y., & Lemoine, J. F. (2015). The impact of culture on creativity: How cultural tightness and cultural distance affect global innovation crowdsourcing work. *Administrative Science Quarterly, 60*, 189–227.

Chua, R. Y. J. (2015). Innovating at cultural crossroads: How multicultural social networks promote ideas flow and creativity. *Journal of Management*. https://doi.org/10.1177/0149206315601183

Chua, R. Y. J., & Iyengar, S. S. (2008). Creativity as a matter of choice: Prior experience and task instruction as boundary conditions for the positive effect of choice on creativity. *Journal of Creative Behavior, 42*(3), 164–180.

Chua, R. Y. J., Morris, M. W., & Ingram, P. (2010). Embeddedness and new idea discussion in professional networks: The mediating role of affect-based trust. *Journal of Creative Behavior, 44*(2), 85–104.

Chua, R. Y. J., Morris, M. W., & Mor, S. (2012). Collaborating across cultures: Cultural metacognition and affect-based trust in creative collaboration. *Organizational Behavior and Human Decision Processes, 118*(2), 116–131.

Coleman, J. S. (1988). Social capital in the creation of human capital. *American Journal of Sociology, 94*, S95–S120.

Coleman, J. S. (1990). *Foundations of social theory*. Cambridge, MA: Harvard University Press.

Cook, J., & Wall, T. (1980). New work attitude measures of trust, organizational commitment and personal need non-fulfilment. *Journal of Occupational Psychology, 53*(1), 39–52.

Cottrell, N. B. (1972). Social facilitation. In C. G. McClintock (Ed.), *Experimental social psychology* (pp. 185–236). New York, NY: Holt, Rinehart, & Winston.

Cox, T. H. (1994). *Cultural diversity in organizations: Theory, research, and practice.* San Francisco, CA: Benett-Koehler.

Cox, T. H., & Blake, S. (1991). Managing cultural diversity: Implications for organizational competitiveness. *The Executive, 5*, 45–56.

Cox, T. H., Lobel, S. A., & McLeod, P. L. (1991). Effects of ethnic group cultural differences on cooperative and competitive behavior on a group task. *Academy of Management Journal, 34*(4), 827–847.

Cramton, C. D., & Hinds, P. J. (2004). Subgroup dynamics in internationally distributed teams: Ethnocentrism or cross-national learning? In R. M. Kramer & B. M. Staw (Eds.), *Research in organizational behavior* (Vol. 26, p. 231–263). Greenwich, CT: JAI Press.

Cronin, M. A., & Weingart, L. R. (2007). Representational gaps, information processing, and conflict in functionally diverse teams. *Academy of Management Review, 32*(3), 761–773.

Crotty, S. K., & Brett, J. M. (2012). Fusing creativity: Cultural metacognition and teamwork in multicultural teams. *Negotiation and Conflict Management Research, 5*(2), 210–234.

Dabbs, J. M., & Ruback, R. B. (1987). Dimensions of group process: Amount and structure of vocal interaction. *Advances in Experimental Social Psychology, 20*, 123–169.

Delbecq, A. L., & Van de Ven, A. H. (1971). A group process model for problem identification and program planning. *The Journal of Applied Behavioral Science, 7*(4), 466–492.

Diehl, M., & Stroebe, W. (1987). Productivity loss in brainstorming groups: Toward the solution of a riddle. *Journal of Personality and Social Psychology, 53*(3), 497.

Diehl, M., & Stroebe, W. (1991). Productivity loss in idea-generating groups: Tracking down the blocking effect. *Journal of Personality and Social Psychology, 61*(3), 392.

DiMarco, M. K., Taylor, J. E., & Alin, P. (2010). Emergence and role of cultural boundary spanners in global engineering project networks. *Journal of Management in Engineering, 26*(3), 123–132.

Dougherty, D. (1992). Interpretive barriers to successful product innovation in large firms. *Organization Science, 3*(2), 179–202.

Dovidio, J. F., Evans, N., & Tyler, R. B. (1986). Racial stereotypes: The contents of their cognitive representations. *Journal of Experimental Social Psychology, 22*(1), 22–37.

Duncan, B. L. (1976). Differential social perception and attribution of intergroup violence: Testing the lower limits of stereotyping of Blacks. *Journal of Personality and Social Psychology, 34*(4), 590.

Duncan, J. (1999). Attention. In R. Wilson & F. Keil (Eds.), *The MIT encyclopedia of the cognitive sciences* (pp. 39–41). Cambridge, MA: MIT Press.

Earley, P. C., & Ang, S. (2003). *Cultural intelligence: Individual interactions across cultures.* Redwood City, CA: Stanford University Press.

Earley, P. C., Ang, S., & Tan, J. S. (2006). *CQ: Developing cultural intelligence at work.* Redwood City, CA: Stanford University Press.

Earley, P. C., & Gibson, C. B. (2002). *Multinational work teams: A new perspective*. New York, NY: Routledge.

Edmondson, A. (1999). Psychological safety and learning behavior in work teams. *Administrative Science Quarterly, 44*(2), 350–383.

Edmondson, A. C. (2003). Speaking up in the operating room: How team leaders promote learning in interdisciplinary action teams. *Journal of Management Studies, 40*(6), 1419–1452.

Elfenbein, H. A., Foo, M. D., White, J., Tan, H. H., & Aik, V. C. (2007). Reading your counterpart: The benefit of emotion recognition accuracy for effectiveness in negotiation. *Journal of Nonverbal Behavior, 31*(4), 205–223.

Ely, R. J., & Thomas, D. A. (2001). Cultural diversity at work: The effects of diversity perspectives on work group processes and outcomes. *Administrative Science Quarterly, 46*(2), 229–273.

Ferrin, D. L., Dirks, K. T., & Shah, P. P. (2006). Direct and indirect effects of third-party relationships on interpersonal trust. *Journal of Applied Psychology, 91*(4), 870.

Fink, A., Grabner, R. H., Gebauer, D., Reishofer, G., Koschutnig, K., & Ebner, F. (2010). Enhancing creativity by means of cognitive stimulation: Evidence from an fMRI study. *Neuroimage, 52*(4), 1687–1695.

Fink, A., Koschutnig, K., Benedek, M., Reishofer, G., Ischebeck, A., Weiss, E. M., & Ebner, F. (2012). Stimulating creativity via the exposure to other people's ideas. *Human Brain Mapping, 33*(11), 2603–2610.

Finke, R. A., Ward, T. B., & Smith, S. M. (1992). *Creative cognition: Theory, research, and applications*. Cambridge, MA: MIT Press.

Fox, J. R., Park, B., & Lang, A. (2007). When available resources become negative resources: The effects of cognitive overload on memory sensitivity and criterion bias. *Communication Research, 34*(3), 277–296.

Frost, P. J. (2003). *Toxic emotions at work: How compassionate managers handle pain and conflict*. Boston, MA: Harvard Business School.

Gelfand, M. J., Erez, M., & Aycan, Z. (2007). Cross-cultural organizational behavior. *Annual Review Psychology, 58*, 479–514.

Gelfand, M. J., Nishii, L. H., Holcombe, K. M., Dyer, N., Ohbuchi, K. I., & Fukuno, M. (2001). Cultural influences on cognitive representations of conflict: Interpretations of conflict episodes in the United States and Japan. *Journal of Applied Psychology, 86*(6), 1059–1074.

Gelfand, M. J., Nishii, L. H., & Raver, J. L. (2006). On the nature and importance of cultural tightness-looseness. *Journal of Applied Psychology, 91*(6), 1225–1244.

Gelfand, M. J., Raver, J. L., Nishii, L., Leslie, L. M., Lun, J., Lim, B. C., . . . & Yamaguchi, S. (2011). Differences between tight and loose cultures: A 33-nation study. *Science, 332*(6033), 1100–1104.

Giambatista, R. C., & Bhappu, A. D. (2010). Diversity's harvest: Interactions of diversity sources and communication technology on creative group performance. *Organizational Behavior and Human Decision Processes, 111*(2), 116–126.

Gibb, J. R. (1961). Defensive communication. *Journal of Communication, 11*(3), 141–148.

Gibson, C. B., & Gibbs, J. L. (2006). Unpacking the concept of virtuality: The effects of geographic dispersion, electronic dependence, dynamic structure, and national diversity on team innovation. *Administrative Science Quarterly, 51*(3), 451–495.

Gibson, C. B., & Zellmer-Bruhn, M. E. (2001). Metaphors and meaning: An intercultural analysis of the concept of teamwork. *Administrative Science Quarterly, 46*(2), 274–303.

Gibson, C. B., & Zellmer-Bruhn, M. E. (2002). Minding your metaphors: Applying the concept of teamwork metaphors to the management of teams in multicultural contexts. *Organizational Dynamics, 31*(2), 101–116.

Govindarajan, V., & Gupta, A. K. (2001). Building an effective global business team. *MIT Sloan Management Review, 42*(4), 63–71.

Guilford, J. P. (1950). Creativity. *American Psychologist, 5*, 444–454.

Haas, M. R. (2006). Acquiring and applying knowledge in transnational teams: The roles of cosmopolitans and locals. *Organization Science, 17*(3), 367–384.

Hackman, J. R. (1990). *Groups that work (and those that don't)*. San Francisco, CA: Jossey-Bass.

Hall, E. T. (1976). *Beyond culture*. Garden City, NY: Anchor.

Harris, M. (1968). *The rise of anthropological theory: A history of theories of culture*. New York, NY: Thomas Y. Crowell.

Harrison, D. A., Price, K. H., Gavin, J. H., & Florey, A. T. (2002). Time, teams, and task performance: Changing effects of surface-and deep-level diversity on group functioning. *Academy of Management Journal, 45*(5), 1029–1045.

Hofstede, G. (1980). *Culture's consequences: International differences in work-related values*. Newbury Park, CA: Sage.

Hofstede, G. (1991). *Cultures and organizations*. London, UK: McGraw-Hill.

Hofstede, G., Hofstede, G. J., & Minkov, M. (2010). *Cultures and organizations. Software of the mind*. New York, NY: McGraw-Hill.

Hong, Y. Y., Chao, M. M., & No, S. (2009). Dynamic interracial/intercultural processes: The role of lay theories of race. *Journal of Personality, 77*(5), 1283–1310.

House, J. S., Landis, K. R., & Umberson, D. (1988). Social relationships and health. *Science, 241*(4865), 540–545.

Imai, L., & Gelfand, M. J. (2010). The culturally intelligent negotiator: The impact of cultural intelligence (CQ) on negotiation sequences and outcomes. *Organizational Behavior and Human Decision Processes, 112*(2), 83–98.

Ingram, P., & Roberts, P. W. (2000). Friendships among competitors in the Sydney hotel industry. *American Journal of Sociology, 106*(2), 387–423.

Jang, S. (2014). *Cultural brokerage in multicultural teams*. (Unpublished doctoral dissertation). Boston, MA: Harvard Business School.

Janssens, M., & Brett, J. M. (2006). Cultural intelligence in global teams: A fusion model of collaboration. *Group & Organization Management, 31*(1), 124–153.

Jehn, K. A., & Mannix, E. A. (2001). The dynamic nature of conflict: A longitudinal study of intragroup conflict and group performance. *Academy of Management Journal, 44*(2), 238–251.

Jehn, K. A., Northcraft, G. B., & Neale, M. A. (1999). Why some differences make a difference: A field study of diversity, conflict, and performance in workgroups. *Administrative Science Quarterly, 44*, 741–763.

Jehn, K. A., Rispens, S., & Thatcher, S. M. (2010). The effects of conflict asymmetry on work group and individual outcomes. *Academy of Management Journal, 53*(3), 596–616.

Kadushin, C. (1982). Social density and mental health. In P. V. Marsden & N. Lin (Eds.), *Social structure and network analysis* (pp. 147–158). Beverly Hills, CA: Sage.

Klafehn, J., Banerjee, P. M., & Chiu, C. Y. (2008). Navigating cultures. In S. Ang & L. Van Dyne (Eds.), *Handbook of cultural intelligence: Theory, measurement and* application (p. 318–331). New York, NY: ME Sharpe, Inc.

Kluckhohn, C. (1954). Culture and behavior. In G. Lindzey (Ed.), *Handbook of social psychology* (Vol. 2, pp. 931–76). Cambridge, MA: Addison-Wesley.

Koopman, P. L., & Wierdsma, A. F. M. (1998). Participative management. In P. J. D. Drenth, H. Thierry, & C. J. De Wolff (Eds.), *Handbook of work and organizational psychology* (Vol. 3: Personnel Psychology, pp. 297–324). Hove, UK: Psychology Press.

Kramer, R. M. (1999). Trust and distrust in organizations: Emerging perspectives, enduring questions. *Annual Review of Psychology, 50*(1), 569–598.

Kurtzberg, T. R. (1998). Creative thinking, a cognitive aptitude, and integrative joint gain: A study of negotiator creativity. *Creativity Research Journal, 11*(4), 283–293.

Lamm, H., & Trommsdorff, G. (1973). Group versus individual performance on tasks requiring ideational proficiency (brainstorming): A review. *European Journal of Social Psychology, 3*(4), 361–388.

Lang, A. (2000). The limited capacity model of mediated message processing. *Journal of Communication, 50*(1), 46–70.

Lau, D. C., & Murnighan, J. K. (1998). Demographic diversity and faultlines: The compositional dynamics of organizational groups. *Academy of Management Review, 23*(2), 325–340.

Leung, A. K. Y., & Chiu, C. Y. (2010). Multicultural experience, idea receptiveness, and creativity. *Journal of Cross-Cultural Psychology, 41*(5–6), 723–741.

Leung, A. K. Y., Maddux, W. W., Galinsky, A. D., & Chiu, C. Y. (2008). Multicultural experience enhances creativity: The when and how. *American Psychologist, 63*(3), 169.

Lewis, J. D., & Weigert, A. (1985). Trust as a social reality. *Social Forces, 63*(4), 967–985.

Lievens, F., Harris, M. M., Van Keer, E., & Bisqueret, C. (2003). Predicting cross-cultural training performance: The validity of personality, cognitive ability, and dimensions measured by an assessment center and a behavior description interview. *Journal of Applied Psychology, 88*(3), 476.

Ma, Z., & Jaeger, A. (2005). Getting to yes in China: Exploring personality effects in Chinese negotiation styles. *Group Decision and Negotiation, 14*(5), 415–437.

Maddux, W. W., & Galinsky, A. D. (2009). Cultural borders and mental barriers: The relationship between living abroad and creativity. *Journal of Personality and Social Psychology, 96*(5), 1047.

Mayer, R. C., Davis, J. H., & Schoorman, F. D. (1995). An integrative model of organizational trust. *Academy of Management Review, 20*(3), 709–734.

Maznevski, M. L. (1994). Understanding our differences: Performance in decision-making groups with diverse members. *Human Relations, 47*(5), 531–552.

McAllister, D. J. (1995). Affect-and cognition-based trust as foundations for interpersonal cooperation in organizations. *Academy of Management Journal, 38*(1), 24–59.

McLeod, P. L., Lobel, S. A., & Cox, T. H. (1996). Ethnic diversity and creativity in small groups. *Small Group Research, 27*(2), 248–264.

Mok, A., & Morris, M. W. (2010). Asian-Americans' creative styles in Asian and American situations: Assimilative and contrastive responses as a function of bicultural identity integration. *Management and Organization Review, 6*(3), 371–390.

Mullen, B., Johnson, C., & Salas, E. (1991). Productivity loss in brainstorming groups: A meta-analytic integration. *Basic and Applied Social Psychology, 12*(1), 3–23.

Nemeth, C. J., Personnaz, B., Personnaz, M., & Goncalo, J. A. (2004). The liberating role of conflict in group creativity: A study in two countries. *European Journal of Social Psychology, 34*(4), 365–374.

No, S., Hong, Y. Y., Liao, H. Y., Lee, K., Wood, D., & Chao, M. M. (2008). Lay theory of race affects and moderates Asian Americans' responses toward American culture. *Journal of Personality and Social Psychology, 95*(4), 991.

O'Reilly, C. A. III, William, K. Y., & Barsade, S. (1998). Group demography and innovation: Does diversity help? In D. H. Gruenfeld (Ed.), *Composition* (pp. 183–207). New York, NY: Elseiver Science/JAI Press.

Parnes, S. J. (1992). *Source book for creative problem solving*. Buffalo, NY: Creative Education Foundation.

Paulus, P. (2000). Groups, teams, and creativity: The creative potential of idea-generating groups. *Applied Psychology, 49*(2), 237–262.

Paulus, P. B., & Brown, V. R. (2003). Enhancing ideational creativity in groups: Lessons from research on brainstorming. In P. B. Paulus & B. A. Nijstad (Eds.), *Group creativity: Innovation through collaboration* (pp. 110–136) (2nd ed.). New York, NY: Oxford University Press.

Paulus, P. B., Larey, T. S., & Dzindolet, M. T. (2001). Creativity in groups and teams. In M. Turner (Ed.), *Groups at work: Theory and research* (p. 319–338). Hillsdale, NJ: Lawrence Erlbaum.

Paulus, P. B., Putman, V. L., Dugosh, K. L., Dzindolet, M. T., & Coskun, H. (2002). Social and cognitive influences in group brainstorming: Predicting production gains and losses. *European Review of Social Psychology, 12*(1), 299–325.

Pelled, L. H., Eisenhardt, K. M., & Xin, K. R. (1999). Exploring the black box: An analysis of work group diversity, conflict, and performance. *Administrative Science Quarterly, 44*, 1–28.

Penley, L. E., & Hawkins, B. (1985). Studying interpersonal communication in organizations: A leadership application. *Academy of Management Journal, 28*(2), 309–326.

Perry-Smith, J. E. (2006). Social yet creative: The role of social relationships in facilitating individual creativity. *Academy of Management Journal, 49*, 85–101.

Polister, P. E. (1980). Network analysis and the logic of social support. In R. H. Price & P. E. Polister (Eds.), *Evaluation and action in the social environment* (pp. 69–87). New York, NY: Academic Press.

Polzer, J. T., Milton, L. P., & Swarm, W. B. (2002). Capitalizing on diversity: Interpersonal congruence in small work groups. *Administrative Science Quarterly, 47*(2), 296–324.

Porath, C. L., & Erez, A. (2007). Does rudeness really matter? The effects of rudeness on task performance and helpfulness. *Academy of Management Journal, 50*, 1181–1197.

Reagans, R., & McEvily, B. (2003). Network structure and knowledge transfer: The effects of cohesion and range. *Administrative Science Quarterly, 48*, 240–267.

Reagans, R., & Zuckerman, E. W. (2001). Networks, diversity, and productivity: The social capital of corporate R&D teams. *Organization Science, 12*(4), 502–517.

Rempel, J. K., Holmes, J. G., & Zanna, M. P. (1985). Trust in close relationships. *Journal of Personality and Social Psychology, 49*(1), 95.

Rietzschel, E. F., Nijstad, B. A., & Stroebe, W. (2007). Relative accessibility of domain knowledge and creativity: The effects of knowledge activation on the quantity and originality of generated ideas. *Journal of Experimental Social Psychology, 43*(6), 933–946.

Rodan, S., & Galunic, C. (2004). More than network structure: How knowledge hetero-geneity influences managerial performance and innovativeness. *Strategic Management Journal*, 25(6), 541–562.

Rubenson, D. L., & Runco, M. A. (1995). The psychoeconomic view of creative work in groups and organizations. *Creativity and Innovation Management*, 4(4), 232–241.

Sanna, L. J. (1992). Self-efficacy theory: Implications for social facilitation and social loafing. *Journal of Personality and Social Psychology*, 62(5), 774.

Schneider, B., & Reichers, A. E. (1983). On the etiology of climates. *Personnel Psychology*, 36, 19–39.

Scott, W. R. (1992). *Organizations: Rational, natural, and open systems*. Upper Saddle River, NJ: Prentice-Hall.

Shenkar, O. (2001). Cultural distance revisited: Towards a more rigorous conceptual-ization and measurement of cultural differences. *Journal of International Business Studies*, 32, 519–535.

Shweder, R., & LeVine, R. (1984). *Culture theory: Essays on mind, self, and emotion*. London, UK: Cambridge University Press.

Smith, K. G., Smith, K. A., Olian, J. D., Sims Jr, H. P., O'Bannon, D. P., & Scully, J. A. (1994). Top management team demography and process: The role of social integra-tion and communication. *Administrative Science Quarterly*, 39, 412–438.

Stahl, G. K., Maznevski, M. L., Voigt, A., & Jonsen, K. (2009). Unraveling the effects of cultural diversity in teams: A meta-analysis of research on multicultural work groups. *Journal of International Business Studies*, 41(4), 690–709.

Stahl, G. K., Maznevski, M. L., Voigt, A., & Jonsen, K. (2009). Unraveling the effects of cultural diversity in teams: A meta-analysis of research on multicultural work groups. *Journal of International Business Studies*, 41(4), 690–709.

Stephan, W. G., & Stephan, C. W. (1985). Intergroup anxiety. *Journal of Social Issues*, 41(3), 157–175.

Sternberg, R. J. (1985). *Beyond IQ: A triarchic theory of intelligence*. New York, NY: Cambridge University Press.

Swann, W. B., Kwan, V. S., Polzer, J. T., & Milton, L. P. (2003). Fostering group identifi-cation and creativity in diverse groups: The role of individuation and self-verification. *Personality and Social Psychology Bulletin*, 29(11), 1396–1406.

Swann, W. B. J., Kwan, V. S. Y., Polzer, J. T., & Milton, L. P. (2003). Fostering group iden-tification and creativity in diverse groups: The role of individuation and self verifica-tion. *Personality and Social Psychology Bulletin*, 29, 1396–1406.

Tajfel, H., & Turner, J. C. (1979). An integrative theory of intergroup conflict. In W. G. Austin, & S. Worchel (Eds.), *The social psychology of intergroup relations* (pp. 33–47). Monterey, CA: Brooks/Cole.

Takeuchi, R., Yun, S., & Tesluk, P. E. (2002). An examination of crossover and spillover effects of spousal and expatriate cross-cultural adjustment on expatriate outcomes. *Journal of Applied Psychology*, 87(4), 655.

Thomas, D. C. (2006). Domain and development of cultural intelligence: The impor-tance of mindfulness. *Group & Organization Management*, 31(1), 78–99.

Thomas, D. C., Stahl, G., Ravlin, E. C., Poelmans, S., Pekerti, A., Maznevski, M., Lazarova, M. B., Elron, E., Ekelund, B. Z., Cerdin, J. L., Brislin, R., Aycan, Z., & Au, K. (2008). Cultural intelligence: Domain and assessment. *International Journal of Cross-Cultural Management*, 8, 123–143.

Tierney, P., & Farmer, S. M. (2002). Creative self-efficacy: Its potential antecedents and relationship to creative performance. *Academy of Management Journal, 45*(6), 1137–1148.

Tihanyi, L., Griffith, D. A., & Russell, C. J. (2005). The effect of cultural distance on entry mode choice, international diversification, and MNE performance: a meta-analysis. *Journal of International Business Studies, 36*(3), 270–283.

Treffinger, D. J., Isaksen, S. G., & Dorval, K. B. (1994). Creative learning and problem solving: An overview. In M. Runco (Ed.), *Problem finding, problem solving, and creativity* (p. 223–236). Norwood, NJ: Albex.

Triandis, H. C. (1989). The self and social behavior in differing cultural contexts. *Psychological Review, 96*(3), 506–520.

Triandis, H. C. (1994). *Culture and social behavior.* New York, NY: McGraw-Hill.

Tsai, W., & Ghoshal, S. (1998). Social capital and value creation: The role of intrafirm networks. *Academy of Management Journal, 41*(4), 464–476.

Tsui, A. S., Egan, T. D., & O'Reilly, C. A. (1992). Being different: Relational demography and organizational attachment. *Administrative Science Quarterly, 37,* 549–579.

Tsui, A. S., Nifadkar, S. S., & Ou, A. Y. (2007). Cross-national, cross-cultural organizational behavior research: Advances, gaps, and recommendations. *Journal of Management, 33*(3), 426–478.

Uzzi, B. (1997). Social structure and competition in interfirm networks: The paradox of embeddedness. *Administrative Science Quarterly, 42,* 35–67.

Uzzi, B. (1999). Embeddedness in the making of financial capital: How social relations and networks benefit firms seeking financing. *American Sociological Review, 64,* 481–505.

Uzzi, B., & Lancaster, R. (2003). Relational embeddedness and learning: The case of bank loan managers and their clients. *Management Science, 49*(4), 383–399.

Vivero, V. N., & Jenkins, S. R. (1999). Existential hazards of the multicultural individual: Defining and understanding "cultural homelessness." *Cultural Diversity and Ethnic Minority Psychology, 5*(1), 6–26.

Walker, G., Kogut, B., & Shan, W. (1997). Social capital, structural holes and the formation of an industry network. *Organization Science, 8*(2), 109–125.

Ward, T. B. (2001). Creative cognition, conceptual combination, and the creative writing of Stephen R. Donaldson. *American Psychologist, 56*(4), 350.

Ward, T. B., Smith, S. M., & Finke, R. A. 1999. Creative cognition. In R. J. Sternberg (Ed.), *Handbook of creativity* (p. 189–212). New York, NY: Cambridge University Press.

Watson, W. E., Kumar, K., & Michaelsen, L. K. (1993). Cultural diversity's impact on interaction process and performance: Comparing homogeneous and diverse task groups. *Academy of Management Journal, 36*(3), 590–602.

Wellman, B. (1988). Structural analysis: From method and metaphor to theory and substance. In B. Wellman & S. D. Berkowitz (Eds.), *Social structures: A network approach* (pp. 19–61). New York, NY: Cambridge University Press.

Wiersema, M. F., & Bantel, K. A. (1992). Top management team demography and corporate strategic change. *Academy of Management Journal, 35*(1), 91–121.

Williams, K. Y., & O'Reilly, C. A. (1998). Demography and diversity in organizations: A review of 40 years of research. *Research in Organizational Behavior, 20,* 77–140.

Zellmer-Bruhn, M. E., Maloney, M. M., Bhappu, A. D., & Salvador, R. B. (2008). When and how do differences matter? An exploration of perceived similarity in teams. *Organizational Behavior and Human Decision Processes, 107*(1), 41–59.

Zhou, J., & Hoever, I. J. (2013). Research on workplace creativity: A review and redirection. *Annual Review of Organizational Psychology and Organizational Behavior, 1,* 333–359.

Zucker, L. G. (1986). Production of trust: Institutional sources of economic structure, 1840-1920. *Research in Organizational Behavior, 8,* 53–111.

10

An Integrated Dual-Pathway Model of Multicultural Experience and Creativity

LAY SEE ONG, YI WEN TAN, AND CHI-YING CHENG ■

Multiculturalism is a ubiquitous phenomenon in today's global world. Culturally diverse societies provide opportunities where people from different cultural groups come together to exchange knowledge and information. Thus, multiculturalism is often touted as a seedbed for creativity. The research on multiculturalism and creativity has well documented the evidence that individuals who are exposed to more than one culture for various reasons can potentially exhibit higher creativity (e.g., Cheng, Sanchez-Burks, & Lee, 2008; Leung & Chiu, 2010; Maddux, Adam, & Galinsky, 2010; Tadmor, Galinsky, & Maddux, 2012).

This line of research generally conceptualizes multicultural experiences in three different ways, which was consistently corroborated to associate with creative benefits. First, multicultural experience defined as the experience of having lived abroad for a period of time was found to positively associate with individual creativity. For example, Maddux and Galinsky's (2009) research showed that individuals who have lived abroad (vs. merely traveled abroad) exhibit significantly higher creativity in problem-solving and idea-generation tasks. In addition, research also showed that bringing intercultural learning experience to the fore enhances individuals' creative performance among those who have spent an extensive amount of time in foreign countries (Maddux et al., 2010). People who have acquired multicultural experience through living abroad for a prolonged period of time could have adhered to a multicultural identity if they identify with or see themselves as part of their exposed cultures (Hong, Wan, No, & Chiu, 2007).

Second, existing research provides support for the idea that individuals with multicultural identities exhibit higher creative benefits.[1] These multicultural individuals are defined as people who have been exposed to two or more cultures for an extensive length of time (e.g., 5 years in each culture) and, more specifically, those who adopt an integration acculturation strategy toward their home and host cultures according to Berry's (1990) acculturation model (Tadmor & Tetlock, 2006). Their higher level of creativity is likely to reflect higher cognitive complexity as a result of constantly negotiating between the multiple cultural knowledge systems (Tadmor et al., 2012; Tadmor, Tetlock, & Peng, 2009). Furthermore, research drawing upon the concept of identity integration (II) has shown that different levels of identity integration explain different levels of creative performance among multicultural individuals (e.g., Cheng et al., 2008). These findings underlie the concept of bicultural identity integration (BII) or multicultural identity integration (MII), which refers to the degree to which individuals with two or more cultural identities perceive their cultural identities as compatible or in conflict.[2] For example, Benet-Martinez and Haritatos (2005) showed that multicultural individuals who see their different cultural identities as compatible and not in conflict (i.e., high BII) tend to be better at accessing the multiple cultural knowledge systems simultaneously than those who see their different cultural identities as incompatible and in conflict (i.e., low BII). Importantly, multiculturals with higher BII are better at integrating ideas from various cultures when performing in creativity tasks as compared to multiculturals with lower BII (Cheng et al., 2008).

Third, multicultural experiences can be simulated in lab settings by presenting stimuli that juxtapose cultural images from two cultures to monocultural individuals who have had limited exposure to cultures other than their own. These images could involve different cultural aspects, including apparel, architecture, arts, cuisine, entertainment, landscape, movie, scenery, and political icons. Research showed that monocultural individuals who were exposed to a slideshow presenting a juxtaposition of two cultures (vs. only one culture) exhibit higher creativity, as reflected in, for example, the generation of a more creative Cinderella story for Turkish children (Leung & Chiu, 2010) and coming up with a more unconventional use of a garbage bag (Cheng, Leung, & Wu, 2011).

A common thread running through the three conceptualizations of multicultural experience is the involvement of knowledge sets. Cultural knowledge sets could be acquired through contacts with diverse cultures or activated through multicultural primes. According to Amabile (1983), there are two main types of knowledge needed for creative performance. The first type is "knowledge about the domain" and the second is "implicit or explicit knowledge of heuristics for generating novel ideas" (pp. 362–365). The former refers to the *what* of creativity—content knowledge that forms fundamental building blocks of the ideas to be used for the creativity task, whereas the latter refers to the *how* and *why* of creativity—normative knowledge that encompasses guides and rules used in the process of the creativity task. In this chapter, we have distinguished between content and normative knowledge to further our understanding of how these two types of knowledge can influence creative performance separately.

In particular, content knowledge refers to the different ideas and representations of people, objects, and events in different cultures that can be used as the contents of creative ideas, that is, content knowledge is the domain knowledge specifically applicable to the creative problem. Adopting the definition from Chiu and Hong (2007), content knowledge involves a network of associations connecting a referent concept (e.g., an object) to other related concepts. For example, when thinking about a concept (e.g., food ware), having multicultural experiences may lead to the activation of a wider range of associated content knowledge (e.g., chopsticks and hand). The possession of different sets of content knowledge can potentially expand the range for creative ideas.

On the other hand, normative knowledge refers to the different rules, routines, principles, and the like that are shared among members within a culture (i.e., norm representations) that can be used to regulate creative processes and outcomes. Norm representations can be understood as behavioral and thought guidelines, which consist of three elements: the antecedent circumstances, the norm itself, and the consequences of the norm (Chiu & Hong, 2007). In other words, there are specific situations where a norm is applicable and, depending on how wide the social acceptance of the norm is, would generate a certain set of consequences (e.g., it is appropriate to use one's hands when eating in India, to use chopsticks in Mainland China, and to use knife and fork in the United States). The knowledge of different norms in different cultures may challenge individuals' beliefs in norms and behavioral routines of their own culture and potentially expand their range for acceptable creative activities and outcomes. For example, when thinking about a concept (e.g., food ware), having multicultural experiences may lead to the activation of a wider range of associated normative knowledge as well as more flexibility in the application of normative knowledge (e.g., it is acceptable to use both hands and chopsticks when eating Indian-Chinese fusion food in the United States).

Drawing upon the accumulative findings of the link between multiculturalism and creativity, we propose an integrative model to account for the distinctive applications of content and normative knowledge sets on creative performance. The understanding of how content and normative knowledge are used during the creative process is important because recent research has shown that perceived cultural norms could influence the way individuals apply their cultural content knowledge (e.g., Zou & Leung, 2015; Zou et al., 2009). Because researchers have repeatedly found that knowledge influences creative performance without specifying the difference between content and normative knowledge (e.g., Amabile, 1983; Batey, Furnham, & Safiullina, 2010; Rietzschel, Nijstad, & Stroebe, 2007; Weisberg, 1999), there is much value in addressing the differing effects of content and normative knowledge on creativity.

Although the overall creative process is believed to consist of five steps, namely, problem formulation, preparation, idea generation, idea evaluation, and idea selection (Amabile, 1983), most researchers have focused on the last three steps as the critical components for creative performance (e.g., Chiu & Kwan, 2010). Idea generation plays an important early step toward creative performance, with existing creativity literature demonstrating a positive correlation between the number of ideas generated and creativity (e.g., Diehl & Stroebe, 1987). With idea

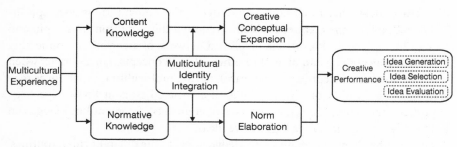

Figure 10.1. The multicultural experience and creative knowledge model (the MEACK model) with dual pathways relating multicultural experience to creative performance.

generation providing the preliminary pool of ideas, these ideas are to be evaluated and selected based on their utility and potential acceptance by the audience (Chiu & Kwan, 2010). Although the three processes are presented sequentially, it is important to note that they may not progress in a linear manner (Chiu & Kwan, 2010). For example, one may have to revisit the idea generation stage if ideas are not deemed acceptable during idea evaluation or if the audience did not accept the selected idea.

In the sections that follow, we will introduce the multicultural experience and creative knowledge (MEACK) model (Figure 10.1). This model depicts how multicultural experience affects the two types of knowledge (i.e., content and normative knowledge) and how these two types of knowledge will in turn influence creative performance that encompasses the processes of idea generation, idea evaluation, and idea selection. The moderating role of MII, an individual difference in the levels of integration among multiple cultural identities accrued from multicultural experiences, will also be discussed.

THE FIRST PATHWAY: THE CONTENT KNOWLEDGE EXPANSION PATHWAY

Drawing from the research evidence on the positive relationship between multiculturalism and creativity, the first pathway examines how multicultural experience leads to the acquisition of more content knowledge sets, which in turn can influence creative performance. Coupled with the influence of MII, we explain how content knowledge facilitates creative conceptual expansion to benefit creative performance.

Multicultural Experience and Content Knowledge

According to Chiu and Hong (2007), culture can be operationalized as knowledge networks which encompass learned routines and conventional knowledge that people in the culture frequently use as a lens to frame their daily experiences.

Both noncultural knowledge (e.g., technical knowledge of a musical instrument) and cultural knowledge (e.g., knowledge of popular music styles in the Singaporean culture) constitute content knowledge for individuals (e.g., a song writer) to start the creative generation process (Amabile, 1983; Brown, Tumeo, Larey, & Paulus, 1998; Nijstad & Stroebe, 2006), with a greater amount of content knowledge increasing the likelihood of novel combinations (Weisberg, 1999). Rietzschel and colleagues (2007)'s work offered direct support for the contribution of content knowledge toward creativity. By manipulating the accessibility of creativity-related domain knowledge, they found that participants primed with relevant knowledge were largely more creative (in originality) as compared to participants who were either not primed or primed with irrelevant knowledge. Similarly, Andrews and Smith (1996) found that product managers with greater knowledge of the marketing environment generated more creative marketing programs as compared to those with less knowledge. Thus, the acquisition of content knowledge is the starting point for incubating novel and useful ideas.

It is reasonable to argue that people who are exposed to different cultures possess different content knowledge sets, thus having access to a greater pool of ideas and concepts (Chiu & Hong, 2005; Hong et al., 2007; Leung, Maddux, Galinsky, & Chiu, 2008; Maddux & Galinsky, 2009). Although there is no direct evidence supporting the notion that multicultural people have a greater creative advantage over monocultural people due to their multiple sets of content knowledge, existing research indicates the importance of availability and accessibility of multiple content knowledge sets for promoting creativity. For example, Cheng and colleagues (2008) found that multiculturals were more creative when presented with a creativity task that tapped into multiple content knowledge sets (i.e., presented with both Asian and American cooking ingredients) than when presented with a creativity task that tapped into only one content knowledge set (i.e., presented with Asian or American cooking ingredients). Although indirect, Chua (2015) provided greater support for the notion by demonstrating the importance of a culturally heterogeneous social network for facilitating creative performance. He found that individuals who had access to a greater variety of culturally novel ideas, through their culturally heterogeneous social network, were more likely to be creative in a task that required multiple content knowledge sets (e.g., ideas to advertise a juice at a global sporting event). In short, being multicultural greatly expands an individual's content knowledge, thereby contributing to higher abilities to access ideas and concepts from multiple cultures (Leung et al., 2008).

Content Knowledge, Creative Conceptual Expansion, and Creative Performance

The idea that being multicultural could potentially expand an individual's content knowledge is congruent with a cognitive process put forth by earlier creative cognition theorists. Ward, Smith, and Vaid (1997) described creative conceptual expansion as a cognitive process where people "construct, stretch, extend, modify, and refine single concepts to fit new situations" (p. 10). For example, when college students were asked to imagine and draw animals that might live on another planet, Ward (1994) found that the creations were extremely similar to the Earth animals. That is, the creations were mostly bilaterally symmetric, with ordinary appendages (e.g., limbs) and sensory organs (e.g., eyes). Here, we can see that the characteristic properties of a concept (i.e., Earth animals) have been expanded and applied to novel situations (i.e., animals on another planet).

There is preliminary support for the presence of this creative conceptual expansion process among multicultural individuals. In a series of six studies, Tadmor, Hong, Chao, Wiruchnipawan, and Wang (2012) showed that having multicultural experience resulted in an expansion of the boundary of the racial categorizations and further resulted in lower intergroup bias and stereotyping (also see Chao, Kung, & Yao, 2015). This effect of conceptual expansion effect on racial categories may have important implications on creativity. Indeed, the research by Tadmor, Chao, Hong, and Polzer (2013) showed that individuals who perceived that racial groups were fixed (vs. malleable, arbitrary social constructions) were also less likely to show high creative performance. In other words, having a fixed view of racial groups (i.e., a nonexpandable boundary of the concept of race) was associated with lower creative performance.

Based on these findings, we argue that multicultural individuals are more adept at retrieving seemingly unrelated ideas from each culture to produce novel combinations through engaging in the creative expansion process (e.g., Chiu & Hong, 2005; Leung et al., 2008; Leung, Qiu, & Chiu, 2014). This effect is consistent with what Leung and Chiu (2010) demonstrated: Participants who had more extensive multicultural experiences were more likely to sample foreign sayings in order to prepare for a creative expansion essay task, as compared to those with fewer multicultural experiences.

The Moderating Role of Multicultural Identity Integration in Content Knowledge and Creative Conceptual Expansion

Although having a variety of knowledge sets is generally beneficial to individual creativity, extant research indicates that the different sets of knowledge relevant to the creativity task may be managed differently, depending on how individuals negotiate their multiple cultural identities. In the introduction, we briefly mentioned Berry's (1990) work on the strategies people use to deal with multicultural experiences. There are four such strategies that can be recategorized to three main themes: (a) low identification with all exposed cultures (marginalization), (b) high identification with only one of the cultures (separation and assimilation), and (c) high identification with all exposed cultures (integration; multiculturalism). Hence, when people highly identify with the multiple cultures that they are exposed to, they are classified as adopting the multiculturalism strategy.

Research has shown that the type of acculturation strategy adopted by multicultural individuals is related to creativity (Tadmor & Tetlock, 2006). Specifically, individuals who had extensive exposure (i.e., 5 years or more) to multiple cultures and acculturated with the multiculturalism strategy were found to exhibit higher creativity, presumably as a result of enhanced integrative complexity through their simultaneous practice with applying multiple cultural meaning systems (Tadmor et al., 2009; Tadmor, Galinsky, et al., 2012). We suppose that higher integrative complexity induced by constantly comparing, contrasting, and integrating multiple cultural knowledge systems can promote creative conceptual expansion.

Even though Berry's taxonomy categorizes people with high identification with all of their exposed cultures as adopting the multiculturalism strategy, Benet-Martinez, Leu, Lee, and Morris (2002) contended that there is variation in how these people perceive and manage their identities. This is especially true when multicultural individuals constantly face the challenge of negotiating between different and sometimes conflicting sets of cultural norms, practices, and values (David, Okazaki, & Saw, 2009). As a result, although multicultural individuals identify with, and have extensive knowledge of their associated cultures, there are individual differences in the way they manage their multicultural identities. In particular, the differences arise in response to their different perceptions of compatibility between those cultures. Building upon the research on BII, we term this individual difference as multicultural identity integration (MII) to capture the psychology of possessing multiple cultural identities.

Specifically, MII measures the extent to which multicultural individuals perceive their multiple cultural identities as being compatible or in conflict. Whereas multicultural individuals with high MII see the identities as compatible and harmonious, those with low MII see the identities as oppositional and in conflict (Benet-Martinez & Haritatos, 2005). Therefore, multicultural individuals with high MII are less likely to experience difficulty in associating themselves with all their cultural identities simultaneously. In contrast, their low-MII counterparts would prefer to keep their cultural identities separate and not be able to associate with all their cultural identities at the same time (see Cheng, Lee, Benet-Martinez, & Nguyen, 2014, for a review). For those with low MII, it is also possible that they only identify with one cultural group in particular contexts, and another cultural group in other contexts.

If multicultural individuals with high (vs. low) MII could sample ideas from a broader set of content knowledge when engaging in creativity tasks, the creative conceptual expansion process is more likely to ensue. Although existing research has demonstrated the importance of recognizing differences or contradictions between concepts in order to stimulate the creative combination process (e.g., Crisp & Turner, 2011), this does not mean that high-MII individuals who tend to see different cultures as compatible with each other do not recognize discrepancies between these cultures. This is evident when multicultural individuals with high MII exhibit cultural frame switching, which requires them to differentiate different sets of cultural knowledge and to apply the one that is culturally appropriate in the corresponding context (i.e., cultural assimilation effect; see Benet-Martinez et al., 2002;

Cheng, Lee, & Benet-Martinez, 2006). Therefore, we argue that high-MII individuals are able to sample ideas from various cultures because they are able to recognize the applicability of these ideas instead of failing to recognize their differences.

Research offers preliminary evidence for creative conceptual expansion to account for higher creative performance among multicultural individuals with high MII. For example, Cheng and colleagues (2008) showed that multiculturals with high MII were more likely to generate creative ideas as compared to those with low MII. Importantly, the difference in creative performance only differed between high- and low-MII individuals when the creativity task involved multiple cultural elements, but not when the task involved only elements from one culture. This implies that high-MII individuals would have sampled ideas and concepts from different knowledge, thus indirectly supporting the moderating role of MII in facilitating conceptual expansion of content knowledge.

Additional indirect but congruent support can be found in Saad and colleagues' (2013) work, in which they sought to understand the mechanism behind the superior creative performance of multiculturals with high MII. Specifically, they found that multiculturals with high MII were able to generate more alternative, expanded uses of a common object in a domain-general unusual uses test (Guilford, 1967) as compared to those with low MII, when they had all their associated cultural identities activated through priming. The heightened ability to expand on the alternative uses of a commonplace object provides indirect support that high-MII individuals are more adept at creative conceptual expansion when multiple cultural identities are activated.

Consistent results were observed among high-MII individuals with compatible gender-professional identities (as opposed to national cultural identities). Cheng and Clerkins (2015) found that senior female engineering students who have high levels of gender-professional identity integration were able to access both of their female and engineer identity-related knowledge sets and performed better in selecting creative product ideas that require knowledge tapping onto the dual identities (i.e., video games designed for middle and high school girls). In contrast, this ability to identify creative video games for schoolgirls was not found among female engineering freshman students who claimed to have high levels of gender-professional identity integration. It is possible that freshmen participants had not accumulated enough engineering-related knowledge; thus, their conceptual expansion may have failed to utilize ideas from both the female and engineer identities to benefit the idea selection process.

We identify at least one boundary condition that limits high-MII individuals' ability to reap the benefits from creative conceptual expansion. Drawing from Hong, Morris, Chiu, and Benet-Martinez (2000)'s work on frame switching, researchers have suggested that when high-MII individuals are primed with cues from a certain culture, they react in an assimilative manner to the primed cultural cues (e.g., Benet-Martinez et al., 2002; Mok & Morris, 2010a; Zou, Morris, & Benet-Martinez, 2008). Hence, although high MII affords higher creative conceptual expansion to benefit creativity, the presence of a cultural prime may direct high-MII individuals to only rely on the content knowledge related to the primed culture, but not the wider sets of content knowledge that are characteristic of diverse cultures.

Past research also distinguished between assimilative and contrast response toward cultural frame switching. Whereas high-MII individuals tend to exhibit an assimilative response to cultural primes, low-MII individuals tend to exhibit a contrastive response (e.g., low-MII Asian Americans behave in a more American way in response to Asian primes). The underlying psychological mechanism for the contrast effect was related to a greater need among low MIIs to protect the unprimed identity from perceived threat and neglect (Mok, Cheng, & Morris, 2010; Mok & Morris, 2010a).

It follows that high-MII individuals who are primed with a given cultural cue may exhibit similar or lower levels of creativity in comparison to low-MII individuals, depending on what kind of cultural cues are made salient in the situation and how they react to the cues (e.g., Benet-Martinez et al., 2002; Mok & Morris, 2010a). For example, it is possible that Chinese American people with high MII who are primed with Chinese culture would perform similarly as their low-MII counterparts who are primed with American culture, with the former group assimilating to the Chinese primes and the latter group contrasting against the American primes. In addition, in cases where both high- and low-MII people are primed with the same culture, it is possible that those with low MII would use the content knowledge of another culture that is *not* primed due to the contrast effect. More important, if the use of content knowledge of the other unprimed culture is more beneficial to the creativity problem, then low-MII people might outperform high-MII people in their creative generations.[3]

Taken together, the aforementioned arguments suggest that in the absence of specific cultural primes, high-MII people are expected to have higher creative performance than low-MII people. However, the relationship between MII and creative performance might not be straightforward when a specific cultural identity is made salient through the use of cultural primes. We can expect that cultural primes will influence multicultural individuals' activation of the corresponding cultural identity, and the cultural knowledge set used for the creative task may not be the same for those with different levels of MII.

THE SECOND PATHWAY: THE ELABORATION OF NORMATIVE KNOWLEDGE PATHWAY

In the second pathway, we argue that multicultural experience can influence creative performance through the use of another type of knowledge—normative knowledge. Next, we will describe this second pathway in detail.

Multicultural Experience and Normative Knowledge

Culture has been thought of as systems comprising social norms that are widely shared among its constituents (Chao & Chiu, 2011; Medin, Unsworth,

& Hirschfeld, 2007). Norms can be thought of as *knowledge representations* consisting of rules, theories, models, worldviews, principles, and the like that are shared among members of a collective (Chao & Chiu, 2011; Medin et al., 2007; Sripada & Stich, 2006). Cultural norms inform members of the conventions that are widely shared and accepted in the culture (Leung et al., 2008), including those governing the domain of creativity (e.g., Erez & Nouri, 2010; Rudowicz, 2003). Since creativity is shaped by social and cultural norms, practices, and values (Morris & Leung, 2010; Runco & Johnson, 2002), it is expected that people who are exposed to different cultures will apply different normative knowledge when performing in creativity tasks, which will lead to downstream consequences on creative performance.

Indeed, various researchers have suggested that different cultures imbue their members with different cultural normative knowledge related to creativity. For instance, Bechtoldt, De Dreu, Nijstad, and Choi (2010) showed that Western cultures value originality more than appropriateness, whereas the reverse is true for Eastern cultures. As Western cultures value individualism, lower power distance, and lower uncertainty avoidance, it is likely that these orientations encourage creative exploration that goes beyond social norms and conventions, such that novelty and uniqueness are widely pursued (Brewer & Chen, 2007; Brewer & Gardner, 1996; Erez & Nouri, 2010; Kim & Markus, 1999; Mok & Morris, 2010a). On the other hand, Eastern cultures value collectivism, higher power distance, higher uncertainty avoidance, and conformity to social norms, with these orientations putting a greater emphasis on pursuing creative ideas within boundaries of existing norms, such as ideas that are deemed more typical or practical (Erez & Nouri, 2010; Harzing & Hofstede, 1996; Westwood & Low, 2003). Importantly, as people with multicultural experience have a broader set of cultural knowledge (Tadmor, Hong, Chiu, & No, 2010), including creativity-related normative knowledge, they are more likely to reduce their reliance on the norms of a single culture (Saad et al., 2013).

The Moderating Role of Multicultural Identity Integration in Normative Knowledge and Norm Elaboration

Similar to the first pathway, we posit that MII also moderates the use of different cultures' creativity-related normative knowledge among multicultural individuals. To elaborate, we expect that people with lower MII will mainly apply the normative knowledge of one culture at one time, depending on which culture is made more accessible in the context (Saad et al., 2013). Conversely, individuals with higher MII are better able to access and apply different sets of normative knowledge simultaneously (Cheng, Sanders, et al., 2008). As researchers also suggested that high-MII individuals may even possibly see themselves as part of a combined emerging culture from the various cultures they are exposed to (Benet-Martinez & Haritatos, 2005), it is possible that their creativity-related normative knowledge grows as it encompasses and intermixes the different sets of normative knowledge associated with the different cultures they are exposed to. We predict that this expanded set of normative knowledge can broaden the range of acceptable creative ideas. We will discuss this point further in the following section.

Regardless of whether high-MII individuals access different sets of normative knowledge simultaneously or from an expanded set of normative knowledge, we suppose that they can arrive at a better understanding of the creativity criteria and goals valued in different cultures and are able to apply this knowledge in a flexible way. We call this capability to flexibly apply a given set of normative knowledge or a combined set of normative knowledge that is deemed applicable in the context to guide creative activities as *norm elaboration*.

Norm Elaboration, Multicultural Identity Integration, and Creativity Performance

As prior research suggested that rules and norms restrict people's brainstorming or idea generation (e.g., Bechtoldt et al., 2010; Woodman, Sawyer, & Griffin, 1993), we argue that high-MII individuals can become less restricted in their generative thoughts than low-MII individuals because they can engage in higher norm elaboration and utilize a wider range of creativity-related normative knowledge. Using the gift idea generation task as an example, an Asian American with low MII may rely on normative knowledge of the Asian culture that values appropriateness as opposed to novelty (Erez & Nouri, 2010; Harzing & Hofstede, 1996; Mok & Morris, 2010a; Westwood & Low, 2003), thus generating more typical gifts that tend to be more appropriate (e.g., gift vouchers). Conversely, Asian Americans with high MII may use normative knowledge of both the Asian and American cultures in generating gift ideas, thus focusing on both novelty and appropriateness norms. For example, they may come up with ideas such as gifting American newlyweds with gift vouchers from their favorite furniture store, placed within a traditional Chinese red packet printed with the word "囍" ("Xi," meaning double happiness). Hence, high-MII individuals who have greater norm elaboration can perform better in idea generation.

Similar creative benefits in terms of idea evaluation and selection should be observed for high-MII individuals. When a creative idea is generated, people may consciously or unconsciously evaluate the ideas to retain the best ideas (Campbell, 1960; Simonton, 1988). People may employ the evaluation processes on their own accord (i.e., internally) or based on the task requirements (i.e., externally; Lubart, 2001), so as to judge the candidate ideas in order to optimize the chance to attain high creative performance. After evaluation, they will then select the ideas that are best for the task. As norms play a vital role in influencing people's assessments of what is considered creative (Lubart, 1999), what is considered best for the task depends on the norms that people refer to.

For example, the norms in the Asian culture will deem appropriate ideas as the preferred solution for the creativity task, whereas the norms in the American culture will deem novel ideas as the preferred solution (Erez & Nouri, 2010;

Harzing & Hofstede, 1996; Mok & Morris, 2010a; Westwood & Low, 2003). Asian Americans with high MII and greater norm elaboration should be able to consider ideas that optimally epitomize both the novelty and appropriateness normative expectations. This also means that they will be more receptive to a wider pool of creative ideas. However, Asian Americans with low MII and lower norm elaboration may only use one set of normative knowledge associated with one of the cultures (e.g., appropriateness as the Asian normative knowledge for creativity) to guide their idea evaluation and selection processes. This practice will lead to a narrower range of creative thoughts.

Basing our example on wedding gifts again, an Asian American with high MII may think of gifting the newlyweds with the paper currencies of different countries, each folded into tiny paper money hearts. In this example, we can appreciate how this Asian American navigates through two sets of cultural norms to arrive at this gift idea. Whereas the norm of the American culture perceives that it is rude to give cash to newlyweds as a wedding present, the Asian culture perceives that cash is the usual form of a wedding present. By creating tiny paper money hearts with different currencies, the Asian American successfully meets the demand of both cultures by giving objects made from money. The high MII individual is receptive to a wider pool of creative ideas that still fall within the norms of appropriateness (for the idea of giving money) and novelty (for the idea of making paper money hearts). For Asian Americans with low MII and guided by the creativity-related normative knowledge of the Asian (American) culture when evaluating and selecting ideas, they may deem the paper money hearts idea as inappropriate (not novel). Thus, high-MII individuals show higher capability to integrate different sets of normative knowledge associated with the respective cultures, thus reaping more creative benefits in terms of idea generation, idea evaluation, and idea selection to contribute to greater creative performance.

Similar to the content knowledge pathway, the boundary condition of cultural primes also applies to the normative knowledge pathway. Under cultural priming, high-MII individuals are expected to employ the normative knowledge of the primed culture, as opposed to making use of the integrated set of normative knowledge of different cultures. Notably, it is also important to take into account high-MII individuals' assimilative responses and low-MII individuals' contrastive responses toward the cultural prime and how that implicates their creative performance.

Finally, it is important to recognize that it is usually the audience, but not the producer of the creativity work, who judges the work's creativity level (Csikszentmihalyi, 1999; Sternberg & Kaufman, 2010). Hence, it is crucial to consider the content knowledge and normative knowledge adhered to by the audience. For example, if the audience is from a monocultural group (e.g., Asians), they may rely on the knowledge associated with that culture (e.g., Asian culture) during idea evaluation. This implies that the creative performance of multicultural individuals (e.g., Asian-Americans) with high MII is not necessarily more favorable than that of multicultural individuals with low MII or of monocultural individuals (e.g., Asians) when the audience is a group of monocultural individuals (e.g., Asians), who only apply creative norms in their culture to the assessment of creative performance.

THEORETICAL IMPLICATIONS

By examining the use of creativity-related content knowledge and normative knowledge by multicultural individuals, our model sheds light on a number of implications in the field of creativity research. First, by addressing how the dual pathways of content knowledge sets and normative knowledge sets impact multicultural individuals' creativity, the model provides new insights for the psychological mechanism(s) that underlie the relation between multicultural experience and creative performance. For example, future research can explore the content knowledge pathway by providing direct support for the higher likelihood of engaging in the creative conceptual expansion process by multicultural individuals and by observing how such cognitive mechanism impacts different phases of the creative process (i.e., idea generation, idea evaluation, and idea selection).

Second, we acknowledge the moderating role of MII in the dual pathways, and its potential interaction with the nature of activated cultural cues in the context. Multicultural individuals do not uniformly receive and use the cultural knowledge sets they acquire from their multicultural encounters. Instead, their idiosyncratic multicultural experiences shape the way they perceive and manage their multiple cultural identities and the corresponding knowledge sets. This also opens up a research avenue to examine how different levels of identity integration result in assimilative or contrastive reactions toward the salient culture in the given context, thus possibly producing boundary conditions on whether multicultural individuals will employ a broader set of content and normative knowledge in approaching a creativity task.

Third, our model suggests the importance of considering the audience of the creative work. As mentioned earlier, it is the audience, not the creator, who judges whether a product or idea is creative (Csikszentmihalyi, 1999; Sternberg & Kaufman, 2010). For example, the American audience, who tends to have a stronger individualistic orientation and a higher need for self-expression, may not appreciate the need for "Otohime" (a.k.a. "Sound Princess"), a commonly used toilet device in Japan that creates a loud flushing sound similar to a toilet being flushed in order to mask the sound of bodily functions, especially for women. This implication is especially relevant for multinational companies as their products face a global audience. In this regard, multicultural individuals with high MII are more likely to enjoy a competitive edge in these companies, as they are at an advantageous position to develop a product or idea that could appeal to audiences coming from different cultural backgrounds. This advantage is due to them being better able to sample ideas from diverse knowledge systems and to take into consideration an integrated set of creativity norms so as to generate ideas more readily accepted as being creative by the global audience (see also Chua, Roth, & Lemoine, 2015). For example, the worldwide coffee chain Starbucks (originated in the United States but with an international audience) produced coffee-flavored moon cakes that combine coffee with the traditional Chinese confectionary served during the Mid-Autumn festival. It is likely that the audience coming from either the American or the Chinese cultural background will evaluate the product as being creative. Thus, we propose that multicultural individuals have the advantage of producing creative ideas that can be appreciated and accepted by a larger audience. Future research can explore whether this implication is true for the idea selection and idea evaluation stages of creative performance.

FUTURE DIRECTIONS

As creativity is a complex and multifaceted phenomenon, the proposed model has much potential to be expanded to incorporate many other components that are involved in the creative process (e.g., Amabile, 1983, 1996; Eysenck, 1993, 1995; Furnham, Batey, Anand, & Manfield, 2008; Guilford, 1950; Woodman & Schoenfeldt, 1989). In this section, we address some of these components in relation to the existing constructs in our model.

First, although both content knowledge and normative knowledge have significant influence on each stage of creative processes, including idea generation, selection, and evaluation, it is plausible that these knowledge sets influence some stages of the creative processes more than others. Specifically, we posit that content knowledge might be more important than normative knowledge in the idea generation stage because generating and brainstorming ideas is driven more by creative conceptual expansion than norm elaboration. The opposite could be true for normative knowledge to be more important in the stages of idea selection and evaluation. Future research could investigate the differential influence exerted by content and normative knowledge on different stages of the creative processes and explore their related psychological mechanisms.

Second, it is possible that differences in how people attain their multicultural experience can result in differences in the levels of acquiring content knowledge and normative knowledge. "Multicultural experience" is a general term that encompasses many ways through which an individual gets to learn or experience more than one culture. Specifically, people may be born and raised in a culture and may be legitimately recognized as a member of that culture (i.e., prescribed cultural affiliation) or choose to engage in diverse cultural experiences out of their own choice (i.e., ascribed cultural affiliation). It was argued that people with prescribed cultural affiliation have a legitimate relationship with the cultural group (Ferenczi, Marshall, & Bejanyan, 2015) because such cultural affiliation is usually determined by uncontrollable factors (e.g., by birth). Chances are that these individuals' developmental years are spent within the culture; thus, they usually have extensive experience with the knowledge of the shared cultural history, values, and behavioral norms out of daily practice (Hall, 1990). In contrast, individuals with ascribed cultural affiliation may be exposed to the culture in the later phase of their lives. For example, these people could be first-generation immigrants who chose to acquire a new cultural affiliation for themselves or cultural sojourners such as expatriates or international students who work or study in another culture for an extensive amount of time. Their normative knowledge of the ascribed culture is acquired through effortful learning. It would be interesting to study the effects of prescribed and ascribed multicultural identities on the acquisition of content knowledge and normative knowledge and on subsequent creative performance, as well as how MII moderates such relationships.

Last, prior research showed that individuals' level of identity integration could be understood as a stable individual difference, as well as a malleable variable. For example, Cheng and Lee (2009, 2013) found that recalling positive cultural experiences such as gaining privilege by having connections with multiple cultural groups induced multicultural individuals' levels of MII. The opposite is true when they recalled negative cultural experiences such as being discriminated against due to one's multicultural status. This finding suggests that identity management can be subjected to external interventions. It is noted that all multicultural individuals are likely to have both positive and negative experiences related to their multiple identities. By bringing their positive (negative) experiences to the fore, MII can be enhanced (decreased) momentarily. Future research could investigate the moderating effect of MII on the dual paths of our model by experimentally manipulating multicultural individuals' level of MII.

Furthermore, prior findings about the malleability of MII shed light on the significant impact of intercultural relations on personal management of multiple identities. It seems likely that the degree of cultural inclusion in a social environment can enhance perceptions of cultural compatibility for multicultural individuals (Cheng & Lee, 2009, 2013), and this suggests the possibility for the change in the level of identity integration in real life. When an inclusive representation of multiculturalism is perceived to be valid in a new environment, multicultural individuals have the opportunities to adopt the new representation and interpret their affiliated cultures as more compatible, thereby enhancing their MII. Future research can employ field studies and longitudinal studies to capture the relationship between cultural inclusion and the development and change of multicultural individuals' levels of MII, as well as how that impacts individual creativity.

CONCLUSION

In this chapter, we propose an integrative model that outlines the process of how multicultural experience may lead individuals to acquire two types of knowledge (content knowledge and normative knowledge) for enhancing creativity and how their level of MII moderates this process. Given today's globalized world and workplace, the need to understand how multicultural experience contributes to creative performance is unprecedentedly important (e.g., the decisions to hire prospective applicants with global learning or living experiences). We hope that this model would help ignite research on the multicultural experience and creative performance link and bring this research to a novel direction, so that a greater understanding of the phenomenon's underlying mechanisms and its interrelations with other related variables can be achieved.

NOTES

1. Following Hong et al. (2007), individuals with multicultural identity are fluent with and identify with more than one culture, and this includes bicultural individuals (i.e., those who are fluent and identify with two cultures).
2. This should be distinguished from another similar concept, multiracial identity integration, which has been used to capture individual difference among individuals with multiple racial identities (Cheng & Lee, 2009).
3. Potentially, this could benefit team-level creative performance if low-MII team members can provide an alternative voice or perspective (e.g., see Mok & Morris, 2010b).

REFERENCES

Amabile, T. M. (1983). The social psychology of creativity: A componential conceptualization. *Journal of Personality and Social Psychology, 45*, 357–376.

Amabile, T. M. (1996). *Creativity in context.* New York, NY: Westview Press.

Andrews, J., & Smith, D. C. (1996). In search of the marketing imagination: Factors affecting the creativity of marketing programs for mature products. *Journal of Marketing Research, 33*, 174–187.

Batey, M., Furnham, A., & Safiullina, X. (2010). Intelligence, general knowledge and personality as predictors of creativity. *Learning and Individual Differences, 20*, 532–535.

Bechtoldt, M. N., De Dreu, C. K. W., Nijstad, B. A., & Choi, H. A. (2010). Motivated information processing, social tuning, and group creativity. *Journal of Personality and Social Psychology, 99*, 622–637.

Benet-Martinez, V., & Haritatos, J. (2005). Bicultural identity integration (BII): Components and psychosocial antecedents. *Journal of Personality, 73*, 1015–1050.

Benet-Martinez, V., Leu, J., Lee, F., & Morris, M. W. (2002). Negotiating biculturalism: Cultural frame switching in biculturals with oppositional versus compatible cultural identities. *Journal of Cross-Cultural Psychology, 33*, 492–516.

Berry, J. W. (1990). Psychology of acculturation. In R. W. Brislin (Ed.), *Applied cross-cultural psychology* (pp. 232–253). Newbury Park, CA: Sage.

Brewer, M. B., & Chen, Y. (2007). Where (who) are collectives in collectivism? Toward conceptual clarification of individualism and collectivism. *Psychological Review, 114*, 133–151.

Brewer, M. B., & Gardner, W. (1996). Who is this "we"? Levels of collective identity and self representations. *Journal of Personality and Social Psychology, 71*, 83–93.

Brown, V., Tumeo, M., Larey, T. S., & Paulus P. B. (1998). Modeling cognitive interactions during group brainstorming. *Small Group Research, 29*, 495–526.

Campbell, D. T. (1960). Blind variation and selective retention in creative thought as in other knowledge processes. *Psychological Review, 67*, 380–400.

Chao, M. M., & Chiu, C.-y. (2011). Culture as norm representations: The case of collective responsibility attribution. In A. K.-y. Leung, C.-y. Chiu, & Y.-y. Hong (Eds.), *Cultural processes: A social psychological perspective* (pp. 65–80). New York, NY: Cambridge University Press.

Chao, M. M., Kung, F. Y. H., & Yao, D. J. (2015). Understanding the divergent effects of multicultural exposure. *International Journal of Intercultural Relations, 47*, 78–88.

Cheng, C.-Y., & Clerkins, C. (2015). *Female professionals' gender-professional identity integration (G-PII) predicts creative idea production and selection.* Unpublished manuscript, Singapore Management University, Singapore.

Cheng, C. Y., & Lee, F. (2009). Multiracial identity integration: Perceptions of conflict and distance among multiracial individuals. *Journal of Social Issues, 65*, 51–68.

Cheng, C.-Y., & Lee, F. (2013). The malleability of bicultural identity integration (BII). *Journal of Cross-Cultural Psychology, 44*, 1235–1240.

Cheng, C.-Y., Lee, F., & Benet-Martinez, V. (2006). Assimilation and contrast effects in cultural frame-switching: Bicultural identity integration (BII) and valence of cultural cues. *Journal of Cross-Cultural Psychology, 37*, 742–760.

Cheng, C.-Y., Lee, F., Benet-Martinez, V., & Nguyen, A.-M. D. (2014). Variations in multicultural experience: Socio-cognitive processes and bicultural identity integration. In V. Benet-Martinez & Y.-y. Hong (Eds.). *The handbook of multicultural identity: Basic and applied psychological perspectives* (pp. 296–299). New York, NY: Oxford University Press.

Cheng, C.-Y., Leung, A. K.-y., & Wu, T.-Y. (2011). Going beyond the multicultural experience-creativity link: The mediating role of emotions. *Journal of Social Issues, 67*, 806–824.

Cheng, C.-Y., Sanchez-Burks, J., & Lee, F. (2008). Connecting the dots within creative performance and identity integration. *Psychological Science, 19*, 1178–1184.

Cheng, C.-Y., Sanders, M., Sanchez-Burks, J., Molina, K., Lee, F., Darling, E., & Zhao, Y. (2008). Reaping the rewards of diversity: The role of identity integration. *Social and Personality Psychology Compass, 2*, 1182–1198.

Chiu, C.-y., & Hong, Y.-y. (2005). Cultural competence: Dynamic processes. In A. Elliot & C. S. Dweck (Eds.), *Handbook of motivation and competence* (pp. 489–505). New York, NY: Guilford.

Chiu, C.-y., & Hong, Y.-y. (2007). Cultural processes: Basic principles. In E. T. Higgins & A. E. Kruglanski (Eds.), *Social psychology: Handbook of basic principles* (pp. 785–809). New York, NY: Guilford.

Chiu, C.-y., & Kwan, L. Y.-Y. (2010). Culture and creativity: A process model. *Management and Organization Review, 6*, 447–461.

Crisp, R. J., & Turner, R. N. (2011). Cognitive adaptation to the experience of social and cultural diversity. *Psychological Bulletin, 137*, 242–266.

Csikszentmihalyi, M. (1999). Implications of a systems perspective for the study of creativity. In R. J. Sternberg (Ed.), *Handbook of creativity* (pp. 313–335). Cambridge, UK: Cambridge University Press.

Chua, R. Y. J. (2015). Innovating at cultural crossroads: How multicultural social networks promote idea flow and creativity. *Journal of Management*. Retrieved from http://jom.sagepub.com/content/early/2015/09/02/0149206315601183.abstract

Chua, R. Y. J., Roth, Y., & Lemoine, J. (2015). How culture impacts creativity: Cultural tightness, cultural distance, and global creative work. *Administrative Science Quarterly*, *60*, 189–227.

David, E. J. R., Okazaki, S., & Saw, A. (2009). Bicultural self-efficacy among college students: Initial scale development and mental health correlates. *Journal of Counseling Psychology*, *56*, 211–226.

Diehl, M., & Stroebe, W. (1987). Productivity loss in brainstorming groups: Toward the solution of a riddle. *Journal of Personality and Social Psychology*, *53*, 497–509.

Erez, M., & Nouri, R. (2010). Creativity: The influence of cultural, social, and work contexts. *Management and Organization Review*, *6*, 351–370.

Eysenck, H. J. (1993). Creativity and personality: Suggestions for a theory. *Psychological Inquiry*, *4*, 147–178.

Eysenck, H. J. (1995). *Genius: The natural history of creativity*. New York, NY: Cambridge University Press.

Ferenczi, N., Marshall, T. C., & Bejanyan, K. (2015). The protective and detrimental effects of self-construal on perceived rejection from heritage culture members. *Frontiers in Psychology*, *6*, 1–12.

Furnham, A., Batey, M., Anand, K., & Manfield, J. (2008). Personality, hypomania, intelligence and creativity. *Personality and Individual Differences*, *44*, 1060–1069.

Guilford, J. P. (1950). Creativity. *American Psychologist*, *5*, 444–454.

Guilford, J. P. (1967). *The nature of human intelligence*. New York, NY: McGraw-Hill.

Hall, S. (1990). Cultural identity and diaspora. In J. Rutherford (Ed.), *Identity, community, culture, difference* (pp. 222–237). London, UK: Lawrence and Wishart.

Harzing, A. W., & Hofstede, G. (1996). Planned change in organizations: The influence of national culture. *Research in the Sociology of Organizations*, *14*, 297–340.

Hong, Y.-y., Morris, M., Chiu, C.-y., & Benet-Martinez, V. (2000). Multicultural minds: A dynamic constructivist approach to culture and cognition. *American Psychologist*, *55*, 709–720.

Hong, Y.-y., Wan, C., No, S., & Chiu, C.-y. (2007). Multicultural identities. In S. Kitayama & D. Cohen (Eds.), *Handbook of cultural psychology* (pp. 323–345). New York, NY: Guilford.

Kim, H., & Markus, H. R. (1999). Deviance or uniqueness, harmony or conformity? A cultural analysis. *Journal of Personality and Social Psychology*, *77*, 785–800.

Leung, A. K.-y., Chen, J., & Chiu, C.-y. (2010). Multicultural experience fosters creative conceptual expansion. In A. K.-y. Leung, C.-y. Chiu & Y.-y. Hong (Eds.), *Cultural processes: A social psychological perspective* (pp. 263–285). New York, NY: Cambridge University Press.

Leung, A. K.-y., & Chiu, C.-y. (2010). Multicultural experience, idea receptiveness, and creativity. *Journal of Cross-Cultural Psychology*, *41*, 723–741.

Leung, A. K.-y., Maddux, W. W., Galinsky, A. D., & Chiu, C.-y. (2008). Multicultural experiences enhances creativity. *American Psychologist*, *63*, 169–181.

Leung, A. K.-y., Qiu, L., & Chiu, C.-y. (2014). Psychological science of globalization. In V. Benet-Martinez & Y.-y. Hong (Eds.), *Oxford handbook of multicultural identity* (pp. 181–201). Oxford, UK: Oxford University Press.

Lubart, T. I. (1999). Creativity across cultures. In R. J. Sternberg (Ed.), *Handbook of creativity* (pp. 339–350). Cambridge, UK: Cambridge University Press.

Lubart, T. I. (2001). Models of the creative process: Past, present and future. *Creativity Research Journal, 13*, 295–308.

Maddux, W. W., Adam, H., & Galinsky, A. D. (2010). When in Rome . . . learn why the Romans do what they do: How multicultural learning experiences facilitate creativity. *Personality and Social Psychology Bulletin, 36*, 731–741.

Maddux, W. W., & Galinsky, A. D. (2009). Cultural borders and mental barriers: The relationship between living abroad and creativity. *Journal of Personality and Social Psychology, 96*, 1047–1061.

Medin, D. L., Unsworth, S. J., & Hirschfeld, L. (2007). Culture, categorisation, and reasoning. In S. Kitayama & D. Cohen (Eds.), *Handbook of cultural psychology* (pp. 615–644). New York, NY: Guilford.

Mok, A., Cheng, C.-Y., & Morris, M. W. (2010). Matching versus mismatching cultural norms in performance appraisal: Effects of the cultural setting and bicultural identity integration. *International Journal of Cross-Cultural Management, 10*, 17–35.

Mok, A., & Morris, M. W. (2010a). Asian-Americans' creative styles in Asian and American situations: Assimilative and contrastive responses as a function of bicultural identity integration. *Management and Organization Review, 6*, 371–390.

Morris, M. W., & Leung, K. (2010). Creativity East and West: Perspectives and parallels. *Management and Organization Review, 6*, 313–327.

Nijstad, B. A., & Stroebe, W. (2006). How the group affects the mind: A cognitive model of idea generation in groups. *Personality and Social Psychology Review, 10*, 186–213.

Rietzschel, E. F., Nijstad, B. A., & Stroebe, W. (2007). Relative accessibility of domain knowledge and creativity: The effects of knowledge activation on the quantity and originality of generated ideas. *Journal of Experimental Social Psychology, 43*, 933–946.

Rudowicz, E. (2003). Creativity and culture: A two-way interaction. *Scandinavian Journal of Educational Research, 47*, 273–290.

Runco, M. A., & Johnson, D. J. (2002). Parents' and teachers' implicit theories of children's creativity: A cross-cultural perspective. *Creativity Research Journal, 14*, 427–438.

Saad, C. S., Damian, R. I., Benet-Martinez, V., Moons, W. G., & Robins, R. W. (2013). Multiculturalism and creativity: Effects of cultural context, bicultural identity, and ideational fluency. *Social Psychological and Personality Science, 4*, 369–375.

Simonton, D. K. (1988). *Scientific genius: A psychology of science.* New York, NY: Cambridge University Press.

Sripada, C. S., & Stich, S. (2006). A framework for the psychology of norms. In P. Carruthers, S. Laurence, & S. Stich (Eds.), *The innate mind, vol 2: Culture and cognition* (pp. 280–301). New York, NY: Oxford University Press.

Sternberg, R. J., & J. C. Kaufman. (2010). Constraints on creativity: Obvious and not so obvious. In J. C. Kaufman & R. J. Sternberg (Eds.), *The Cambridge handbook on creativity* (pp. 467–482). Cambridge, England: Cambridge University Press.

Tadmor, C. T., Chao, M. M., Hong, Y.-y., & Polzer, J. T. (2013). Not just for stereotyping anymore: Racial essentialism reduces domain-general creativity. *Psychological Science, 24*, 99–105.

Tadmor, C. T., Galinsky, A. D., & Maddux, W. W. (2012). Getting the most out of living abroad: Biculturalism and integrative complexity as key drivers of creative and professional success. *Journal of Personality and Social Psychology, 103*, 520–542.

Tadmor, C. T., Hong, Y.-y., Chao, M. M., Wiruchnipawan, F., & Wang, W. (2012). Multicultural experiences reduce intergroup bias through epistemic unfreezing. *Journal of Personality and Social Psychology, 103*, 750–772.

Tadmor, C. T., Hong, Y.-y., Chiu, C.-y., & No, S. (2010). What I know in my mind and where my heart belongs: Multicultural identity negotiation and its cognitive consequences. In R. Crisp (Ed.), *The psychology of social and cultural diversity* (pp. 115–144). West Sussex, UK: Blackwell.

Tadmor, C. T., & Tetlock, P. E. (2006). Biculturalism: A model of the effects of second-culture exposure on acculturation and integrative complexity. *Journal of Cross-Cultural Psychology, 37*, 173–190.

Tadmor, C. T., Tetlock, P. E., & Peng, K. (2009). Acculturation strategies and integrative complexity: The cognitive implications of biculturalism. *Journal of Cross-Cultural Psychology, 40*, 105–139.

Ward, T. B. (1994). Structured imagination: The role of category structure in exemplar generation. *Cognitive Psychology, 27*, 1–40.

Ward, T. B., Smith, S. M., & Vaid, J. (1997). Conceptual structures and processes in creative thought. In T. B. Ward, S. M. Smith, and J. Vaid (Eds.), *Creativity thought: An investigation of conceptual structures and processes* (pp. 1–27). Washington, D.C.: American Psychological Association.

Weisberg, R. W. (1999). Creativity and knowledge: A challenge to theories. In R. J. Sternberg (Ed.), *Handbook of creativity* (pp. 226–259). Cambridge, England: Cambridge University Press.

Westwood, R., & Low, D. R. (2003). The multicultural muse: Culture, creativity and innovation. *International Journal of Cross Cultural Management, 3*, 235–259.

Woodman, R. W., Sawyer, J. E., & Griffin, R. W. (1993). Toward a theory of organizational creativity. *Academy of Management Review, 18*, 293–321.

Woodman, R. W., & Schoenfeldt, L. F. (1989). Individual differences in creativity: An interactionist perspective. In J. A. Glover, R. R. Ronning, & C. R. Reynolds (Eds.), *Handbook of creativity* (pp. 3–32). New York, NY: Plenum.

Zou, X., & Leung, A. K.-y. (Eds.). (2015). Intersubjective norms [Special Issue]. *Journal of Cross-Cultural Psychology, 46* (10).

Zou, X., Morris, M., Benet-Martinez, V. (2008). Identity motives and cultural priming: Cultural (dis)identification in assimilative and contrastive responses. *Journal of Experimental Social Psychology, 44*, 1151–1159.

Zou, X., Tam, K. P., Morris, M. W., Lee, S.-L., Lau, I. Y.-M., & Chiu, C.-y. (2009). Culture as common sense: Perceived consensus versus personal beliefs as mechanisms of cultural influence. *Journal of Personality and Social Psychology, 97*, 579–597.

PART FOUR

Policy and Applied Perspectives

11

Innovation in Cultural and Creative Industries

SHYHNAN LIOU AND CHIA HAN YANG ■

This chapter proposes a dual-mechanism model of innovation to understand the development of cultural and creative industries (CCIs) by bringing insights from culture and creativity research. First, we introduce the development and evolution of various countries' CCIs, together with the challenges they currently encounter for future development. Second, as shown in Figure 11.1, drawing upon research on culture and creativity and successful cases of CCIs, we introduce a dual-mechanism framework that pertains to the processes underlying the reciprocal relationship between culture and creativity and multicultural convergence to gain a more nuanced understanding of how CCIs develop. Lastly, we derive from this framework major propositions for overcoming the challenges faced by CCIs.

DEFINING CULTURAL AND CREATIVE INDUSTRIES

The terms "culture" and "industry" were first mentioned together in the book *Dialectic of Enlightenment*, which gives rise to the concept of "cultural industry" (Horkheimer & Adorno, 1947).[1] Cultural industries were used to permeate war propaganda during World War II, rendering culture as a tool for mind control. Thus, the early perception toward CCI was widely negative. The formal definition of cultural industries began to take shape in the postindustrial era when consumerism became part of the mainstream culture in the late 1990s (Jameson, 1991). The role of cultural industries shifted from being used to propagate war ideologies, to one that advocated postmodernist ideologies, that is, the consumption of cultural goods and cultural specificities (Bauman, 1993). The rise of cultural industries during this period became the flowerbed for new industry models (e.g., cultural production and consumption, creative productions) and new academic areas of study (e.g., cultural economics; Throsby, 2001).

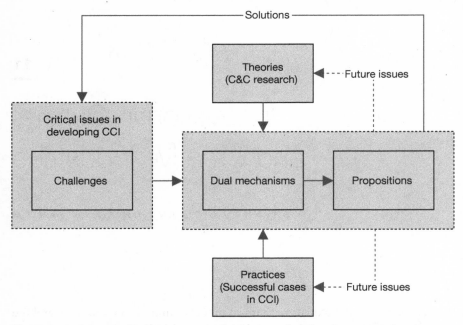

Figure 11.1. Framework of innovation in developing cultural and creative industries.

This trend of cultural industries continued to evolve until the late 20th century, when creative industries became a major focus for industry policy. When the British Labor government returned to power in 1997, then Prime Minister Tony Blair first raised the concept of "creative industries" and established the Creative Industries Task Force (CITF). This was the first time a governmental department had implemented and developed an industrial model based on the concept of culture. The Labor Party government subsequently proposed the Creative Industries Mapping Document in 1998 and 2001, which defined creative industries as "industries that originated from the creativity, skill, and talent of the individual, who creates wealth and employment opportunities through the generation and application of intellectual property rights." Around the same time, British scholar John Howkins published his book *The Creative Economy* (2002). Creative industries and economics soon became a significant field of learning in industrial development and academic research. Creative industries also brought about various types of economic values and job employment. In 2001, the production values of creative industries as defined by the British government leapt to second place among the country's economic sectors. Opportunities were created for participation by 120,000 firms, which helped resolve the issue of unemployment at that time.

With the Western countries increasing their investment in creative industries in 2000, Taiwan and China have further extended the concept of creative industries to the concept of cultural and creative industries (CCIs).[2] These CCIs build on the cultural foundation of traditional Chinese society and emphasize the role of culture in the process of industrial development. In 2010, the government formally stipulated and promulgated the Development of the Cultural and Creative Industries Act, in which the CCI was defined as "industries that originate from creativity or cultural accumulation and through the formation and application of intellectual property, and which have the potential to create wealth and employment opportunities and promote the esthetic attainment of the entire populace, thereby enhancing the living environment of all the citizens." Although this definition seems to have constricted the original scope of creative industries, it is nonetheless within the concept proposed by UNESCO and consistent with the industrial classifications proposed by other countries, with its emphasis on culture as the foundation and on cultivating industries through creativity. Categorizations of CCI of different countries and organizations are listed in Table 11.1, from which the major similarities and differences in terms of cultural contents and the main media for cultural transmission can be discerned.[3]

Overall, despite the various terminologies and classifications by different countries (e.g., cultural industries, creative industries, CCIs), the developmental context appears to be the same: These industries adhere to the concepts of deindustrialization that characterize modern experiential economy within postindustrial societies. In modern experiential economy, the production model has

Table 11.1. CATEGORY OF CULTURAL AND CREATIVE INDUSTRIES IN DIFFERENT NATIONS/ORGANIZATIONS

Nation/Organization	Category of CCI/CI
UNESCO	Visual art, Performing art, Craft, Publishing, Film, Advertising, Architecture, Music, Multimedia, Audio/Video product, Cultural tourism, Sport
United Kingdom	Antique, Performing art, Craft, Fashion design, Publishing, Broadcast & TV, Film, Advertising, Architecture, Music, Software
South Korea	Film & TV, Broadcast, Game, Animation, Art, Advertising, Publishing, Creative design, Craft, Traditional clothing, Traditional food, Software, Internet
Australia	Stage art, Design, Literature, Film & TV, Broadcast, Library, Community cultural development, Museum, Zoo/Botanical garden, Multimedia
Singapore	Media, Design, Pop music, Publishing, Art supporting service
Hong Kong	Advertising, Architecture, Antique & craft, design, Film, Digital entertainment, Music, Performing art, Publishing, Software, TV & broadcasting
Taiwan	Visual art, Performing art, Cultural asset, Craft, Film, Broadcast & TV, Publishing, Advertising, Product design, Visual design, Branding & fashion, Architecture, Digital content, Pop music, Creative life

CCI, cultural and creative industry; CI, creative industry.

transformed progressively from Fordism and the pursuit of large-scale standardization to post-Fordism, which emphasizes mass customization and flexible accumulation in order to reflect personal identity and heterogeneity. Correspondingly, productions have evolved from tangible assets (land, labor, and capital) to intangible assets (knowledge and creativity). As a result, price and functionality are no longer competitive factors. Instead, cultural capital and symbolic meanings represented by the products, as well as their connection to consumers' personal experiences and lifestyles, are critical in today's consumer market (Baudrillard, 1998). In this chapter, we apply the theoretical perspective of culture and creativity research to understand various important challenges that emerge from the process of industrializing culture and creativity.

EMERGENT CHALLENGES IN DEVELOPING CULTURAL AND CREATIVE INDUSTRIES

Among the countries that invest heavily in CCIs, Taiwan is in the forefront. To illustrate our propositions, we will use the CCIs in Taiwan as the basis for our discussions. In this section, we will first discuss the background of CCIs in the context of Taiwan, and later, we will discuss the critical challenges faced in CCI development. These discussions are not only specific to Taiwan's CCIs; they can also apply to the emerging challenges in developing global CCIs.

Taiwan first proposed the concept of CCI in 2002. In the report *Challenge 2008: The Six-Year National Development Plan*, culture, arts, and design fields that formerly belonged to different industrial categories were grouped together under the *Development Plans for the Cultural and Creative Industries* and classified as national key development industries. Although this policy change occurred within the developmental context of the Western countries shifting from cultural industries to creative industries and was influenced by the prevailing international trends during that period, CCI was formerly initiated in Taiwan by the Integrated Community Development (ICD) policy launched by the Taiwanese government in 1994. This policy was the foundation on which subsequent classifications and definitions of the CCI were made.

The original intention of the ICD policy was derived from the slogan "making culture in line with everyday life; making everyday life in line with culture." Its aim was to decentralize the implementation targets of the policy from the county level to the local communities and encourage local residents to participate in the discussions on local cultural issues and to develop a sense of community awareness. It was hoped that such a bottom-up approach would help address cultural and economic issues such as the loss of traditional cultures and the decline of local industries. Results were positive after this policy was implemented for several years. However, when the Taiwanese government referred to the case of community building in Japan, they became aware that sustainable management of communities lies in empowering local communities and managing local cultural industries. They then devised important policies for local industries to discover cultural resources unique to the local regions, thereby achieving economic benefits that could be channeled to the promotion of sustainable community development. Since then, culture-oriented industries started to grow and produced a fusion of ideas and academic discourses in Taiwan, leading to the emergence of the policy direction of "making culture in line with industrialization; making industrial developments in line with culture." In this context, the Taiwanese government decided to put forward its own definition of CCI based on the aforementioned foundation in community building and formally promulgated the Development of the Cultural and Creative Industries Act in 2010. In this Act, 15 CCI classifications were clearly listed under that definition.

Based on our critical review from recent literature on CCI development in Taiwan (2014 and 2015), and the large-scale interviews conducted with different parties relevant to Taiwan's CCIs (e.g., government officials, academics, entrepreneurs), we identified six emergent challenges of CCI development.[4]

Definition, Scope, and Categorization of the Cultural and Creative Industries

A common argument regarding CCI is its definition, which has led to debates about "real versus fake" CCIs and the criteria for inviting investments within the CCI sector (Hartley, 2005).[5] Using Taiwan's CCIs as an example, after promulgation of the Development of the Cultural and Creative Industries Act in 2010, 15 categories of CCI were made based on legal effectuality for defining and standardizing the meaning of CCI. However, having a legal definition and classification may result in the possible exclusion of other new creative industrial developments, which in turn introduces constraints on the evolution of CCI.

An example is the exclusion of technological industries in most countries' definition of CCI. In fact, today's e-commerce model, which is being driven by digital technologies, embodies the original spirit of integrating culture and creativity. Yet it is unclear whether e-commerce technologies are being considered as targets for CCI-related government policies and injection of resources. In Taiwan, the 15 CCI categories under the Development of the Cultural and Creative Industries Act face the issues of unclear definition and overlapping coverage, which currently is one major source of debate among the different stakeholders.

Debates Over the Commercialization and Industrialization of Culture

Since various stakeholders have been unable to reach a consensus regarding CCI's impacts on cultural evolution and regeneration, the process of industrializing culture has become a major source of debate (Baumol & Bowen, 1993; Ryan, 1991). An issue that has yet to be resolved for today's CCI is whether culture should be industrialized or commercialized. Does the subjectivity of culture become diluted upon industrialization, thereby diminishing the value of cultural capitals (Bourdieu, 1984; Throsby, 2001)? This question involves the varying conceptualizations of culture and the evolution process of CCI.

Culture can incorporate market demand and add creative value through the introduction of interdisciplinary elements, such as the integration of culture with technology, design, business models, tourism, and other aspects. This can result in the reinterpretation and regeneration of culture, increasing its public appeal and making it more acceptable by the mass market. On the other hand, there is the risk of excessive transformation, causing it to become entertainment segments that are common, mundane, and easily accessible. In this case, the unique value that the cultural contents originally hold will be lost (Poster, 2004).

Competition Among Cultures and Cultural Hegemony

After culture has been industrialized and commercialized, a possible challenge that it faces is the competitive market situation. Under this situation, the various cultural capitals will be transformed and become attached to specific commodities or service processes, thereby becoming the subjects of competition in the consumption markets. In a free market with competition and limited demand, indigenous cultural contents that are weaker or more vulnerable to begin with may receive less commercialization or suffer from market erosion in the face of stronger overseas cultural contents, causing them to gradually lose their visibility. Eventually, there will be market monopoly and the appearance of an exclusive phenomenon known as "cultural hegemony" (Hesmondhalgh, 2007; Scott, 2005).

This debate is often manifested in the form of Eastern and Western cultures competing for the same CCI markets. Examples are local movies produced by European or Asian countries where English is not the native language, which are originally intended to promote understanding of the regional cultures. However, since these movies compete in the same limited market as those produced by English-speaking countries, they end up suffering from a lack of market visibility. Therefore, attempts at industrialization of indigenous or local cultures with the aim of bringing them to the awareness of the public may fail under market competition. Over time, these cultures will gradually lose their cultural identity and competitiveness to survive. Eventually, they might disappear and become extinct cultures (Lampel & Shamsie, 2006).

Ignorance of Content Creation and Overemphasis on Production

In current industrialization in the CCI chain, the majority of employment opportunities and growth momentum in CCI still resides in the downstream production side of the industrial chain, rather than the creation of cultural contents located upstream (Pratt, 2004). For example, countries have increasingly focused on their indigenous cultures, which have led to many new opportunities for the creation of indigenous crafts. However, many newly created crafts businesses mainly focus on the downstream production chain. There are very few opportunities to cultivate upstream issues that are related to the preservation of the cultural discourses. Given increased commercial opportunities, the newer generations of indigenous people would naturally gravitate toward the downstream pathways, hence resulting in fewer of them being involved in the cultivation of upstream tasks pertaining to creation and transmission of the cultural heritage.

Practitioners of newly created CCI businesses tend to focus their participation in the downstream production and marketing ends, as that can maintain a certain economic scale and size in order to obtain immediate benefits to help stabilize their businesses. This leads to an imbalance between investments made in the upstream and downstream of the industrial chain. In the long term, without exploring and creating cultural contents in the upstream, the existing limited cultural contents will be overproduced as a popular entertainment and lose the original cultural identity (Deuze, 2009; Murdock, 2003).

Limited Market Size and Changes in Aesthetic Lifestyles

The development of CCIs around the world has suffered the predicament of limited growth caused by small market size. When people tend to pursue cultural consumption, they are seeking to fulfill a higher level of satisfaction in the need hierarchy. Hence, it will clearly be difficult to promote CCIs when these businesses are massively produced, given a limited consumption market. In addition, the proliferation of minority cultures is not an activity that can occur overnight. Whether a location or society has sufficient capacity for cultural consumption is dependent on the lifestyle of consumers developed by their aesthetic experience and training (Potts, 2009; Turow & McAllister, 2009).

An example is the performing arts industry, where newly established performance groups operate based on a nondiversified business model due to lack of resources. Their profits are often comprised solely of earnings from the staging of performances. Given limited scale and high competitiveness within the market of minority cultures, most of these groups often find it difficult to persist and drop out of the industry one after another.

To summarize, since the consumption pattern of CCI businesses is positioned more toward the economic end of the manufacturing industries, further growth of the CCI sector requires progressive transition toward capturing more cultural contents and opening up the aesthetics economy. It will certainly be difficult to sustain growth if rapid changes are introduced to elevate the public's preference for the cultural market without adequate support at the upstream of developing new cultural contents.

Debate Over the Necessity of Developing Cultural and Creative Industry Parks

Besides issues relating to the nature of CCIs, another challenge comes from policy decision. During the initial period when the Taiwanese government was trying to develop the CCIs, they adopted an approach based on mass production and clustering following the approach used by the Ministry of Economic Affairs to develop the manufacturing and technological industries. Consequently, with the release of state-owned land over the past decade, large numbers of CCI Parks were established in the various cities and counties.[6]

The concept of industrial parks is to tap the cluster effect for reducing transactional costs associated with the industrial chain. However, as the industrial orientations and qualities of CCI are much more diverse and difficult to integrate, the transactional costs within the industrial chain are low. Rather, there is much need for the practitioners to keep direct contact with the market, but less need for maintaining clustering and cooperation within the production end of similar industries (Costa, 2008; Lorenzen & Frederiksen, 2008). Hence, the policies on CCI Parks have not been effective in their support and development of the industries to date. Additionally, there are often contentions over the misallocation of resources and policy failures.

INNOVATION IN CULTURAL AND CREATIVE INDUSTRIES

The aforementioned analyses of the challenges for today's CCIs are not only specific to Taiwan. Based on our analysis of successful CCI cases, together with the insights garnered from the frontier theories used in research on culture and creativity, we develop a dual-mechanism framework for understanding different phenomena associated with CCI, and propose future directions for further developments. As shown in Figure 11.2, the dual-mechanism model attests to (1) the reciprocal process between culture and creativity and (2) the process of multicultural convergence. We derive eight major propositions from the model, which we describe in the following section.

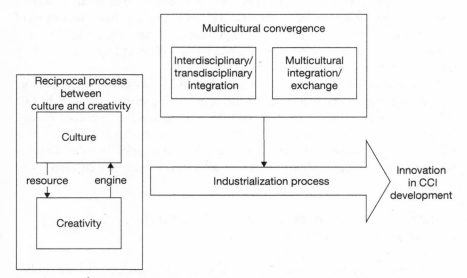

Figure 11.2. Dual mechanisms for innovation in developing cultural and creative industries.

THE RECIPROCAL PROCESS BETWEEN CREATIVITY AND CULTURE

Creativity and culture mutually influence each other, as discussed in Chapters 1 and 2 in this volume. The fundamental questions underlying this reciprocal process include, first, how culture serves as a source of creativity in creative industries; and second, how creativity in CCIs facilitates cultural development.

Culture as Creative Resources in Cultural and Creative Industries

In CCIs, culture is not only passively re-created but also serves as a resource for creativity. Basically, culture can offer some conventional knowledge for answering three fundamental questions about life, namely: What is the most important thing for people (i.e., value system)? What is the right thing to do (i.e., norm system)? What is true (i.e., belief system; Chiu, Leung, & Hong, 2010)? Through informing its members how to make sense of these fundamental questions, culture provides them a sense of consensual validity to fulfill (a) epistemic security required in uncertain circumstances (Chiu, Morris, Hong, & Menon, 2000; Kosic, Kruglanski, Pierro, & Mannetti, 2004), (b) existential security for creating life goals and comprehending phenomena that occur in life (Greenberg, Solomon, & Pyszczynski, 1997), and self-identity and belongingness needs (Jetten, Postmes, & Mcauliffe, 2002; Pickett, Bonner, & Coleman, 2002). In turn, these functions of culture also serve to motivate individuals to pursue and adhere to cultural values and beliefs (Li, Kwan, Liou, & Chiu, 2013). We assert that cultures also provide creative resources for the development of CCIs.

According to several CCI cases in Taiwan, we argue that deriving symbolic meanings from socially shared consensus and exploring local emotional adherence serve as sources of creativity for developing creations and services in CCIs. For example, ethnic Chinese have a long-established cultural tradition and practice of incense burning, such as lighting up joss sticks in religious rituals and daily life as well as appreciating incense fragrances in related events. For example, Fushan Kodo (see Figure 11.3) develops cultural and creative products by relating to the tradition of incense burning as a source of creativity.[7] The products of Fushan Kodo, including circle incense, powder incense, sandalwood timber, and agarwood, are designed to be suitable for contemporary daily uses. In this context, the traditional incense culture not only serves as a source for designing new cultural and creative products but also creates cultural symbolic meaning and local emotional attachment to the products through redefining the culture itself in contemporary style of living. This can also promote product marketing by associating the products with a lifestyle that values slow and relaxed living.

Another example is the Dream Works of the Mei established by the Sinyi Township Farmers' Association at Nantou County, Taiwan, in 2007. The Dream Works of the Mei is situated in a mountainous area where indigenous, Hakka, and

Figure 11.3. Sampled cases in major propositions.

Hoklo Taiwanese people live together. To promote local products, the Farmers' Association uses local indigenous cultures as the basis of creativity to market agricultural products through a storytelling strategy. For example, indigenous life, festivals, and local animals were adopted to inspire different creative designs, such as naming brewing products as Boar Astray, Elder's Speaking, Dancing Plum, and Singing Millet. By doing so, the Farmers' Association branded the products based heavily on cultural symbolic meaning and local attachment. The various indigenous stories associated with these products also facilitate market differentiation and segmentation, thus alleviating the difficulties experienced by traditional farmers' associations regarding the kind of strategies used to market local products.

As another example, the former Head of the Department of Architecture at the Massachusetts Institute of Technology designed a series of tableware featuring the theme of home (JIA Inc.). Specifically, he adopted the cultural value pertaining to the custom and etiquette of ethnic Chinese dining, in which family members tend to actively interact with each other and gather to eat on a round table. Then, he designed the tableware by using an idyllic image depicting a lotus pond covered with lotus leaves, demonstrating an excellent example of drawing creative materials from the culture. The aforementioned examples show a common approach of exploring stories implicated in conventional cultures and relinking them to cultural memories and emotions. Therefore, we propose that culture constitutes an important resource of creativity for developing CCIs.

Proposition 1: Culture provides symbolic meanings and emotional attachment for products and experiences offered by CCIs.

However, deriving creativity from cultural resources has its limits. For example, although Rhic Talif,[8] a Taiwanese ethnic writer and artist, was already a renowned fashion designer in the metropolis, he frequently experienced a lack of creative thoughts. Consequently, he returned to his hometown and used stories associated with driftwood as cultural memories for creating carving artworks. These works have been recognized by the international folk art community because their creative expressions have effectively manifested modern art and successfully promoted the aesthetic value of the East Coast of Taiwan. However, Rhic Talif encountered difficulties in continually promoting creative industries in his hometown. In an interview, Rhic Talif revealed that young people in his hometown are not as deeply bounded in emotions and memories associated with the hometown culture as people of his generation are, let alone applying and representing these cultural implications in creative activities. This challenge is similar to the one experienced by Tiehua Music Village, a community attempting to promote local music creation as a basis for developing and nurturing Amis music tradition. Instead of appreciating Amis traditional music, most audience and young tribal members prefer popular music from the metropolis of Taipei. This implies that indigenous cultures must identify new ways of self-expression.

Different Cultures Provide Distinctive Creative Standards

In addition to serving as a resource of creativity, culture is a standard for identifying creativity (Chiu & Kwan, 2010; Liou & Lan, in press; Morris & Leung, 2010). Creativity emphasizes novelty and usefulness, and novelty is contrary to what is known in order to transcend the existing and the familiar. Culture is an important force to dictate what is familiar and what is novel. For example, the two movies *The Last Emperor* and *Crouching Tiger, Hidden Dragon* were enthusiastically welcomed in the Western market, where consumers found the scenes of ostentatious Chinese courts and swordsmen flying over the eaves and running on the walls extremely novel. However, the two movies were not as passionately received in ethnic Chinese communities because Chinese people are already familiar with these scenes. Another example is *Inferno Affairs*, a movie dubbed as the most popular movie ever in Hong Kong. However, Hollywood's adoption of the same plot in filming *The Departed* with an impeccable cast was indifferently received in the US market. The reason for such indifference might be attributable to how in *Inferno Affairs*, the interwoven social relations in the undercover schemes between the police and underworld gangs rightly reflect the complexity of collective life in ethnic Chinese societies, presenting a social milieu that the audience in Hong Kong can identify with. However, in the United States, an individualistic society that values individual heroes, the social milieu and background depicted in *The Departed* seem unfamiliar and distant. Therefore, it is important to show cultural sensitivity in order to enhance novelty and emotional identification when using culture as a resource of creativity for CCI development. Culture matters in defining what is creative.

Recent research also reveals cultural variations in the conception of creativity (Liou & Lan, in press; Morris & Leung, 2010). For example, comparing Eastern and Western cultures indicates that Eastern cultures value usefulness more, whereas Western cultures value novelty more (Morris & Leung, 2010). Furthermore, culture's distinctive influence on creativity is recognized in each stage of the creativity process such as idea generation and idea selection (Chiu & Kwan, 2010). Relatedly, more researchers have applied the norm theory as opposed to the trait theory to interpret culture's influence on creativity and to examine under which situations creativity is norm-based and thus generates the corresponding cultural effects. In a recent cross-cultural comparative study, Liou and Lan (in proess) corroborated these cultural differences in the lay conception of creativity. Therefore, we propose that CCIs must take into account the cultural differences reflected in the creativity criteria and processes.

Proposition 2: Creative preferences and creative evaluation criteria differ across cultures.

Creativity as the Engine for Driving the Continuation and Transmission of Cultures

Creativity is a mechanism for producing new knowledge, and the evolution and progress of human cultures are based on the accumulation and constant production of knowledge (Tomasello, 2001). The role of innovation in facilitating cultural evolution pertains to a dialectical process in that innovation transcends culture in the beginning yet will eventually become a part of it (Li, Kwan, Liou, & Chiu, 2013). Creative workers should propose novel perspectives and practices that dissent from those in their cultures and convince members of their culture to accept the proposal as a part of their social cultures (Chiu & Kwan, 2010). According to the notion of cultural dynamics (Morris, Hong, Chiu, & Liu, 2015), cultures are not stable values or characteristics within individuals that are passed down through socialization and self-reproduction. Rather, cultural influences on human life are situational and dynamic, particularly when multicultural interactions and exchanges are prevalent in the globalized world. On a micro level, cultural dynamics describes how individuals obtain, use, and change culture; on a macro level, it describes the diffusion and modification of cultural customs and systems. Recent studies have indicated that culture does not feature the stable and static deep structure of history, but it changes corresponding to economic growth and decline (Greenfield, 2013; Twenge, Campbell, & Freeman, 2012). For example, Grossmann and Varnum's (2015) content analyses revealed that under economic growth and urbanization, human social culture has gradually shifted from a collectivist culture to an individualist one.

Such dynamic process and multiplicity of culture should be considered when developing CCIs. Creativity and culture, which activate each other and coevolve, are the resource and engine of developing CCIs. Therefore, applying innovation to transforming, continuing, and regenerating culture in a contemporary context is an active mission for CCIs.

Constitutes of the Innovation Mechanisms for Facilitating Cultural Continuation

The introduction of digital technology vivifies and diffuses cultural contents in the Internet environment because digitalized content can be transformed into re-created elements for new design. Design thinking (e.g., Brown, 2008) pertains to applying innovative methods for solving practical problems through emphasizing the experiences and needs of users in the context of their life. Combining digital technology and design thinking can facilitate interdisciplinary value-adding creations that are likely to improve the visibility and appeal of CCI products in the market. For example, Bright Ideas Design[9] is a design team committed to promoting culture and art as well as employing technology to create new images from traditional cultures. This team is adept at using novel and lively technological language and designs to reinterpret cultures through entertainment technology (e.g., multimedia, animation, game, and virtual reality), thus introducing intangible cultural assets and traditional arts into popular design trends. Another example, the entrepreneurial team of Pinkoi, which is composed of designers and e-commerce engineers, develops a product design website that serves as a platform for designers and consumers to co-create products and for designers to market their designs and share stories.

Proposition 3: Accounting for the core of culture, the use of digital technology and design thinking facilitates the transformation and preservation of culture.

Cultural Preservation and Regeneration of Local Spaces and Folk Customs

People cannot easily experience the historical memories associated with cultural spaces. For example, Hayashi Department Store was the second department store in Taiwan when it opened in 1932 during the period of Japanese colonization. After being abandoned for several decades, Hayashi reopened as a cultural and creative department store in 2014, and the new management team creatively enriched the department store by decorating it with physical objects that are associated with its cultural contents and historical elements. For example, to enable customers to re-experience the culture represented by the department store, the first floor was organized into an experiential Japanese living room and kitchen that demonstrate and sell foods. The Japanese shrine built on the top floor of the department store during Japanese colonization was preserved, and exhibition spaces were created to exhibit Japanese and Tainan local cultures. Such a "coding" process enables continuity and proliferation of the culture by engaging customers in a spatial journey to appreciate the past stories embodied by the department store.

Another example is the role of the Ten-Drum Cultural Creative Group in preserving and regenerating the sugar culture at Rende, Tainan. In 2007, this traditional drum performing group entered the abandoned factory of the Taiwan Sugar Corporation at Rende and developed the place into the Ten Drum Culture Village that spans 7.5 hectares. Initially, this park only served as a paid performance venue for traditional drum performers, and the performing arts culture was not yet integrated with the local sugar culture. Subsequently, after the park gained publicity as drum performance became popular among tourists, Ten-Drum began to incorporate the culture and historical memories of the sugar industry in the village. For example, Ten-Drum reopened the abandoned sugar factory as a tourist attraction, adopted the culture of the sugar industry as a drum-performing element, integrated drum music and the history of the sugar factory in filmmaking, and used the park as the basis for organizing activities facilitating the communal development of the Rende District and preservation of the sugar industry. Consumers who attend the events organized by the park participate in the re-expression and transformation of the sugar industry culture, thus contributing to cultural preservation and reconstruction.

In Tainan City of Taiwan, the tradition of the matchmaker Yue Lao,[10] the god of marriage and love in Chinese mythology, is an example illustrating the regeneration of traditional folk customs. The local Yue Lao temple is famous for granting people's wish for sustaining satisfactory relationships. As a result of news disseminated on the social networking websites and the holding of matchmaking events, numerous Western tourists were attracted to the temple. As the owner of Hsieh Guest House noted,[11] he rebuilt an old house in Tainan (i.e., a project under "Old House, New Life") not just to provide a hostel for backpackers to rest in but to offer a complete experience of living in Tainan. For example, the owner of Hsieh Guest House decimated the local tradition of praying to Yue Lao for good marriages to the international community, noting that achieving a satisfying marital life is a common urge for most people. Similarly, the story regarding the longing for the loved one's return described in the "Romance in Anping," a song set against the Anping Port in Tainan City and depicting cross-cultural romance, is emotionally moving because people from various cultures share common sentiments regarding cross-cultural romantic relationships. Another example is the coming-of-age ceremony for 16 year olds in Tainan.[12] Although the traditional customs and the social motivation for this ceremonial activity no long exist, the social need of protecting young children remains the same (i.e., an existential motivation). Therefore, social media and contemporary lifestyle are aptly used to regenerate this cultural activity, reinforcing its value for social and emotional attachment.

Proposition 4: The preservation and regeneration of cultural spaces and folk customs should embody the interactive experiences that reflect present-day life.

Innovation Mechanism for Multicultural Convergence

The second process for promoting CCI development is multicultural convergence. Based on the common conception that culture refers to a set of traditional knowledge shared by an interdependent group of people who share a common history (Chiu, Leung, & Hong, 2010), researchers have categorized culture in the form of national culture (Lehman, Chiu, & Schaller, 2004), religious culture (Shariff, Purzycki, & Sosis, 2014), political culture (Malka, 2014), and professional culture (Chiu, Kwan, & Liou, 2014; also see Chapter 6 of this volume). We argue that CCI innovation can tap into the prospects of transdisciplinary integration and multicultural convergence in the international community for new developmental visions.

Transdisciplinary integration refers to the cooperation among stakeholders from various professional disciplines in the CCI chain. Whereas *interdisciplinary research* refers to research that involves crossing the boundaries of several academic disciplines with contrasting research paradigms to create new theories and knowledge for the purpose of solving a common problem, *transdisciplinary research* refers to research projects that integrate academic researchers from different unrelated academic disciplines and nonacademic participants to pursue a common research goal and to create new theory and knowledge (Chiu, Kwan, & Liou, 2014).

Stakeholders participating in the innovation process of the CCI chain consist of the formulators and executors of government policies, creative workers (e.g., research and development professionals, literary and artistic creators), designers, engineers, marketing personnel, communal members, and consumers. Transdisciplinary integration among these stakeholders from different professional disciplines involves heterogeneous cultural exchanges and co-creation. Each disciplinary or professional culture has its own language, mode of analysis, and standard of validation (Chiu, Kwan, & Liou, 2014). These stakeholders individually hold distinctive viewpoints and values and interact with each other to achieve transdisciplinary integration. Both interdisciplinary and transdisciplinary integrations provide the impetus for culture mixing in the CCI chain, thus potentially providing insights for resolving challenges faced by CCIs and creating new opportunities.

INTERDISCIPLINARY INTERACTION AMONG VARIOUS PROFESSIONAL DISCIPLINES

Master Liu of Bamboola Taiwan possesses unique crafting techniques for bamboo weaving and carving, and the products he designed are widely embraced by the public. However, he claimed that he cannot cooperate with other designers because they lack crafting ingenuity to understand the gist of his creations. Thus, cooperation with other designers inevitably involves coping with issues unrelated to the creations and the use of abstract terminology. He also experienced great discomfort and distrust in the marketing and accounting operations of retail stores. He solemnly stated that he is only interested in creating his own craft.

Green-in-hand, a new cultural and creative brand in Taiwan, demonstrates the importance of interdisciplinary interaction. In collaboration with local farmers, this brand began to deliver and present the fundamental values of Taiwanese agricultural lifestyle by providing well-designed agricultural goods in 2006. Their model provides a good storytelling and marketing channel by incorporating cultural and creative elements to traditional farm goods, and helps farmers shorten delivery length to contribute more revenue to the original producers upstream of agricultural industry. With design thinking, they present various products, including rice, tea, honey, and wine, to showcasae Taiwanese lifestyle. The managing team creates a platform to call for the participation of farmers, designers, literacy experts, storytellers, and salespersons, thereby building a cooperation mechanism necessary for interdisciplinary integration and ideation. This mechanism aims to enhance their competitive advantage by recognizing the values of Taiwanese lifestyle, including the land, climate, taste, good memory, hard work, village life, and the story of real farmers, in their products.

These examples indicate that CCI development can harness knowledge exchange between different professional disciplines. As Chiu, Kwan, and Liou (2013) have succinctly delineated the different steps of the co-creation mechanism necessary for interdisciplinary integration and research, they posit to "enhance awareness of cultural differences through critical reflections on one's professional socialization experiences. Next, encourage team members to broaden their abilities by learning from dissimilar others and subscribe to growth beliefs. And ensure the salience of an interdisciplinary learning culture by increasing affective bonding between participants from diverse disciplinary backgrounds. Lastly, build intellectual bridges between different disciplinary groups and grow a culture of cross-disciplinary innovation" (pp. 146–148).

Proposition 5: Innovative stakeholders from different disciplines (e.g., creators, designers, engineers, and marketers) in CCIs rely on the establishment of a co-creation mechanism to promote transdisciplinary interaction.

Transdisciplinary Integration in the Chain of Cultural and Creative Industries

To resolve the bottleneck impeding CCI development, it is important to extract cultural content and apply creative design in the upstream of the value chain. The history of the Sio House in Tainan provides an example. Since 1919, this site was originally the office of the state-owned salt business during Japanese colonization and is now one of the cultural heritage sites in Tainan. After stationing in this building in 2010, the Tainan-based Huang Sun Enterprise Co. Ltd. experienced an internal transdisciplinary process of both collaboration and conflict dynamically. This investment marked Huang Sun's first endeavor in branching out to CCIs. Initially, to achieve a rapid marketing success in tourism, the marketing department of this enterprise organized an event featuring the 365-color birthday salt collection and successfully obtained market visibility. Nevertheless, the product and exhibition were neither closely connected to the cultural and historical space of the building nor the local cultural elements. After gaining initial success, the design department of the enterprise introduced design concept to their products to further improve product quality and diversity. After stabilizing its business operations, Huang Sun invited cultural and historical workers as well as creators and artists to this site. They helped the enterprise deliberate how to reestablish historical significance of this site and the salt industry in Taiwan, re-express the cultural heritage of the salt industry, and transform this site into an exhibition platform for local artists and designers. This enables the Sio House to become the definer of the salt culture. This example indicates different phases of collaboration between a dominant discipline and the other disciplines.

Shiang Ye Industry is an example of a successful transformation from a traditional manufacturing industry to a design-based creative industry. Established in 1978 in Kaohsiung, Shiang Ye was initially an original equipment manufacturer (OEM) of a chair manufacturing factory accepting foreign orders. The internal resources and organization of the enterprise were concentrated on the manufacturing department. After 2000, Shiang Ye implemented transdisciplinary collaboration to transform its operating mode. The company collaborated with Taipei Design Center in Milan and design departments at various universities in Taiwan, combined manufacturing and design resources, developed new chair designs to participate in international design competitions, and won grand prizes from the Red Dot and the IF competitions. Subsequently, after the second-generation founder obtained a design-related degree in Europe and returned to Taiwan, Shiang Ye had begun to actively invest in establishing its own brands, gradually developed an original brand manufacturer (OBM) operating mode, and initiated design–business transdisciplinary collaboration. To prevent conflicts arising from transdisciplinary collaboration, Shiang Ye also established a new department run by the second-generation founder to develop contemporary chairs with novel design styles. The traditional manufacturing department that provided prototype testing and technical support for its own brands continued to be the main source of revenue of the company. By gaining more market recognition from the winning of design awards, the company then integrated its manufacturing, design, and business operations to achieve mass production advantage. Shiang Ye successfully transformed from a traditional chair manufacturer to a creative furniture designer. However, such transformation had to overcome the conflict between the professional cultures of manufacturing engineers and designers. As the leading research and development engineer of Shiang Ye noted, "Sometimes a simple design requires completely modifying the whole manufacturing process." Moreover, the second-generation owner of the company noted that Shiang Ye would never have transformed into a design-oriented creative company without the support from the company's founder.

Proposition 6: The CCI chain depends on balancing upstream and downstream developments for promoting transdisciplinary integration.

Using Multicultural Integration to Generate Creative Expressions in Cultural and Creative Industries

Our dual-mechanism model also proposes multicultural convergence as a source of creative expressions (Leung, Maddux, Galinsky, & Chiu, 2008), as this process incorporates into products the significance of the local culture as a strategy for entering the international market, encourages self-presentation through the cultural lens, and promotes appreciation and sharing of diverse cultures.

Taiwan has experienced multicultural integration and is thus accustomed and open to different cultures. Multicultural integration is frequently observed in CCI activities. For example, the Rose House afternoon tea cafe is committed to combining the elegance of Western afternoon tea with the idyllic lifestyle of Taiwan against the context of a tense, metropolitan life commonly experienced by Taiwanese people. Rose House was established in 1990 at Taichung, Taiwan, by a famous rose artist and Western-style painter. This cafe was the first to introduce the culture of English afternoon tea into Taiwan. Its name was originated from Saint-Exupéry's *Le Petit Prince*, a book that has influenced the life of its founder. Based on the rose philosophy in the book, the founder integrated English afternoon tea with art, local spaces, and dietary habits in Taiwan, successfully creating a trend of local afternoon tea culture that has continued for nearly two decades and providing multiple perspectives to interpret the Chinese implication of the word "rose." In 2001, Rose House established a branch in London and subsequently in places such as New York, Japan, Australia, and Vancouver with the tea drinking business model that combines English culture, Taiwanese culture, and the concepts of afternoon tea and Western painting. In recent years, Rose House extended its multicultural interactions to new spatial domains by bringing its service to various cultural heritage sites such as the Yilan Museum of Art, Former British Consulate at Takao, and Taichung City Hall, thus developing cross-cultural interaction between the English afternoon tea culture and the local historical culture. This extension also introduces the use of gallery and design exhibition hall as venues for cultural diffusion.

As another example, the Taiwan National Palace Museum has reached out to other cultures to promote its collections of cultural relics among visitors. In the last decade, the development of the Taiwan National Palace Museum has centered on the core ideal of "old is new." The museum introduced CCIs to its historical collections and derived new cultural and business value by collaborating with international designers in branding creation. This branding model is most famous for the museum's collaboration with the famous Italian design brand ALESSI. Specifically, the two parties signed an agreement stipulating their joint project, "East–West Brand Integration for Creating New Cultural Opportunities," in 2005 and subsequently released series of products, including the Chin Family in 2007 and Orientales in 2008. Their CCI products, including wine caps, salt and pepper shakers, juicers, and key chains based on the image of Emperor Qianlong's portrait, are widely popular in the European market and have successfully illustrated the business application of Chinese culture to benefit market extension and multinational cultural diffusion. However, this collaboration was criticized within the Chinese market for the limited understanding of the essence of Chinese culture as reflected in product design, the Oriental stereotype illustrated by the products, and its superficial extraction and simplification of Chinese culture. These criticisms reveal the presence of cultural conflict and misinterpretation that may arise during multicultural interaction.

Proposition 7: Multicultural integration can improve the innovation of CCIs.

From Local Cultural Self-Awareness to International Recognition

To gain acceptance of the international market, the challenge of CCIs lies in how to promote other cultures' receptivity toward one's local culture and to differentiate the local culture from other dominant cultures (e.g., Chiu, Liou, & Kwan, 2016; Liou, Kwan, & Chiu, 2016). Hugh Hu is an entrepreneur who received comprehensive design training in the West. When Hu visited the design industries in Japan, the Netherlands, and Germany, he realized that cultural exchanges facilitate people's reflection on their own cultural values and spark innovation. He mentioned that the Hong Kong–based brand, Shanghai Tang, strategized to enter the mainstream Western market by incorporating the Chinese cultural essence in its design. For example, the brand is famous for styling the *qipao*, a traditional Chinese dress, to present the beautiful demeanor of a woman and at the same time creating fashion with the use of various design elements. By doing so, people who identify themselves as contemporary Chinese would feel comfortable using this brand without the hard feeling of crossing the cultural border. Although the clothing of Shanghai Tang is both traditional and fashionable, the brand actually reflects the stereotypes of Chinese in the eyes of the Westerners. Shanghai Tang uses strong, fluorescent, and garish colors to present uniqueness. As its products have been precisely designed and positioned for commercial ends, whether or not its products can be accepted in China is no longer crucial because its original intention is to highlight the style of Oriental fashion for entering the Western mainstream market. From our perspective, Shanghai Tang is a Western brand established by Hong Kong people with an intention to benefit from the booming rise of China through exaggerating the Oriental design expressions in order to stand out in the Western market.

The Kwong Xi paper factory is another example to show how multicultural exchanges can diversify CCI development. Kwong Xi was originally a traditional paper manufacturer in Central Taiwan, where the water quality is good for papermaking in the region. They exported their papers to Japan and Korea and owned a high market share. However, after 1990s, due to high competition from China's paper producers, the whole paper industry in Taiwan experienced offshore industry migration into China. Besides, a strong earthquake in Central Taiwan in 1999 also made this local industry suffer. As a result, the owner of the Kwong Xi paper factory studied the cases of industrial transformation in Western countries and took the lead in creating the operational model of tourism factory in papermaking even before the Taiwanese government began to promote this concept in 2003. Referring to the successful cases in other cultures, Kwong Xi paper factory created a dual-track model to combine traditional papermaking and cultural tourism. Not only did they organize the experience tour in their site to promote the paper crafts culture and to preserve the authenticity of the papermaking process, they also created new paper products such as eatable paper. The success of the tourism factory in turn contributes back to the original papermaking business and helps this factory recover from the reduction of market share since 2000.

Proposition 8: Assuming an open attitude to enrich different cultures through multicultural exchanges can help diversify CCIs.

Summary

As summarized in Figure 11.2, the first mechanism explains how the reciprocal process between culture and creativity can be the source of innovation that drives the industrialization process of the CCIs to enter the consumer market. The second mechanism explains how multicultural convergence in the forms of transdisciplinary collaboration and cross-cultural interaction can provide the impetus for effective and meaningful transformation. These mechanisms serve to enhance diversity of the industrialization process and to inform a balanced focus between cultural preservation and commercialization. Figure 11.2 shows the structure of these proposed dual mechanisms for innovation in CCI development.[13]

DISCUSSION

In this section, we draw on the dual mechanisms of the reciprocal culture–creativity link and multicultural convergence to further explore the solutions that overcome the challenges faced by CCIs outlined earlier and the potentiality for future development, as summarized in Table 11.2. Implications of the dual mechanisms for theory and industry practice are also raised in the following.

First, the disputes over the definition of CCI arose mainly from the fact that previous definitions of CCI were still limited to conventional industrial classification without paying sufficient attention to the nature of innovation in creative industries, which thus restricted the possible emergence of new industries inspired by CCI. The reciprocal process between creativity and culture can continuously create the new segment of CCI and release the limited boundary of current industry category. For example, current examples that include the newly emerging social enterprises and social innovation, lifestyle design for elderly people, and smart cities can be incorporated into the new category of CCI through this culture and creativity reciprocal process. In addition, the transdisciplinary collaboration and cross-national multicultural interaction can both create the new segment of CCI. Therefore, to advance the CCI development within the context of experience economy should engage in establishing and enhancing both a culture–creativity reciprocal mechanism and a mechanism for multicultural convergence as innovation dynamics for developing new industries, and blurring the divisions among industrial categories.

Second, regarding the debate of culture and commercialization, the reciprocal mechanism between culture and creativity proposed by this study may allay the apprehension that the process of cultural industrialization could be harmful to the culture because the proposed culture-based mechanism adopts creativity to promote, continue, and regenerate culture. In other words, culture can provide a comprehensive basis of commercialization to enrich the cultural value after industrialization, and creativity can provide the diversity of commercializing culture to enhance cultural evolution. In addition, this mechanism will facilitate people's understanding of their native cultures and the co-prosperity of diverse cultures in the context of a sound interdisciplinary industry chain and an industrial ecology involving multicultural convergence. It means that positive interdisciplinary and transdisciplinary co-creation can help cultural continuity after industrialization. Meanwhile, enhancing multicultural interaction in the commercialization process can effectively facilitate culture diffusion.

Third, cultural competition entails economic competition and can certainly accelerate the clash of civilization between strong economies and disadvantaged cultures. However, the threats posed by cultural diversity, as well as the value of global biodiversity, are the unconventional truth that the world must acknowledge. As indicated in the present study's discourse, cultural cultivation as a source for creativity can strengthen the competitiveness of indigenous culture in the market, and creativity serving as an engine for cultural diversity can also avoid the dominance of cultural hegemony. In addition, the innovation mechanism for multicultural convergence also reveals that transdisciplinary collaboration can find new ways of presenting local culture in the dominant market, and cross-national multicultural interaction can facilitate cultural mixing and avoid cultural hegemony. These mechanisms that result in mutual enrichment will create a healthy ecosystem for the diverse agglomeration of CCIs.

Table 11.2. Solutions to the Challenges of Cultural and Creative Industry from Proposed Dual Mechanisms

Challenge/Debate	The Reciprocal Process Between Creativity and Culture		Multicultural Mixing Mechanism	
	Culture serves as a source for creativity in CCI	Creativity serves as an engine driving cultural evolution	Transdisciplinary collaboration for innovation in CCI	Cross-national multicultural interactions for promoting CCI
1. Definition/scope/category of CCI	The reciprocal process between creativity and culture can continuously create the new segment of CCI and widen the limited boundary of current industry category		Transdisciplinary collaboration and cross-national multicultural interaction can both create the new segment of CCI	
2. Debate about culture and commercialization/industrialization	Culture provides a comprehensive basis of commercialization to enrich the cultural value after industrialization	Creativity can provide the diversity of commercializing culture to enhance cultural evolution	Positive interdisciplinary/transdisciplinary co-creation helps culture continuity after industrialization	Enhancing multicultural interaction in the commercialization process can help culture diffusion
3. Competition of culture and cultural hegemony	Cultural cultivation as a source for creativity can empower cultural representation in the market	Creativity serving as an engine for cultural diversity can avoid cultural hegemony	Transdisciplinary collaboration can find new ways of presenting local culture in the dominant market	Cross-national multicultural interaction can facilitate cultural mixing and avoid cultural hegemony
4. Ignorance of content creation and overemphasis on production	Recognizing the value of (indigenous) cultures can encourage CCI entrepreneurs to explore cultural content and cultivation	Creativity can drive cultural evolution to regenerate the content creation aspect of CCI	Good transdisciplinary collaboration mechanism can benefit both the upstream creation and downstream production in CCI	With an awareness of cultural self-identity, local culture can enrich other cultures to enable product attractiveness

5. Limited size of market and the change of aesthetic lifestyle	Recognize the value of (indigenous) cultures can reshape the aesthetic lifestyle and commitment in local cultural goods	Creativity as an engine can expand the scale of CCI and its potential market	New horizontal and vertical integration talents by transdisciplinary collaboration can create new market for CCI	Awareness of cross-national multicultural interaction can cultivate new aesthetic lifestyle to create new market for CCI
6. Debate about the necessity of developing industrial park for CCIs	The reciprocal process between creativity and culture can create a culture-based ecosystem for developing CCI instead of only building a regional industrial park			Transdisciplinary collaboration and cross-national multicultural interaction can create a culture-based ecosystem for developing CCI instead of only building a regional industrial park

CCI, cultural and creative industry.

Fourth, regarding the imbalance between cultural creation and production, the current excessive enthusiasm for developing cultural products and businesses in the CCI indicates that businesses in the CCI misunderstand this industry as a commercial model for saving the consumer market. They do so while neglecting upstream development and enrichment of cultural content as well as overlooking the balance of the industry value chain. We find that recognizing the value of indigenous cultures can encourage CCI entrepreneurs to explore the cultural contents. On the other hand, the reciprocal process also reveals that creativity can drive cultural evolution to regenerate the content creation aspect of CCI. These measures can solve the problem of ignoring the upstream content creation. In addition, from the view of multicultural convergence, good transdisciplinary collaboration mechanism can benefit both upstream creation and downstream production in CCI. With awareness of culture self-identity, local culture can also enrich other cultures to enable product attractiveness. It shows that the innovation dynamics derived from upstream culture and creative operation as well as the industry system collaboratively created by interdisciplinary enterprises will remind related businesses of the importance of balancing CCI developments.

Fifth, regarding the limited size of market, limitation and individualization in the market segmentation of the CCIs are inevitable industrial characteristics due to cultural diversity. In the future, related businesses can actively train creative talents for cultural development while implementing both interdisciplinary and transdisciplinary integration of talents. By doing so, these businesses can not only strengthen the innovation mechanism of the CCIs but expand industrial scale through association to create new job types. As a result, the mechanism of reciprocal process indicates that recognizing the value of indigenous cultures can reshape the aesthetic lifestyle and commitment in local cultural goods, and creativity as an engine can also expand the scale of CCI and its potential market. This mechanism will facilitate the expansion of market size in CCI. Meanwhile, the mechanism of multicultural convergence finds that new horizontal and vertical integration talents by transdisciplinary collaboration can create new markets for CCI, and awareness of cross-national multicultural interaction can also cultivate new aesthetic lifestyle to create new markets for CCI.

Last, to solve the debate of CCI parks, CCIs that emphasize both local origins and diversity will essentially differ from previous innovation systems and industrial parks clustered spatially. The mechanism of reciprocal process between creativity and culture can create a culture-based ecosystem for developing CCIs instead of only building a regional industrial park. The mechanism for transdisciplinary collaboration and cross-national multicultural interaction can also provide more talents, stakeholders, and newly created enterprise in this culture-based ecosystem, thereby developing a creative milieu as a creative city.

This study analyzed the current status of CCI development and applied the basic research on culture and creativity to frame these industrial problems and propose developmental strategies for and solutions to these problems. The approach adopted in this study is an example of how theory and practice can co-develop.

Future development can advance the mechanism that facilitates the reciprocal reinforcement between theory and practice.

NOTES

1. The concept of CCI was derived from the historical evolution of cultural industries. This section describes this three-phase development from cultural industries, creative industries, to today's CCI.
2. Regarding this concept of culture-based industries, the various countries have yet to arrive at a standardized name that is within the existing scope proposed by UNESCO. Presently, many European countries continue to use the original term "cultural industries." The United Kingdom, Australia, New Zealand, and Hong Kong use "creative industries." Taiwan and China are among the few regions that use "CCI." Japan uses the term "contents industry," whereas the United States is the sole country using the term "intellectual property industries."
3. The definition and classification used by the various countries also reflect their respective historical industrial bases and the focus of their future industrial policies. Common categories classified by all countries include movies and television, performing arts, process design, and publishing. Separately, the United Kingdom particularly emphasizes the fields of arts and antiques, fashion design, and software services. The specialties of South Korea are games, animation, and traditional foods. Australia is one of the few countries in the world that emphasizes the cultural domains, such as museums, zoos, and botanical gardens. Taiwan's foci, which include digital contents and creative life industries, are also categories that few other countries had proposed.
4. The interviewees are listed in Appendix A.
5. In Taiwan, the debate about "real versus fake" CCIs happened in 2015, because Taipei City Government aimed to review the qualification of stationed enterprises in one of its cultural parks. The definition and scope of CCIs were discussed again to examine the balance of cultural and commercial elements in each enterprise.
6. There are currently five state-level CCI parks in Taiwan, which are located in Huashan of Taipei, Taichung, Tainan, Hualien, and Chiayi. The number of other CCI parks in various localities that were established by the private sector or through conversion of old and abandoned spaces is too numerous to count. In addition, China already has approximately 2,000 CCI parks as of the end of 2014.
7. From 1992, Fushan Kodo (富山沉香) was established in Kaohsiung in Taiwan and successfully transformed the traditional joss sticks shop into a chain department store for religion related goods.
8. http://rahictalif.com/
9. http://www.brightideas.com.tw/
10. The tradition of matchmaking (i.e., connecting the red string of fate) in the Yue Lao temples in Tainan City has extended to matchmaking services available on the Internet. According to the statistics of the Tainan Grand Matsu Temple, its matchmaker successfully matches more than 300 couples on average each year. Wang Hao-yi noted that the matchmaker temples in Tainan feature individual functions. For example, the matchmaker worshipped in the Sacrificial Rites Martial Temple

helps "solve the problem of unrequited love," the matchmaker in the Tainan Grand Matsu Temple helps "strengthen relations," the matchmaker in the Grand Guanyin Pavilion Temple "protects and makes relationships last forever," and the matchmaker in the Chongqing Temple helps "chop down the peach tree" (i.e., terminate love affairs).

11. https://www.facebook.com/TainanOldHouseInn

12. The Seventh Maiden Goddess in the folk belief of Tainan is allegedly the Maiden Immortal Qi Xing that is regarded as the protector of children. Legends have also indicated that this ceremony was related to the dock workers in the district of Wutiao Port to the west of Tainan. In the past, businesses gathered in the suburb of the port, and numerous child workers under the age of 16 assisted with the loading and unloading at the dock.

13. The sources of data in each proposition are summarized in Appendix B.

REFERENCES

Adorno, T. W., & Horkheimer, M. (1947). *Dialektik der Aufklärung: Philosophische Fragmente* (Amsterdam: Querido). *Dialectic of Enlightenment* (J. Cumming, Trans.). New York, NY: Herder and Herder.

Baudrillard, J. (1998). *The consumer society: Myths and structures* (Vol. 53). London, UK: Sage.

Bauman, Z. (1993). *Postmodern ethics*. Oxford, UK: Blackwell.

Baumol, W. J., & Bowen, W. G. (1993). *Performing arts—the economic dilemma: A study of problems common to theater, opera, music and dance*. Aldershot, UK: Gregg Revivals.

Bourdieu, P. (1984). *Distinction: A social critique of the judgment of taste*. Cambridge, MA: Harvard University Press.

Brown, T. (2008). Design thinking. *Harvard Business Review, 86*, 84–92.

Chiu, C. Y., & Kwan, L. Y. Y. (2010). Culture and creativity: A process model. *Management and Organization Review, 6*, 447–461.

Chiu, C. Y., Kwan, L. Y. Y., & Liou, S. (2013). Culturally motivated challenges to innovations in integrative research: Theory and solutions. *Social Issues and Policy Review, 7*, 149–172.

Chiu, C. Y., Kwan, L. Y. Y., & Liou, S. (2014). Professional and disciplinary cultures. In A. B. Cohen (Ed.), *Culture reexamined: Broadening our understanding of social and evolutionary influences* (pp. 11–30). Washington, DC: American Psychological Association.

Chiu, C. Y., Leung, K-Y., & Hong, Y-Y. (2010). Cultural processes: An overview. In A. K-Y. Leung, C-Y. Chiu, & Y-Y. Hong (Eds.), *Cultural processes: A social psychological perspective* (pp. 3–22). New York, NY: Cambridge University Press.

Chiu, C. Y., Liou, S., & Kwan, L. Y. Y. (2016). Institutional and cultural contexts of creativity and innovation in China. In A. Lewin, M. Kenny, & J. Murmann (Eds.), *China's innovation challenge: Overcoming the middle income trap* (pp. 368–394). New York, NY: Cambridge University Press.

Chiu, C. Y., Morris, M. W., Hong, Y. Y., & Menon, T. (2000). Motivated cultural cognition: The impact of implicit cultural theories on dispositional attribution varies as a function of need for closure. *Journal of Personality and Social Psychology*, *78*(2), 247–259.

Costa, P. (2008). Creativity, innovation and territorial agglomeration in cultural activities: the roots of the creative city. In P. Cooke & L. Lazzeretti (eds), *Creative cities, cultural clusters and local economic development* (pp. 183–210). Cheltenham: Edward Elgar.

Deuze, M. (2009). Convergence culture and media work. In J. Holt & A. Perren (Eds.), *Media industries: History, theory and method* (pp. 144–155). Oxford, UK: Wiley-Blackwell.

Greenberg, J., Solomon, S., & Pyszczynski, T. (1997). Terror management theory of self-esteem and cultural worldviews: Empirical assessments and conceptual refinements. *Advances in Experimental Social Psychology*, *29*, 61–139.

Grossmann, I., & Varnum, M. E. (2015). Social structure, infectious diseases, disasters, secularism, and cultural change in America. *Psychological Science*, *26*(3), 311–324.

Hartley, J. (2005). *Creative industries*. Oxford, UK: Blackwell.

Hesmondhalgh, D. (2007). *The cultural industries*. London, UK: Sage.

Howkins, J. (2002). *The creative economy: How people make money from ideas*. London, UK: Penguin.

Jameson, F. (1991). *Postmodernism: Or the cultural logic of late capitalism*. Durham, NC: Duke University Press.

Jetten, J., Postmes, T., & McAuliffe, B. J. (2002). "We're all individuals": Group norms of individualism and collectivism, levels of identification and identity threat. *European Journal of Social Psychology*, *32*(2), 189–207.

Kosic, A., Kruglanski, A. W., Pierro, A., & Mannetti, L. (2004). The social cognition of immigrants' acculturation: Effects of the need for closure and the reference group at entry. *Journal of Personality and Social Psychology*, *86*(6), 796–813.

Lampel, J., & Shamsie, J. (2006). Uncertain globalization: Evolutionary scenarios in future development of the cultural industries. In J. Lampel, J. Shamsie, TK Lant (Eds.), *The business of culture: Strategic perspectives on entertainment and media* (pp. 275–286). London, UK: Lawrence Erlbaum.

Lehman, D. R., Chiu, C. Y., & Schaller, M. (2004). Psychology and culture. *Annual Review of Psychology*, *55*, 689–714.

Leung, A. K. Y., Liou, S., Qiu, L., Kwan, L. Y. Y., Chiu, C. Y., & Yong, J. C. (2014). The role of instrumental emotion regulation in the emotions–creativity link: How worries render individuals with high neuroticism more creative. *Emotion*, *14*(5), 846–856.

Leung, A. K. Y., Maddux, W. W., Galinsky, A. D., & Chiu, C-. Y. (2008). Multicultural experience enhances creativity: The when and how? *American Psychologist*, *63*, 169–181.

Li, C., Kwan L. Y. Y., Liou, S., & Chiu, C. Y. (2013). Culture, group processes, and creativity. In M. Yuki & M. Brewer (Eds.), *Culture and group processes* (pp. 143–165). Oxford, UK: Oxford University Press.

Liou, S., Kwan, L. Y. Y., & Chiu C. Y. (2016). Historical and cultural obstacles to frame-breaking innovations in China. *Management and Organization Review*. doi: 10.1017/mor.2016.3

Liou, S., & Lan, X. (in press). Situational salience of norms moderates cultural differences in the originality and usefulness of creative ideas generated or selected by teams. *Journal of Cross-cultural Psychology*. doi: 10.1177/0022022116640897.

Liou, S., & Yang, C. H. (2015). Challenges and trends of developing cultural and creative industries. Paper presented at *The 2015 International Conference of Culture and Creativity*. Tainan, Taiwan.

Liou, S., & Yang, C. H. (forthcoming). *The developing creative industries: Evolution and innovation*. Tainan, Taiwan: NCKU.

Lorenzen, M., & Frederiksen, L. (2008). Why do cultural industries cluster? Localization, urbanization, products and projects. In P. Cooke & L. Lazzeretti (Eds.), *Creative cities, cultural clusters and local economic development* (pp. 155–179). UK: Edward Elgar.

Malka, A. (2014). Political culture and democracy. In A. B. Cohen (Eds.), *Culture reexamined: Broadening our understanding of social and evolutionary influences* (pp. 129–153). Washington, DC: American Psychological Association.

Morris, M. W., Hong Y.-Y., Chiu, C.-Y., & Liu, Z. (2015). Normology: Integrating insights about social norms to understand cultural dynamics. *Organizational Behavior and Human Decision Processes, 129*, 1–13.

Morris, M. W., & Leung, K. (2010). Creativity East and West: Perspectives and parallels. *Management and Organization Review, 6*, 313–327.

Murdock, G. (2003). Back to work. In A. Beck (Ed.), *Understanding the cultural industries* (pp. 15–35). London, UK: Routledge.

Pickett, C. L., Bonner, B. L., & Coleman, J. M. (2002). Motivated self-stereotyping: Heightened assimilation and differentiation needs result in increased levels of positive and negative self-stereotyping. *Journal of Personality and Social Psychology, 82*(4), 543–562.

Poster, M. (2004). Consumption and digital commodities in the everyday. *Cultural Studies, 18*(2-3), 409–423.

Potts, J. (2009). Why creative industries matter to economic evolution. *Economics of Innovation and New Technology, 18*(7), 663–673.

Pratt, A. C. (2004). The cultural economy: A call for spatialized "production of culture" perspectives. *International Journal of Cultural Studies, 7*(1), 117–128.

Ryan, B. (1991). The contradictions of the artist-capitalist relation. In B. Ryan (Ed.), *Making capital from culture: The corporate form of capitalist cultural production* (pp. 41–49). New York, NY: Walter de Gruyter.

Scott, A. J. (2005). *On Hollywood: The place, the industry*. Princeton, NJ: Princeton University Press.

Shariff, A., Purzycki, B., & Sosis, R. (2014). Religions as cultural solutions to social living. In A. B. Cohen (Ed.), *Culture reexamined: Broadening our understanding of social and evolutionary influences* (pp. 217–238). Washington, DC: American Psychological Association.

Throsby, D. (2001). *Economics and culture*. Cambridge, UK: Cambridge University Press.

Tomasello, M. (2001). Cultural transmission: A view from chimpanzees and human infants. *Journal of Cross-Cultural Psychology, 32*(2), 135–146.

Turow, J., & McAllister, M. (2009). *The advertising and consumer culture reader*. New York, NY: Routledge.

Twenge, J. M., Campbell, W. K., & Freeman, E. C. (2012). Generational differences in young adults' life goals, concern for others, and civic orientation, 1966–2009. *Journal of Personality and Social Psychology, 102*(5), 1045–1062.

APPENDIX 11A

Interviewees for Critical Issues in Developing Cultural and Creative Industries

Interviewee	Title and Affiliation at Time of Interview	Date and Location of Interview
Tze-San, Yeh	Director, Cultural Bureau in Tainan City Government	April 10, 2013; Tainan, Taiwan
Hao-Yi Wang	Historical Researcher	August 27, 2013; Tainan, Taiwan
Erik, Gau	Cultural Entrepreneur (Design)	August 27, 2013; Tainan, Taiwan
Aaron, Yi	Cultural Curator, Professor	August 30, 2013; Taipei, Taiwan
Hugh, Hu	Founder, NDD Design Company	September 20, 2013; Tainan, Taiwan
Hun-Wen, Huang	Director, Tainan Cultural Center	January 12, 2014; Tainan, Taiwan
Terry Ou'Young	Historical Researcher	January 15, 2015; Tainan, Taiwan
Aurora, Yang	Cultural Entrepreneur (Salt)	January 16, 2015; Tainan, Taiwan
Robert, Huang	Cultural Entrepreneur (Tea)	April 2, 2015; Taichung, Taiwan
Huang-Zang, Huang	Cultural Entrepreneur (Paper Craft)	November 1, 2015; Nantou, Taiwan

APPENDIX 11B

Sources of Data in Each Proposition

	Dual Mechanisms for Innovation in CCI Development		Source of Literature	Evidence From Practical Cases Selected Cases	Time of Interview and Site Investigation
Mechanism 1: Reciprocal Process Between Creativity and Culture	Culture as creative resources in cultural and creative industries	Proposition 1: According to shared consensus, culture provides symbolic meanings and emotional attachment for products and experiences offered by CCIs	• Greenberg, Solomon, & Pyszczynski (1997) • Chiu, Morris, Hong, & Menon (2000) • Pickett, Bonner, & Coleman (2002) • Jetten, Postmes, & Mcauliffe (2002) • Kosic, Kruglanski, Pierro, & Mannetti (2004) • Chiu, Leung, & Hong (2010) • Li, Kwan, Liou, & Chiu (2013)	Fushan Kodo (http://www.53.com.tw) Dream Works of the Mei (http://www.52313.com.tw/hsinifa. html) JIA Inc. (http://www.jia-inc.com)	December 2013 August 2014
		Proposition 2: Different cultures vary in their effects on creativity processes and standards, thus engendering distinctive preferences for and evaluations of the creative expressions and experiences of CCIs	• Chiu & Kwan (2010) • Morris & Leung (2010) • Morris & Leung (2012) • Liou & Lan (in press)	Rhic Talif (http://rahictalif.com) Tiehua Music Village (http://www.tiehua.com.tw/) Film (The Last Emperor; Crouching Tiger, Hidden Dragon; Inferno Affairs)	Novmber 2012 November 2012 July 2015

Mechanism	Proposition	References	Cases	Date
Creativity as the engine for driving the continuation and rebirth of cultures	Proposition 3: Accounting for the core of culture, the employment of technology, design, and business facilitates the transformation and innovation mechanism for promoting culture continuity	• Tomasello (2001) • Chiu & Kwan (2010) • Twenge, Campbell & Gentile (2013) • Greenfield (2013) • Li, Kwan, Liou, & Chiu (2014) • Morris, Hong, Chou, & Liu (2015) • Grossmann & Varnum (2015) • Liou, S. & Yang, C.-H. (forthcoming)	Bright Ideas Design (http://www.brightideas.com.tw/) Pinkoi (http://www.pinkoi.com) Fandora (http://fandorashop.com/tw/)	April 2015 April 2015
	Proposition 4: The preservation and regeneration of cultural spaces and folk customs must embody the interactive experiences of present-day life	• Liou & Yang (forthcoming) • Liou & Yang (2015)	Hayashi Department Store (http://www.hayashi.com.tw/) Ten Drum Culture Village (http://www.tendrum-cultrue.com.tw/) Hsieh Guest House	June 2014 May 2015 December 2013 July 2015 November 2015
Mechanism 2: Innovation Mechanism for Multicultural Convergence	Interdisciplinary integration in the innovation of cultural and creative industries	Proposition 5: Innovative stakeholders from different disciplines (e.g., creators, designers, engineers, and marketers) in CCIs rely on the establishment of a co-creation mechanism to promote interdisciplinary interaction	• Chiu, Leung, & Hong (2010) • Chiu, Kwan, & Liou (2013) • Chiu, Kwan, & Liou (2014)	Age Ceremony for 16 Year Olds Bamboola Taiwan (http://www.bamboola.com.tw/) Green-in-hand (http://www.greeninhand.com/)

August 2013
October 2014
August 2015
May 2013

November 2015

	Proposition	References	Case	Date
	Proposition 6: The CCI chain depends on the balanced upstream and downstream development for promoting transdisciplinary integration	• Liou & Yang (forthcoming) • Liou & Yang (2015)	Sio House (http://www.sio-house.com.tw/) Shiang Ye (http://www.shiangye.com/)	July 2013 December 2013 November 2015 November 2012
Multicultural exchanges and co-prosperity	Proposition 7: Multicultural mixing can improve the innovation performance of CCIs	• Chiu, C. Y., Liou, S., & Kwan, L. Y. (2016) • Leung, Maddux, Galinsky, & Chiu (2008)	Rose House (http://www.rosehouse.com) National Palace Museum (http://www.npm.gov.tw/)	April 2015 January 2016 February 2013
	Proposition 8: Assuming an open and mutually enlightening attitude to enrich one another's cultures in the multicultural exchanges under globalization will create diversity in homogenous CCIs	• Chiu, Liou & Kwan (2016) • Liou, Kwan, & Chiu (2016)	Shanghai Tang (http://www.shanghaitang.com/) Kwong Xi Paper Factory (http://www.taiwanpaper.com.tw/)	November 2015 November 2015

CCI, cultural and creative industry.

12

Time To Be Innovative, Hong Kong

Time Orientation, Creativity, and Entrepreneurial Activities

MARTA K. DOWEJKO, KEVIN AU, AND YINGZHAO XIAO ■

Hong Kong has been consistently ranked among the top 10 economies worldwide based on GDP per capita and economy-level innovativeness. On the surface, the economy is doing well and is well prepared to tackle future economic challenges. Yet a closer look reveals that Hong Kong is facing difficulties in establishing solid foundations for innovation and accompanying entrepreneurial activities. In fact, while its innovation inputs, defined as preparedness of human capital, good infrastructure, market and business sophistication, and efficiency of institutions, have been assessed as strong and occupying the second position globally, its R&D activities and the innovative outputs are what presented a challenge in developing local innovativeness (Cornell University, INSEAD, and WIPO, 2014). It does not come as a surprise since Hong Kong's R&D expenses (0.75% of GDP) are ranked among one of the lowest in developed economies. Taking away the spending that is flowing to the universities and public research facilities (0.5%), some are amazed by how the local private sector can use the meager spending of 0.25% GDP to sustain a truly competitive economy. As a result, Hong Kong's innovation efficiency ratio, measured as a share of output to input scores, was assessed at 0.66, meaning that out of one unit of innovation input Hong Kong is producing two thirds of innovation output unit (Cornell University, INSEAD, and WIPO, 2014). In comparison to other countries such as South Korea or the United Kingdom, which have efficiency ratios closer to one, Hong Kong appears to be less capable of turning its resources into innovative outcomes. Indeed, even the government's audit documents (2013, p. 15) assessing the innovation situation in Hong Kong call it "modest."

Hong Kong is therefore stuck between high creative potential and low innovation outputs. Many attribute this paradoxical situation to inadequate innovation policies and to the overpowering risk aversion conventionally recognized in Hong Kong society. In addition to these commonly accepted views, we argue that Hong Kong's cultural time orientation, which drives norms, collective behaviors, and social consensus prevalent in the city's cultural makeup, has also played a significant part in dampening the innovation incentives and, in the long term, undermining the innovative activity.

As shown later, we analyze Hong Kong's innovativeness from the cultural perspective and we explore the notion of time orientation as the main driver for creating a paradoxical situation whereby an innovation-ready economy is struggling to achieve its full potential. We argue that the city's specific relationship with time, which is not aligned with conventional innovation-driving time orientations, creates obstacles to translating creative outputs into commercially viable innovation. This in-depth indigenous study of Hong Kong's business and institutional environments is the result of a year-long research project.[1] The rest is organized as follows: We first lay the theoretical arguments that connect the concepts of creativity, innovation, and culture; then, we discuss the time orientation as specific cultural dimension and describe the innovation-enhancing time orientation configurations. We follow with the in-depth analysis of Hong Kong's creative and innovative outputs and present the vicious circle of crouching innovation as the consequence of cultural conditioning spurring from the city's time orientation. We conclude our analysis by providing a series of recommendations that could help alleviate the negative consequences of Hong Kong's time orientation.

CREATIVITY, INNOVATION, AND CULTURE

Although creativity and innovation represent two sides of the same coin, not all products of our creativity turn into innovations. Creativity resides in the creation of new and original ideas; it is related to the inventor's individual skills and often driven by his or her personal experience. Innovation represents the development of useful creative ideas and encompasses the trade-off between the creativity of the inventor and the actual market need (Chiu & Kwan, 2010). Put differently, the target audience needs to recognize the value of the idea and be willing to accept it for the creative output to be turned into innovation, since innovation is "the successful implementation of creative ideas" (Amabile, 1996, p. 1). As Figure 12.1 presents, creativity and innovation, both driven by complex processes, are connected and influenced by cultural norms, collective behaviors, and social consensus at multiple stages of development (Morris & Leung, 2010).

Cultures encapsulate shared norms, collective actions, and social consensus. Culture, which is defined as "shared motives, values, beliefs, identities, and interpretations or meanings of significant events that result from common experiences of members of collectives that are transmitted across generations" (House, Hanges, Javidan, Dorfman, & Gupta, 2004, p. 15), constitutes an important

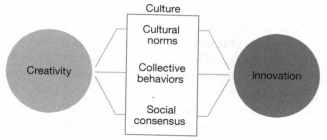

Figure 12.1. Creativity, innovation, and culture.

reference point for individuals in their creative and innovation processes. Culture inspires people to develop new ideas, but it also creates perceptual and conceptual boundaries within which people operate and search for original ideas to solve existing problems (Simonton & Ting, 2010) and provides a reference point for assessing the value of ideas. Since most individuals are intrinsically and extrinsically motivated to accept, share, and follow cultural norms, their creative process may be restricted to fit within the prescribed cultural frame of mind.

Culture also impacts people's choice of which new ideas to develop. It may induce conformity in behaviors, inspire people to stand up to current norms and expectations (Chao, Zhang, & Chiu, 2010; Chiu & Kwan, 2010; Morris & Leung, 2010; Simonton & Ting, 2010), or increase self-censorship of ideas to implement based on their utility in a broader context (Erez & Nouri, 2010). Finally, culture drives audiences to accept or reject new ideas for implementation (Chiu & Kwan, 2010; Daghfous, Petrof, & Pons, 1999; Dwyer, Mesak, & Hsu, 2005; Norenzayan, Artran, Faulkner, & Schaller, 2006) and impacts the development of institutional environment for innovation (Li & Zahra, 2012; Mowery & Rosenberg, 1993). Although culture itself is not sufficient to explain differences in creativity and innovativeness of nations, some cultures are thought to be more conducive of creativity than others. Multiple studies provide conceptual and empirical arguments for individualistic, risk-tolerant, and egalitarian cultures as usually more beneficial to fostering creativity and innovation (Efrat, 2014; Erez & Nouri, 2010; S. Shane, 1993; S. A. Shane, 1992; Taylor & Wilson, 2012; Williams & McGuire, 2010).

TIME ORIENTATION AS A CULTURAL DIMENSION

A plethora of studies discuss the importance of uncertainty avoidance or individualism on innovation outcomes in global economies. We strive to move away from the earlier well-studied, conventional cultural dimensions and focus on the notion of time orientation (Butler, 1995). Time orientation as cultural dimension describes culture's inclination toward considering activities from the past, present, or future perspectives. It reflects the extent to which a culture believes it can control time and the value it assigns to its changing. The most well-known studies of time as cultural dimension include Hofstede's long-term orientation that reflects pragmatism (Hofstede, Hofstede, & Minkov, 2010) and Trompenaars' time dimension that encompasses the extent of synchronicity of actions, the magnitude of time horizon, and the relativity of scheduling (Trompenaars & Hampden-Turner, 2012). Time is an important aspect of any social interaction; it captures movement, dynamics, and activities. In the creativity and innovation context, it helps us to define how quickly a new idea should be put into an experiment, it determines the speed of a prototype development, and it measures the pace at which the idea is turned into a new business. Time is not an object existing independently of the actors as the theory of relativity had established (Einstein, 1931). For a given activity or community, time can thus be constructed in a unique way, and it must therefore be understood as a cultural phenomenon that can affect the organizing of activities including that of creativity and innovation (Gardet et al., 1976; Trompenaars & Hampden-Turner, 2012; Zampetakis, Bouranta, & Moustakis, 2010).

And yet, in the modern era, time is measured objectively with precision and independently from individual actions. We adhere to time zones and accept standard time and calendars by which we live and do business. However, time evolves as a social and cultural phenomenon with many symbolic notions attached to it. It can be constructed differently within the same location and culture. People recognize that a period of 1 month can be perceived differently depending on where we are and what we are doing. One month in a wilderness of Tasmania might drag indefinitely, whereas a month in Hong Kong may pass at a blink of an eye and be rich in many life-changing opportunities. Likewise, an hour can feel like a long time when waiting for a conference to start, but it can feel like only a brief moment when pitching to investors.

Differences in how we perceive time can have an impact on our actions and interactions, as well as on our expectations, memories, and perceptions (Zimbardo & Boyd, 1999). Flaherty (1991) argues that time seems to move slowly during periods when there is almost nothing happening. That is to say, when you are waiting without anything to do, time seems to run slowly. The same feeling also appears during periods that are unusually eventful; for example, a dangerous situation that calls for your immediate action can seem to last forever. Time is a social construct that allows members of culture to coordinate their activities (Durkheim, 1893), and it is dependent on situations and individuals involved in them (Butler, 1995; Clark, 1990).

Time varies across situations and settings, and it is essential to our development and progress. However, relatively few studies explore how the perception and relationship with time impacts the ways people develop and assess new ideas, plan their life events, and put their skills to work in the field of creativity and innovation (Lichtenstein, Carter, Dooley, & Gartner, 2007; Perlow, Okhuysen, & Repenning, 2002; Zampetakis et al., 2010). We argue that as a specific cultural dimension, time orientation may be one of the most crucial determinants of our capability to innovate.

There are four main conceptual facets of time orientation as a cultural dimension: the relationship between and the duration of past, present, and future; the sequencing of actions; the pace of getting to desired outcomes; and the perceived objectivity of the time concept (Butler, 1995; Orlikowski & Yates, 2002). The notions of past, present, and future can vary in length from one culture to another (Butler, 1995). They can also vary in importance and be seen in connection or in disconnection to one another. Figure 12.2 illustrates findings from chosen cultures on relatedness and dominance of past, present, and future timeframes (Cottle, 1967; Trompenaars & Hampden-Turner, 2012).[2] Hong Kong is a culture where all dimensions are of similar importance, but where the present is slightly dominant and disconnected from its past and future.

As for our actions, cultures may adopt a synchronous or chronological view of how things should be done; they can also adopt a linear or cyclic view of time (Clark, 1990; Trompenaars & Hampden-Turner, 2012). Furthermore, different cultures may value a slow or fast pace of accomplishing objectives and moving through time. Finally, time can be seen as an exogenous and absolute value that is independent of human action, as a socially constructed and culturally relative

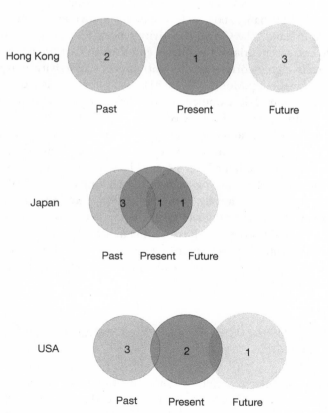

Figure 12.2. How cultures relate to past, present, and future.

concept, or as realized through people's recurrent activities that produce meaningful temporal structures (Orlikowski & Yates, 2002).

We argue that an innovative mindset requires people to assume the subjective and nonlinear vision of time. It requires the implementation of cycles, iterations, and the synchronicity of actions. It is nurtured through feedback loops; it assumes that, sometimes, one needs to slow down or take a step back to achieve his or her goals. Innovation and creativity require a subjective approach to time as they are defined through meaningful temporal events and achievement of milestones (Orlikowski & Yates, 2002). As our case study will reveal, Hong Kong has a very different relationship with time, which impacts its ability to turn its creative outputs into innovation.

CREATIVITY AND INNOVATION IN ENTREPRENEURSHIP

Entrepreneurship pursues opportunities without regard to resources currently at hand, as it is an "activity that involves the discovery, evaluation, and exploitation of opportunities to introduce new goods and services, ways of organizing markets, processes, and raw materials through organizing efforts that previously had not existed" (S. Shane, 2003, p. 4). Creativity, innovation, and entrepreneurship go hand in hand. The Global Creativity report (Florida et al., 2011) linked creativity to entrepreneurial activity rates and showed that the overall creativity of economies is highly correlated with entrepreneurial activity as measured by Global Entrepreneurship Monitor ($r = 0.81$). Since creativity is required for each stage of entrepreneurial development, culture or institutions also affect entrepreneurship in multiple stages (Baker, Gedajlovic, & Lubatkin, 2005). For example, culture defines incentives and thus affects whether professors would publish their inventions in journals or commercialize them in a new venture (Li & Zahra, 2012). Also, time orientation affects whether investors would push a startup for sale quickly to secure short-term gain or nurture it long term to create an epoch-changing company. Alternatively, time orientation may influence prospective entrepreneurs with creative minds to focus on popular ideas at present, on ideas connecting with traditions, or on those leading to the future. To this end, we continue our analysis within the entrepreneurship context to explain how the cultural makeup can be the driving force of the disconnection between creativity and innovation in Hong Kong.

ENTREPRENEURIAL CREATIVITY AND INNOVATION IN HONG KONG

Hong Kong is characterized culturally and institutionally in several distinctive ways. First, it is very much a Chinese society regarded as collective, which is high in power distance and emphasizes the concepts of "saving face" and social recognition (Hui, Au, & Fock, 2004; Lau, Shaffer, & Au, 2007). Meanwhile, being historically a trading port and refugee sanctuary, its eclecticism contributes to low uncertainty avoidance and a can-do, entrepreneurial spirit that drive local creativity. In addition, the British colonial governance brought the rule of law and the efficient and trustworthy government. Together with the hardworking population and international opportunities, these elements have allowed Hong Kong to develop, in a few decades, a modern society—open, wealthy, and based on convenience (Fuller, 2010). Hong Kong has also been home to an increasingly diverse population who speaks at least two languages and has an above-average understanding of Eastern and Western cultures and know-how, which further increases their capacity to spot opportunities at cultural and technological cross-roads and, potentially, deliver radical innovation (Chiu & Kwan, 2010). Although it has suffered from economic stagnation and social unrest in the past decade, international observers continue to rate Hong Kong as well-governed, competitive, and technologically advanced (WEF, 2014). To the external observer, Hong Kong looks like one of the most innovative economies in the world and in the cross-country rankings, such as Global Innovativeness Index (2014), it has been consistently outperforming many other markets in the region.

However, to the trained insider eye, Hong Kong has been struggling with a paradoxical situation. Although its creative potential is well established and well documented across various domains of activities, its innovation products are not, which causes a serious imbalance in innovation inputs and outputs. For example, Hong Kong is the second economy in the world with the largest number of YouTube video uploads per working citizen. However, when it comes to actual global entertainment and media outputs or creative goods exports, Hong Kong lags behind other developed economies, taking the 18th and 73rd place, respectively (Global Innovativeness Index, 2014).

We have noticed the same pattern in Hong Kong entrepreneurship setting. In our recent study of local entrepreneurship conducted within the Empowering Young Entrepreneurs (EYE) Program, we asked a cohort of potential entrepreneurs to self-assess the strength of their individual creativity based on three different measures taken at three different stages of program participation (Dowejko, Au, & Shen, 2014).[3] The first measurement was taken at the registration stage to the program. Specifically, we asked 902 applicants to identify their strengths from a pre-established list of skills that are empirically associated with entrepreneurial actions (Mueller & Thomas, 2001; Ward, 2004). A whopping 74.6% reported creative thinking as their strength, which was the most common skill indicated by study participants.

The second measure was taken 2 months later with 635 participants who remained in the program after the entrepreneurial skill training. This time, we asked them to assess their creativity through evaluating their idea generation behaviors (Amabile, 1983; Zhang & Bartol, 2010). Again, 82% reported high frequency of use of creative techniques related to problem identification and 84% were frequently exploring creative ways of information search. In terms of idea generation, 64% of respondents reported a frequent use of creative techniques, such as generation of multiple alternatives or out-of-the-box solutions, for problem solving.

Finally, the third measurement of creativity was taken at the midpoint of the EYE program, 4 months after its commencement, with its remaining 335 participants, who underwent the team formation processes. They were asked to assess multiple institutional complexity factors influencing their decision to become an entrepreneur (Greenwood, Raynard, Kodeih, Micelotta, & Lounsbury, 2011). The perceived supply and use of technology and creative ideas was enumerated as one of the eight potential factors and study participants indicated it as one of the three most important factors influencing their choice of becoming an entrepreneur, together with availability of business opportunities and knowledge and the availability of funding sources. Over 90% indicated that the use and supply of technology and creative ideas positively impacted their decision to start a business.

From these responses, one would expect the startup ideas assessed within the study to be highly creative and radical. However, the drop in reported frequency of use of creative techniques from problem identification and information search to idea generation suggests that there is a disconnection between creative inputs and outputs.

We captured this disconnect in the business proposals submitted by the participants to the EYE Program and analyzed them based on their innovativeness in introducing new products or services, devising new technologies, or accessing new markets. Whereas 72% of startups formed by our initial respondents offered varying degrees of innovation, the assessment from multiple external judges has confirmed that only 32% of submitted projects could be considered as highly innovative and putting their high levels of self-proclaimed creativity into practice. Out of the 148 business ideas presented by study participants, most of them were focusing on traditional industries (69.6%), where they provided an online solution (84.3%) to the existing problem or were using an international expansion as adopted innovation strategies (57%). Examples include online trading platforms connecting more or less niche communities or businesses, traveling sites, networking apps, or location-based services. Incremental innovation was prevalent and the innovation increments offered by startups in our sample were small.

The truth is, based on our research, innovation has been held hostage by local culture and its time orientation. This lower than expected performance can be explained by Hong Kong's collective behavior that favors the traditional ways of doing business inculcated within local industries and other stakeholders, social consensus over the benefits of short-termism in approaching personal and organizational development, and cultural norms that reinforce the fear of failure and emphasize conformity to social pressures, all of which are further fortified by the economic prosperity (Figure 12.3).

To elaborate, creativity and the entrepreneurial spirit of Hong Kong are still present, but they remain dormant and pared down by how people construct their life timelines. Although Hong Kong is institutionally and demographically ready to take the entrepreneurial risk and produce important creative outputs, there are other factors that temper the spirit down. Ironically, we connect the dormant entrepreneurial spirit to the economic prosperity of Hong Kong (Dowejko & Au, 2015). As one of our interviewees pointed out, "good is the enemy of great."

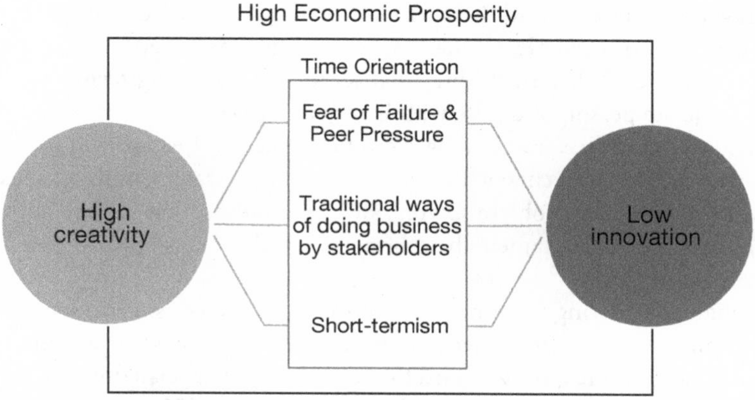

Figure 12.3. Hong Kong innovation paradox.

The necessity-driven entrepreneurship is no longer needed and the opportunity-driven entrepreneurship is pared down by the number of opportunities that are easier to achieve and readily available within the local economy, reinforcing conformism in behaviors.

A wealthy modern Hong Kong does not motivate new generations to set up their businesses the way poverty motivated Li Ka-shing to build his empire. Local society has developed high levels of risk aversion in their career choices. Parents do not want their children to go through the same hurdles of necessity-driven entrepreneurship and direct them toward less risky careers. These days, fresh graduates are looking for job safety and often pick the "easy way" by finding employment in well-established sectors and companies. Our EYE Program survey has revealed that potential entrepreneurs indeed face an increased pressure from their closest friends and family when they decide to launch a business and that it might be one of the key factors preventing people from taking the leap. For those who decided to discontinue their participation in the program, the pressure from friends not to pursue the entrepreneurial career increased by 436% within the first 4 months in the EYE Program, as compared to the 25% increase for those who continued on their entrepreneurial journey. Such strong impact seriously limits the conversion of entrepreneurial intentions into actions as peer pressure proved to be an important factor influencing the entrepreneurship rates and the overall innovativeness that comes with it. Simply put, the culture-induced pressure from closest peers negatively impacts life timelines of prospective entrepreneurs by delaying or canceling the conversion of creative ideas into entrepreneurial and innovative activities.

TIME ORIENTATION OF HONG KONG

In Hofstede's research, Hong Kong has been categorized as a culture with long-term orientation, where the society nurtures pragmatic virtues oriented to reap future rewards (Hofstede et al. 2010). Yet, in comparison to other economies that draw on Confucian traditions, Hong Kong's score of 61 out of 100 is rather below average. For example, China score is 87, Taiwan's is 93, and Singapore's is 72 (Hofstede et al. 2010). In cultures that score higher on long-term orientation, people associate personal success with invested effort instead of luck; they value thrift and perseverance, and emphasize future success; they are willing to learn from other cultures and change their traditions if necessary. Common sense and consensus rein in their problem solving, and the middle way is favored above ideological or political fundamentalism because which norms apply depends very much on the situation.

Although considering the timespan cultures take into consideration when planning for future events, Hofstede's long-term orientation does not account for the speed at which cultures work toward the future or for the relatedness of the past, present, and future. This paints an incomplete picture of Hong Kong's relationship with time and requires a further analysis based on an extended definition of time orientation we offered by Trompenaars and Hampden-Turner (2012) and Orlikowski and Yates (2002).

The pace of life in Hong Kong is fast. Its tempo of work is quick, if not very quick. Fast is the general impression of locals and visitors and the image projected in the media reports. In the language of time orientation, Hong Kong can be characterized by the disconnection of past, present, and future; the preference for chronological arrangement of actions; the fast pace of getting to desired outcomes; and the linearity and objectivity of the time concept.

All aspects of past, present, and future are considered of high importance and are seen in extended terms, but they are also disconnected from each other. This implies that people may have the tendency for considering their past, present, and future separately and for not weighting their relationship and mutual influence. In short, the time is now. Compared to the majority of other countries, the present looms large compared to the past and the future among Hong Kong people (Trompenaars & Hampden-Turner, 2012). On one hand, Hong Kong citizens have high respect for tradition and for older generations and do much to improve the living standards of their elderly. On the other hand, Hong Kong has very few heritage sites that are being preserved to cultivate the history of Hong Kong. For example, a controversial decision of demolishing an officially recognized heritage site to accommodate a modern hotel in one of the districts, Stanley, was taken by the authorities despite the local community being quite vocal about holding the opposing view. Another example comes from the business environment and illustrates a time-driven, collective behavior. In family businesses, where the second generation of entrepreneurs is coming to power, older generations have trouble accepting new ways of doing business (present) and stick to their traditional ways of doing things (past). However, the second generation (present), just like their predecessors, is not very receptive to improvements in business model development either. They are very reluctant about working with startup businesses (future) that could potentially positively impact their businesses and industries. The "don't fix it if it's not broken" attitude prevails, especially in the favorable economic conditions of today's Hong Kong.

In addition to time disconnection, Hong Kong people's relationship with time events is chronological and not synchronic (Trompenaars & Hampden-Turner, 2012). This means that they live their life and organize their activities in planned stages. They value the order in which life goals are accomplished, they refuse delaying their career development for the sake of personal development, and they avoid going back to things that were supposed to be accomplished at an earlier age (Orlikowski & Yates, 2002). This may create tensions in the society; for instance, many local citizens aspire to buy an apartment at the age of 30, but they cannot afford it because of the city's skyrocketing real estate prices. To make things worse, local culture imposes on them to buy an apartment in order to get married as an expected (and sequential) course of life. This creates frustration in younger generations because not owning the flat prevents them from starting families and getting on with their lives.

Not only life events need to be accomplished in a prescribed order, but they are also required to be completed at a fast pace. In fact, Hong Kong is one of the very few places in the world where most of the white-collar workers aspire to retire at the age of 35. This creates additional time pressure on their careers and personal development and reinforces the sequential perception of time. Get rich quick is a local mantra, and short-termism is a generally accepted planning horizon mindset.

Finally, in Hong Kong, people see time as linear, independent, and an objective phenomenon on which they have no influence and that runs independently of their objectives and lifecycles. Governance is administration led, and monitoring from the legislators and the court is passive. Business is dominated by the market, believing intervention and planning are less important if not futile (Au & White, 2010). The popular way of getting on is to find out the trend and ride with the wave. Also, recent political debates and the 1997 handover might have an adverse effect on people who may feel helpless and unable to control their lives. Hence, one's role becomes to race against the clock and to fulfil life objectives in line with the passing time. Personal objectives precede organizational ones, making innovation more difficult to complete (Gilson & Roe, 1999). This feeling is further reinforced by peers who, driven by the economic prosperity of Hong Kong, mutually encourage each other to stick to the known, easy, and faster ways of career development. Indeed, living in Hong Kong can sometimes be compared to joining traffic on a highway. You see all the cars passing by at full speed, and you feel the pressure to join them at full speed as well. Choosing your own speed is not a viable option.

We suggest the roots of this time orientation are in the trading background of Hong Kong and its return of sovereignty to China. Historically, Hong Kong has been a trading port that took in many refugees in the 1970–1980s, so people treat the city as a place of quick exchange, sojourning, and short-term gain amid uncertainty. The colonial government maintained a noninterventionist doctrine that left an imprint on the policies and beliefs of the Hong Kong public. Long-term planning is seldom considered necessary. Also, the historically rooted trading and arbitrage business mentality combined with the legacy of British banking practices, manufacturers' reliance on short-term loans, and the financial, instead of engineering or operational background of locally active venture capital investors have contributed to creating the short-term investment mentality (Au & White, 2010).

The British rule before 1997 and the "one country–two systems" arrangement with China may also have influenced the way people think about their future in Hong Kong (Cheung, 2009). The handover of Hong Kong to China should have aligned the city with long-term planning of the nation. However, portraying Hong Kong by some outlets as being passed on from one powerful country to another, as a former colony now returning to the motherland, ironically negates its economic achievements and social development as one of the most modern and self-sustainable cities in Asia. Its history is misguidedly shaped as a shame and failure. Detached from their historical roots, many residents may feel they are losing their past and disconnected from the future. Meanwhile, the political and social systems only continue to unfold with widespread dispute. Even with the Basic Law and the promise of 50 years unchanged lifestyle, many residents only see a transitional city and economy that belonged, or will belong, to a different political arrangement in the long term. They find it difficult to foresee what the future may hold for them. Indeed, the uncertainty of the future only strengthens the "right here, right now" mindset.

CONSEQUENCES OF HONG KONG'S TIME ORIENTATION: VICIOUS CIRCLE OF CROUCHING INNOVATION

Consequently, Hong Kong is stuck in an innovation deadlock, in which the local economy has entrapped itself throughout the years. It results from negative reinforcement of innovation-limiting activities that are the consequence of government, university, population, and business behaviors, to a large extent determined by Hong Kong's specific time orientation. Cultural cues driven by fast-paced and disconnected views of temporal structures create a short-term orientation in the society and in institutions that rely on traditional ways of doing business and prosperity-driven conformist behaviors. There is little room for meaningful feedback loops and long-term innovation cycles, and business and institutional environments are promoting fast solutions geared toward achieving short-term gains. We call it the vicious circle of "crouching" innovation, whereby innovative outputs go unnoticed in some areas and are limited in others (Figure 12.4). We briefly describe this cycle next.

Overreliance on Public Funds

According to statistics from UNESCO (2014), Hong Kong allocates yearly 0.75% of its GDP to research and development, which is an equivalent of US$352 per

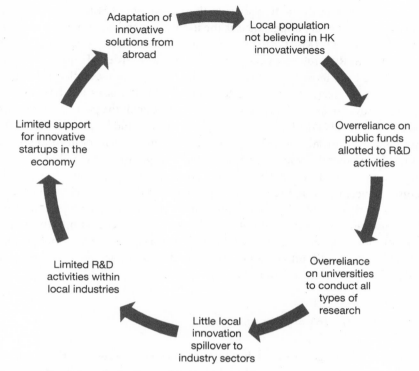

Figure 12.4. Vicious circle of crouching innovation.

capita. In comparison, countries such as Singapore, Israel, or South Korea are allotting from 2% to almost 4% of their yearly GDP, or around US$1,100 per capita, on research activities. Proportion-wise, Hong Kong government and business enterprises are the largest contributors of R&D money, responsible for 47.3% and 47.6% of funding, respectively. Although it is quite usual for the government and local firms to shoulder most research activities, the imbalance in Hong Kong results from the augmented role of the Hong Kong government in providing for research undertakings. In other economies, business enterprises provide up to 72% of funding, as in South Korea or China. Although in Hong Kong the government is to a large extent matching industry's research expenses one-to-one, in other economies it is playing a rather complementary role. This is a result of the traditional mindset in doing business in Hong Kong. In the past, Hong Kong relied on trading and logistics, which engendered little innovation compared to other industry sectors. In consequence, investment in research and development is not deemed necessary to the economic prosperity of today. Short-term orientation and known ways of doing business prevail.

Further, in line with short-termism, government-issued support funds, such as Small Entrepreneur Research Assistance Programme (SERAP), were until recently, more likely to be approved for companies with currently high marketability of the product under development. In fact, the commercial viability of the project accounted for 30% of the vetting score in the assessment of SERAP applications, being judged as of equal importance as the innovation and technology content of submitted projects (HKCTC, 2013). The commercial viability was important in ensuring that SERAP funding would be repaid by the awardees. However, it could also limit the long-term innovativeness of the local economy. Projects that may potentially have greater impact long term or serve as the basis for development of future innovations were less likely to be supported with the government funds. Also, a highly regulated administration of such funds could be detrimental to the awarded firm's innovativeness. Measures that were initially introduced to protect the fund from potential fraudulent behaviors acted against the flexibility in developing research activities and were slowing down the technological development. In consequence, firms that operate in fast-paced environments were potentially forced to work with obsolete solutions simply because the new generation of technology they were using had not been foreseen and budgeted into their fund administration. The short-term planning and fast-paced and rigid implementation that had been built into the fund administration acted against the innovation speed and scope of the fund awardees.

Overreliance on Universities

The pivotal role of government funding is reflected in how the R&D money is being spent. With such limited resources the priority in receiving funds is accorded to universities. Indeed, Hong Kong's research and development activities rely heavily on universities. In 2010, the government put down money to finance 42% of university research (UGC, 2014), and 52.2% of all research activities were performed by local tertiary institutions (UNESCO, 2014). In comparison, universities in Singapore were generating 28.8% of local R&D activities, and in South Korea only one in ten research projects was conducted at local universities. As a result, Hong Kong–based universities are bearing much more responsibility for both types of research: advancing frontiers of basic knowledge research and the more grounded and functional applied research. This means that local tertiary institutions are accountable for two important research outcomes: delivering world-class peer-reviewed basic research and contributing to the economic advancement through knowledge transfer of applied research. For university researchers, it is a difficult choice to make since applied research is less likely to gain worldwide peer recognition and basic research may not be immediately applicable within the local economy. What makes the choice even more difficult is that in most local institutions the career advancement path has traditionally been designed to account for basic research achievement while putting less emphasis on the achievements in applied research fields. If we add to this that Hong Kong has a relatively small population of researchers compared to other countries, with 2,925 researchers per million people (UNESCO, 2014),[4] the pressure on universities to deliver becomes very apparent. As a result, conducting applied or contractual research is occasionally treated as a side activity and a necessary evil. In fact, while the total number of university research projects has increased by 7.6% since 2009, the proportion of contractual research at universities has decreased by 10.2% from 2009 to 2013 (UGC, 2014). This reflects a linear time approach to organizing activities, whereby the tradeoff between basic and applied research is seen as a zero-sum game.

University–Industry Spillovers

The increased research burden combined with basic research priority limits the innovation spillover effect that tertiary institutions might have on the local economy. Also, collaboration between universities and the enterprise sectors has traditionally been relatively weak in Hong Kong. Things are improving though, and in recent years more emphasis has been put on commercializing university technologies, rejuvenating Knowledge Transfer Offices, and opening up of local universities to industry cooperation. The Innovation and Technology Commission has recently set up a new Technology Start-up Support Scheme for Universities (TSSSU) to encourage students and professors from six local universities to commercialize university-based R&D results and launch technology spinoffs (Audit Commission, 2013).

Until recently, however, there were two principal ways in which universities in Hong Kong could develop cooperative R&D projects with the industry. They could either apply for matching funds from the government within the Innovation and Technology Commission's University-Industry Collaboration Programme (UICP) or work directly with local and foreign businesses on research projects. For both types of funding the numbers and value of research projects have been increasing in recent years. Nevertheless, out of 23,500 research projects conducted at local publicly funded universities in the 2012/13 academic year, industry collaborations represent only a fraction of research activities, amounting to 2.1% across all universities (UGC, 2014), furthering the traditional divide between universities and businesses. Similarly, the most recent statistics reported by Knowledge Transfer Offices of publicly funded universities revealed that, until 2013, university technology had been licensed to a total of 219 outside organizations and a cumulative number of 72 active spinoff companies were funded as a result of university research (UGC, 2013). A panel of experts assessed the limited R&D transfer, driven by the predominant focus on present and traditional tasks and goals for universities and businesses alike, perhaps "poses" a true challenge within the Hong Kong economy (Dowejko & Au, 2015).

Industry R&D

Local firms still lack capabilities and the mindset to adopt technologies streaming from universities and to commercialize them. They also conduct limited research and development activities themselves. According to a recent survey with

1,001 local businesses from the Intellectual Property Department (2012), only 6% of local firms carried out R&D activities in 2012. Within the remaining 94%, one in four businesses stated there were "no research and development needs for their business." This mindset was even more prominent for small companies, with less than 10 employees. A recent report revealed that there are two reasons for such a state of mind among small and medium-sized enterprises (SMEs) (Dowejko & Au, 2015). First, most of them operate in industries that benefit from the close proximity to Mainland China, such as trading, retail, and hospitality industries. Since the demand for their products and services remains high, they do not see the need to change the ways they do business. This is very much in line with Hong Kong's tendency to focus on the present and treat it in disconnection from future developments in neighboring markets. Second, most of the businesses are represented by family firms, which very often value traditional business models and stability of the environment and often succumb to intergenerational pressures to maintain the status quo. As a result, they lock in the capital and resources that could feed innovation and potentially kick-start new industries. Indeed, when enquired, only 12.9% of local businesses with fewer than 10 employees have registered any trademark, patent, or design in Hong Kong (HKIPD and Mercado Solutions Associates, 2012).

Innovative Startup Support

The short-term and present-oriented mindset that keeps local enterprise innovation in a deadlock also tampers with how well-established businesses interact with local startups. Interfirm linkages among mature local firms and startups appear to be weak, especially since homegrown SMEs see startups as money-draining pits and not prospective cooperation partners, as noticed in the recent report on entrepreneurship and innovation in Hong Kong (Dowejko & Au, 2015). They tend to emphasize how new businesses have an unstoppable appetite for financial resources while bringing nothing to the table. What they fail to see is that by unlocking their reserves of financial and nonfinancial resources to startups, they gain the opportunity to revamp their businesses, rejuvenate their industries, or even kick-start new ones. Few of the well-established businesses embraced this logic. One of the practices is to invest in startups by acquiring their technology and assimilating them into a larger firm's operations. Within this practice, large businesses hire startup's founding teams as their employees to facilitate their work on the idea. However, this type of strategic thinking is still limited. In fact, a panel of experts evaluated Hong Kong's lack of focus on high-growth startups as a potential challenge (Dowejko & Au, 2015).

Adaptation From Abroad

Instead of working with innovative startups, creating their own solutions, or working together with other businesses on creating new approaches, many local companies are leaning toward adopting solutions that were tested on other markets and are currently successful elsewhere. One of the major challenges indicated by recent reports was that local businesses often rely on borrowing existing ideas without engaging in a full cycle of innovation processes (Dowejko & Au, 2015). Despite the fact that Hong Kong has recently become quite prolific in trademark registration practices, with over 5,600 trademarks per million inhabitants registered by Hong Kong residents locally and abroad and a 71% growth rate since 2008 (WIPO, 2012), local manufacturers still often resort to producing licensed goods or designing for well-known brands over creating their own brands. In the recent study by HKTDC, there were 83%, 61%, and 40% of companies engaging in OEM, ODM, and OBM businesses,[5] respectively (HKTDC, 2008). In fact, the number of industrial design applications filed by Hong Kong residents has remained the same since 2008 and accounted for 1,172 applications per million inhabitants locally and abroad (WIPO, 2012). Although these numbers seem high, the lack of growth in this area is a signal that the industry is stagnating. Similarly, local retailers choose short-term gains and are still likely to opt for foreign brands with well-established current notoriety instead of supporting up-and-coming local brands in developing their product portfolios.

In our sample of existing businesses studied through EYE Program surveys, 17% of companies admitted there was nothing innovative about their market, product, or technology and 18% claimed being involved in innovation in all three areas. Within those businesses that reported some kind of innovation, the largest group, accounting for 36% of companies, was introducing new products to existing markets with the help of existing technology.

This behavior is further reinforced by the "not-invented-here" syndrome that is driven by the focus on the present and short-term outlook, whereby it is easier to obtain necessary administrative approvals for market adaptations than for market innovations. At the operational level, government officers have a limited understanding of strategic objectives for developing innovation and fostering entrepreneurship in local industries and sometimes create unnecessary obstacles to implementing new solutions in existing industries. In such situations, entrepreneurs are better off implementing solutions new to Hong Kong but not new to other markets, because it is easier to obtain necessary permits based on examples from other countries. The situation is much more complicated when a startup tries to implement a solution that is new to local and foreign markets. Lack of precedence makes it much harder to receive favorable opinions from operational-level officers. Oftentimes, ideas copied from other markets are better received than homegrown ideas, and local bureaucracy sometimes inadvertently acts as an obstacle in commercializing and developing innovative business ideas. Therefore, despite efforts made by CreateHK, a government agency launched to support creative industries and design capability in Hong Kong, the city appears to remain stuck in the mentality of low value-added small business activities that address immediate needs with widely accepted solutions, which is reinforced by limiting the promotion of creativity to selected industries only.

Hong Kong Innovativeness

As a result, Hong Kong society has been operating with a conviction that Hong Kong is less capable of innovation than other economies and has been discouraged from commercializing its creative outputs in favor of focusing on fast-tracking personal career objectives or choosing market adaptation as an innovation strategy. In particular, potential entrepreneurs do not commercialize their original ideas because of a pervasive lack of faith on behalf of their would-be business supporters in their capability to deliver creative solutions to more technical problems. Consequently, only few take steps toward implementing creative outputs. Patenting activity statistics reveal that in 2012 Hong Kong residents had filed 223 patent applications per million inhabitants in Hong Kong and abroad. In comparison, in the same period Singapore's citizens filed 919 patent applications and South Koreans filed for as many as 4,076 patents. Also, because of the size of the local market, most patent and design applications by Hong Kong residents are filed abroad, which lowers the visibility of local innovation. In 2012 alone, only 11% of all patents by Hong Kong residents were filed locally (WIPO, 2012).

Local innovation is not well packaged to capture public attention and inspire other less creative industries to follow in the creative footsteps of homegrown visionaries. Cross-fertilization is limited across sectors because a chronological, linear, and present-focused approach to updating and revamping industries is applied within the economy. As a consequence, local businesses and society do not benefit from local creativity and are reluctant to invest in research and development activities. This means the burden of fostering innovation in Hong Kong is transferred onto the public funds' shoulders and into universities. This reiterates the cycle of local noninnovation.

RECOMMENDATIONS FOR FAST-TRACKING LOCAL INNOVATION

To break the negative spiral and ignite the self-propelling innovation process, multiple measures need to be introduced at different stages of the cycle (Figure 12.5). These changes do not need to be revolutionary, but it is essential that they are implemented in sync. Otherwise, the inertia of the spiral would counteract the change and restore the equilibrium as it was. In other words, coordinating smaller, targeted moves across multiple stakeholder activities rather than making big changes in a single area of influence is recommended to inspire positive change in driving innovation (Mahmood & Rufin, 2005). Such synchronized and incremental implementation could potentially impact the time orientation of Hong Kong culture and promote the cyclical, interconnected, and synchronous perception of how innovation should be developed. We briefly present the logic behind cyclical and interconnected actions later and offer four main recommendations for change.

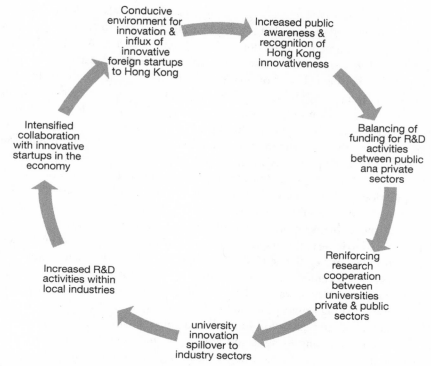

Figure 12.5. Igniting the self-propelling innovation process.

First, local businesses need to get more involved with creating innovative outputs. It would be unreasonable to assume that the government could increase its R&D contributions ad infinitum, but it is not unreasonable to expect the development of long-term focused incentives for local businesses to increase their research and development spending. For example, inadequate policy attention has been given to promoting innovation and collaboration among local firms in Hong Kong. Initiatives such as the newly launched Technology Start-up Support Scheme for Universities (TSSSU) or the recently introduced Enterprise Support Scheme (ESS), which relaxes the fast commercialization condition of SERAP, are both great ways of creating the R&D dialogue across different groups of stakeholders and battling the short-termism of local innovators. Also, the proposed Innovation and Technology Bureau (ITB) is a big step toward unifying and reinforcing innovation-related policies of Hong Kong and putting more emphasis on long-term planning and cyclic development of the city's innovation capacity. To further address the innovation issue, activities of agencies such as CreateHK could be extended to cater to all types of industries instead of focusing on creative ones. This would help enhance synchronicity through developing cross-fertilization practices across different sectors of the economy.

To foster collaboration further, more matching grants, such as the newly introduced ESS, could be developed to create investment and resource-sharing incentives. This could not only energize local innovation but also unlock resources for local startups and promote long-term planning. Also, establishing stronger ties between the government's incubation and R&D centers, such as ASTRI or NAMI, and further development of contract and collaborative research capabilities could positively impact the inclusion of smaller and younger businesses in creating innovation in Hong Kong. Similarly, local universities are not quite engaging in dialogue with their alumni networks and only recently began to foster multidisciplinary collaboration. Tapping into alumni networks and nurturing the collaborative spirit through undergraduate education could be helpful in building connections between past, present, and future. It could also inspire change in the mindset of local enterprises and positively influence the strengthening of cooperation practices between firms at different stages of development, thus effectively connecting the old with the new, the past with the future.

Second, more intensive promotion of updated strategic industries for Hong Kong could contribute to the shaping and restructuring of existing small businesses (Research Office of Legislative Council Secretariat, 2015). The establishment of five strategic R&D centers in 2006 that built on Hong Kong's industrial heritage was an important step toward enhancing local innovativeness and building a bridge between Hong Kong's past and future; however, these efforts have not seen their continuation and extension in small and young business activities just yet. As a consequence, Hong Kong is still relying on imitation and not innovation in most of its business endeavors. Engaging younger generations though further opening of R&D centers to the public and through promoting cooperation with other stakeholders from the government sector, such as InvestHK or CreateHK, could help to modify the local conviction of Hong Kong's noninnovativeness and shift local focus toward the future and long-term planning. It could also potentially release the pressure to conform to safe and fast-tracked careers.

Third, increasing entrepreneurial migration through further relaxation of immigration policies and encouraging the return of second-generation emigrants could improve the innovative output of Hong Kong and encourage the rejuvenation of traditional businesses and sectors. An additional influx of human capital stock with a diversified cultural background (and time orientation) could be helpful in shifting Hong Kong's fast-paced, linear, and temporally disconnected view of doing business. Reinstating capital investor visas but shifting its investment requirements toward private equity and seed capital, creating professional incentives for attracting immigrants with postgraduate degrees, and facilitating the career shift and return to Hong Kong for nonlocal graduates of Hong Kong universities constitute examples of changes that could improve the research and development capability of Hong Kong. Also, bridging the period between the entrepreneurship visa application and approval to allow for gestation activities could increase the number of foreign startups with time-sensitive ideas to choose Hong Kong over other entrepreneurship hubs.

Finally, increased efforts in promoting existing innovation outputs should be helpful in changing the perception of local innovativeness. Hong Kong innovations often escape our attention because many of them constitute parts of more complex products or are commercialized under foreign licenses. Patent-wise, Hong Kong specializes in audiovisual technology, electrical machinery, solar energy, semiconductors, furniture, games, and consumer products.[6] In semiconductor technology, the Hong Kong–based company ASM Pacific Technology is a world leader in the semiconductor assembly and packaging equipment market. Similarly, the award-winning company and international patent-holder Hot Toys, which produces high-end figurines, cosbaby figures, and toy vehicles, is the worldwide industry leader of licensed collectible toys from international movies, such as *Toy Story, Monsters Inc., The Avengers, Batman*, and *Indiana Jones*. Also, many of the local innovations are simply taken for granted because they became a part of local culture and are no longer noticed as out of the ordinary. For example, the Octopus card, which serves as public transport ticket and micropayment card accepted in most convenience stores and supermarkets across the city, became an inseparable part of locals' daily routine. It has been implemented outside Hong Kong as well, though none of these implementations seems to be as successful as the original one. Similarly, Hong Kong's toy industry has been perceived as an integral part of local reality, so we no longer pay attention to the fact that Hong Kong is one of the top 20 leading economies creating innovation in games and toys.[7] For instance, a Hong Kong–based company with foreign origins, Hanson Robotics, is a world leader in creating interactive animatronic robots, which are capable of maintaining eye contact, recognizing faces and understanding speech, holding conversations, and simulating a real person's personality.

Applying simultaneous and targeted changes at each stage of the innovation cycle would speed up positive change and create an environment that is conducive to innovation. In particular, relaxing institutional cues of sequential and fast-paced innovation (non) incentives to accommodate a long-term vision and planning would be beneficial to changing Hong Kong's relationship with time. This, in turn, will attract more local and foreign startups to innovate in Hong Kong and reestablish public recognition of Hong Kong's creative and innovative spirit.

CONCLUSION

Although we cannot reset Hong Kong's clock, we can try to modulate it by helping to develop culturally meaningful and socially accepted development timelines for the city and its residents. In particular, long-term planning and vision for economic development that is deeply rooted in the past achievements and future geopolitical advantages has the capability of shaping the social consensus and driving innovative collective behaviors in institutional and business environments.

Rather than concentrating on one-off remedies to address immediate troubles in commercializing specific innovations, this chapter suggests that the institutional and business decision makers should shift their attention toward addressing deeper, culturally laden challenges of the local business culture to foster long-term outlook, future orientation, and cross-fertilization of business sectors. For example, the ongoing discussion on the future of cryptocurrency in Hong Kong and globally has deeper implications not only for the thriving financial industry of Hong Kong but also for its logistics, e-commerce, and information and technology sectors, just to name few. We encourage all stakeholders to take a broader look and consider the issue from the legal, banking, trading, and social perspectives.

The case of Hong Kong illustrates the difficulties of converting creative outputs into products of innovation when cultural conditioning drives the conflict between the readiness and predisposition to innovate. Understanding the time orientation and its implications for innovation behavior gives policymakers and entrepreneurs a deeper insight into how to address challenges for innovation acceptance and adoption, depending on the country's cultural makeup. It may also give scholars in creativity and entrepreneurship another cultural dimension to consider in their future research (Zampetakis et al., 2010). The history of local entrepreneurialism and the current creative spirit of Hong Kong provide solid foundations to foster innovation and revive the entrepreneurial spirit of the city. Realignment of the elements that currently lead to institutional and business inefficiencies has the potential of reinstating the positive cultural cues that will turn the vicious cycle of innovation into a virtuous one.

NOTES

1. The research accompanied the Empowering Young Entrepreneurs Program was run by The Chinese University of Hong Kong and jointly sponsored by Google HK (http://entrepreneurship.bschool.cuhk.edu.hk/eyeprogram). It encompassed three waves of surveys with 902 potential entrepreneurs, numerous business case studies, a policy workshop, analysis of archival datasets and reports, and 55 interviews with entrepreneurship and innovation experts from academic, policy-making, legal, media, and commercial backgrounds.

2. The methodology adopted to measure approaches to time is from Cottle, T. J. (1967), who referred to it as the "circle test." The question asked was as follows: "Think of the past, present, and future as being in the shape of circles. Please draw three circles in the space available, representing past, present, and future. Arrange three circles in any way you want that best show how you feel about the relationship of the past, present, and future. You may use different sizes of circles. When you have finished, label each circle to show which one is the past, which one the present, and which one the future" (Trompenaars and Hampden-Turner (2012: 154–155). For clarity sake, we also used different shades to highlight circles that represent past, present, and future and we assigned numbers, from the most to the least dominant, to further emphasize the importance of each timeframe to a given culture.

3. Please refer to Appendix 1 for a brief description of our sample and of the EYE Program design.

4. In comparison, Singapore has 6,307, South Korea has 5,451, and the United States has 4,650 researchers per million people.

5. OEM stands for original equipment manufacturing; ODM, original design manufacturing; OBM, original brand manufacturing.
6. Based on the Relative Specialization Index (RSI) calculated with data from WIPO Statistics database for years 2004–2012.
7. Based on Relative Specialization Index (RSI) calculated with data from WIPO Statistics database for the years 2004–2012.

REFERENCES

Amabile, T. M. (1983). *The social psychology of creativity.* New York, NY: Springer-Verlag.

Amabile, T. M. (1996). *Creativity and innovation in organizations.* Boston, MA: Harvard Business School Press.

Au, K., & White, S. (2010). Hong Kong's venture capital system and the commercialization of new technology. In D. Fuller (Ed.), *Innovation policy and the limits of laissez-faire: Hong Kong's policy in comparative perspective* (pp. 145–180). Hampshire, UK: Palgrave Macmillan.

Baker, T., Gedajlovic, E., & Lubatkin, M. (2005). A framework for comparing entrepreneurship processes across nations. *Journal of International Business Studies, 36*(5), 492–504.

Butler, R. (1995). Time in organizations: Its experience, explanations and effects. *Organization Studies, 16*(6), 925–950.

Chao, M. M., Zhang, Z.-X., & Chiu, C. Y. (2010). Adherence to perceived norms across cultural boundaries: The role of need for cognitive closure and ingroup identification. *Group Processes and Intergroup Relations, 13*(1), 69–89.

Cheung, B. L. A. (2009). *Hong Kong's experience: Cultural inheritance and institutional innovation.* Hong Kong: Commercial Press.

Chiu, C. Y., & Kwan, L. Y. Y. (2010). Culture and creativity: A process model. *Management and Organization Review, 6*(3), 447–461. doi:10.1111/j.1740-8784.2010.00194.x

Clark, P. (1990). Chronological codes and organizational analysis. In J. Hassard & D. Pym (Eds.), *The theory and philosophy of organizations: Critical issues and new perspectives* (pp. 137–163). London, UK: Routledge.

Audit Commission. (2013). Chapter 10: Innovation and Technology Commission, Innovation and Technology Fund: Management of Projects. The Government of the Hong Kong Special Administrative Region: Hong Kong.

Cornell University, INSEAD, & WIPO. (2014). *The Global Innovation Index 2014: The human factor in innovation.* Second printing. Fontainebleau, Ithaca, and Geneva. https://www.globalinnovationindex.org/userfiles/file/reportpdf/GII-2014-v5.pdf

Cottle, T. J. (1967). The circles test: An investigation of perceptions of temporal relatedness and dominance. *Journal of Projective Techniques and Personality Assessment, 31*(5), 58–71.

Daghfous, N., Petrof, J. V., & Pons, F. (1999). Values and adoption of innovations: A cross-cultural study. *Journal of Consumer Marketing, 16*(4), 314–331.

Dowejko, M. K., & Au, K. (2015). *Crouching tigers, hidden dragons: Eight action plans for invigorating Hong Kong's startups and awakening local innovation.* Hong Kong: Center for Entrepreneurship, The Chinese University of Hong Kong.

Dowejko, M. K., Au, K., & Shen, N. (2014). *Entrepreneurship ecosystem of Hong Kong* (Interim Report). Hong Kong: Center for Entrepreneurship, The Chinese University of Hong Kong.

Durkheim, E. (1893). *De la division du travail social: étude sur l'organisation des sociétés supérieures*. Paris, France: Alcan.

Dwyer, S., Mesak, H., & Hsu, M. (2005). An exploratory examination of the influence of national culture on cross-national product diffusion. *Journal of International Marketing, 13*(2), 1–27.

Efrat, K. (2014). The direct and indirect impact of culture on innovation. *Technovation, 34*(1), 12–20. doi:10.1016/j.technovation.2013.08.003

Einstein, A. (1931). *Relativity: The special and general theory*. New York, NY: Crown.

Erez, M., & Nouri, R. (2010). Creativity: The influence of cultural, social, and work contexts. *Management and Organization Review, 6*(3), 351–370. doi:10.1111/j.1740-8784.2010.00191.x

Flaherty, M. G. (1991). *A watched pot: How we experience time*. New York, NY: New York University Press.

Florida, R., Mellander, C., Stolarick, K., Silk, K., Matheson, Z., & Hopgood, M. (2011). *Creativity and prosperity: The Global Creativity Index*. Toronto, Ontario: Martin Prosperity Institute.

Fuller, D. (Ed.). (2010). *Innovation policy and the limits of laissez-faire: Hong Kong's policy in comparative perspective*. Hampshire, UK: Palgrave Macmillan.

Gardet, L., Gurevich, A. J., Kagame, A., Larre, C., Lloyd, G. E. R., Neher, A., . . . Ricoeur, P. (1976). *Cultures and time*. Paris, France: UNESCO Press.

Gilson, R. J., & Roe, M. J. (1999). Lifetime employment: Labor peace and evolution of Japanese corporate governance. *Columbia Law Review, 99*, 508–540.

Greenwood, R., Raynard, M., Kodeih, F., Micelotta, E. R., & Lounsbury, M. D. (2011). Institutional Compexity and organizational responses. *The Acacemy of Management Annals, 5*(1), 317–371.

HKCTC. (2013). *Funding Schemes under the Innovation and Technology Commission*. Hong Kong: Hong Kong Council for Testing and Certification.

HKIPD, & Associates, M. S. (2012). *Survey on Business Attitudes to Intellectual Property*. Hong Kong: HKSAR Intellectual Property Department.

HKTDC. (2008). *Study on OEM, ODM, and OBM: Extending the supply chain and added value*. Hong Kong: Hong Kong Trade Development Council.

Hofstede, G., Hofstede, G. J., & Minkov, M. (2010). *Cultures and organizations: Software of the mind*. Revised and expanded 3rd ed. New York, NY: McGraw-Hill.

House, R. J., Hanges, P. J., Javidan, M., Dorfman, P. W., & Gupta, V. (Eds.). (2004). *Culture, leadership and organizations: The GLOBE study of 62 societies*. Thousand Oaks, CA: Sage.

Hui, M. K., Au, K., & Fock, H. (2004). Empowerment effects across cultures. *Journal of International Business Studies, 35*(1), 46–60.

Lau, V. P., Shaffer, M. A., & Au, K. (2007). Entrepreneurial career success from a Chinese perspective: Conceptualization, operationalization, and validation. *Journal of International Business Studies, 38*, 126–146.

Li, Y., & Zahra, S. A. (2012). Formal institutions, culture, and venture capital activity: A cross-country analysis. *Journal of Business Venturing, 27*(1), 95–111. doi: 10.1016/j.jbusvent.2010.06.003

Lichtenstein, B. B., Carter, N. M., Dooley, K. J., & Gartner, W. B. (2007). Complexity dynamics of nascent entrepreneurship. *Journal of Business Venturing, 22*(2), 236–261.

Mahmood, I. P., & Rufin, C. (2005). Government's dilemma: The role of government in imitation and innovation. *Academy of Management Review, 30*(2), 338–360.

Morris, M. W., & Leung, K. (2010). Creativity East and West: Perspectives and parallels. *Management and Organization Review, 6*(3), 313–327.

Mowery, D. C., & Rosenberg, N. (1993). The U.S. national innovation system. In R. R. Nelson (Ed.), *National innovation systems: A comparative analysis.* Oxford, UK: Oxford University Press.

Mueller, S. L., & Thomas, A. S. (2001). Culture and entrepreneurial potential: A nine country study of locus of control and innovativeness. *Journal of Business Venturing, 16*(1), 51–75. doi:10.1016/s0883-9026(99)00039-7

Norenzayan, A., Artran, S., Faulkner, J., & Schaller, M. (2006). Memory and mystery: The cultural selection of minimally counterintuitive narratives. *Cognitive Science, 30*(3), 531–553.

Orlikowski, W. J., & Yates, J. (2002). It's about time: Temporal structuring in organizations. *Organization Science, 13*(6), 684–700.

Perlow, L. A., Okhuysen, G., & Repenning, N. P. (2002). The speed trap: Exploring the relationship between decision making and temporal context. *Academy of Management Journal, 45*(5), 931–955.

Secretariat, R. O. o. L. C. (2015). *Four pillars and six industries in Hong Kong: Review and outlook.* Hong Kong: Research Office of Legislative Council Secretariat.

Shane, S. (1993). Cultural influences on national rates of innovation. *Journal of Business Venturing, 8*(1), 59–73. doi:10.1016/0883-9026(93)90011-s

Shane, S. (2003). *A general theory of entrepreneurship. The individual-opportunity nexus.* Cheltenham, UK: Edward Elgar.

Shane, S. A. (1992). Why do some societies invent more than others? *Journal of Business Venturing, 7*(1), 29–46. doi:10.1016/0883-9026(92)90033-n

Simonton, D. K., & Ting, S.-S. (2010). Creativity in Eastern and Western civilizations: The lessons from historiometry. *Management and Organization Review, 6*(3), 329–350.

Taylor, M. Z., & Wilson, S. (2012). Does culture still matter?: The effects of individualism on national innovation rates. *Journal of Business Venturing, 27*(2), 234–247. doi:10.1016/j.jbusvent.2010.10.001

Trompenaars, F., & Hampden-Turner, C. (2012). *Riding the waves of culture: Understanding diversity in global business* (3rd ed.). New York, NY: McGraw-Hill.

UGC. (2013). *Institutions' annual report on knowledge transfer recurrent funding.* Hong Kong: University Grants Committee.

UGC. (2014). Statistics on UGC-funded universities in Hong Kong. Retrieved from University Grants Committee. https://cdcf.ugc.edu.hk/cdcf/statEntry. action?language=EN

UNESCO. (2014). GERD data by country. Retrieved from UNESCO Institute for Statistics. http://uis.unesco.org/

Ward, T. B. (2004). Cognition, creativity, and entrepreneurship. *Journal of Business Venturing, 19*(2), 173–188. doi:10.1016/s0883-9026(03)00005-3

WEF. (2014). The Global Competitiveness Report 2013–2014: Full data edition. K. Schwab & X. Sala-i-Martin (Eds.). Geneva, Switzerland: World Economic Forum. http://www3.weforum.org/docs/WEF_GlobalCompetitivenessReport_2013-14.pdf

Williams, L. K., & McGuire, S. J. (2010). Economic creativity and innovation implementation: The entrepreneurial drivers of growth? Evidence from 63 countries. *Small Business Economics, 34*(4), 391–412. doi:10.1007/s11187-008-9145-7

WIPO. (2012). Patent, trademark, and industrial design applications statistics by country. Retrieved from http://www.wipo.int/ipstats/en/office_stats_reports.html

Zampetakis, L. A., Bouranta, N., & Moustakis, V. S. (2010). On the relationship between individual creativity and time management. *Thinking Skills and Creativity, 5*, 23–32.

Zhang, X., & Bartol, K. M. (2010). Linking empowering leadership and employee creativity: The influence of psychological empowerment, intrinsic motivation, and creative process engagement. *Academy of Management Journal, 53*(1), 107–128.

Zimbardo, P. G., & Boyd, J. N. (1999). Putting time in perspective: A valid, reliable Individual-Differences metric. *Journal of Personality and Social Psychology, 77*(6), 1271–1288.

APPENDIX 12.1

Description of the EYE Program and Its Participants

The first edition of the EYE Program was officially launched in January 2014 and concluded in October of the same year. It was run by the Chinese University of Hong Kong with financial and in-kind support of Google Hong Kong. The EYE Program was run free of charge for all participants and involved three principal stages. First, the participants underwent an in-depth training of entrepreneurial skills, which included business, user experience design, and technology. Then, they were asked to form teams and present new or ongoing startup ideas to a panel of external expert judges, who assessed their feasibility, innovativeness, and potential sustainability. Out of 148 business proposals submitted, 80 were admitted to the pitching stage and 40 selected teams underwent a mentorship process, where one mentor was coaching one team for 2 months. The mentor–team matching was a complex process that encouraged both parties to get to know each other before committing to a mentoring relationship. In the final stage, 20 teams were selected by an independent panel to undergo a second pitch process and 6 winning teams got a chance to visit Google's headquarters in Mountain View and get a taste of the Silicon Valley's startup ecosystem. Overall, the EYE Program entailed entrepreneurship training, mentorship, networking events, and extensive press coverage for participating entrepreneurs and their startups.

We have collected primary quantitative data from the participants of the EYE Program, young entrepreneurs aged below 35, in a three-stage survey as described in the chapter. The participants of the program were admitted based on their interest in entrepreneurship and their official Hong Kong residency status. Prior entrepreneurship experience was not required.

Our typical EYE Program participant was a Chinese male. He is between 21 to 25 years old and has already graduated from the university with a bachelor's degree. He studied in Hong Kong and is quite versed in business. He feels strongly about his creative thinking and business management skills, but he wishes he knew more about fundraising and coding. He briefly worked as an employee, but he feels ready to start his own business. He already has an idea and a draft of his business plan, but he has no experience in entrepreneurship and this is why he enrolled in the EYE Program.

The typical EYE Program team is made of two to four persons (62.8% of all teams) with mainly male co-founders (62.2% are male-only teams), all being enrolled in the EYE Program (77.3% of teams with two to four members and 43.9% of total). Their expertise is mostly one-dimensional in business (31.8%) or combines business and technology (19.6%). They came up with the business idea during the program (87.2% of the projects are new), and it was a joint effort (83% not related to experience). Most of them had no external mentor or advisor to help them refine the business proposal (88.5%). They are looking for initial funding between HK$100,000 and HK$500,000 (43%).

Tables and figures are indicated by an italic *t* and *f* following the page number.